The POWER of FAITH

Other Titles by Smith Wigglesworth

Ever Increasing Faith

Experiencing God's Power Today

Greater Works

Smith Wigglesworth Devotional

Smith Wigglesworth on Faith

Smith Wigglesworth on Healing

Smith Wigglesworth on Heaven

Smith Wigglesworth Only Believe

Smith Wigglesworth on Spirit-Filled Living

Smith Wigglesworth on Spiritual Gifts

Smith Wigglesworth on the Holy Spirit

Wigglesworth on the Anointing

The POWER of FAITH

Smith WIGGLESWORTH

Whitaker House

Whitaker House gratefully acknowledges and thanks Glenn Gohr and the entire staff of the Assemblies of God Archives in Springfield, Missouri, for graciously assisting us in compiling Smith Wigglesworth's works for publication in this book.

Unless otherwise indicated, all Scripture quotations are taken from the *New King James Version* (NKJV), © 1979, 1980, 1982, 1984 by Thomas Nelson, Inc. Used by permission. All rights reserved. All Scripture quotations marked (KJV) are taken from the King James Version of the Holy Bible.

Publisher's note: This new edition from Whitaker House has been updated for the modern reader. Words, expressions, and sentence structure have been revised for clarity and readability. Although the more modern Bible translation quoted in this edition was not available to Smith Wigglesworth, it was carefully and prayerfully selected in order to make the language of the entire text readily understandable while maintaining his original premises and message.

THE POWER OF FAITH

Titles included in this anthology:
Smith Wigglesworth on Spirit-Filled Living
ISBN-13: 978-0-88368-534-1   © 1998 by Whitaker House
Smith Wigglesworth on Power to Serve
Now published as *Smith Wigglesworth Only Believe*
ISBN-13: 978-0-88368-7   © 1998 by Whitaker House
Experiencing God's Power Today
ISBN-13: 978-0-88368-596-9   © 2000 by Whitaker House
Smith Wigglesworth on God's Transforming Power
Now published as *Smith Wigglesworth on Heaven*
ISBN-13: 978-0-88368-954-7   © 1998 by Whitaker House

ISBN-13: 978- 0-88368-608-9
ISBN-10: 0-88368-608-2
Printed in the United States of America
© 2000 by Whitaker House

Whitaker House
1030 Hunt Valley Circle
New Kensington, PA 15068
www.whitakerhouse.com

Library of Congress Cataloging-in-Publication Data
Wigglesworth, Smith, 1859–1947.
The power of faith / by Smith Wigglesworth
p.   cm.
ISBN 0-88368-608-2 (pbk. : alk. paper)
1. Spiritual life—Pentecostal churches. I. Title.
BV4501.2 W51942   2000
252'.0994—dc21   00-010230

3 4 5 6 7 8 9 10 11 12 13 14 ⊔⊔ 16 15 14 13 12 11 10 09 08 07 06

CONTENTS

INTRODUCTION

An encounter with Smith Wigglesworth was an unforgettable experience. This seems to be the universal reaction of all who knew him or heard him speak. Smith Wigglesworth was a simple yet remarkable man who was used in an extraordinary way by our extraordinary God. He had a contagious and inspiring faith. Under his ministry, thousands of people came to salvation, committed themselves to a deeper faith in Christ, received the baptism in the Holy Spirit, and were miraculously healed. The power that brought these kinds of results was the presence of the Holy Spirit, who filled Smith Wigglesworth and used him in bringing the good news of the Gospel to people all over the world. Wigglesworth gave glory to God for everything that was accomplished through his ministry, and he wanted people to understand his work only in this context, because his sole desire was that people would see Jesus and not himself.

Smith Wigglesworth was born in England in 1859. Immediately after his conversion as a boy, he had a concern for the salvation of others and won people to Christ, including his mother. Even so, as a young man, he could not express himself well enough to give a testimony in church, much less preach a sermon. Wigglesworth said that his mother had the same difficulty in expressing herself that he did. This family trait, coupled with the fact that he had no formal education because he began working twelve hours a day at the age of seven to help support the family, contributed to Wigglesworth's awkward speaking style. He became a plumber by trade, yet he continued to devote himself to winning many people to Christ on an individual basis.

In 1882, he married Polly Featherstone, a vivacious young woman who loved God and had a gift of preaching and evangelism. It was she who taught him to read and who became his closest confidant and strongest supporter. They both had compassion for the poor and needy in their community, and they opened a mission, at which Polly preached. Significantly, people were miraculously healed when Wigglesworth prayed for them.

In 1907, Wigglesworth's circumstances changed dramatically when, at the age of forty-eight, he was baptized in the Holy Spirit. Suddenly, he had a new power that enabled him to preach, and even his wife was amazed at the transformation. This was the beginning of what became a worldwide evangelistic and healing ministry that reached thousands. He eventually ministered in the United States, Australia, South Africa, and all over Europe. His ministry extended up to the time of his death in 1947.

Several emphases in Smith Wigglesworth's life and ministry characterize him: a genuine, deep compassion for the unsaved and sick; an unflinching belief in the Word of God; a desire that Christ should increase and he should decrease (John 3:30); a belief that he was called to exhort people to enlarge their faith and trust in God; an emphasis on the baptism in the Holy Spirit with the manifestation of the gifts of the Spirit as in the early church; and a belief in complete healing for everyone of all sickness.

Smith Wigglesworth was called "The Apostle of Faith" because absolute trust in God was a constant theme of both his life and his messages. In his meetings, he would quote passages from the Word of God and lead lively singing to help build people's faith and encourage them to act on it. He emphasized belief in the fact that God could do the impossible. He had great faith in what God could do, and God did great things through him.

Wigglesworth's unorthodox methods were often questioned. As a person, Wigglesworth was reportedly courteous, kind, and gentle. However, he became forceful when dealing with the Devil, whom he believed caused all sickness. Wigglesworth said the reason he spoke bluntly and acted forcefully with people was that he knew he needed to get their attention so they could focus on God. He also had such anger toward the Devil and sickness that he acted in a seemingly rough way. When he prayed for people to be healed, he would often hit or punch them at the place of their problem or illness. Yet, no one was hurt by this startling treatment. Instead, they were remarkably healed. When he was asked why he treated people in this manner, he said that he was not hitting the people but that he was hitting the Devil. He believed that Satan should never be treated gently or allowed to get away with anything. About twenty people were reportedly raised from the dead after he prayed for them. Wigglesworth himself was healed of appendicitis and kidney stones, after which his personality softened and he was more gentle with those who came to him for prayer for healing. His abrupt manner in ministering may be attributed to the fact that he was very serious about his calling and got down to business quickly.

Although Wigglesworth believed in complete healing, he encountered illnesses and deaths that were difficult to understand. These included the deaths of his wife and son, his daughter's lifelong deafness, and his own battles with kidney stones and sciatica.

He often seemed paradoxical: compassionate but forceful, blunt but gentle, a well-dressed gentleman whose speech was often ungrammatical or confusing. However, he loved God with everything he had, he was steadfastly committed to God and to His Word, and he didn't rest until he saw God move in the lives of those who needed Him.

In 1936, Smith Wigglesworth prophesied about what we now know as the charismatic movement. He accurately predicted that the established mainline denominations would experience revival and the gifts of the Spirit in a way that would surpass even the Pentecostal movement. Wigglesworth did not live to see the renewal, but as an evangelist and prophet with a remarkable healing ministry, he had a tremendous influence on both the Pentecostal and charismatic movements, and his example and influence on believers is felt to this day.

Without the power of God that was so obviously present in his life and ministry, we might not be reading transcripts of his sermons, for his spoken messages were often disjointed and ungrammatical. However, true gems of spiritual insight shine through them because of the revelation he received through the Holy Spirit. It was his life of complete devotion and belief in God and his reliance on the Holy Spirit that brought the life-changing power of God into his messages.

As you read this book, it is important to remember that Wigglesworth's works span a period of several decades, from the early 1900s to the 1940s. They were originally presented as spoken rather than written messages, and necessarily retain some of the flavor of a church service or prayer meeting. Some of the messages were Bible studies that Wigglesworth led at various conferences. At his meetings, he would often speak in tongues and give the interpretation, and these messages have been included as well. Because of Wigglesworth's unique style, the sermons and Bible studies in this book have been edited for clarity, and archaic expressions that would be unfamiliar to modern readers have been updated.

In conclusion, we hope that as you read these words of Smith Wigglesworth, you will truly sense his complete trust and unwavering faith in God and take to heart one of his favorite sayings: "Only believe!"

Smith Wigglesworth on

SPIRIT-FILLED LIVING

CONTENTS

CHAPTER ONE

EXTRAORDINARY

The people in whom God delights are the ones who rest upon His Word without doubting. God has nothing for the man who wavers, *"for let not that man suppose that he will receive anything from the Lord"* (James 1:7). Therefore, I would like us to get this verse deep into our hearts until it penetrates every fiber of our being:

Only believe, only believe.
All things are possible; only believe.

God has a plan beyond anything that we have ever known. He has a plan for every individual life, and if we have any other plan in view, we miss the grandest plan of all. Nothing in the past is equal to the present, and nothing in the present can equal the things of tomorrow. Tomorrow should be so filled with holy expectations that we will be living flames for Him. God never intended His people to be ordinary or commonplace. His intentions were that they should be on fire for Him, conscious of His divine power, realizing the glory of the Cross that foreshadows the crown.

SANCTIFIED UNTO GOD

God has given us a very special Scripture:

Now in those days, when the number of the disciples was multiplying, there arose a complaint against the Hebrews by the Hellenists, because their widows were neglected in the daily distribution. Then the twelve summoned the multitude of the disciples and said, "It is not desirable that we should leave the word of God and serve tables. Therefore, brethren, seek out from among you seven men of good reputation, full of the Holy Spirit and wisdom, whom we may appoint over this business....” And the saying pleased the whole multitude. And they chose Stephen, a man full of faith and the Holy Spirit, and Philip. (Acts 6:1–3, 5)

During the time of the inauguration of the church, the disciples were pressured by many responsibilities. The practical things of life could not be attended to, and many were complaining concerning the neglect of their widows. Therefore, the disciples decided upon a plan, which was to choose seven men to do the work of caring for the needs of these widows—men who were *“full of the Holy Spirit.”* What a divine thought. No matter what kind of work was to be done, however menial it may have been, the person chosen had to be *“full of the Holy Spirit.”* The plan of the church was that everything, even everyday routines, must be sanctified to God, for the church had to be a Holy Spirit church. Beloved, God has never ordained anything less.

ENDUED WITH POWER

I want to stress one thing. First and foremost, I would emphasize these questions: Have you received the Holy Spirit since you believed? Are you filled with divine power?

The heritage of the church is to be so equipped with power that God can lay His hand upon any member at any time to do His perfect will. There is no stopping point in the Spirit-filled life. We begin at the Cross, the place of disgrace, shame, and death, and that very death brings the power of resurrection life. Then, being filled with the Holy Spirit, we go on *“from glory to glory”* (2 Cor. 3:18). Let us not forget that possessing the baptism in the Holy Spirit means that there must be an ever increasing holiness. How the church needs divine anointing. It needs to see God's presence and power so evidenced that the world will recognize it. People know when the tide is flowing; they also know when it is ebbing.

The necessity for seven men to be chosen for the position of serving tables was very evident. The disciples knew that these seven men were men ready for active service, and so they chose them. In Acts 6:5, we read, *“And the saying pleased the whole multitude. And they chose Stephen, a man full of faith and the Holy Spirit, and Philip.”*

14

There were others, but Stephen and Philip stand out most prominently in the Scriptures. Philip was a man so filled with the Holy Spirit that a revival always followed wherever he went. Stephen was a man so filled with divine power that although serving tables might have been all right in the minds of the other disciples, God had a greater vision for him. God filled him with a baptism of fire, with power and divine anointing, that took him on to the climax of his life when he saw right into the open heavens (Acts 7:56).

Had we been there with the disciples at that time, I believe we would have heard them saying to each other, "Look here. Neither Stephen nor Philip are doing the work we called them to. If they do not attend to business, we will have to get someone else." That is the human way of thinking, but divine order is far above our finite planning. When we please God in our daily service, we will always find that everyone who is faithful in the little things, God will make ruler over much (Matt. 25:21).

Stephen is such an example to follow. He was a man chosen to serve tables, who had such a revelation of the mind of Christ and of the depth and height of God that there was no standing still in his experience. He went forward with leaps and bounds. Beloved, there is a race to be run, a crown to be won. We cannot stand still. I say to you, be vigilant. Be vigilant. Let no one *"take your crown"* (Rev. 3:11).

ABOVE THE ORDINARY

God has privileged us in Christ Jesus to live above the ordinary human plane of life. Those who want to be ordinary and live on a lower plane can do so, but as for me, I will not. The same unction, the same zeal, the same Holy Spirit power is at our command as it was at the command of Stephen and the apostles. We have the same God that Abraham and Elijah had, and we do not need to lag behind in receiving any gift or grace. We may not possess all the gifts as abiding gifts, but as we are full of the Holy Spirit and divine unction, it is possible, when there is a need, for God to make evident every gift of the Spirit through us as He may choose to use.

Stephen, an ordinary man, became extraordinary under the Holy Spirit's anointing until, in many ways, he stands supreme among the apostles. *"And Stephen, full of faith and power, did great wonders and signs among the people"* (Acts 6:8). As we go deeper in God, He enlarges our capacity for understanding and places before us a wide-open door. I am not surprised that this man chosen to serve tables was afterwards called to a higher plane.

You may ask, "What do you mean? Did he stop taking care of his responsibilities?" No, but he was lost in the power of God. He lost sight of everything in the natural and steadfastly fixed his gaze upon Jesus, *"the author and finisher of our faith"* (Heb. 12:2), until he was transformed into a shining light in the kingdom of God. May we be awakened to believe His Word and to understand the mind of the Spirit, for there is an inner place of purity where we can see God. Stephen was just as ordinary a person as you and I, but he was in the place where God could move him so that he, in turn, could affect those around him. He began in a humble place and ended in a blaze of glory. Dare to believe Christ.

FACING THE OPPOSITION

As you go on in this life of the Spirit, you will find that the Devil will begin to get restless and will cause a dispute in the church; it was so with Stephen. Any number of people may be found in the church who are very proper in a worldly sense—always correctly dressed, the elite of the city, welcoming everything into the church but the power of God. Let us read what God says about them:

> *Then there arose some from what is called the Synagogue of the Freedmen (Cyrenians, Alexandrians, and those from Cilicia and Asia), disputing with Stephen. And they were not able to resist the wisdom and the Spirit by which he spoke.* (Acts 6:9–10)

The Freedmen, or Libertines, could not stand the truth of God. With these opponents, Stephen found himself in the same predicament as the blind man whom Jesus healed. As soon as the blind man's eyes were opened, the Pharisees threw him out of the synagogue. (See John 9:1–38.) They did not want anybody in the synagogue who had his eyes open. As soon as you receive spiritual eyesight, out you go! These Freedmen, Cyrenians, and Alexandrians rose up full of wrath in the very place where they should have been full of the power of God, full of love divine, and full of reverence for the Holy Spirit. They rose up against Stephen, this man *"full of the Holy Spirit"* (Acts 6:3).

16

Beloved, if there is anything in your life that in any way resists the power of the Holy Spirit and the entrance of His Word into your heart and life, drop on your knees and cry aloud for mercy. When the Spirit of God is waiting at your heart's door, do not resist Him; instead, open your heart to the touch of God. Resistance is good if it is applied to fighting evil. For instance, there is a resisting to the point of *"bloodshed, striving against sin"* (Heb. 12:4), but resisting the Holy Spirit (Acts 7:51) will drive you into sin.

MIGHTY FOR GOD

Stephen spoke with remarkable wisdom, and things began to happen. You will find that there is always a moving when the Holy Spirit has control. Brought under conviction by the message of Stephen, his opponents resisted, they lied, they did anything and everything to stifle that conviction. Not only did they lie, but they got others to lie against Stephen, who would have laid down his life for any one of them. Stephen was used by God to heal the sick, perform miracles, and yet they brought false accusations against him (Acts 6:13–14). What effect did these false charges have on Stephen? *"And all who sat in the council, looking steadfastly at him, saw his face as the face of an angel"* (v. 15).

Something had happened in the life of this man. Chosen for menial service, he became mighty for God. How was it accomplished in him? It was because his aim was high. Stephen was faithful in little, and God brought him to full fruition. Under the inspiration of divine power by which he spoke, the council could not help but listen to his holy, prophetic words. Beginning with Abraham and Moses, Stephen continued unfolding the truth. What a marvelous exhortation! Take your Bible and read it. Listen in as the angels listened in. As light upon light, truth upon truth, revelation upon revelation, found its way into their hearts, they gazed at him in astonishment. Their hearts perhaps became warm at times, and they may have said, "Truly, this man is sent by God"—but then he hurled the truth at them:

> *You stiffnecked and uncircumcised in heart and ears! You always resist the Holy Spirit; as your fathers did, so do you. Which of the prophets did your fathers not persecute? And they killed those who foretold the coming of the Just One, of whom you now have become the betrayers and*

murderers, who have received the law by the direction of angels and have not kept it. (Acts 7:51–53)

Then what happened? These men were moved; they were *"cut to the heart, and they gnashed at him with their teeth"* (v. 54).

There are two occasions in the Scriptures where people were *"cut to the heart."* After Peter had delivered that inspired sermon on the Day of Pentecost, the people were *"cut to the heart"* (Acts 2:37) with conviction, and there were added to the church 3,000 souls (v. 41). Here is Stephen, speaking under the inspiration of the Holy Spirit, and the men of this council who were being *"cut to the heart"* rose up as one man to slay him. As you read Acts 7, beginning with verse fifty-five, what a picture you have before you. As I close my eyes, I have a vision of this scene in every detail: the howling mob with their vengeful, murderous spirits, ready to devour this holy man, and he *"being full of the Holy Spirit, gazed into heaven and saw the glory of God."* What did he see there? From his place of helplessness, he looked up and said: *"I see the heavens opened and the Son of Man standing at the right hand of God!"* (v. 56).

Is that the position that Jesus left earth to take? No. He went to *sit* at the right hand of the Father (Heb. 12:2); but in support of the first martyr, in behalf of the man with that burning flame of Holy Spirit power, God's Son *stood up* in honorary testimony of him who, called to serve tables, was faithful unto death.

But is that all? No, I am so glad that is not all. As the stones came flying at Stephen, pounding his body, crushing his bones, striking his temple, mangling his beautiful face, what happened? How did this scene end? With a sublime, upward look, this man, chosen for an ordinary task but filled with the Holy Spirit, was so moved upon by God that he finished his earthly work in a blaze of glory, magnifying God with his last breath. Looking up into the face of the Master, he said, *"'Lord, do not charge them with this sin.' And when he had said this, he fell asleep"* (Acts 7:60).

Friends, it is worth everything to gain the Holy Spirit. What a divine ending to the life and testimony of a man who was chosen to serve tables.

CHAPTER TWO

DIVINE REVELATION

Praise the Lord. Praise the Lord. "Only believe! Only believe! All things are possible; only believe." There is something very remarkable about that chorus. God wants to impress it so deeply on our hearts that in our corners, rooms, and private places, we will get engrossed in this divine truth: if we will only believe, He can get in us and out of us for others what otherwise would never be possible. Oh, for this truth to grab hold of us so that God will come to us afresh and say, "Only believe." Beloved, this song will help you. I trust the Lord will give me something to make you ready for everything so that you will be on God's schedule and in the place He has designed for you.

The possibilities are within the reach of all. Let us consider the words from Matthew 16:13: *"He asked His disciples, saying, 'Who do men say that I, the Son of Man, am?'"* The response is found in verse sixteen: *"Simon Peter answered and said, 'You are the Christ, the Son of the living God.'"*

This is a blessed truth. Lord, help me to convey it. I am deeply convinced that there is such a marvelous work done in our hearts when the presence of the Incoming One is revealed. He brings new life in God. Our human souls recognize a tremendous, divine treasure within this truth: that we are in a place where God intends that we will not only be able to bind and loose things on earth and in heaven (v. 19), but also by the grace of God to stand in the situations of the day so that the gates of hell will not be able to triumph against us (v. 18). Beloved, what I desire above all is that my life will be an example in every way of this truth. I want His Word to be a light within me, a flame of fire burning in my bones, presenting itself within my being as reality. God's Word is to be believed in everything that it declares.

19

Let us read the wonderful words of John 1:12–13:

But as many as received Him, to them He gave the right to become children of God, to those who believe in His name: who were born, not of blood, nor of the will of the flesh, nor of the will of man, but of God.

How marvelous to be born of God and to have His nature. This divine nature came to us as we received the Word of God. And Jesus said to His disciples, *"Who do men say that I, the Son of Man, am?'...Simon Peter answered and said, 'You are the Christ, the Son of the living God'"* (Matt. 16:13, 16). Peter's response is wonderful. Who do you say that He is? Oh, glory to God, who do you say He is? *"The Christ, the Son of the living God."* The truth comes to us, and we are blessed, *"for flesh and blood has not revealed this...but My Father who is in heaven"* (v. 17). To have this revelation that He is the Son of God is a revelation that He was manifested to destroy the works of the Devil (1 John 3:8). Sometimes it is important that we encourage one another with these divine relationships. The baptism in the Holy Spirit unfolds not only the operations of God, but also the position we have by the Holy Spirit in this world.

THE ROCK AND THE KEY

My message is to believers, and I know the Lord is going to bless His Word to us. It is a perfect revelation to me and to you. I know that God declares it to us by His own Son. The new birth is a perfect place of royalty where we reign over the powers of darkness, bringing everything to perfect submission to the rightful owner, who is the Lord. He rules within and reigns there, and our bodies have become temples of the Holy Spirit (1 Cor. 6:19).

He said to Peter, *"On this rock I will build My church"* (Matt. 16:18). What rock was it? The rock is the living Word. *"On this rock I will build My church."* Who is the rock? The Son of the living God. He is the rock.

But what are the keys? The keys are the divine working by faith in the things of God. *"And I will give you the keys of the kingdom of heaven"* (v. 19). Remember this: it is the key that has life within it. It is life divine. The key holds the power to enter in. That verse opens and unlocks all the dark things and brings life and liberty to the captive. *"On this rock I will build My church, and the gates of Hades shall not prevail against it"* (v. 18).

Now let us see how it works. It works; it always works; it never fails to work. Now let me bring before you the truth because you know you cannot depend upon yourself in this, so I want to help you. You will never be able to get anything by your own initiative. You cannot do it. It is divine life flowing through you that empowers you to act. You are in the right position when you allow the glory of the new life to cause you to act.

INTERPRETATION OF A MESSAGE IN TONGUES:

Out of the depths I cried, and the Lord heard my cry and brought me into a large place on sea, on land, in a large place.

OPPORTUNITY FOR ACTION

On a ship one day, some people said to me, "We are going to have a program. Would you be a participant in the entertainment?"

"Oh, yes, I will be in anything that is going to be helpful," I replied, and I believe God was in it.

So they said to me, "What can you do? What place will you take in the entertainment?"

"I can sing," I offered.

So they said to me, "Where would you like to be scheduled in the entertainment? We are going to have a dance."

I said, "Put me down just before the dance."

That evening, I was longing for my turn to come because there had been a clergyman there trying to sing and entertain them, and it seemed so out of place. My turn came, and I sang: "If I Could Only Tell Him As I Know Him." I sang the song, and when I finished, the people said, "You have spoiled the dance." Well, I was there for that purpose, to spoil the dance.

A preacher came to me afterwards and said, "How dare you sing that?" "Why," I said, "how dare I not sing it?" It was my opportunity. He was going to India, and when he got there, he wrote in his periodical and mailed it to England. He said, "I did not seem to have any chance to preach the Gospel, but there was a plumber on board who seemed to have plenty of opportunities to preach to everybody. He said things that continue to stick with me. He told me that the book of Acts was written only because the apostles acted."

You see, I was in the drama of life-acting in the name of Jesus. And so that opened the door and provided me a place that I could speak all the time. The door was open in every way. Glory to God.

The next morning, a young man and his wife came to me and said, "We are in a terrible state. We are looking after a gentleman and lady in the first class; she is a great teacher of Christian Science. She has been taken seriously ill, and the doctor gives her little hope. We have told her about you, and she said she would like to see you." I said, "All right."

That was my opportunity. Opportunity is a wonderful thing. Opportunity is the great thing of the day. And so when I went into the lady's first-class room, I saw that she was very sick. I said, "I am not going to speak to you about anything, not even about your sickness. I am simply going to lay my hands upon you in the name of Jesus, and the moment I do, you will be healed." As soon as I laid my hands upon her, the fever left her, and she was perfectly healed.

However, she was terribly troubled in her mind and heart, and for three days she became worse. I knew it would have been easy to share the Bread of Life with her and to bring her into liberty, but God would not allow it. Just before she got saved, she felt that she would be lost forever. Then God saved her. Hallelujah.

She asked, "What will I do?"

I said, "What do you mean?"

"Oh," she said, "for three years I have been preaching all over England; we live in a great house in India, and we have a great house in London. I have been preaching Christian Science, and now what can I do? You know my salvation is so real. I am a new woman altogether."

Filled with joy, she said, "Will I be able to continue smoking cigarettes?"

"Yes, smoke as many as ever you can; smoke night and day if you can."

Then she asked, "You know we play cards—bridge and other things. Can I play?"

"Yes, play all night through; go on playing."

And she said, "You know we have a little wine, just a little with our friends in the first-class. Should I give it up?"

"No, drink all you want."

Later, she called a maid to her, and said, "I want you to take this telegram and stop that order for a thousand cigarettes." She called her husband and said, "I cannot go into all these things again."

We do not have to go down to bring Him up or up to bring Him down. He is near to you. He is in your heart. It is a living word of faith that we preach. (See Romans 10:6–8.) God wants you all to know that if you only dare to act upon the divine principle that is written there, the gates of hell will not prevail. Praise the Lord.

REIGNING IN LIFE

And so, beloved, it is for all of us. Do not forget this. Every one of you can know this union, this divine relationship, this great power. It will keep you aware that God has come to reveal that everything is subject to you. Through His grace, you have received the *"gift of righteousness"* to *"reign in life through the One, Jesus Christ"* (Rom. 5:17). It is a lovely phrase—reigning in life through Jesus. Love for the Lord is welling up in my heart.

There are two ways to enter into this divine relationship. I am here to say that it does not matter how many times we have failed. There is one keynote in Pentecost: holiness unto the Lord. I find the association with my Lord brings purity and makes my whole being cry out after God, after holiness. Holiness is power. Holiness unto the Lord. Why do I know this? Because I see Jesus my Lord. I see Him; He is so beautiful.

When Jesus went to the tomb of Lazarus, he saw Mary and her friends weeping. Jesus also wept. He wept because of their grief and unbelief. He could not weep because Lazarus was dead. Jesus was and still is *"the resurrection and the life"* (John 11:25). But their sorrow moved Him to groan in His spirit, and He wept. The sequel to that glorious triumph was the great union with His Father. He said to His Father, *"And I know that You always hear Me, but because of the people who are standing by I said this, that they may believe that You sent Me"* (v. 42).

Oh, the blessedness of the truth. That word moves me tremendously. I know that He hears me. Since I know that He hears me, then I know that I have the petition that I desired (1 John 5:15). Glory to God. Not a power in the world can take that knowledge away from you. Every soul is privileged to go into the Holiest of Holies through the blood of the Lamb.

CHAPTER THREE

A FACE-TO-FACE ENCOUNTER WITH GOD

*Then Jacob was left alone; and a Man wrestled with him
until the breaking of day.*
—Genesis 32:24

L ooking back on our spiritual journeys, we will see that we have held on to our own way too much of the time. When we come to the end of ourselves, God can begin to take control. The Scripture asks: *"Can two walk together, unless they are agreed?"* (Amos 3:3). We cannot enter into the profound truths of God until we relinquish control, for *"flesh and blood cannot inherit the kingdom of God; nor does corruption inherit incorruption"* (1 Cor. 15:50).

Jacob's name means "supplanter." When Jacob came to the end of his plans, God had a better plan. How slow we are to see that there is a better way.

The glory is never so wonderful as when we realize our helplessness, throw down our sword, and surrender our authority to God. Jacob was a diligent worker, and he would go through any hardship if he could have his own way. In numerous situations, he had his way; all the while, he was ignorant of how gloriously God preserved him from calamity. There is a good; there is a better, but God has a best, a higher standard for us than we have yet attained. It is a better thing if it is God's plan and not ours.

GOD HAS A PLAN

Jacob and his mother had a plan to secure the birthright and the blessing, but God planned the ladder and the angels. Isaac, Jacob's father, agreed that Jacob should go *"to Padan Aram, to the house of Bethuel* [his] *mother's father"* (Gen. 28:2). On his way there, Jacob rested his head on a stone. In his dream, he saw a *"ladder...and its top reached to heaven"* (v. 12). Above the ladder, Jacob saw God and heard Him say: *"The land on which you lie I will give to you and your descendants"* (v. 13). He also heard God tell him: *"I am with you and will keep you wherever you go, and will bring you back to this land; for I will not leave you"* (v. 15). What a good thing for Jacob that in the middle of carrying out his own plan, God found him at the right place. The trickery to obtain the birthright had not been the honorable thing to do, but here at Bethel, he found that God was with him.

Many things may happen in our lives, but when the veil is lifted and we see the glory of God, His tender compassion covers us all the time. How wonderful to be where God is. Jacob experienced twenty-one years of wandering, fighting, and struggling. Listen to his conversation with his wives: *"Your father has deceived me and changed my wages ten times, but God did not allow him to hurt me"* (Gen. 31:7). To his father-in-law, Jacob said:

> *Unless the God of my father...had been with me, surely now you would have sent me away empty-handed. God has seen my affliction and the labor of my hands.* (v. 42)

GOD'S WAY IS BEST

Jacob had been out in the bitter frost at night watching the flocks. He was a thrifty man, a hard worker, a planner, a supplanter. We see supplanters in our world today. They may experience a measure of blessing, but God is not first in their lives. We are not judging them, but there is a better way. It is better than our best. It is God's way. Scripture tells us: *"There is a way that seems right to a man, but its end is the way of death"* (Prov. 16:25).

There is a way that God establishes. In our human planning, we may experience blessings of a kind, but we also undergo trials, hardships, and barrenness that God would have kept from us if we had followed His way. I realize through the anointing of the Holy Spirit that there is a freshness, a glow, a security in God where you can know that God is with you all the time. There is a place to reach where all that God has for us can flow through us to a needy world all the time: *"For as the heavens are higher than the earth, so are My ways higher than your ways, and My thoughts than your thoughts"* (Isa. 55:9).

ALONE WITH GOD

Jacob was given time to think: *"Then Jacob was left alone; and a Man wrestled with him until the breaking of day."* Oh, to be left alone with God! In the context of the Scripture, we read that several things had preceded his being alone. His wives and his children had been sent ahead. His sheep, oxen, camels, and donkeys had gone ahead. He was alone.

Often, you will find that you are left alone. Whether you like it or not, you will be left alone like Jacob was left alone. His wives could not make atonement for him; his children could not make atonement for him; his money was useless to help him.

What made Jacob come to that place of loneliness, weakness, and knowledge of himself? He recalled the memory of the grace with which God had met him twenty-one years before, when he saw the ladder and the angels and heard the voice of God: *"Behold, I am with you and will keep you wherever you go, and will bring you back to this land; for I will not leave you until I have done what I have spoken to you"* (Gen. 28:15). He remembered God's mercy and grace.

He was returning to meet his brother Esau, who had become very rich. Esau had been blessed abundantly in the things of this world. He had authority and power to take all that Jacob had and to take vengeance upon him. Jacob knew this. He also knew that there was only one way of deliverance. What was it? Only God could keep Jacob safe. God had met him twenty-one years before when he had left home empty-handed. Now, he was returning with wives, children, and goods, but he was lean in soul and impoverished in spirit. Jacob said to himself, "If I do not get a blessing from God, I can never meet Esau," and he made up his mind he would not go on until he knew that he had favor with God. Jacob was left alone. Unless we get alone with God, we will surely perish. God intervenes when conflict exists. The way of revelation is plain. The Holy Spirit's plan is so clear that we have to say it was God after all.

Jacob was left alone. He knelt alone. The picture is so real to me. Alone! He began to think. He thought about the ladder and the angels. I think as he began to pray, his tongue stuck to the roof of his mouth. Jacob had to get rid of a lot of things. It had all been Jacob! As he got alone with God, he knew it. If you get alone with God, you will find it to be a place of revelation. Jacob was left alone, alone with God. We stay too long with our relations, our camels, and our sheep. Jacob was left alone. Hour after hour passed. He began to feel the presence of God, but he still had not received the desired blessing.

THE WAY TO VICTORY

If ever God is disappointed with you when you wait in His presence, it will be because you are not fervent. If you are not serious and intense, you disappoint God. If God is with you and you know it, be in earnest. Pray and believe: *"Hold fast the confidence and the rejoicing of the hope firm to the end"* (Heb. 3:6). If you do not, you disappoint God.

Jacob was that way. God said, "You are not real enough; you are not hot enough; you are too ordinary; you are no good to Me unless you are filled with zeal—white hot!" The Angel of the Lord said, *"Let Me go, for the day breaks"* (Gen. 32:26). Jacob knew if God went without blessing him, he could not meet Esau. If you are left alone with God and you cannot get to a place of victory, it is a terrible time. You must never let go, whatever you are seeking— fresh revelation, light for your path, some particular need—never let go. Victory is ours if we are earnest enough. All must pass on; nothing less will please God. *"Let Me go, for the day breaks."* He was wrestling with equal strength. Nothing is obtained that way.

You must always master that with which you are wrestling. If darkness covers you, if a fresh revelation is what you need, or if your mind needs to be relieved, always get the victory. God says you are not earnest enough. You say, "The Word does not say that." But it was in God's mind. In wrestling, the strength is in the neck, chest, and thigh; the thigh is the source of strength. So God touched his thigh. With that strength gone, defeat is sure. What did Jacob do? He hung on. God intends for people to be severed by the power of His power, so hold fast; He will never let go. If we let go, we will fall short.

Jacob said, *"I will not let You go unless You bless me!"* (v. 26). And God blessed him: *"Your name shall no longer be called Jacob, but Israel"* (v. 28). The change of Jacob to Israel was wonderful!

Israel! Victory all the time! God is building all the time. God is sufficient all the time. Now Jacob has power over Esau, power over the world, power over the cattle. All is in subjection as he comes out of the great night of trial. The sun rises upon him. Oh, that God may take us on.

What happened after that? Read how God blessed and honored him. Esau meets him. There is no fighting now. What a blessed state of grace! They kiss each other: *"When a man's ways please the LORD, He makes even his enemies to be at peace with him"* (Prov. 16:7).

"What about all these cattle, Jacob?"

"Oh, they are a present."

"I have plenty; I don't want your cattle. What a joy it is to see your face again!"

What a wonderful change! Who caused it? God.

HOLDING ON TO GOD

Could Jacob hold God? Can you hold God? Yes, you can. Sincerity can hold Him, dependence can hold Him, weakness can hold Him, for *"when* [you are] *weak, then* [you are] *strong"* (2 Cor. 12:10). I'll tell you what cannot hold Him: self-righteousness cannot hold Him; pride cannot hold Him; assumption cannot hold Him; high-mindedness cannot hold Him—thinking you are something when you are nothing, puffed up in your imagination. You can hold Him in your prayer closet, in the prayer meeting, everywhere: *"If anyone hears My voice and opens the door, I will come in to him and dine with him, and he with Me"* (Rev. 3:20).

Can you hold Him? You may sometimes think that He has left you. Oh, no! He does not leave Jacob, Israel. What changed his name? The wrestling? What changed his name? The holding on, the clinging, the brokenness of spirit? If You do not help me, I am no good, no good for the world's need. I am no longer salt. Jacob obtained the blessing because of the favor of God and his yieldedness to God's will. God's Spirit was working in him to bring him to a place of helplessness. God worked to bring him to Bethel, the place of victory. Jacob remembered Bethel, and through all the trying circumstances, he had kept his vow. (See Genesis 28:20–22.)

When we make vows and keep them, God helps us. We must call upon God and give Him an account of the promise. *"And Jacob called the name of the place Peniel: 'For I have seen God face to face, and my life is preserved'"* (Gen. 32:30). How did he know? Do you know when God blesses you? Do you know when you have victory? Over twenty years later, the vision of the ladder and the angels remained with Jacob.

We must have a perfect knowledge of what God has for us. He knew that he had the favor of God, and that no man could hurt him. Let us in all our seeking see that we have the favor of God. Keep His commandments. Walk in the Spirit. Be tenderhearted and lovable. If we do these things, we will be appreciated by others, and our ministry will be a blessing to those who hear. God bless you. God bless you for Jesus' sake.

CHAPTER FOUR

THE LIVING WORD

When He had come down from the mountain, great multitudes
followed Him. And behold, a leper came and worshiped Him,
saying, "Lord, if You are willing, You can make me clean." Then
Jesus put out His hand and touched him, saying, "I am willing; be
cleansed." Immediately his leprosy was cleansed.
—Matthew 8:1–3

When I read these words, my heart is moved, for I realize that Jesus is just as much present with us as He was in Jerusalem when He walked the earth. How it changes our whole nature as we comprehend what Jesus meant when He said: *"You search the Scriptures, for in them you think you have eternal life; and these are they which testify of Me"* (John 5:39). This living Word is not given to us just because of the narratives or the wonderful parables that Jesus taught, but that we, through it, might be changed. Beloved, His presence is so remarkable that if we will but call on Him, believing that He has the giving of eternal life at His command, we will be changed in body, soul, and spirit.

THE SENTENCE OF DEATH

When Jesus was on earth and beheld suffering humanity, He was moved with compassion. He met the most difficult problems; one of the hardest conditions to meet was leprosy. The moment that leprosy was pronounced upon a person, it meant that he was doomed. Just as there was no remedy at that time for a leper, there is no earthly power that can deliver us from sin. Leprosy was the disease that had a death sentence, and sin means death to the spiritual man unless it is cleansed by the blood of Jesus. Here was a leper with the seal of death on him, and there was only one hope. What was it? If he could come to Jesus, he would be healed. But how could a leper come to Jesus? When a leper came near other people, he had to cry out: *"Unclean! Unclean!"* (Lev. 13:45)—so how could a leper ever get near to Jesus?

The difficulty was tremendous, but when faith lays hold, impossibilities must yield. When we touch the Divine and believe God, sin will drop off; disease will go; circumstances will change. I can almost read the thoughts of the people as they passed by the leper: "You poor leper! If you had been where we were, you would have seen the most remarkable things happen, for people were delivered from all kinds of diseases today." The leper might have asked, "Where were you?" They would have answered, "We have been with Jesus!" Oh, the thrill of life when we have been with Jesus.

WATCHING FOR JESUS

Let me give you a little picture. Every night when Jesus left the disciples and made His way up the mountainside, they would watch Him as far as the eye could see, until He disappeared. On the next day, the crowds would gather and watch for His appearing. They were so taken up with watching for Jesus that when they saw Him coming down the mountain, they could not keep quiet. Their hearts were full of the thought of seeing Him, but where was the leper? The leper, too, had come, but the eyes of the people were not on the leper now. They were watching for Jesus. The leper kept close to the crowd, and as Jesus drew nearer, he began his chant, *"Unclean! Unclean!"*

The crowd immediately moved away from him, leaving the path clear for the leper to be the first to get to Jesus. No one could turn him back. No one could stop a man whose heart was set on reaching Jesus. No power on earth can stop a sinner from reaching the side of the Master, if he has faith that will not be denied. Perhaps some have awful diseases in their bodies, or their souls are far away from God. They have been prayed for, and have prayed themselves, but the thing is not removed, and they are in the place where the leper was. He knew that Jesus could heal him, but how could he get near Him?

Jesus makes one great sweeping statement from that day to this as He says, *"I am willing; be cleansed."* Immediately, the man's leprosy was cleansed.

THE PLACE OF HEALING

When you are in the place God wants you to be, you will be healed. Let go of what is hindering you, and you will be established in God. You do not need to wait for a healing service; you can be healed right where you are. You do not need to wait for an altar call; you can be saved now, right where you are.

We have another narrative of a simple act of faith. Here is a man, a centurion, who is very influential. His expression is lovely. He is a man of authority, having soldiers under him, and he has a servant who is sick. He comes right up beside Jesus and says, *"My servant is lying at home paralyzed, dreadfully tormented"* (Matt. 8:6). And Jesus says to him, *"I will come and heal him"* (v. 7).

ROOM FOR JESUS

Listen. There is a marvelous fact in the Scriptures, which may be hard to understand. Jesus said, *"Foxes have holes and birds of the air have nests, but the Son of Man has nowhere to lay His head"* (v. 20). Is this true? Yes, but at the same time, it is not true. He could have had a dozen beds. Then why did He not use them? For the simple reason that the people loved Jesus and wanted Him, yet they dared not have Him in their house. If He would go to their homes, such convicting truths would fall from His lips that they could not stand in His presence. They wanted this holy, lovely Jesus, this beautiful Nazarene, and yet they did not want Him. Thus the Son of Man did not have any place to lay His head, so He spent His nights on the Mount of Olives.

The centurion said, *"Lord, I am not worthy that You should come under my roof. But only speak a word, and my servant will be healed"* (v. 8). The centurion knew that Jesus did not have to be physically present to heal the sick servant. He believed that just a word from Jesus would be sufficient. Jesus was amazed at this man's faith, and He told the centurion, *"Go your way; and as you have believed, so let it be done for you"* (v. 13). The servant was healed as Jesus spoke.

But some do not want Jesus to come to their homes, and it is not because they have such great faith. They do not want Him to come because of the changes they would have to make in their lives. They know that if Jesus were to live in their hearts, their lives would be totally transformed. How many there are who refuse salvation because they know they cannot continue to live in the same old ways; therefore, they do not invite Christ to their homes. Beloved, let us not be afraid to ask Him to come in to stay. Ask Him to give you grace to come to Him. It is only a step to Jesus. He is not looking at our unworthiness, but at His worthiness. My whole heart cries out to God that I might touch Him afresh.

CHRIST LIVING WITHIN

The greatest gift to mankind is to be able to say, "Christ lives in me!" How wonderful to have the knowledge that He dwells within. How I praise God for His wonderful Word, the Word that *"became flesh and dwelt among us, and we beheld His glory, the glory as of the only begotten of the Father, full of grace and truth"* (John 1:14). John says:

That which was from the beginning, which we have heard, which we have seen with our eyes, which we have looked upon, and our hands have handled, concerning the Word of life. (1 John 1:1)

That was their natural knowledge of Him. Jesus came into the world in His human nature. Because of that, they could say they had seen and touched eternal life. In holiness and purity, in majesty and power, the Son of God walked the earth. Everyone who touched Him was healed. When He spoke, it was done. Oh, that we might have the divine knowledge of His greatness, whereby we would be constantly changing, going on *"from glory to glory"* (2 Cor. 3:18), until we grow up into His perfect likeness (Eph. 4:15).

CHAPTER FIVE

OUR LIVING HOPE

Blessed be the God and Father of our Lord Jesus Christ,
who according to his abundant mercy has begotten us again to a
living hope through the resurrection of Jesus Christ from the dead.
—1 Peter 1:3

A farmer surveys his land, eagerly scanning the first ears of corn poking through the soil. He knows that first beginnings often indicate the outcome of the harvest. In the same manner, we can be assured of resurrection because Jesus Christ has risen from the dead. And *"as He is, so are we in this world"* (1 John 4:17). Christ is now getting the church ready for translation. In Peter, we read that we are *"begotten...again to a living hope through the resurrection of Jesus Christ from the dead."* Oh, to be changed. Just as in the flesh Jesus triumphed by the Spirit, we can be like Him in His victory. What a living hope He gives!

Although Paul and Peter were together very little, they both were inspired to bring before the church the vision of this wonderful truth that the living are being changed. If Christ did not rise, our faith is vain. We are still in our sins (1 Cor. 15:17). But Christ has risen and become the firstfruits (v. 23), and we now have the glorious hope that we will also be changed. We who were *"not a people...are now the people of God"* (1 Pet. 2:10). We have been lifted from the mire to be among princes. Beloved, God wants us to see the preciousness of it. It will drive away the dullness of life. Jesus gave all for this treasure. He purchased the field because of the pearl, *"the pearl of great price"* (Matt. 13:46)—the lowest level of humanity. Jesus purchased it, and we are the pearl of great price for all time. Our inheritance is in heaven, and in 1 Thessalonians 4:18, we are told to *"comfort one another with these words."*

What could be better than the hope that in a little while, the change will come? It seems like such a short time ago that I was a boy. Soon, I will be changed by His grace and be more than a conqueror with *"an inheritance incorruptible and undefiled and that does not fade away"* (1 Pet. 1:4). The inheritance is in you. It is something that is accomplished by God for you. When my daughter was in Africa, she often wrote of things corroding. We have a corruptible nature, but as the natural decays, the spiritual is at work. As the corruptible is doing its work, we are changing.

When will it be seen? When Jesus comes. Most beautiful of all, we will be like Him. What is the process? Grace! What can work it out? Love! It cannot be translated into human phrases. God so loved that He gave Jesus (John 3:16).

There is something very wonderful about being undefiled in the presence of my King, never to change, only to be more beautiful. Unless we know something about grace and the omnipotence of His love, we will never be able to grasp it. But believers can say:

> Love, fathomless as the sea.
> Grace flowing for you and for me.

OUR PLACE IS RESERVED

He has prepared a beautiful place for us, and we will have no fear of anyone else taking it; it is reserved. When I went to certain meetings, I would have a reserved seat. I could walk in at any time, and my seat would be unoccupied. What is good about having a reservation? You have a place where you can see Him; it is the very seat you would have chosen. He knows just what you want! He has designed the place for you. Because of His love, you will have joy instead of discord throughout eternity. Will you be there? Is it possible to miss it? We *"are kept by the power of God through faith for salvation ready to be revealed in the last time"* (1 Pet. 1:5).

What is distinctive about it? It will be the fullness of perfection, the ideal of love. The poor in spirit, the mourners, the meek, the hungry and thirsty, the merciful, the pure—all will be ready to be revealed at the appearing of Jesus Christ. You could not remain there unless you had experienced His purifying, perfecting, and establishing. You will be ready when His perfect will has been worked out in you. When you are refined enough, you will go. But there is something to be done yet to establish you, to make you purer. A great price has been paid: *"The genuineness of your faith [is] much more precious than gold that perishes"* (v. 7). And we must give all and yield all as our Great Refiner puts us in the melting pot again and again. He does this so that we will lose the chaff (Matt. 3:12), so that the pure gold of His presence will be clearly seen, and His glorious image will be reflected. We must be steadfast and immovable, until all His purposes are worked out.

STANDING FIRM THROUGH TRIALS

Praising God in a meeting is a different thing than thanking Him for the trials you face in your life. There must be no perishing though we are tried by fire. What is going to appear at the appearing of Jesus? Faith! Your heart will be established by the grace of the Spirit, which doesn't crush, but refines; doesn't destroy, but enlarges. Oh, beloved, the Enemy is a defeated foe, and Jesus not only conquers but displays the spoils of His conquest. The pure in heart will see God (Matt. 5:8). *"If therefore your eye is good, your whole body will be full of light"* (Matt. 6:22).

What is it? It is loyalty to the Word by the power of the blood. You know your inheritance within you is more powerful than all that is without. How many have gone to the stake and through fiery persecution? Did they desire it? Faith tried by fire had power to stand all ridicule, all slander. We need to have the faith of the Son of God, *"who for the joy that was set before Him endured the cross"* (Heb. 12:2). Oh, the joy of pleasing Him. No trial, no darkness, nothing is too hard for me. If only I may see the image of my Lord again and again. In the melting pot, He removes the skimmings until His face is seen. When the metal reflects Him, it is pure. Who is looking into our hearts? Who is the Refiner? My Lord. He will remove only what will hinder. Oh, I know the love of God is working in my heart.

GETTING READY FOR REVIEW

I remember going to the Crystal Palace when General Booth had a review of representatives of the Salvation Army from all nations. It was a grand sight as company after company with all their distinctive characteristics passed a certain place where he could view them. It was a wonderful scene. We are going to be presented to God. The trials are getting us ready for the procession and the presentation. We are to be a joy to look at, to be to His praise and glory. No one will be there but those who have been tried by fire. Is it worth it? Yes, a thousand times. Oh, the ecstasy of exalted pleasure. God reveals Himself to our hearts.

Peter speaks of *"sincere love"* (1 Pet. 1:22). What does it mean to have *"sincere love"*? It means that even when you are misused or shamed, it never alters; this love is only more refined, making you more like Him. *"Sincere love"* is full of appreciation for those who do not see eye to eye with you. Jesus illustrated it on the cross when He said, *"Father, forgive them"* (Luke 23:34). And Stephen demonstrated it as he was being stoned. He said, *"Lord, do not charge them with this sin"* (Acts 7:60). *"Sincere love"* is the greatest thing God can give to my heart.

We are saved by an incorruptible power—a process always refining, a grace always enlarging, a glory always increasing. We are neither barren nor unfruitful in the knowledge of our Lord Jesus Christ. *"The spirits of just men made perfect"* (Heb. 12:23) are stored in the treasury of the Most High. We are purified as sons and are to be as holy and blameless as He is. Through all eternity, we will gaze at Him with pure, genuine love. God will be glorified as the song is continuously sung: *"Holy, holy, holy, Lord God Almighty"* (Rev. 4:8).

How can we be sad, or hang our heads, or be distressed? If we only knew how rich we are. May God's name be blessed.

CHAPTER SIX

OUR RISEN CHRIST

We praise God that our glorious Jesus is the risen Christ. Those of us who have tasted the power of the indwelling Spirit know something about how the hearts of those two disciples burned as they walked to Emmaus with the risen Lord as their companion. (See Luke 24:13–31.)

Note the words of Acts 4:31: *"And when they had prayed, the place where they were assembled together was shaken."* There are many churches where they never pray the kind of prayer that you read of here. A church that does not know how to pray and to shout will never be shaken. If you live in a place like that, you might as well write over the threshold: *"Ichabod"—"The glory has departed from Israel!"* (1 Sam. 4:21). It is only when men have learned the secret of prayer, power, and praise that God comes forth. Some people say, "Well, I praise God inwardly," but if there is an abundance of praise in your heart, your mouth cannot help speaking it.

WHAT IS INSIDE WILL COME OUT

A man who had a large business in London was a great churchgoer. The church he attended was beautifully decorated, and his pew was delightfully cushioned—just enough to make it easy to sleep through the sermons. He was a prosperous man in business, but he had no peace in his heart. There was a boy at his business who always looked happy. He was always jumping and whistling. One day he said to this boy, "I want to see you in my office."

When the boy came to his office, the man asked him, "How is it that you can always whistle and be happy?" "I cannot help it," answered the boy. "Where did you get this happiness?" asked the gentleman. "I got it at the Pentecostal mission." "Where is that?"

38

The boy told him, and the man began attending. The Lord reached his heart, and in a short while, he was entirely changed. One day, shortly after this, he found that instead of being distracted by his business as he formerly had been, he was actually whistling. His disposition and his whole life had been changed.

The shout cannot come out unless it is within. The inner working of the power of God must come first. It is He who changes the heart and transforms the life. Before there is any real outward evidence, there must be the inflow of divine life. Sometimes I say to people, "You weren't at the meeting the other night." They reply, "Oh, yes, I was there in spirit." I say to them, "Well, next time come with your body also. We don't want a lot of spirits here and no bodies. We want you to come and get filled with God." When all the people come and pray and praise as did these early disciples, there will be something happening. People who come will catch fire, and they will want to come again. But they will have no use for a place where everything has become formal, dry, and dead.

The power of Pentecost came to loose men. God wants us to be free. Men and women are tired of imitations; they want reality; they want to see people who have the living Christ within, who are filled with Holy Spirit power.

GOD IS ALWAYS ON TIME

I received several letters and telegrams about a certain case, but when I arrived I was told I was too late. I said, "That cannot be. God has never sent me anywhere too late." God showed me that something different would happen than anything I had ever seen before. The people I went to were all strangers. I was introduced to a young man who lay helpless, and for whom there was no hope. The doctor had been to see him that morning and had declared that he would not live through the day. He lay with his face to the wall, and when I spoke to him, he whispered, "I cannot turn over." His mother said that they had had to lift him out of bed on sheets for weeks, and that he was so frail and helpless that he had to stay in one position.

The young man said, "My heart is so weak." I assured him, "*God is the strength of* [your] *heart and* [your] *portion forever'* (Ps. 73:26). If you will believe God, it will be so today."

Our Christ is risen. He is a living Christ who lives within us. We must not have this truth merely as a theory. Christ must be risen in us by the power of the Spirit. The power that raised Him from the dead must animate us, and as this glorious resurrection power surges through our beings, we will be freed from all our weaknesses. We will *be strong in the Lord and in the power of His might*" (Eph. 6:10). There is a resurrection power that God wants you to have and to have today. Why not receive your portion here and now?

I said to these people, "I believe your son will rise today." They only laughed. People do not expect to see signs and wonders today as the disciples saw them of old. Has God changed? Or has our faith diminished so that we are not expecting the greater works that Jesus promised? We must not sing in any minor key. Our message must rise to concert pitch, and there must be nothing left out of it that is in the Book.

It was wintertime, and I said to the parents, "Will you get the boy's suit and bring it here?" They would not listen to the request, for they were expecting the boy to die. But I had gone to that place believing God. We read of Abraham:

(As it is written, "I have made you a father of many nations") *in the presence of Him whom he believed; God...gives life to the dead and calls those things which do not exist as though they did.* (Rom. 4:17)

God, help us to understand this. It is time people knew how to shout in faith as they contemplate the eternal power of our God, to whom it is nothing to *give life to your mortal bodies* (Rom. 8:11) and raise the dead. I come across some who would be giants in the power of God, but they have no shout of faith. Everywhere, I find people who become discouraged even when they are praying simply because they are just breathing sentences without uttering speech. You cannot win the victory that way. You must learn to take the victory and shout in the face of the Devil, "It is done!" There is no man who can doubt if he learns to shout. When we know how to shout properly, things will be different, and tremendous things will happen. In Acts 4:24 we read, *they raised their voice to God with one accord.* It surely must have been a loud prayer. We must know that God means for us to have life. If there is anything in the world that has life in it, it is this Pentecostal revival we are in. I believe in the baptism of the Holy Spirit with the speaking in tongues, and I believe that every man who is baptized in the Holy

40

Spirit will *"speak with other tongues, as the Spirit* [gives him] *utterance"* (Acts 2:4). I believe in the Holy Spirit. And if you are filled with the Spirit, you will be superabounding in life, and living waters will flow from you.

At last I persuaded the parents to bring the boy's clothes and lay them on the bed. From the human viewpoint, the young man lay dying. I spoke to the afflicted one, "God has revealed to me that as I lay my hands on you, the place will be filled with the Holy Spirit, the bed will be shaken, and you will be shaken and thrown out of bed. By the power of the Holy Spirit, you will dress yourself and be strong." I said this to him in faith. I laid hands on him in the name of Jesus, and instantly the power of God fell and filled the place. I felt helpless and fell flat on the floor. I knew nothing except that a short while after, the place was shaken. I heard the young man walking over to me, saying, "For Your glory, Lord! For Your glory, Lord!"

He dressed himself and cried, "God has healed me." The father fell, the mother fell, and another who was present fell also. God manifested His power that day in saving the whole household and healing the young man. It is the power of the risen Christ we need. Today, that young man is preaching the Gospel.

GOD IS AT WORK

For years we have been longing for God to come forth, and, praise Him, He is coming forth. The tide is rising everywhere. I was in Switzerland not long ago, preaching in many places where the Pentecostal message had not been heard. Today, there are nine new Pentecostal assemblies in different places going on blessedly for God. All over the world it is the same; this great Pentecostal work is in motion. You can hardly go to a place now where God is not pouring out His Spirit upon all flesh, and His promises never fail. Our Christ is risen. His salvation was not a thing done in a corner. Truly He was a man of glory who went to Calvary for us in order that He might free us from all that would mar and hinder, that He might transform us by His grace and bring us out from under the power of Satan into the glorious power of God. One touch of our risen Christ will raise the dead. Hallelujah!

Oh, this wonderful Jesus of ours comes and indwells us. He comes to abide. It is He who baptizes us with the Holy Spirit and makes everything different. We are to be a *"kind of firstfruits"*

41

(James 1:18) unto God and are to be like Christ who is the firstfruit. We are to walk in His footsteps and live in His power. What a salvation this is, having this risen Christ in us. I feel that everything else must go to nothingness, helplessness, and ruin. Even the best thought of holiness must be on the decrease in order that Christ may increase. All things are under the power of the Spirit.

GOD IS WITH YOU

Dare you take your inheritance from God? Dare you believe God? Dare you stand on the record of His Word? What is the record? If you will believe, you will see the glory of God. You will be sifted as wheat. You will be tested as though some strange thing tried you. You will be put in places where you will have to put your whole trust in God. There is no such thing as anyone being tested beyond what God will allow. There is no temptation that will come, but God will be with you right in the temptation to deliver you (1 Cor. 10:13), and when you have been tried, He will bring you forth as gold (Job 23:10). Every trial is to bring you to a greater position in God. The trial that tries your faith will take you on to the place where you will know that the faith of God will be forthcoming in the next test. No man is able to win any victory except through the power of the risen Christ within him. You will never be able to say, "I did this or that." You will desire to give God the glory for everything.

If you are sure of your ground, if you are counting on the presence of the living Christ within, you can laugh when you see things getting worse. God wants you to be settled and grounded in Christ and to become steadfast and unmovable in Him. The Lord Jesus said, *"I have a baptism to be baptized with, and how distressed I am till it is accomplished!"* (Luke 12:50). Assuredly, He was obedient to the will of His Father in Gethsemane, in the judgment hall, and, after that, on the cross, where He, *"through the eternal Spirit offered Himself without spot to God"* (Heb. 9:14). God will take us right on in like manner, and the Holy Spirit will lead every step of the way. God led Him right through to the empty tomb, to the glory of the Ascension, to a place on the throne. The Son of God will never be satisfied until He has us with Himself, sharing His glory and sharing His throne.

CHAPTER SEVEN

PRESSING THROUGH

I f anything stirs me in my life, it is words such as these: *"We never saw anything like this!"* (Mark 2:12). These words were spoken following the healing of a paralyzed man. His four friends removed a portion of the roof in order to *"let down the bed on which the paralytic was lying"* (v. 4). Jesus healed the man, and

Immediately he arose, took up the bed, and went out in the presence of them all, so that all were amazed and glorified God, saying, "We never saw anything like this!" (v. 12)

Something should happen all the time to cause people to say, "We never saw anything like that." God is dissatisfied with stationary conditions. So many people stop at the doorway when God in His great plan is inviting them into His treasury. He opens the storehouse of the Most High, *"the unsearchable riches of Christ"* (Eph. 3:8), to us. God wants to move us into this divine position so that we are completely new creations (2 Cor. 5:17). You know that the flesh profits nothing. Paul said in Romans that *"the carnal mind is enmity against God; for it is not subject to the law of God, nor indeed can be"* (Rom. 8:7). As we cease to live in the old life and come to know the resurrection power of the Lord, we enter a place of rest, faith, joy, peace, blessing, and life everlasting. Glory to God!

May the Lord give us a new vision of Himself and fresh touches of divine life. May His presence shake off all that remains of the old life and bring us fully into His newness of life. May He reveal to us the greatness of His will concerning us, for there is no one who loves us like Him. Yes, beloved, there is no love like His, no compassion like His. He is filled with compassion and never fails to take those who will fully obey Him into the Promised Land.

THE SWEET PRESENCE OF GOD

In God's Word, there is always more to follow, always more to know. If only we could be like children in taking in the mind of God, what wonderful things would happen. Do you apply the whole Bible to your life? It is grand. Never mind those who take only a part. You take it all. When we get such a thirst that nothing can satisfy us but God, we will have a royal time.

The child of God must have reality all the time. After the child of God comes into the sweetness of the perfume of the presence of God, he will have the hidden treasures of God. He will always be feeding on that blessed truth that will make life full of glory. Are you dry? There is no dry place in God, but all good things come out of hard times. The harder the place you are in, the more blessing can come out of it as you yield to His plan. Oh, if only I had known God's plan in its fullness, I might never have had a tear in my life. God is so abundant, so full of love and mercy; there is no lack to those who trust in Him. I pray that God will give us a touch of reality, so that we may be able to trust Him all the way.

It is an ideal thing to get people to believe that when they ask, they will receive (Matt. 21:22). But how could it be otherwise? It must be so when God says it. Now we have a beautiful word brought before us in the case of this paralyzed man, helpless and so weak that he could not help himself get to Jesus. Four men, whose hearts were full of compassion, carried the man to the house, but the house was full. Oh, I can see that house today as it was filled, jammed, and crammed. There was no room, even by the door. It was crowded inside and out.

THE WAY TO JESUS

The men who were carrying the sick man said, "What will we do?" But there is always a way. I have never found faith to fail, never once. May the Holy Spirit give us a new touch of faith in God's unlimited power. May we have a living faith that will dare to trust Him and say, "Lord, I do believe."

There was no room, *"not even near the door"* (Mark 2:2), but these men said, "Let's go up on the roof." Unbelieving people would say, "Oh, that is silly, ridiculous, foolish!" But men of faith say, "We must get our friend help at all costs. It is nothing to move the roof. Let's go up and go through." Lord, take us today, and let us go through; let us drop right into the arms of Jesus. It is a lovely place to drop into, out of your self-righteousness, out of your self-consciousness, out of your unbelief. Some people have been in a strange place of deadness for years, but God can shake them out of it. Thank God, some of the molds have been broken. It is a blessed thing when the old mold gets broken, for God has a new mold. He can perfect the imperfect by His own loving touch.

PAID IN FULL

I tell you, friends, that since the day that Christ's blood was shed, since the day of His atonement, He has paid the price to meet all the world's needs and its cries of sorrow. Truly Jesus has met the needs of broken hearts and sorrowful spirits, withered limbs and broken bodies. God's dear Son paid the debt for all, for He *"took our infirmities and bore our sicknesses"* (Matt. 8:17). He was *"in all points tempted as we are, yet without sin"* (Heb. 4:15). I rejoice to bring Him to you today, even though it is in my crooked Yorkshire speech, and say to you that He is the only Jesus; He is the only plan; He is the only life; He is the only help; but thank God, He has triumphed to the utmost. He came *"to seek and to save that which was lost"* (Luke 19:10), and He heals all who come to Him.

As the paralyzed man was lowered through the roof, there was a great commotion, and all the people gazed up at this strange sight. We read, *"When Jesus saw their faith, He said to the paralytic, 'Son, your sins are forgiven you'"* (Mark 2:5). What had the forgiveness of sins to do with the healing of this man? It had everything to do with it. Sin is at the root of disease. May the Lord cleanse us from outward sin and from inbred sin and take away all that hinders the power of God to work through us.

"Some of the scribes were sitting there and reasoning in their hearts" (v. 6). They asked: *"Who can forgive sins but God alone?"* (v. 7). But the Lord answered the thoughts of their hearts by saying,

> *"Which is easier, to say to the paralytic, 'Your sins are forgiven you,' or to say, 'Arise, take up your bed and walk'? But that you may know that the Son of Man has power on earth to forgive sins;"* He said to the paralytic, *"I say to you, arise, take up your bed, and go to your house."*
>
> (vv. 9–11)

45

Jesus healed that man. He saw also the faith of the four men. There is something in this for us today. Many people will not be saved unless some of you are used to stir them up. Remember that you are your *"brother's keeper"* (Gen. 4:9). We must take our brother to Jesus. When these men carried the paralyzed man, they pressed through until he could hear the voice of the Son of God, and liberty came to the captive. The man became strong by the power of God, arose, took up his bed, and went forth before them all.

I have seen wonderful things like this accomplished by the power of God. We must never think about our God in small ways. He spoke the word one day and made the world. That is the kind of God we have, and He is just the same today. There is no change in Him. Oh, He is lovely and precious above all thought and comparison. There is none like Him.

CLAIM HIS PROMISES

I am certain today that nothing will profit you but what you take by faith. As you *"draw near to God...He will draw near to you"* (James 4:8). Believe and claim the promises, for they are *"Yes"* and *"Amen"* to all who believe (2 Cor. 1:20). Let us thank God for this full Gospel, which is not hidden under a bushel today (Matt. 5:15). Let us thank Him that He is bringing out the Gospel as *"in the days of His flesh"* (Heb. 5:7). All the time, God is working right in the very middle of us, but I want to know, what are you going to do with the Gospel today? There is a greater blessing for you than you have ever received in your life. Do you believe it? Will you receive it?

CHAPTER EIGHT

RIGHTEOUSNESS

You have loved righteousness and hated lawlessness;
therefore God, Your God has anointed You with the oil of gladness
more than Your companions.
—Hebrews 1:9

As we are filled with the Holy Spirit, God purposes that like our Lord, we should love righteousness and hate lawlessness. I see that there is a place for us in Christ Jesus where we are no longer under condemnation but where the heavens are always open to us. I see that God has a realm of divine life opening up to us where there are boundless possibilities, where there is limitless power, where there are untold resources, and where we have victory over all the power of the Devil. I believe that, as we are filled with the desire to press on into this life of true holiness, desiring only the glory of God, nothing can hinder our true advancement.

PRECIOUS FAITH

Peter began his second letter with these words:

Simon Peter, a bondservant and apostle of Jesus Christ, to those who have obtained like precious faith with us by the righteousness of our God and Savior Jesus Christ.
(2 Pet. 1:1)

Through faith, we realize that we have a blessed and glorious union with our risen Lord. When He was on earth, Jesus told us, "*I*

47

am in the Father and the Father in Me" (John 14:11). *"The Father who dwells in Me does the works"* (v. 10). And He prayed to His Father, not only for His disciples, but for those who would believe on Him through their testimonies: *"that they all may be one, as You, Father, are in Me, and I in You; that they also may be one in Us, that the world may believe that You sent me"* (John 17:21). What an inheritance is ours when the very nature, the very right-eousness, the very power of the Father and the Son are made real in us. This is God's purpose, and as by faith, we take hold of the purpose, we will always be conscious that *"He who is in* [us] *is greater than he who is in the world"* (1 John 4:4). The purpose of all Scripture is to move us to this wonderful and blessed elevation of faith where our constant experience is the manifestation of God's life and power through us.

Peter went on to write to those who have obtained *"like pre-cious faith,"* saying, *"Grace and peace be multiplied to you in the knowledge of God and of Jesus our Lord"* (2 Pet. 1:2). We can have the multiplication of this grace and peace only as we live in the realm of faith. Abraham attained to the place where he became a *"friend of God"* because he *"believed God"* (James 2:23). He *"be-lieved God, and it was accounted to him for righteousness"* (v. 23). Righteousness was credited to him on no other ground than that he *"believed God."* Can this be true of anybody else? Yes, it can be true for every person in the whole wide world who is saved and is blessed along with faithful Abraham. The promise that came to him because of his faith was that in him all the families of the earth would be blessed (Gen. 18:18). When we believe God, there is no telling where the blessings of our faith will end.

Some are anxious because, when they are prayed for, the thing that they are expecting does not happen that same night. They say they believe, but you can see that they are really in turmoil from their unbelief. Abraham believed God. You can hear him saying to Sarah, "Sarah, there is no life in you, and there is nothing in me; but God has promised us a son, and I believe God." That kind of faith is a joy to our Father in heaven.

EYES OF FAITH

One day I was having a meeting in Bury, in Lancashire, Eng-land. A young woman from a place called Ramsbottom came to be healed of an enlargement of her thyroid gland. Before she came she said, "I am going to be healed of this goiter, Mother." After one meeting she came forward and was prayed for. The next meeting she got up and testified that she had been wonderfully healed. She said, "I will be so happy to go and tell Mother about my healing."

She went to her home and testified how wonderfully she had been healed. The next year when we were having the convention, she came again. From a human perspective, it looked as though the goiter was just as big as ever, but that young woman was believing God. Soon she was on her feet giving her testimony, saying, "I was here last year, and the Lord wonderfully healed me. I want to tell you that this has been the best year of my life." She seemed to be greatly blessed in that meeting, and she went home to testify more strongly than ever that the Lord had healed her.

She believed God. The third year, she was at the meeting again, and some people who looked at her said, "How big that goiter has become." But when the time came for testimonies, she was on her feet and testified, "Two years ago, the Lord gloriously healed me of a goiter. Oh, I had a most wonderful healing. It is grand to be healed by the power of God." That day someone questioned her and said, "People will think there is something the matter with you. Why don't you look in the mirror? You will see your goiter is bigger than ever." The young woman went to the Lord about it and said, "Lord, You so wonderfully healed me two years ago. Won't You show all the people that You healed me?" She went to sleep peacefully that night still believing God. When she came down the next day, there was not a trace or a mark of that goiter.

THE MIRROR OF FAITH

God's Word is from everlasting to everlasting. His Word cannot fail. God's Word is true, and when we rest in its truth, what mighty results we can get. Faith never looks in the mirror. The mirror of faith is the perfect law of liberty:

> *But he who looks into the perfect law of liberty and continues in it, and is not a forgetful hearer but a doer of the work, this one will be blessed in what he does.* (James 1:25)

To the man who looks into this perfect law of God, all darkness is removed. He sees his completeness in Christ. There is no darkness in faith. Darkness is only in nature. Darkness exists when the natural replaces the divine.

Grace and peace are multiplied to us through a knowledge of God and of Jesus Christ. As we really know our God and Savior, we will have peace multiplied to us like the multiplied fires of ten thousand Nebuchadnezzars. (See Daniel 3:10–30.) Our faith will increase even though we are put into a den of lions, and we will live with joy in the middle of the whole thing. What was the difference between Daniel and the king that night when Daniel was put into the den of lions? Daniel's faith was certain, but the king's was experimental. The king came around the next morning and cried, *"Daniel, servant of the living God, has your God, whom you serve continually, been able to deliver you from the lions?"* (Dan. 6:20). Daniel answered, *"My God sent His angel and shut the lions' mouths"* (v. 22). The thing was done. It was done when Daniel prayed with his windows open toward heaven. All our victories are won before we go into the fight. Prayer links us to our lovely God, our abounding God, our multiplying God. Oh, I love Him. He is so wonderful!

HOLINESS OPENS THE DOOR

You will note as you read 2 Peter 1:1–2 that this grace and peace are multiplied through the knowledge of God, but that first our faith comes through the righteousness of God. Note that righteousness comes first and knowledge afterwards. It cannot be otherwise. If you expect any revelation of God apart from holiness, you will have only a mixture. Holiness opens the door to all the treasures of God. He must first bring us to the place where we, like our Lord, "[love] *righteousness and* [hate] *lawlessness,"* before He opens up to us these good treasures. When we *"regard iniquity in* [our hearts]*, the Lord will not hear"* us (Ps. 66:18), and it is only as we are made righteous, pure, and holy through the precious blood of God's Son that we can enter into this life of holiness and righteousness in the Son. It is the righteousness of our Lord Himself made real in us as our faith remains in Him.

After I was baptized with the Holy Spirit, the Lord gave me a blessed revelation. I saw Adam and Eve turned out of the Garden for their disobedience. They were unable to partake of the Tree of Life, for the cherubim with flaming sword kept them away from this tree. When I was baptized, I saw that I had begun to eat of this Tree of Life, and I saw that the flaming sword surrounded it. It was there to keep the Devil away. Oh, what privileges are ours

50

when we are born of God. How marvelously He keeps us so that the Wicked One cannot touch us. I see a place in God where Satan cannot come. We are *"hidden with Christ in God"* (Col. 3:3). He invites us all to come and share this wonderful hidden place. We dwell *"in the secret place of the Most High"* and *"abide under the shadow of the Almighty"* (Ps. 91:1). God has this place for you in this blessed realm of grace.

Peter went on to say:

> *As His divine power has given to us all things that pertain to life and godliness, through the knowledge of Him who called us by glory and virtue, by which have been given to us exceeding great and precious promises, that through these you may be partakers of the divine nature.*
>
> (2 Pet. 1:3–4)

DARE TO BELIEVE GOD

"Faith is the substance of things hoped for" (Heb. 11:1) right here in this life. It is here that God wants us to share in His divine nature. It is nothing less than the life of the Lord Himself imparted and flowing into our whole beings, so that our very bodies are quickened, so that every tissue, every drop of blood, and our bones, joints, and marrow receive this divine life. I believe that the Lord wants this divine life to flow right into our natural bodies. God wants to establish our faith so that we will grasp this divine life, this divine nature of the Son of God, so that our *"spirit, soul, and body be preserved blameless at the coming of our Lord Jesus Christ"* (1 Thess. 5:23).

When the woman who had suffered for twelve years from a flow of blood was healed, Jesus perceived that power had gone out of Him (Mark 5:25–34). The woman's faith reached out, and His power was imparted. Immediately, the woman's being was charged with life, and her weakness departed. The conveying of this power produces everything you need, but it comes only as your faith reaches out to accept it. Faith is the victory. If you can believe, the healing power is yours.

I suffered for many years from hemorrhoids, until my whole body was thoroughly weak; the blood used to gush from me. One day I got desperate and took a bottle of oil to anoint myself. I said to the Lord, "Do what You want to, quickly." I was healed at that very moment. God wants us to have an activity of faith that dares to believe God. There is what seems to be faith, an appearance of faith, but real faith believes God right to the end.

What was the difference between Zacharias and Mary? The angel came to Zacharias and told him his wife Elizabeth would bear a son (Luke 1:13). Zacharias began to question this message, saying, *"I am an old man, and my wife is well advanced in years"* (v. 18). Gabriel, the angel of the Lord, rebuked him for his unbelief and told him, *"You will be mute and not able to speak until the day these things take place, because you did not believe my words"* (v. 20).

Note the contrast when the angel came to Mary. She said, *"Behold the maidservant of the Lord! Let it be to me according to your word"* (v. 38). And Elizabeth greeted Mary with the words, *"Blessed is she who believed, for there will be a fulfillment of those things which were told her from the Lord"* (v. 45).

God wants us to believe His Word in the same way. He wants us to come with a boldness of faith, declaring, "You have promised it, Lord. Now do it." God rejoices when we manifest a faith that holds Him to His Word. Can we get there?

FAITH CLAIMS THE VICTORY

The Lord has called us to this glory and power. As our faith claims His promises, we will see this evidenced. I remember one day I was holding a meeting. My uncle came to that meeting and said, "Aunt Mary would like to see Smith before she dies." I went to see her, and she was assuredly dying. I said, "Lord, can't You do something?" All I did was stretch out my hands and lay them on her. It seemed as though there was an immediate touch of the glory and power of the Lord. Aunt Mary cried, "It is going all over my body." That day she was made perfectly whole.

One day I was preaching, and a man brought a boy who was wrapped up in bandages. It was impossible for him to walk, so it was difficult for them to get him to the platform. They passed him over about six seats. The power of the Lord was present to heal, and it entered right into the child as I placed my hands on him. The child cried, "Daddy, it is going all over me." They took off the boy's bandages and found nothing wrong with him.

The Lord wants us to be walking letters of His Word. Jesus is the Word and is the power in us. It is His desire to work in and through us *"for His good pleasure"* (Phil. 2:13). We must believe that He is in us. There are boundless possibilities for us if we dare to act in God and dare to believe that the wonderful power of our living Christ will be made clear through us as we lay our hands on the sick in His name (Mark 16:18).

The *"exceedingly great and precious promises"* (2 Pet. 1:4) of the Word are given to us that we might be *"partakers of the divine nature"* (v. 4). I feel the Holy Spirit is grieved with us when we know these things but do not do greater deeds for God. Does not the Holy Spirit show us wide-open doors of opportunity? Will we not let God lead us to greater things? Will we not believe God to take us on to greater demonstrations of His power? He calls us to forget the things that are behind, reach toward the things ahead, and *"press toward the goal for the prize of the upward call of God in Christ Jesus"* (Phil. 3:13–14).

CHAPTER NINE

UTTERMOST SALVATION

Many people say that the fifth chapter of Matthew is for the millennial age and that people cannot live it now. Consequently, they avoid this chapter without carefully investigating it. But for the spiritually mature, there is a little heaven on earth in the truth of this passage. Mature Christians can reach a place where they have no fellowship with darkness and where the world does not know them.

After I was baptized in the Holy Spirit, I saw distinctly that God had allowed me to eat of that Tree of Life of which Adam and Eve were not able to eat. I saw that when the Holy Spirit came in, He wonderfully revealed Christ to me so that I was nourished by His presence, strengthened, and filled with great joy. Praise His name! I know that the baptism of the Holy Spirit brings us into possession of all the fullness of God. People often sing, "Oh, that will be glory for me. When by His grace, I shall look on His face," but I saw that God had changed that song for me so that I can sing:

> Oh, now it is glory for me,
> Now it is glory for me,
> For as by His grace,
> I look on His face,
> Now it is glory for me.

A SPIRIT OF POVERTY

Let me come to this wonderful chapter God has given. I will begin with the third verse, *"Blessed are the poor in spirit, for theirs is the kingdom of heaven"* (Matt. 5:3). The people who have grasped this idea and have identified themselves with the Lord Jesus Christ have come to a place where they now see that all things are possible with God. We have come to a place of an unlimited supply in God, and in our poverty of spirit, we are entitled to all that God has, *"for theirs is the kingdom of heaven."* In spite of my meekness, humility, and helplessness, all that God has is mine.

When Jesus came to Sychar, a city of Samaria, *"being wearied from His journey"* (John 4:6), He sat down by a well. His disciples were not with Him because they had gone to buy food in a nearby city (v. 8). When they returned, they saw Him at peace. He was not looking for food but was quite relaxed. When Jesus was not interested in eating the food they had bought, *"the disciples said to one another, 'Has anyone brought Him anything to eat?'"* (v. 33). This shows us the possibility for man to live in God, to be absorbed in God, with no consciousness of the world under any circumstances, except as we bring help to it. And He said to them, *"Behold, I say to you, lift up your eyes and look at the fields, for they are already white for harvest!"* (v. 35). That is His food, the spiritual life in God, which is joy in the Holy Spirit.

He comes to enrapture our souls, to break every bond of mere human affection and replace in us the divine instead of the earthly, the pure instead of the unholy, the eyes of faith that see God instead of human feelings. The divine Son of God is to be in us, mightily moving through us, as we cease to be. This poverty of spirit spoken of in this Beatitude helps us.

A Spirit of Mourning

We must live in such a pure atmosphere that God will shine in and through our souls. Oh, this uttermost salvation (Heb. 7:25)! I am satisfied that as we get to know the Son of God, we will never be weak anymore. The tide will turn. Let us look at the next verse in Matthew 5: *"Blessed are those who mourn, for they shall be comforted"* (v. 4).

Did Jesus mean mourning over death? No, He meant mourning over our sons and daughters who have not yet reached heaven, who know nothing about the things of the Spirit of Life. When God places within us a mourning cry to move the powers of God, then He will send a revival in every home.

It is impossible to get this spiritual mourning over lost souls without having the very next thing that God says, *"[you] shall be comforted."* As though God could give you a spirit of mourning over a needy soul, then not give you victory! Beloved, it is the mighty power of God in us. And when the Spirit brings us to this mourning attitude over lost souls and over all the failures that we see in professing Christians, until we can go into the presence of God with that mourning spirit, nothing will happen. But when that happens, rejoice; God will bring you through.

A Spirit of Meekness

God wants us to rejoice today. He has brought us into this blessed place that we may mourn and then rejoice. Let us go on with the chapter because much depends on the next verse: *"Blessed are the meek, for they shall inherit the earth"* (Matt. 5:5).

You say, "Don't talk to me about being meek; I will never be able to be like that." Take the case of Moses. He surely was not meek when he killed the Egyptian. But when God got Moses into His hand in the land of Midian, He molded him so that he became the meekest man in all the earth. I do not care what your temper is like. If you get only a little touch of heaven, God can mold you so that you can be the meekest person on the earth.

I used to have such a bad temper that it made me tremble all over. It would make me furious with its evil power. I saw that this temper had to be destroyed; it could not be patched up. One day the power of God fell upon me. I came to the meeting and fell down before the Lord. The people began asking, "What sin has Wigglesworth been committing?" This went on for two weeks. Every time I came to the altar, God used to sweep through me with such a manifestation of my helplessness that I would go down before God and weep right through. Then the preacher or the leader was broken up and came beside me. God started a revival that way. God had broken me up, and revival began through His revival in me. Oh, it was lovely! At last my wife said, "Since my husband had that touch, I have never been able to cook anything that he was not pleased with. It is never too cold and never too hot."

Only God can make people right. Only melted gold is minted. Only moistened clay accepts the mold. Only softened wax receives the seal. Only broken, contrite hearts receive the mark as the Potter turns us on His wheel. Oh, Lord, give us that blessed state where we are perfectly and wholly made meek.

A Spirit of Hunger and Thirst

The Beatitudes of the Spirit are truly lovely. *"Blessed are those who hunger and thirst for righteousness, for they shall be filled"*

(Matt. 5:6). Oh, yes, praise the Lord! We must emphasize that God will not fail to fill us. No man can *"hunger and thirst after righteousness"* unless God has put the desire in him. And I want you to notice that this righteousness is the righteousness of Jesus.

In 1 John 5:4–5, we find these verses: *"This is the victory that has overcome the world; our faith. Who is he who overcomes the world, but he who believes that Jesus is the Son of God?"* Righteousness is more than paying our way. We hear someone say, "Oh, I never do anything wrong to anybody. I always pay my way." This is simply life in the flesh, but there is a higher *"law of the Spirit of life in Christ Jesus"* (Rom. 8:2). I must see that Jesus is my perfect righteousness. He came by the power of God:

> *For what the law could not do in that it was weak through the flesh, God did by sending His own Son in the likeness of sinful flesh, on account of sin: He condemned sin in the flesh.* (Rom. 8:3)

We must see that if we get this righteousness of God, sin is destroyed. There are beautiful words in the ninth verse of the first chapter of Hebrews: *"You have loved righteousness and hated lawlessness; therefore God, Your God, has anointed You with the oil of gladness more than Your companions."*

But the climax of divine touches of heaven never leaves you stationary but rather increases your thirst and appetite for greater things. Something within makes you press on until you are empty of everything else so that you may be filled with what God is pressing in. This righteousness is a walk with God. It is a divine inheritance. It is seeing the face of Jesus until you cannot be satisfied without drinking of His Spirit and being overflowed continually with His blessings. I cannot be satisfied without Christ's righteousness. He gives us thirst for the immensity of God's power. It is a divine problem that is solved in only one way: having Him. And having Him, we have all things.

A SPIRIT OF MERCY

I pray that God will bring you to a death of self and a life of righteousness, which will please God. Thus we understand in some measure what God has for us in the next verse of Matthew 5: *"Blessed are the merciful, for they shall obtain mercy"* (v. 7).

I believe this is truly a spiritual condition, which is higher than the natural law. Sometimes when we talk about mercy, we think of being kind, amiable, or philanthropic toward others. We think those are respected positions. So they are, but the world has that. Beloved, we should have all that, but we should have much more. We will never understand the meaning of the mercy of Jesus until He fills us with Himself. My blessed Lord! Can there ever be one like Him? Can you think of such rarity, such beauty, such self-sacrifice? *"Blessed are the merciful."* We must have heaven's riches to give to souls in poverty. You cannot be filled with the Lord and not be merciful. You cannot have the baptism with power without this supernatural mercy, this divine touch of heaven that stops satanic forces, frees the oppressed, and strengthens the helpless. That is the spirit that God wants to give us. Oh, for heaven to bend down upon us with this deep inward cry for a touch of Him, His majesty, His glory, His might, His power!

It is a very remarkable thing that the merciful always obtain mercy. Look at the measure of this spiritual life: first full, then pressed down, then shaken together, and then running over (Luke 6:38). This divine touch of heaven is lovely. It is the most charming thing on earth, sweeter than all. I am just running over with new wine this morning. God wants you to have this new wine. It thrills the human heart. How it mightily sweeps you right into heaven!

I ask you all, needy souls, whatever you want, to *"come boldly to the throne of grace"* (Heb. 4:16). Come, and the Lord bless you.

CHAPTER TEN

COUNT IT ALL JOY

Count it all joy when you fall into various trials.
—James 1:2

This letter was addressed *"to the twelve tribes which are scattered abroad"* (v. 1). Only one like the Master could stand and say to the people, *"Count it all joy"* when they were disbursed everywhere, driven to their wits' end, and persecuted. The Scriptures say that *"they wandered in deserts and mountains, in dens and caves of the earth"* (Heb. 11:38). These people were separated from each other, but God was with them.

GOD IS FOR YOU

It does not matter where you are if God is with you. He who is for you is a million times greater than all who can be against you (Rom. 8:31). Oh, if by the grace of God, we could only see that the blessings of God's divine power come to us with such sweetness, whispering to us, "Be still, My child. All is well." Be still and see the salvation of the Lord.

What would happen if we learned the secret to asking once and then believing? What an advantage it would be if we could come to a place where we know that everything is within reach of us. God wants us to see that every obstacle can be removed. God brings us into a place where the difficulties are, where the pressure is, where the hard corner is, where everything is so difficult that you know there are no possibilities on the human side. God must do it. All these places are in God's plan. God allows trials, difficulties, temptations, and perplexities to come right along our path, but there is not a temptation or trial that can come to us without God providing a way out (1 Cor. 10:13). You do not have the way out; it is God who can bring you through.

Many saints come to me and want me to pray for their nervous systems. I guarantee there is not a person in the whole world who could be nervous if he or she understood 1 John 4. Let us read verses sixteen through eighteen:

And we have known and believed the love that God has for us. God is love, and he who abides in love abides in God, and God in him. Love has been perfected among us in this: that we may have boldness in the day of judgment; because as He is, so are we in this world. There is no fear in love; but perfect love casts out fear, because fear involves torment. But he who fears has not been made perfect in love.

Let me tell you what perfect love is. The one *"who believes that Jesus is the Son of God"* is the one *"who overcomes the world"* (1 John 5:5). What is the evidence and assurance of salvation? He who believes in his heart on the Lord Jesus (Acts 16:31). Every expression of love is in the heart. When you begin to pour out your heart to God in love, your very being, your whole self, desires Him. Perfect love means that Jesus has taken hold of your intentions, desires, and thoughts and purified everything. Perfect love cannot fear (1 John 4:18).

GOD WILL DELIVER YOU

What God wants is to saturate us with His Word. His Word is a living truth. I would pity one who has gone a whole week without temptation because God tries only the people who are worthy. If you are passing through difficulties, trials are rising, darkness is appearing, and everything becomes so dense you cannot see through, hallelujah! God will see you through. He is a God of deliverance, a God of power. He is near to you if you will only believe. He can anoint you with fresh oil and make your cup run over (Ps. 23:5). Jesus is the *"balm in Gilead"* (Jer. 8:22), the *"rose of Sharon"* (Song 2:1).

I believe that God wants to align us with such perfection of blessing and beauty that we will say, *"Though He slay me, yet will I trust Him"* (Job 13:15). When the hand of God is on you, and the clay is fresh in the Potter's hands, the vessel will be made perfect as you are pliable in God's hands. Only melted gold is minted. Only moistened clay is molded. Only softened wax receives the seal. Only broken, contrite hearts receive the mark as the Potter turns us on His wheel. He can put His stamp on you today. He can mold you anew and change your vision. He can remove the difficulty. The Lord of Hosts is here, waiting for your affection. Remember His question, *"Simon, son of Jonah, do you love Me more than these?"* (John 21:15). He never lets the chastening rod fall upon anything except what is marring the vessel. If there is anything in you that is not yielded and bent to the plan of the Almighty, you cannot preserve what is spiritual only in part. When the Spirit of the Lord gets perfect control, then we begin to be changed by the expression of God's light in our human frame. The whole body begins to have the fullness of His life manifested until God so has us that we believe all things.

DRAW NEAR TO GOD

If God brings you into oneness and fellowship with the Most High God, your nature will tremble in His presence. But God can chase away all the defects, the unrest, the unfaithfulness, the wavering, and He can establish you with such comfort that you rest in the Holy Spirit by the power of God. God invites us to higher heights and deeper depths; therefore, we can sing:

> Make me better, make me purer,
> By the fire that refines,
> Where the breath of God is sweeter,
> Where the brightest glory shines.
> Take me higher up the mountain
> Into fellowship with Thee,
> In Thy light I'll see the fountain,
> And the blood that cleanses me.

I am realizing these days that there is a sanctification of the Spirit where the thoughts are holy, where life is beautiful and pure. As you come closer to God, the Spirit reveals His holiness and shows us a new plan for the present and the future. The height and depth, the breadth and length of God's inheritance for us are truly wonderful.

61

We read in Romans 8:10, *"And if Christ is in you, the body is dead because of sin, but the Spirit is life because of righteousness."* What a vision, beloved. *"The body is dead"* because sin is being judged and destroyed. The whole body is absolutely put to death; consequently, there is His righteousness, His beauty, the life of the Spirit, freedom, and joy. The Spirit lifts the soul into the presence of heaven. Oh, this is glorious.

EXPERIENCE HIS JOY

"Count it all joy when you fall into various trials." Perhaps you have been counting it all sadness until now. Never mind. Tell it to Jesus now. Express your deepest feelings to Him:

> He knows it all, He knows it all,
> My Father knows, He knows it all,
> The bitter tears, how fast they fall,
> He knows, my Father knows it all.

Sometimes I change the words to this song. I would like to sing it as I change it:

> The joy He gives that overflows,
> He knows, my Father knows it all.

Sorrow may come at night, but *"joy comes in the morning"* (Ps. 30:5). So many believers never look up. When Jesus raised Lazarus from the dead, He lifted His eyes and said, *"Father, I thank You that You have heard Me"* (John 11:41). Beloved, God wants us to have some resurrection touch about us. We may enter into things that will bring us sorrow and trouble, but through them, God will bring us to a deeper knowledge of Himself. Never use your human plan when God speaks His Word. You have your cue from an Almighty Source who has all the resources that never fade away. His treasury is past measuring, abounding with extravagances of abundance, waiting to be poured out upon us.

Hear what the Scripture says: *"God...gives to all liberally and without reproach"* (James 1:5). The almighty hand of God comes to our weakness and says, "If you will dare to trust Me and not doubt, I will abundantly satisfy you from the treasure house of the Most High." He forgives and supplies. He opens the door into His fullness and makes us know that He has done it all. When you come to Him again, He gives you another overflow without measure, an expression of a Father's love.

Who desires anything from God? He can satisfy every need. He satisfies the hungry with good things (Luke 1:53). I believe a real weeping would be good for us. You are in a poor way if you cannot weep. I do thank God for my tears, which help me. I like to weep in the presence of God. I ask you in the name of Jesus, will you cast *"all your care upon Him, for He cares for you"* (1 Pet. 5:7)? I am in great need today; I want an overflow. Come on, beloved, let us weep together. God will help us. Glory to God. How He meets the needs of the hungry!

CHAPTER ELEVEN

A LIVING FAITH

We appreciate cathedrals and churches, but God does not dwell in temples made by hands but in the sanctuary of the heart. Here is true worship: *"God is Spirit, and those who worship Him must worship in spirit and truth"* (John 4:24). The Father seeks *"such to worship Him"* (v. 23). The church is the body of Christ. Its worship is a heart worship, a longing to come into the presence of God. God sees our hearts and will open our understanding. The Lord delights in His people. He wants us to come to a place of undisturbed rest and peace that is found only in God. Only simplicity will bring us there. As Jesus placed a little child in the middle of the disciples, He said: *"Unless you are converted and become as little children, you will be no means enter the kingdom of heaven"* (Matt. 18:3). He did not mean that we should seek to have a child's mind, but a child's meek and gentle spirit. It is the only place to meet God. He will give us that place of worship.

How my heart cries out for a living faith and a deep vision of God. The world cannot produce it. It is a place where we see the Lord, a place where we pray and know that God hears. We can ask God and believe Him for the answer, having no fear but a living faith to come into the presence of God. *"In [His] presence is fullness of joy; at [His] right hand are pleasures forevermore"* (Ps. 16:11).

CHANGED BY GOD

God is looking for people He can reveal Himself in. I used to have a tremendous temper, going white with passion. My whole nature was outside God that way. God knew His child could never

64

be of service to the world unless he was wholly sanctified. I was difficult to please at the table. My wife was a good cook, but I could always find something wrong with the meal. I heard her testify in a meeting that after God sanctified me, I was pleased with everything.

I had men working for me, and I wanted to be a good testimony to them. One day, they waited after work was over and said, "We would like that spirit you have." Our human spirit has to be controlled by the Holy Spirit. There is a place of death and life where Christ reigns in the body. Then all is well. This Word is full of stimulation. It is by faith that we come into a place of grace. Then all can see that we have been made new. The Holy Spirit arouses our attention. He has something special to say: if you will believe, you can be sons of God, like Him in character, spirit, longings, and actions until all know that you are His child.

The Spirit of God can change our nature. God is the Creator. His Word is creative, and if you believe, His creative power can change your whole nature. You can become *"children of God"* (John 1:12). You cannot reach this altitude of faith alone. No man can keep himself. The all-powerful God spreads His covering over you, saying, *"If you can believe, all things are possible to him who believes"* (Mark 9:23). The old nature is so difficult to manage. You have been ashamed of it many times, but the Lord Himself offers the answer. He says, "Come, and I will give you peace and strength. I will change you. I will operate on you by My power, making you a *'new creation'* (2 Cor. 5:17) if you will believe." He invites us to:

> Leave it there, leave it there.
> Take your burden to the Lord
> And leave it there.

Jesus says, *"Learn from Me, for I am gentle and lowly in heart, and you will find rest for your souls"* (Matt. 11:29). The world has no rest. It is full of troubles, but in Christ, you can move and act in the power of God with a peace that *"surpasses all understanding"* (Phil. 4:7). An inward flow of divine power will change your nature. *"Therefore the world does not know us, because it did not know Him"* (1 John 3:1).

What does it mean? I have lived in one house for fifty years. I have preached from my own doorstep; all around know me. They know me when they need someone to pray, when there is trouble, when they need a word of wisdom. But at Christmas time when they call their friends to celebrate, would they invite me? No. Why? They would say, "He is sure to want a prayer meeting, but we want a dance."

Wherever Jesus came, sin was revealed, and men don't like sin to be revealed. Sin separates us from God forever. You are in a good place when you weep before God, repenting over the least thing. If you have spoken unkindly, you realized it was not like the Lord. Your keen conscience has taken you to prayer. It is a wonderful thing to have a sensitive conscience. When everything is wrong, you cry to the Lord. It is when we are close to God that our hearts are revealed. God intends us to live in purity, seeing Him all the time. How can we?

> *Beloved, now we are children of God; and it has not yet been revealed what we shall be, but we know that when He is revealed, we shall be like Him, for we shall see Him as He is. And everyone who has this hope in Him purifies himself, just as He is pure.* (1 John 3:2–3)

CHRIST'S PRECIOUS SACRIFICE

As the bridegroom is to the bride, our Lord, the Lamb of God, is the hope of the church. He became poor for us that we might be made rich. What an offering! He suffered, He died, He was buried, He rose, and He is coming for us. How we love Him.

I am praying that God will create children in this meeting. *"But as many as received Him, to them He gave the right to become children of God, to those who believe in His name"* (John 1:12). When we believe, we receive Him. When we receive Him, anything can happen: *"With God all things are possible"* (Matt. 19:26).

When I am leaving anywhere by train or ship, people come to see me off; I preach to them. It is God's plan for me; it is an order. The captain and the stewards hear me. "Oh!" they say. "Another preacher on board." The world thinks there is something wrong with you if you are full of zeal for God. The world does not know us, but we are sons of God and possess His power. As we look to Jesus, our lives are changed. He is God's Son.

No man who sins has power. Sin makes a man weak, taking away his dignity and power. The Holy Spirit gives joy. It is God's plan. Heaven opens. As you pray, you know He hears. As you read the Word of God, it is alive. Remember that sin dethrones, but purity strengthens. Temptation is not sin, but the Devil is a liar and tries to take away peace. You must live in the Word of God. There is *"now no condemnation"* (Rom. 8:1). Who is he that can condemn you? Christ, but He won't condemn you because He died to love you. Don't condemn yourself. If there is anything wrong, come to Christ's blood: *"If we walk in the light as He is in the light, we have fellowship with one another, and the blood of Jesus Christ His Son cleanses us from all sin"* (1 John 1:7).

WITNESSES OF CHRIST

Jesus came to destroy the works of the Devil. You can enter into a new experience with God. All should fear God. He creates in our hearts such a love for Jesus that we are living in a new realm. We are children of God with power, filled with all the fullness of God:

Beloved, if our heart does not condemn us, we have confidence toward God. And whatever we ask we receive from Him, because we keep His commandments and do those things that are pleasing in His sight....By this we know that He abides in us, by the Spirit whom He has given us.
(1 John 3:21–22, 24)

Paul went on to impart some spiritual gifts. Did Paul give the gifts? No. The Holy Spirit gives gifts, and Jesus gives gifts. No man can give spiritual gifts.

I am here ministering faith. Before leaving home, I received a wire asking if I would go to Liverpool. If I know God is sending me, my faith rises. A woman with cancer and gallstones was very discouraged. The woman said, "I have no hope." "Well," I said, "I have not come from Bradford to go home with a bad report." God said to me, "Establish her in the fact of the new birth." When she had the assurance that her sin was gone and she was born again, she said, "That is everything to me. Cancer is nothing now. I have got Jesus." The battle was won. God delivered her, and she got up and dressed. She was free, happy in Jesus.

When God speaks, you can rely completely on His Word. Will you believe that God makes you His children? Life and immortality are ours in the Gospel. This is our inheritance through the blood of Jesus: life forevermore. Believe, and the Lord will fill you with life so that you will witness for Him as you wait for His return.

CHAPTER TWELVE

KEEPING THE VISION

N othing really matters if the Lord loves me, and He does, He does. I was describing to a few people last night how God has blessed this ministry with success. His hand has been upon us. I encountered the same kind of thing in Switzerland where there were nine churches formed and another four being formed. I went back there and found all the people praising the Lord. Just as our brother tonight asked the people who were healed through my ministry to stand up, they stood up. The same thing happened—just the same—and people are being healed during my absence. There is the sequel. There is the power manifested.

I told you when I was here before that if this work ceased, you could count on it that the mission had been Wigglesworth's; if it was of God, it would not cease. Humanity is the failure everywhere, but when humanity is filled with God's divinity, there is no such thing as failure, and we know that the baptism of the Holy Spirit is not a failure. There are two sides to the baptism of the Holy Spirit. The first condition is that you possess the baptism; the second condition is that the baptism possesses you. The first has to happen before the second can occur. God can so manifest His divine power that all souls can possess, if they are eligible, this blessed infilling of the baptism of the Holy Spirit. There is no limit to it. It cannot be measured. It is without limit because God is behind it, in the middle of it, and through it.

After reading all of the epistles, I would say that God is through all, under all, and over all in this work. I pray that the Holy Spirit will be with us. I trust that we will witness the demonstration of the Spirit's power, of the anointing that is received, because every person in this place must see the need of being filled with the Holy Spirit. It is important; no, it is more than important.

You neglect it at your peril. From time to time, I see people very negligent, cold, and indifferent. After they get filled with the Holy Spirit, they become ablaze for God. I believe God wants the same portion for every soul in this meeting, but even greater than that because we are in the kingdom.

Ministers of God are to be flames of fire, nothing less than flames, nothing less than holy, mighty instruments with burning messages, with hearts full of love, with depths of consecration where God has taken full charge of their bodies, and they exist only to manifest the glory of God. Surely this is the ideal and purpose of this great plan of salvation for man: that we might be *"filled with all the fullness of God"* (Eph. 3:19). We are called to be ministers of life and instruments pointing to the saving power for humanity. God works mightily in us, proving and manifesting His grace. This glorious baptism is to be a witness of Jesus, and oh, beloved, we must reach the ideal identification with the Master. It is the same baptism, the same power, the same revelation of the King of Kings. God must fill us with this divine, glorious purpose for God. Clearly, we are to be children of God who testify to His power, which fills the earth.

INTERPRETATION OF A MESSAGE IN TONGUES:

The Lord is the Life, the Truth, and the manifestation of bringing into life and power of sonship, built upon the Rock, the Rock Christ Jesus, established with the truth of salvation, our heritage, for we have to go forth with ministry of life unto life, and death unto death, for the Holy Spirit is that ministry.

EQUIPPED FOR SERVICE

Beloved, I want us to turn to this wonderful Word of God. I want you to see how we can be equipped with His power. I want you to keep your minds fixed on this fact, for it will help to establish you. It will strengthen you if you think about Paul, who was *"one born out of due time"* (1 Cor. 15:8). Paul was *"a brand plucked from the fire"* (Zech. 3:2), chosen by God to be an apostle to the Gentiles (Eph. 3:1). I want you to see him, first as a persecutor, furious to destroy those who were bringing glad tidings to the people. See how madly he rushed them into prison, urging them to blaspheme that holy name. Then see this man changed by the

power of Christ and the Gospel of God. See him divinely transformed by God, filled with the Holy Spirit. As you read the ninth
chapter of Acts, you see how special his calling was. In order for
Paul to understand how he might be able to minister to the needy,
God's Son said to Ananias, *"For I will show him how many things
he must suffer for My name's sake"* (Acts 9:16).

You will find that the cup of suffering from heaven is united
with a baptism of fire. I don't want you to think I mean suffering
with diseases. I mean suffering in persecution, with slander, strife,
bitterness, abusive scoldings, and with many other evil ways of suffering; but none of these things will hurt you. Instead, they will
kindle a fire of holy ambition. As the Scripture says, *"Blessed are
those who are persecuted for righteousness' sake, for theirs is the
kingdom of heaven"* (Matt. 5:10).

To be persecuted for Christ's sake is to be united with a
blessed people, with those chosen to cry under the altar, *"How
long?"* (Rev. 6:9–10). Oh, to know that we may cooperate with Jesus. If we suffer persecution, rejoice in that day. Beloved, God
wants witnesses, witnesses of truth, witnesses to the full truth,
witnesses to the fullness of redemption, witnesses to the deliverance from the power of sin and disease, witnesses who can claim
their territory, because of the eternal power working in them,
eternal life beautifully, gloriously filling the body, until the body is
filled with the life of the Spirit. God wants us to believe that we
may be ministers of that kind.

Read Acts 20. See how Paul was lost in the zeal of his ministry,
and see how those first disciples gathered together on the first day
of the week to break bread. See their need for breaking bread. As
they were gathered together, they were caught up with the ministry. In Switzerland, the people said to me, "How long can you
preach to us?" I said, "When the Holy Spirit is upon me, I can
preach forever!"

If it were only man's ability or college training, we might be
crazy before we began, but if it is the Holy Spirit's ministry, we will
be as sound as a bell that has no flaw in it. It will be the Holy Spirit
at the first, in the middle, and at the end. I do not want to think of
anything during the preaching so that the preaching will reflect
nothing except, "Thus says the Lord." The preaching of Jesus is
that blessed incarnation, that glorious freedom from bondage, that
blessed power that liberates from sin and the powers of darkness,

71

that glorious salvation that saves you from death to life, and from the power of Satan to God.

I see that Paul was lost in this glorious theme. In the middle of Paul's sermon, Eutychus, a young man, was too drowsy to be aware of his surroundings, and he sank into a deep sleep until he fell from the third-story window in which he had been sitting (Acts 20:9). I have often offered a pound note to anyone who fell asleep in my meetings—you can try it if you want to.

TAKE EACH OPPORTUNITY

I want you to notice that he preached from evening to midnight, and in the middle of the night, this thing happened. If you turn to Philippians, you will see a wonderful truth there where Paul said, *"I may attain to the resurrection"* (3:11). Hear the words spoken to Martha, that wonderful saying when Jesus said to her, *"I am the resurrection and the life. He who believes in Me, though he may die, he shall live"* (John 11:25). Paul desired to attain it, and it is remarkable evidence to me that you never attain anything until opportunity comes. On the activity of faith, you will find that God will bring so many things before your notice that you will have no time to think over them. You will jump into them and bring authority by the power of the Spirit. If you took time to think, you would miss the opportunity.

I was in San Francisco riding down the main street one day. I came across a group in the street, so the driver stopped, and I jumped out of the car. Rushing across to where the commotion was, I found, as I broke through the crowd, a body laid on the ground apparently in a tremendous seizure of death. I got down and asked, "What is wrong?" He replied in a whisper, "Cramp." I put my hand underneath his back and said, "Come out in the name of Jesus," and the boy jumped up and ran away. He never even said, "Thank you."

Likewise, you will find out that with the baptism of the Holy Spirit, you will be in a position where you must act because you have no time to think. The Holy Spirit works on the power of divine origin. It is the supernatural, God filling until it becomes a freeing power by the authority of the Almighty. It sees things come to pass that could not come to pass in any other way.

Returning to Paul's position: it is midnight, and death comes as a result of a fall from a window. The first thing Paul does is the most absurd thing to do, yet it is the most practical thing to do in the Holy Spirit: he fell on the young man. Yes, fell on him, embraced him, and left him alive. Some would say he fell on him, crushed life into him, and brought him back. It is the activity of the Almighty. We must see that in any meeting, the Holy Spirit can demonstrate His divine power until we realize that we are in the presence of God.

I want you to understand that the Holy Spirit is in this meeting. This is a meeting where all can be saved, where all can be healed, where the power of the resurrection of Jesus Christ is clearly in evidence, where we see nothing but Jesus. We are here for the importance of impressing on you that this same Jesus is present here.

THE BLESSING OF THE LORD'S SUPPER

I wish every meeting included a celebration of the Lord's Supper. I would love to see the saints gather together at every meeting in order to remember Christ's death, His resurrection, and His ascension. What a thought that Jesus Himself instituted this glorious memorial for us. Oh, that God would let us see that it is *"as often"* (1 Cor. 11:25) as we do it. It is not weekly, not monthly, not quarterly, but *"as often"* as we do it, and in remembrance of Him. What a blessed remembrance it is to know that He took away our sins. What a blessed remembrance to know that He took away my sins and my diseases. What a blessed remembrance to know that *"He always lives to make intercession"* (Heb. 7:25) for the saints—not the sinners. He has left us to do that: *"I pray for them. I do not pray for the world but for those whom You have given Me, for they are Yours"* (John 17:9). He has left us to pray for the world. He is there interceding for us to keep us right, holy, ready, mighty, and filled with Himself so that we might bring the fragrance of heaven to the world's needs. Can we do it? Yes, we can. We can do it.

THE NEED FOR HUMILITY

Let me read this Scripture to you so that we might get our minds perfectly fortified with this blessed truth that God has for us: *"Serving the Lord with all humility"* (Acts 20:19). None of us will be able to be ministers of this new covenant of promise in the power of the Holy Spirit without humility. It seems to me that the way to get up is to get down. It is clear to me that in the measure the death of the Lord is in me, the life of the Lord will abound in me. To me, the baptism of the Holy Spirit is not a goal; it is an in-filling that allows us to reach the highest level, the holiest position that it is possible for human nature to reach. The baptism of the Holy Spirit comes to reveal Him who is filled fully with God. So I see that to be baptized with the Holy Spirit is to be baptized into death, into life, into power, into fellowship with the Trinity, where we cease to be and God takes us forever. Paul said, *"I have been crucified with Christ; it is no longer I who live, but Christ lives in me"* (Gal. 2:20). I believe that God wants to put His hand upon us so that we may reach ideal definitions of humility, of human help-lessness, of human insufficiency, until we will rest no more upon human plans, but have God's thoughts, God's voice, and God the Holy Spirit to speak to us. Now here is a word for us: *"And see, now I go bound in the spirit"* (Acts 20:22). There is the Word. Is that a pos-sibility? Is there a possibility for a person to align himself so com-pletely with the divine will of God?

Jesus was a man, flesh and blood like us, while at the same time, He was the incarnation of divine authority, power, and maj-esty of the glory of heaven. He bore in His body the weaknesses of human flesh. He was tempted *"in all points...as we are, yet without sin"* (Heb. 4:15). He is so lovely, such a perfect Savior. Oh, that I could shout "Jesus" in such a way that the world would hear. There is salvation, life, power, and deliverance through His name. But, beloved, I see that *"the Spirit drove Him"* (Mark 1:12), that He was *"led by the Spirit"* (Luke 4:1), and here comes Paul *"bound in the spirit"* (Acts 20:22).

What an ideal condescension of heaven that God should lay hold of humanity and possess it with His holiness, His righteous-ness, His truth, and His faith so that he could say, *"'I go bound'* (v. 22); I have no choice. The only choice is for God. The only desire or ambition is God's. I am bound with God." Is it possible, beloved?

If you look at the first chapter of Galatians, you will see how wonderfully Paul rose to this state of bliss. If you look at the third chapter of Ephesians, you see how he became *"less than the least of all saints"* (v. 8). In Acts 26, you will hear him say: *"King Agrippa, I was not disobedient to the heavenly vision"* (v. 19). In order to keep the vision, he yielded not to flesh and blood. God laid hold of him; God bound him; God preserved him. I ought to say, however, that it is a wonderful position to be preserved by the Almighty. We ought to see to it in our Christian experience that when we commit ourselves to God, the consequences will be all right. He who *"seeks to save his life will lose it, and whoever loses his life will preserve it"* (Luke 17:33).

What is it to be bound by the Almighty, preserved by the Infinite? There is no end to God's resources. They reach right into glory. They never finish on the earth. God takes control of a man in the baptism of the Holy Spirit as he yields himself to God. There is the possibility of being taken and yet left—taken charge of by God and left in the world to carry out His commands. That is one of God's possibilities for humanity: to be taken over by the power of God while being left in the world to be salt as the Scripture describes (Matt. 5:13).

A Fresh Vision for Each Day

Now, beloved, I am out to win souls. It is my business to seek the lost. It is my business to make everybody hungry, dissatisfied, mad, or glad. I want to see every person filled with the Holy Spirit. I must have a message from heaven that will not leave people as I found them. Something must happen if we are filled with the Holy Spirit. Something must happen at every place. Men must know that a man filled with the Holy Spirit is no longer a man. I told you when I was here last year that God has no room for ordinary men. A man can be swept by the power of God in his first stage of revelation of Christ, and from that moment on, he has to be an extraordinary man. In order to be filled with the Holy Spirit, he has to become a free body for God to dwell in. No man can have the Trinity abiding in him and be the same as he was before. I appeal to you who have been filled with the Holy Spirit, whatever the cost, let God have His way. I appeal to you people who have got to move on, who cannot rest until God does something for you. I appeal to you as I could never have appealed to you unless God had been speaking to me since I left this place. Let me tell you what He has been saying. God has been revealing to me that any man who does not sin yet remains in the same place spiritually for a week is a backslider. You say, "How is it possible?" Because God's revelation is available to anyone who will wholeheartedly be committed to following God.

Staying the same for two days would almost indicate that you had lost the vision. The child of God must have a fresh vision every day. The child of God must be more active by the Holy Spirit every day. The child of God must come into line with the power of heaven, where he knows that God has put His hand upon him. He must be able to say:

> I know the Lord, I know the Lord,
> I know the Lord has laid His hand on me,
> He filled me with the Holy Spirit.
> How do I know? Oh, the Spirit spoke through me.
> I know the Lord has laid His hand on me,
> I know the Lord has laid His hand on me—Glory.
> He healed the sick, and He raised the dead,
> I know the Lord has laid His hand on me.

Jesus went about doing good, for God was with Him. God anointed Him. Beloved, is that not the ministry to which God would have us become heir? Why? Because the Holy Spirit has to bring us a revelation of Jesus, and the purpose of being filled with the Holy Spirit is to give us a revelation of Jesus. He will make the Word of God just the same life as was given by the Son, as new, as fresh, as effective as if the Lord Himself were speaking.

I wonder how many of you are a part of the bride of Christ? The bride loves to hear the Bridegroom's voice (John 3:29). Here it is, the blessed Word of God, the whole Word, not just part of it. No, we believe in the whole thing. Day by day, we find out that the Word itself gives life. The Spirit of the Lord breathes through us. He makes the Word come alive in our hearts and minds. So I have within my hands, within my heart, within my mind, this blessed reservoir of promises that is able to do so many marvelous things.

I believe that the Lord will deliver some of the people in this meeting tonight. Some of you have most likely been suffering because you have a limited revelation of Jesus, a limited revelation of the fullness of Jesus, and there may be some who need to be delivered. I can see that we are surrounded by faith in a great way, differently from other places. Nevertheless, the Lord has been wonderfully manifesting Himself. Since I left you last year, I have seen wonderful things. God has indeed been manifesting Himself.

I must tell you one of those cases. In Oakland, California, I held meetings at a theater. Only to glorify God, I tell you that Oakland was in a very serious state. There was very little Pentecostal work there, and so a large theater was rented. God worked especially in filling the place until we had to have overflow meetings. In these meetings, we had a rising flood of people getting saved by rising up voluntarily, up and down the place, getting saved the moment they rose. Then we had a large number of people who needed help in their bodies, rising up in faith and being healed.

One of them was an old man who was ninety-five years of age. He had been suffering for three years until he gradually got to the place that for three weeks he was consuming only liquids. He was in a terrible state, but this man was different from the others. I got him to stand while I prayed for him, and he came back and told us with such a radiant face that new life had come into his body. He said, "I am ninety-five years old. When I came into the meeting, I was full of pain with cancer in the stomach. I have been healed so that I have been eating perfectly, and I have no pain." Similarly, many people were healed.

I believe that tonight God wants me to help some of you in this meeting. I want a manifestation to the glory of God. Anybody in this meeting who has pain in the head, in the feet, shoulders, or legs, if you want deliverance, rise up, and I will pray for you. You will find that God will so manifest His power that you will go out of this meeting free. If there is anyone in this meeting in pain, from the head to the feet, anywhere, if you will rise, I will pray for you, and the Lord will deliver you. I hope you are expecting big things.

If you look at Acts 2, you will find that the Holy Spirit came, and there was a manifestation of the divine power of God. It brought conviction as the Word was spoken in the Holy Spirit.

In Acts 3, we see that a man was healed at the Beautiful Gate, through the power of the Spirit. It was such a miraculous, wonderful evidence of the power of the Spirit that 5,000 men, women, and we don't know how many children, were saved by the power of God. God manifested His divine power to prove that He is with us.

Now, how many would like to give their hearts to God tonight? How many would like to be saved?

CHAPTER THIRTEEN

THE INCARNATION OF MAN

I especially want to speak to those who are saved. God wants you to be holy. He wants you to be filled with the power that will keep you holy. He wants you to have a revelation of what sin and death are, and what the Spirit and life of the Spirit are. Look at these two significant verses:

> *There is therefore now no condemnation to those who are in Christ Jesus, who do not walk according to the flesh, but according to the Spirit. For the law of the Spirit of life in Christ Jesus has made me free from the law of sin and death.* (Rom. 8:1–2)

"No condemnation." This is the primary thought for me because it means so much; it contains so much truth. If you are without condemnation, you are in a place where you can pray through. You can have a revelation of Christ. For Him to be in you brings you to a place where you cannot, if you follow the definite leadings of the Spirit of Christ, have any fellowship with the world. I want you to see that the Spirit of the Lord would reveal this fact to us. If you love the world, you cannot love God, and the love of God cannot be in you (1 John 2:15). God wants a clear decision, because if you are in Christ Jesus, you are a *"new creation"* (2 Cor. 5:17). You are in Him; therefore, you walk in the Spirit and are free from condemnation.

INTERPRETATION OF A MESSAGE IN TONGUES:

It is the Spirit alone that, by revelation, brings the whole truth, visiting the Son in your hearts, and reveals unto you the capabilities of sonship that are in you after you are created after the image of Him.

FREE FROM SIN

So the Spirit of the Lord would bring you into revelation. He wants you without condemnation. What will that mean? Much in every way, because God wants all His people to be clear witnesses so that the world will know we belong to God. More than that, He wants us to be *"the salt of the earth"* (Matt. 5:13); to be *"the light of the world"*(v. 14); to be like cities built on a hill so that they cannot be hidden (v. 14). He wants us to be so *"in God"* (1 John 4:15) that the world will see God in us. Then they can look to Him for redemption. That is the law of the Spirit. What will it do? *"The law of the Spirit of life in Christ Jesus"* will make you *"free from the law of sin and death"* (Rom. 8:2). Sin will have no dominion over you (Rom. 6:14). You will have no desire to sin, and it will be as true of you as it was of Jesus when He said, *"The ruler of this world is coming, and he has nothing in Me"* (John 14:30). Satan cannot influence; he has no power. His power is destroyed: *"The body is dead because of sin, but the Spirit is life because of righteousness"* (Rom. 8:10).

To be filled with God means that you are free. You are filled with joy, peace, blessing, and strength of character. You are transformed by God's mighty power.

Notice there are two laws. *"The law of the Spirit of life in Christ Jesus"* makes you *"free from the law of sin and death"* (v. 2). *"The law of sin and death"* is in you as it was before, but it is dead. You still have your same flesh, but its power over you is gone. You are the same person, but you have been awakened into spiritual life. You are a *"new creation"* (2 Cor. 5:17), created in God afresh after the image of Christ. Now, beloved, some people who conform to this truth do not understand their inheritance, and they go down. Instead of becoming weak, you have to rise triumphantly over *"the law of sin and death."* In Romans, we read, *"I thank God; through Jesus Christ our Lord! So then, with the mind I myself serve the law of God, but with the flesh the law of sin"* (7:25).

God wants to show you that there is a place where we can live in the Spirit and not be subject to the flesh. We can live in the Spirit until sin has no dominion over us. We reign in life and see the covering of God over us in the Spirit. Sin reigned unto death, but Christ reigned over sin and death, and so we reign with Him in life.

Not a sick person here could be said to be reigning in life. Satanic power reigns there, and God wants you to know that you have to reign. God made you like Himself, and in the Garden of Gethsemane, Jesus restored to you everything that was lost in the Garden of Eden. Through the agony He suffered, He purchased our blessed redemption.

OUR GLORIOUS REDEMPTION

People say, "Could anything be greater than the fellowship that prevailed in the Garden of Eden when God walked and talked and had fellowship with man?" Yes, redemption is greater. Nothing but what was local was in the garden, but the moment a man is born again, he is free from the world and lives in heavenly places. He has no destination except heaven.

Redemption is, therefore, greater than the Garden of Eden, and God wants you to know that you may receive this glorious redemption not only for salvation, but also for the restoration of your bodies. They are redeemed from the curse of the law. You have been made free, and all praise and glory are due the Son of God. Hallelujah! No more Egypt places! No more sandy deserts! Praise the Lord! Free *"from the law of sin and death"* (Rom. 8:2). How was it accomplished? These verses from Romans answer that question. Pay particular attention to verse three. It contains the supreme truth:

> *For what the law could not do in that it was weak through the flesh, God did by sending His own Son in the likeness of sinful flesh, on account of sin: He condemned sin in the flesh, that the righteous requirement of the law might be fulfilled in us who do not walk according to the flesh but according to the Spirit.* (Rom. 8:3–4)

Righteousness was fulfilled in us! Brother and sister, I tell you there is a redemption. There is an atonement in Christ. There is a personality of Christ to dwell in you. There is a Godlikeness for you to attain, a blessed resemblance to Christ. The God in you will not fail if you believe the Word of God.

INTERPRETATION OF A MESSAGE IN TONGUES:
The living Word is sufficient for you. Eat it. Devour it. It is the Word of God.

FILLED WITH GOD

Jesus came to destroy the works of the Devil. God was manifested in Him. The fullness of God resided in Jesus, and He walked about glorified, filled with God. Incarnate! May I embody Christ? Yes. How can I be so filled with God that all my movements, my desires, my mind, and my will are so controlled by a new power that I no longer exist, for God has filled me? Praise the Lord! Certainly it can be so. Did you ever examine the condition of your new birth into righteousness? Did you ever investigate it? Did you ever try to see what there was in it? Were you ever able to fathom the fullness of redemption that came to you through believing in Jesus?

Before *"the foundation of the world,"* redemption was all completed (Matt. 25:34). It was set in order before the Fall. This redemption had to be so mighty and had to redeem us all so perfectly that there would be no deficiency in the whole of redemption.

Let us see how it came about: *"In the beginning was the Word, and the Word was with God, and the Word was God"* (John 1:1). He became flesh. Then, He became the voice and the operation of the Word. By the power of God through the Holy Spirit, He became the Authority. Now, let me go further with you.

BORN OF GOD

You are born of an incorruptible power of God (1 Pet. 1:23), born of the Word, who has the personality and nature of God. You were begotten of God, and *"you are not your own"* (1 Cor. 6:19). You can believe that you have *"passed from death into life"* (John 5:24) and have become *"heirs of God and joint heirs with Christ"* (Rom. 8:17) in the measure in which you believe His Word. The natural flesh, the first order, has been changed into a new order, for the first order was Adam, the natural, and the last order was Christ, the heavenly. Now you have been changed by a heavenly power existing in an earthly body, and that power can never die. I want you to see that you are born of a power and have existing in you the power that God used to create the world. It is *"the law of the Spirit of life in Christ Jesus"* that makes you *"free from the law of sin and death"* (v. 2).

Now, let us look at the law without the Spirit, *"the law of sin and death."* Here is a man who has never come into the new law.

He is still in the law of Adam, never having been regenerated, never having been born again. He is led captive by the Devil at his will. There is no power that can convert a man except the power of the blood of Jesus. The carnal mind is *"not subject to the law of God, nor indeed can be"* (Rom. 8:7). Carnality is selfishness and uncleanness. It cannot be subject to God. It interferes with you by binding you and keeping you in bondage. But God destroys carnality by a new life, which is so much better, and fills you *"with joy inexpressible and full of glory"* (1 Pet. 1:8). The half can never be told. Everything that God does is too big to tell. His grace, His love, His mercy, and His salvation are all too big to understand.

Do you not know that ours is an abundant God, *"who is able to do exceedingly abundantly above all that we ask or think"* (Eph. 3:20)? We are illuminated and quickened by the Spirit, looking forward to the Rapture when we will be caught up and lifted into the presence of God. God's boundaries are enormous, wonderful, and glorious!

A RISEN SAVIOR

Now, let me touch on another important point. Can you think about Jesus being dead in the grave? Do you think that God could do anything for us if Jesus were still there? After His crucifixion and until He was laid in the grave, everything had to be done for Him, and I want you to see that a dead Christ can do nothing for you. He carried the cross, so don't you carry it. The Cross covered everything, and the Resurrection brought everything to life. When He was in the grave, the Word of God says that He was raised by the operation of God through the Spirit. Jesus was awakened by the Spirit in the grave, and this same Spirit dwells in your mortal bodies. Jesus rose by the quickening power of the Holy Spirit:

> *But if the Spirit of Him who raised Jesus from the dead dwells in you, He who raised Christ from the dead will also give life to your mortal bodies through His Spirit who dwells in you.* (Rom. 8:11)

If you will allow Jesus to have charge of your bodies, you will find that this Spirit will quicken you and will free you. Talk about divine healing! You cannot remove it from the Scriptures. They are full of it. You will find, also, that all who are healed by the power of

God, especially believers, will find their healing an incentive to make them purer and holier. If divine healing merely made the body whole, it would be worth very little. Divine healing is the marvelous act of the providence of God coming into your mortal bodies, and after being touched by the Almighty, can you ever remain the same? No. Like me, you will eagerly worship and serve God.

Chapter Fourteen

Filled with God

You may be filled with all the fullness of God.
—Ephesians 3:19

Some people come with very small expectations concerning God's fullness, and a lot of people are satisfied with a thimbleful. You can just imagine God saying, "Oh, if they only knew how much they could take away!" Other people come with a larger container, and they go away satisfied. God is longing for us to have such a desire for more, a desire that only He can satisfy.

You women would have a good idea of what I mean from the illustration of a screaming child being passed from one person to another. The child is never satisfied until he gets to the arms of his mother. You will find that no peace, no help, no source of strength, no power, no life, nothing can satisfy the cry of the child of God but the Word of God. God has a special way of satisfying the cries of His children. He is waiting to open the windows of heaven until He has moved in the depths of our hearts so that everything unlike Himself has been destroyed. No one needs to go away empty. God wants you to be filled. My brother, my sister, God wants you today to be like a watered garden, filled with the fragrance of His own heavenly joy, until you know at last that you have touched the immense fullness of God. The Son of God came for no other purpose than to lift, to mold, and to remold, until *"we have the mind of Christ"* (1 Cor. 2:16).

Ask Largely of God

I know that dry ground can be flooded (Isa. 44:3). May God prevent me from ever wanting anything less than a flood. I will not

84

settle for small things when I have such a big God. Through the blood of Christ's atonement, we may have riches and riches. We need the warming atmosphere of the Spirit's power to bring us closer and closer until nothing but God can satisfy. Then we may have some idea of what God has left after we have taken all that we can. It is like a sparrow taking a drink of the ocean and then looking around and saying, "What a vast ocean! What a lot more I could have taken if I only had room."

Sometimes you have things you can use, and you don't know it. You could be dying of thirst right in a river of plenty. There was once a boat in the mouth of the Amazon River. The people on board thought they were still in the ocean. They were dying of thirst, some of them nearly mad. They saw a ship and asked if they would give them some water. Someone on the ship replied, "Dip your bucket right over; you are in the mouth of the river." There are a number of people today in the middle of the great river of life, but they are dying of thirst because they do not dip down and take from the river. Dear friend, you may have the Word, but you need an awakened spirit. The Word is not alive until it is moved upon by the Spirit of God, and in the right sense, it becomes Spirit and Life when it is touched by His hand alone.

Beloved, *"there is a river whose streams shall make glad the city of God, the holy place of the tabernacle of the Most High"* (Ps. 46:4). There is a stream of life that makes everything move. There is a touch of divine life and likeness through the Word of God that comes from nowhere else. We think of death as the absence of life, but there is a death-likeness in Christ, which is full of life.

There is no such thing as an end to God's beginnings. We must be in Christ; we must know Him. Life in Christ is not a touch; it is not a breath; it is the almighty God; it is a Person; it is the Holy One dwelling in the temple *"not made with hands"* (Heb. 9:11). Oh, beloved, He touches, and it is done. He is the same God over all, *"rich to all who call upon Him"* (Rom. 10:12). Pentecost is the last thing that God has to touch the earth with. If you do not receive the baptism of the Holy Spirit, you are living in a weak and impoverished condition, which is no good to yourself or anybody else. May God move us on to a place where there is no measure to this fullness that He wants to give us. God exalted Jesus and gave Him a name above every name. You notice that everything has been put under Him.

It has been about eight years since I was in Oakland, California, and since that time, I have seen thousands and thousands healed by the power of God. In the last five months of the year, we had over 7,000 people in Sweden saved by the power of God. The tide is rolling in. Let us see to it today that we get right into the tide, for it will hold us. God's heart of love is the center of all things. Get your eyes off yourself; lift them up high, and see the Lord, for in Him, there *"is everlasting strength"* (Isa. 26:4).

If you went to see a doctor, the more you told him about yourself, the more he would know. But when you come to Doctor Jesus, He knows all from the beginning, and He never prescribes the wrong medicine. Jesus sends His healing power and brings His restoring grace, so there is nothing to fear. The only thing that is wrong is your wrong conception of His redemption.

TAKE AUTHORITY OVER SATAN

He was wounded that He might be able to identify with your weaknesses (Heb. 4:15). He took your flesh and laid it upon the cross that *"He might destroy him who had the power of death, that is, the devil, and release those who through fear of death were all their lifetime subject to bondage"* (Heb. 2:14–15).

You will find that almost all the ailments that you experience come as a result of Satan, and they must be dealt with as satanic; they must be cast out. Do not listen to what Satan says to you, for the Devil is a liar from the beginning (John 8:44). If people would only listen to the truth of God, they would realize that every evil spirit is subject to them. They would find out that they are always in the place of triumph, and they would *"reign in life through the One, Jesus Christ"* (Rom. 5:17).

Never live in a place other than where God has called you, and He has called you from on high to live with Him. God has designed that everything will be subject to man. Through Christ, He has given you authority over all the power of the Enemy. He has worked out your eternal redemption.

I was finishing a meeting one day in Switzerland. When the meeting ended and we had ministered to all the sick, we went out to see some people. Two boys came to us and said that there was a blind man present at the meeting that afternoon. He had heard all the words of the preacher and said he was surprised that he had not been prayed for. They went on to say that this blind man had heard so much that he would not leave until he could see. I said, "This is positively unique. God will do something today for that man."

We got to the place. The blind man said he had never seen. He was born blind, but because of the Word preached in the afternoon, he was not going home until he could see. If ever I have joy, it is when I have a lot of people who will not be satisfied until they get all that they have come for. With great joy, I anointed him and laid hands on his eyes. Immediately, God restored his vision. It was very strange how the man reacted. There were some electric lights. First he counted them; then he counted us. Oh, the ecstatic pleasure that this man experienced every moment because of his sight! It made us all feel like weeping and dancing and shouting. Then he pulled out his watch and said that for years he had been feeling the raised figures on the watch in order to tell the time. But now, he could look at it and tell us the time. Then, looking as if he had just awakened from some deep sleep, or some long, strange dream, he realized that he had never seen the faces of his father and mother. He went to the door and rushed out. That night, he was the first person to arrive for the meeting. All the people knew him as the blind man, and I had to give him a long time to talk about his new sight.

I wonder how much you want to take away today. You could not carry it if it were substance, but there is something about the grace, the power, and the blessings of God that can be carried, no matter how big they are. Oh, what a Savior. What a place we are in, by grace, that He may come in to commune with us. He is willing to say to every heart, *"Peace, be still"* (Mark 4:39), and to every weak body, *"Be strong"* (Deut. 31:6).

Are you going halfway, or are you going all the way to the end? Do not be deceived by Satan, but believe God.

CHAPTER FIFTEEN

JOINT HEIRS WITH CHRIST

I used to have a hard heart, and God had to completely break me. I used to be critical of people who preached divine healing and did certain things that I thought they should not do. Then God began to put me through a testing and to subdue me. I fell down before God, and then the hardness and all the bitterness were taken away. I believe God wants to remove the critical sprit from us. He wants to replace it with His Spirit. As the Scripture says:

> But if the Spirit of Him who raised Jesus from the dead dwells in you, He who raised Christ from the dead will also give life to your mortal bodies through His Spirit who dwells in you. (Rom. 8:11)

Here the power of God is dealing with our *"mortal bodies,"* but the power of the Spirit today wants to revive us both in spirit and body:

> For if you live according to the flesh you will die; but if by the Spirit you put to death the deeds of the body, you will live. For as many as are led by the Spirit of God, these are sons of God. For you did not receive the spirit of bondage again to fear, but you received the Spirit of adoption by whom we cry out, "Abba, Father." The Spirit Himself bears witness with our spirit that we are children of God, and if children, then heirs; heirs of God and joint heirs with Christ, if indeed we suffer with Him, that we may also be glorified together. (vv. 13–17)

THE PRIVILEGES OF ADOPTION

The thought that especially comes to me today is that of our relationship to our heavenly Father. The Spirit brings us to a place where we see that we are children of God. And because of this glorious position, we are not only children but heirs, and not only heirs, but joint heirs. Because of that, *"all the promises of God in Him are Yes, and...Amen"* (2 Cor. 1:20). If the Spirit of God *"who raised Jesus from the dead dwells in you, He who raised Christ from the dead will also give life to your mortal bodies through His Spirit who dwells in you"* (Rom. 8:11).

It brings me into a living place to believe that as an adopted child, I may grasp the promises. I see two wonderful things: I see deliverance for the body, and I see the power of the Spirit in sonship raising me up and pressing me onward to resurrection through faith in the Lord Jesus Christ. That promise is found in His Word:

> *Jesus spoke these words, lifted up His eyes to heaven, and said: "Father, the hour has come. Glorify Your Son, that Your Son also may glorify You, as You have given Him authority over all flesh, that He should give eternal life to as many as You have given Him. And this is eternal life, that they may know You, the only true God, and Jesus Christ whom You have sent."* (John 17:1–3)

It is no small thing to be brought into fellowship with the Father through Jesus Christ. The Spirit that is in you not only puts to death all other power, but He is showing us our privilege and bringing us into a faith where we can claim all we need. The moment a man comes into the knowledge of Christ, he is made an heir of heaven. By the Spirit, he is being changed into the image of the Son of God. It is in that image that we can definitely look into the face of the Father and see that the things we ask for are done: *"And if children, then heirs; heirs of God and joint heirs with Christ, if indeed we suffer with Him, that we may also be glorified together"* (Rom. 8:17).

And the glory is not only going to be revealed, but it is already revealed in us. We are being changed *"from glory to glory"* (2 Cor. 3:18). I want you to know what it means to be children of God. I want you to know that the Spirit that raised Jesus from the dead is

89

dwelling in your mortal body, making you His child. *"We shall be like Him, for we shall see Him as He is"* (1 John 3:2). It does not mean that we will have faces like Jesus, but we will have the same Spirit. When they look at us and see the glory, they will say, "Yes, it is the same Spirit," for they will see the radiance of the glory of Jesus Christ. Beloved, we are being changed: *"For the earnest expectation of the creation eagerly waits for the revealing of the sons of God"* (Rom. 8:19).

All of us who are born of God and have the power of the Holy Spirit within are longing for the evidence of our adoption. You say, when will these things happen? Paul, in a spirit of expectation, wrote:

> *For we know that the whole creation groans and labors with birth pangs together until now. Not only that, but we also who have the firstfruits of the Spirit, even we ourselves groan within ourselves, eagerly waiting for the adoption, the redemption of our body.* (vv. 22–23)

Waiting for Deliverance

Within me this afternoon, there is a cry and a longing for deliverance. Praise God, it is coming! There is a true sense even now in which you may live in the resurrection power. The Holy Spirit is working in us and bringing us to a condition where we know He is doing a work in us. I never felt so near heaven as last night when the house was shaking with an earthquake, and I thought my Lord might come. More than crossing the sea and seeing my children, I would rather see Jesus. Praise God, we are delivered by the power of the Spirit: *"Because the creation itself also will be delivered from the bondage of corruption into the glorious liberty of the children of God"* (v. 21).

Do not ask how can this be. The sovereign grace and power of God are equal to all these things. I have been changed by the power of the Holy Spirit, and I know that there is a better man in me than the natural man.

Brothers and sisters, are you really *"waiting for the adoption"* (v. 23)? The baptism of the Holy Spirit links heaven to earth, and God wants us to be so filled with the Spirit and walk in the Spirit so that while we live here on earth, our heads will be right up in heaven. Brothers and sisters, the Spirit can give you patience to wait. The baptism in the Holy Spirit is the essential power in the body that will bring rest from all your weariness and give you a hopeful expectation that each day may be the day we go up with Him. We must not be foolish people, folding our hands and giving up everything. I find there is no time like the present to be up and active. We need our bodies to be strengthened by the Spirit; otherwise, we would be entirely worn-out. The Holy Spirit Himself will pray through you and help you to remember the things for which you should pray, for *"the Spirit also helps in our weaknesses"* (v. 26). Is there anyone who could say, "I have no need for the Holy Spirit"?

THE NEED FOR TRANSFORMATION

The highest purpose God has for us is that we will be transformed into the image of His Son. We have seen in part God's purpose in filling us with the Spirit that He might conform us to the image of His Son. Paul wrote:

> *For whom He foreknew, He also predestined to be conformed to the image of His Son, that He might be the first-born among many brethren. Moreover whom He predestined, these He also called; whom He called, these He also justified; and whom He justified, these He also glorified.* (Rom. 8:29–30)

Where are you standing? I believe there are two kinds of people: the whosoever will and the whosoever won't. I want you to examine yourselves to see where you stand. If you stand on these truths that God has given, you will be amazed to see how God will make everything happen so that you will be conformed to the image of His Son.

It is a sad thing today to see how people are astonished at the workings of God. Millions of years ago He purposed in His heart to do this mighty thing in us. Are you going to refuse it, or are you going to yield? I thank God He planned ahead for me to be saved. Some will receive Christ, but others will not believe in Him for salvation. You see it is a mystery, but God purposed it *"before the foundation of the world"* (Eph. 1:4). And if you yield, He will put in you a living faith, and you cannot get away from the power of it. Oh, brothers and sisters, let us come a little nearer. How amazing it is that we can be transformed so that the thoughts of Christ will be first in our minds. How blessed that when everybody around you is interested in everything else, you are thinking about Jesus Christ.

WHAT IS YOUR RESPONSE?

Friends, it is the purpose of God that you should rise into the place of sonship. Don't miss the purpose God has in His heart for you. Realize that God wants to make of you the firstfruits (James 1:18) and separate you unto Himself. God has lifted some of you up again and again. It is amazing how God in His mercy has restored and restored, and *"whom He called, these He also justified; and whom He justified, these He also glorified"* (Rom. 8:30). The glorification is still going on and is going to exceed what it is now.

Within your heart there surely must be a response to this call. It does not matter who is against us: *"What then shall we say to these things? If God is for us, who can be against us?"* (v. 31). If there are millions against you, God has purposed it and will bring you right through to glory. Human wisdom has to stand still. It is *"with the heart one believes unto righteousness"* (Rom. 10:10).

Brothers and sisters, what do you want? That is the question. What have you come here for? We have seen God work in horribly diseased bodies. Our God is able to heal and to meet all of our needs. The Scripture says: *"He who did not spare His own Son, but delivered Him up for us all, how shall He not with Him also freely give us all things?"* (Rom. 8:32).

Do you need to be healed of a critical spirit? The Scripture warns: *"Who shall bring a charge against God's elect?"* (v. 33). I tell you, it is bad business for the man who harms God's anointed (1 Chron. 16:21–22). *"Who is he who condemns?"* (Rom. 8:34). How much of that there is today: brother condemning brother, everybody condemning one another. You also go about condemning yourself. The Devil is the *"accuser of [the] brethren"* (Rev. 12:10). But there is power in the blood to free us, to keep us, and to bring us healing.

Do not let the Enemy cripple you and bind you. Why don't you believe God's Word? There is a blessed place for you in the Holy Spirit. Instead of condemning you, Christ is interceding for you. Rest in this promise:

For I am persuaded that neither death nor life, nor angels nor principalities nor powers, nor things present nor things to come, nor height nor depth, nor any other created thing, shall be able to separate us from the love of God which is in Christ Jesus our Lord. (Rom. 8:38–39)

Beloved, you are in a wonderful place. Because God has called and chosen you, He wants you to know that you have power with Him. Because you are sons and joint heirs, you have a right to healing for your bodies and to be delivered from all the power of the Enemy.

CHAPTER SIXTEEN

APPREHEND YOUR APPREHENSION

Read Philippians 3. It contains wonderful words that encourage us to be filled with all the fullness of God. God's Word is our food. If we do not edify ourselves with it, our needs will not be met. Let us preach by our lives, actions, presence, and praise, always being living letters of Christ. We should strive to be examples to all men of the truth contained in the Word of God.

Follow the truth, and do not abandon it. Always be watchful for divine inspiration. If we were to go all the way with God, what would happen? Seek the honor that comes from God alone. Paul spoke about the desire to attain. He said that he reached for *"the goal for the prize of the upward call of God in Christ Jesus"* (Phil. 3:14). There is no standing still. We are renewed by the Spirit. Although we are always striving for more of God, we have a sense of contentment in Him.

FOLLOW GOD'S COMMAND

Abraham left his home and followed God to a new land (Gen. 12:1–4). We never get into a new place until we come out of the old one. We must model God's personality. We can never be satisfied to stay where we are spiritually, for the truth continues to enlighten us. We must move on, or we will perish. We must be obedient to the Holy Spirit who guides us.

Paul was a man who had kept the law blamelessly. He had tried in his humanity to follow an ideal standard. Then Paul saw a light from heaven, and he was made new. Are you new? He was not with the other apostles, but he had been told of *"the Word of life"* (1 John 1:1). He had not yet attained to these ideal principles, but he had zeal. Before him was a challenge. He was to *"go into the city"* (Acts 9:6) where he would be told what to do. The present was nothing to him; he was motivated to follow God's command. Everything that had been important to him before, he now counted *"loss for the excellence of the knowledge of Christ Jesus* [his] *Lord"* (Phil. 3:8). His chief goal was to *"gain Christ"* (v. 8).

When Judas and the soldiers came after Jesus in the garden, Jesus spoke, and the men fell backward (John 18:6). He, the Creator, submitted Himself to these men. Yet He said, *"Let these go their way"* (v. 8), referring to the disciples. When they abused Him, He did not retaliate. Paul understood these Christlike principles. He recognized the power of Christ, which is able to lift our humanity.

JESUS IS OUR EXAMPLE

Jesus' followers sought to make Him a King, but Jesus retired to pray. Paul desired to *"gain Christ and be found in Him"* (Phil. 3:8–9). Oh, can I gain Him? Is it possible to change and change, having His compassion, His love?

In an effort to prevent Jesus from being taken, Peter cut off Malchus's ear (John 18:10). Jesus put it on again. See the dignity of Christ, who comes to create a new order of life. May we *"gain Christ and be found in Him"* that we might have the *"righteousness which is from God by faith"* (Phil. 3:8–9).

Jesus identified Himself with us. He came to be a firstfruit (1 Cor. 15:23). How zealous is the farmer as he watches his crops to see the first shoots and blades of the harvest. Jesus was a firstfruit, and God will have a harvest! What a lovely position to be children of God, perfectly adjusted in the presence of God and *"found in Him"* (Phil. 3:9)! You say, "It is a trying morning," or "I am in a needy place." He knows and understands your needs. When Jesus saw a great crowd coming toward Him, He said to Philip, *"Where shall we buy bread, that these may eat?"* (John 6:5). Jesus knew where the food would come from. He was testing Philip's faith. From a little boy's lunch, Jesus fed over five thousand. They were all filled, and twelve baskets of bread were left over (v. 13).

HE IS HERE

Did you ever walk a while on the way to Emmaus? The two who walked with Jesus thought He was a stranger. If we only knew that He is by our sides! He made Himself known to them in the breaking of the bread (Luke 24:30–31). The same day, He appeared again and said, *"Peace to you"* (v. 36). Oh, to be found in the place where He is! How did He get there? He was there all the time. We need to have our eyes open. He is always there to bring us to the place where we are confident; the Lord is with us. There is such a place. Abraham walked there. Jesus lived it. Paul desired it. Have you got it?

"Found in Him" (Phil. 3:9). It is there where we can receive *"the righteousness which is from God by faith"* (v. 9). Abraham received it. God gave him righteousness because he believed, and God credited him with righteousness. God adds in order to take away. He takes away hindrances and imparts the biggest blessing: the rest of faith. God *"will keep him in perfect peace, whose mind is stayed on* [Him]*"* (Isa. 26:3).

EXPERIENCE HIS RESURRECTION POWER

Jesus had what Paul desired. Paul knew Jesus by revelation as we do. He did not know Him from being with Him in His human ministry as the other apostles did. Paul saw that Jesus lived in resurrection power. Paul wanted to gain the rest of faith, so he refused all hindrances and pressed on. He wanted to remove any interference that stood in the way of his knowing Christ. Before facing the Cross, Jesus told His disciples to *"stay here and watch"* (Mark 14:34) while He went further in the garden to pray. Jesus went to the place of apprehension to attain. We also must watch and pray if we are to *"know Him and the power of His resurrection"* (Phil. 3:10).

One day Jesus came upon a funeral procession. A widow's only son had died, and Jesus' great heart had compassion for her. He touched her son in his coffin and said, *"Young man, I say to you, arise"* (Luke 7:14). Death had no power; it could not hold him: *"He who was dead sat up and began to speak"* (v. 15). Oh, compassion is greater than death, greater than suffering. Oh, God, give it to us.

One day, I saw a woman with tumors. In the condition she was in, she could not live out that day. I said, "Do you want to live?" She could not speak, but she was able to move her finger. In the name of Jesus, I anointed her with oil. Mr. Fisher, who was with me, said, "She's gone!"

It had been a little blind girl who had led me to this dying mother's bedside. Compassion broke my heart for that child. I had said to the mother, "Lift your finger." Carrying the mother across the room, I put her against the wardrobe. I held her there. I said, "In the name of Jesus, death, come out." Like a fallen tree, leaf after leaf, her body began moving. Upright instead of lifeless, her feet touched the floor. "In Jesus' name, walk," I said. She did, back to her bed.

I told this story in the service. There was a doctor there who said, "I'll prove that." He saw her and confirmed that the story was true. She told the doctor: "It is all true. I was in heaven, and I saw countless numbers all like Jesus. He pointed, and I knew I had to go. Then I heard a voice saying, 'Walk, in the name of Jesus.'"

There is power in His resurrection. There is a *"righteousness which is from God by faith"* (Phil. 3:9). Are we able to comprehend it? Can we have it? It is His love. It is His life in us. It is His compassion.

See that apprehension is apprehended. Miss it not. Oh, miss Him not! It is the *"righteousness which is from God by faith"*—the rest of faith.

CHAPTER SEVENTEEN

SONSHIP

Behold what manner of love the Father has bestowed on us,
that we should be called children of God! Therefore the world
does not know us, because it did not know Him.
Beloved, now we are children of God.
—1 John 3:1–2

God has done something marvelous for the believer. He has taken him out of the world. It is a remarkable word that Jesus said: *"I do not pray that You should take them out of the world....They are not of the world"* (John 17:15–16). It is a great truth for us to understand. In this glorious position of God's own, we come to a place where we know with confidence, we say it without fear of contradiction from our own hearts or even outside voices, *"Beloved, now we are children of God."*

I want us to examine ourselves in the light of the Word. God has definitely purposed that we should inherit all of the Scriptures, but we must meet the requirements necessary to claim them. Remember this, there are any number of things you may quote without possessing the essential reality of them. I want us to have something more than the literal word. Words are of no importance unless the believer has the assurance of the abiding of those words.

Let me say a few things that are contained in the Scriptures that should be ours. Here is one: *"Beloved, now we are children of God."* That is Scripture. That is divine. That is for us, but it is another thing altogether to have it. Here is another word: *"He who practices righteousness is righteous, just as He is righteous"* (1 John 3:7). There is another word I want to give you. It is a verse that is used by most believers: *"He who is in you is greater than he who is in the world"* (1 John 4:4). That is quoted by many people, but may God reveal to us that the meaning is more than just saying it. You can quote these words without being in the place of victory.

Any person who has come to the place of this word, *"He who is in you is greater than he who is in the world,"* is mightier than all the powers of darkness, mightier than the power of disease, mightier than his own self. There is something reigning supremely great in him more than in the world when he is in that place. But we must come to the place of knowledge. It is not sufficient for you to quote the Word of God. You never come to a place of righteousness and truth until you are in possession of the promises contained in the Word.

INTERPRETATION OF A MESSAGE IN TONGUES:

God, who has divinely brought forth the Word by the power of His might through His Son, gave it displacement in the human soul that the human may be dried up, withered by God, coming in by the force of living power.

Beloved, God wants us to be something more than ordinary people. Remember this: if you are ordinary, you have not reached the ideal principles of God. The only thing that God has for a man is to be extraordinary. God has no room for an ordinary man. There are millions of ordinary people in the world. But when God takes hold of a man, He makes him extraordinary in personality, power, thought, and activity.

"Beloved, now we are children of God." It is a divine plan fashioned by His divine will. God has not given anything that He does not mean for us to attain. God means for us to possess all these things. *"Beloved, now we are children of God."* God has such purposes to perform in us that He has a great desire to utter these words in our hearts that we may rise, that we may claim, that we may be ambitious, that we may be covetous, that there may be something in us that nothing can satisfy unless we not only tow the line but live in the line and claim the whole thing as ours.

You will never reach ideal purposes in any way unless you become the living epistle of the Word by the power of the Holy Spirit. You become the living force of the revelation of God, the incarnation of the personality of His presence in the human soul. Then you know that you are His children. Look at Christ. He is the most beautiful of all. He is utterly glorious, passionate for God, filled with all the fullness of God. He came to earth in the glory of the majesty of His Father, and He stood in the earth in human form. Read Romans 8:3 with me. It is a good word to concentrate on:

For what the law could not do in that it was weak through the flesh, God did by sending His own Son in the likeness of sinful flesh, on account of sin: He condemned sin in the flesh.

Jesus came in human form, *"born of a woman"* (Gal. 4:4), and took on the weaknesses of human flesh. Look at Hebrews 2:14, for there will be a blessing for you:

Inasmuch then as the children have partaken of flesh and blood, He Himself likewise shared in the same; that through death He might destroy him who had the power of death, that is, the devil.

I like to think about the manifestation of the power of God. God came and resided in flesh, in weakness, under the law—for you. He came in human form, worshipped in it, lived in it, and moved in it. They recognized Him as the Son of God.

INTERPRETATION OF A MESSAGE IN TONGUES:
Yes, it was the purpose of the Almighty to move through weakness and quicken it by His mighty power until flesh became the habitation of God in the Spirit.

Beloved, there is the principle. The remarkable position of every soul is to be so inhabited by Jesus as to become a living personality of God's ideal Son. It is very remarkable and beautiful. God has these divine plans for us because so many people believe that because they are in the flesh that they are always to be in the place of weakness. Friends, your weaknesses have to be swallowed up with the ideal of Him who never failed.

Every time He was tried, He came out victorious. He *"was in all points tempted as we are, yet without sin"* (Heb. 4:15). The purpose for His temptations was so that He might be able to help all who are tempted and tried and oppressed in any way. He was the great embodiment of God to human life. He came to expose our weaknesses that we might behold His mightiness. Through Him, we can be strong in the Lord. Praise the Lord!

It's all right now, it's all right now,
For Jesus is my Savior and it's all right now.

It is always all right when He is almighty. Then we are all right. The Word of God says:

Therefore, having been justified by faith, we have peace with God through our Lord Jesus Christ, through whom also we have access by faith into this grace in which we stand, and rejoice in hope of the glory of God.
(Rom. 5:1–2)

It is a great position to be saved by this immensity of power, this great inflow of life, this great fullness of God. This wonderful inhabiting of the Spirit comes right into the human soul and shakes the husks away, shakes the mind!

DIVINELY ADJUSTED

Many people have lost out because their minds prevent them from letting God reach their hearts. May God show us that the only thing that is ever going to help us is the heart. *"For with the heart one believes unto righteousness"* (Rom. 10:10). It is the heart where we believe in faith. It is the heart that is inhabited by the Spirit. It is the heart that is moved by God. The mind is always secondary.

The heart conceives, the mind reflects, and the mouth is operated. But you must not try to reverse the order. Some people are all tongue, neither head nor heart. But when He comes, there is perfect order. It is as right as rain. Look how it comes! The heart believes and then like a ventilator, it flows through and quickens the members of the mind. Then the tongue speaks of the glory of the Lord.

INTERPRETATION OF A MESSAGE IN TONGUES:
Oh, it was the love that flowed from Calvary that moved with compassion for the mighty need of the world's cry. It entered the heart of the Father, unveiled His love to the world, gave us His Son in affection, and the work was done.

101

Praise the Lord! Then it is done. It is perfectly done. The Scriptures are perfect, the sacrifice is perfect, the revelation is perfect, and everything is so divinely adjusted by God Almighty that every person who comes into infinite revelation touched by God sees that the whole canon of Scripture is perfect from the beginning to the end. Not a single thing in the Scriptures clashes with or contradicts the Spirit and makes trouble.

When the power of God surges through the whole life, the Word becomes the personality of the subject. We become the subjects of the Spirit of the living God, and we are moved by the power of God until *"we live and move and have our being"* (Acts 17:28) within this flow of God's integrity. What a wonderful adjustment for weaknesses! Do you believe it is possible?

"God is able to make all grace abound" (2 Cor. 9:8). God is able to shake us thoroughly, to send a wind and blow the chaff away until it will never be seen anymore. God is able to refine us in a way that everyone would desire to proclaim His praises:

> It is better to shout than to doubt,
> It is better to rise than to fail,
> It is better to let the glory out,
> Than to have no glory at all.

"Beloved, now we are children of God." I don't want to leave the subject until I feel that God has given you the hope and ability to bring you into the very place He has made for you. It is as easy as possible if you can reach out by faith.

I am the last man to say anything about fasting, praying, or anything that has been a source of blessing to others. But I have learned by personal experience that I can get more out of one moment's faith than I can get out of a month's yelling. I can get more by believing God in a moment than I can get by screaming for a month. Also, I am positive that blessing comes out of fasting when the fasting is done in the right way. But I find so many people who make up their minds to fast, and they finish with a thick head, troubled bones, and sleepy conditions. I am satisfied that that is no way to fast. A way to fast is described in many Scriptures.

Praying and fasting go together. The Spirit leads you to pray. The Spirit holds on to you until you forget even the hour or the day, and you are so caught up by the power of the Spirit that you want nothing, not even food or drink. Then God gets His plan through because He has you through and through. So the Lord of Hosts, I trust, will *"surround* [us] *with songs of deliverance"* (Ps. 32:7) and give us inward revelations until our whole beings will be uplifted.

Now I can understand clearer than ever Psalm 24: *"Lift up your heads, O you gates!"* (v. 7). Human hindrances, thoughts, and efforts can block the Spirit. *"Lift up your heads, O you gates! And be lifted up, you everlasting doors! And the King of glory shall come in"* (v. 7). Let Him in! Oh, if He comes in, what a wonderful Jesus! You say, "He is in." I believe that when you let God in, you gladly give Him full possession of your heart. The difficulty is that some people are on the edge, waiting to see which way to go. Friends, that is a dangerous position to be in. May God the Holy Spirit wake us up to see we must rise to the challenge of His call.

Who dares to believe God? Who dares to claim his rights? What are your rights? *"Now we are children of God."* This is a position of absolute rest, a position of faith. It is a place of perfect trust and perfect habitation where there are no disturbances. You experience peace like a river. Look at the face of God. Hallelujah! The very Word that comes to judge comes to help.

The law came as a judgment, but when the Spirit comes and breathes through the law, He comes to lift us higher and higher. Hallelujah! We must go a little further. God comes to us and says, "I will make it all right if you dare believe."

All the great things of God come to us as we realize our sinfulness before Him. Instead of hiding as Adam and Eve did when they realized they were naked (Gen. 3:7–10), we should come to God to be clothed. We cannot associate with the evil of this world. If you can be attracted by anything earthly, you have missed the greatest association that God has for you. If your property, your money, your friends, or any human thing can attract you from God, you are not His child in this respect. I will prove it by the next words:

> *Beloved, now we are children of God; and it has not yet been revealed what we shall be, but we know that when He is revealed, we shall be like Him, for we shall see Him as He is. And everyone who has this hope in Him purifies himself, just as He is pure.* (1 John 3:2–3)

Hallelujah! So you see, beloved, the importance of coming into line with God's Word. Let us encounter the Word; let us face God and see if this thing really is so.

ASSOCIATION WITH GOD

"Beloved, now we are the children of God." What is the reality of it? God clearly explains: *"if children, then heirs; heirs of God and joint heirs with Christ"* (Rom. 8:17). But look at the tremendous, gigantic power of God behind our inheritance. First, we are adopted; then we receive an inheritance; then we are made coheirs with Jesus. There you come into it. Will you shiver like someone hesitating on the edge of a pool? Or will you take a plunge into omnipotence and find the waters are not as cold as people told you? Dare you let the warmth of the power of God make you see your inheritance in the Spirit? No, you will see something better than that. God touches our souls, making our whole bodies cry out for the living God. Glory!

Do you want God? Do you want fellowship in the Spirit? Do you want to walk with Him? Do you desire communion with Him? Everything else is no good. You want the association with God, and God says, *"I will come in to* [you] *and dine with* [you], *and* [you] *with Me"* (Rev. 3:20). Hallelujah! We can attain spiritual maturity, fullness of Christ, a place where God becomes the perfect Father and the Holy Spirit has a rightful place now as never before.

The Holy Spirit breathes through us, enabling us to say, "You are my Father; You are my Father." Because you have been adopted, *"God has sent forth the Spirit of His Son into your hearts, crying out, 'Abba, Father!'"* (Gal. 4:6). Oh, it is wonderful. May God the Holy Spirit grant to us that richness of His pleasure, that unfolding of His will, that consciousness of His smile upon us. There is *"no condemnation"* (Rom. 8:1). We find that *"the law of the Spirit of life"* makes us *"free from the law of sin and death"* (v. 2). Glory!

The Spirit is having His perfect way because if we see the truth as clearly as God intends for us to see it, we will all be made so much richer, looking forward to the Blessed One who is coming again. Here we are, face to face with the facts. God has shown us different aspects of the Spirit. He has shown us the pavilion of splendor. He has revealed to us the power of the relationship of sonship. He has shown us that those who are God's children bear His image. They actively claim the rights of their adoption. They speak, and it is done. They bind the things that are loose, and loose the things that are bound (Matt. 16:19). And the perfection of sonship is so evident that more and more people are becoming children of God. They joyfully sing:

I know the Lord, I know the Lord,
I know the Lord's laid His hands on me.
Oh, I know the Lord, I know the Lord,
I know the Lord's laid His hands on me.

Do you believe it? Let us see you act it. Beloved, God the Holy Spirit has a perfect plan to make us a movement. There is a difference between a movement and a monument. A movement is something that is always active. A monument is something that is erected on a corner and neither speaks nor moves, but there is a tremendous lot of humbug and nonsense to get it in place. It is silent and does nothing. A movement is where God comes into the very being of a person, making him active for God. He is God's property, God's mouthpiece, God's eyes, and God's hands. God will *"sanctify you completely"* (1 Thess. 5:23).

The sanctification of the eyes, the hands, the mouth, the ears—to be so controlled by the Spirit who lives within us—is a wonderful place for God to bring us to. *"Beloved, now we are children of God; and it has not yet been revealed what we shall be"* (1 John 3:1-2). What a great thought: to be heirs, *"joint heirs with Christ"* (Rom. 8:17); to receive revelations and kindnesses from God; to have God dwell within man. The believer is filled, moved, and intensified until he takes wing. It would not take a trumpet to rouse him, for he is already on the wing, and he will land very soon. He would hear God's voice no matter how much noise surrounded him.

We read in 1 Corinthians 2:9: *"But as it is written: 'Eye has not seen, nor ear heard, nor have entered into the heart of man the things which God has prepared for those who love Him.'"*

Everything that is going to help you, you have to make yours. *"God has prepared."* He has stored it up already. You don't need a stepladder to get to it. It is ready to be handed out to you when you become joined with Him. When you walk with Him, He will either drop everything He has on you or take you where you are to remain forever.

Beloved, it is impossible in our finite condition to estimate the lovingkindness or the measureless mind of God. When we come into like-mindedness with the Word, instead of looking at the Word, we begin to see what God has for us in the Word. This is a very inexhaustible subject, but I pray that God will make us an inexhaustible people. I want you to be able to say:

Me with a quenchless thirst inspire,
A longing, infinite desire
Fill my craving heart.
Less than Thyself You do not give,
Thy might within me now to live.
Come, all Thou hast.

God, please come and make it impossible for me to ever be satisfied but to always have a quenchless thirst for You, the living God. Then I will not be overtaken. Then I will be ready. Then I will have shining eyes, filled with delight as they look at the Master.

THE SON OF GOD REVEALED

You ask, "Can we see the Master?" Here, look at Him. His Word is Spirit and life-giving. This is the breath, the Word of Jesus. Through the Holy Spirit, men have written and spoken. Here is the life. Here is the witness. Here is the truth. Here is the Son of God *"revealed from faith to faith"* (Rom. 1:17), from heart to heart, from vision to vision, until we all come into perfect unity of fellowship into the fullness of Christ.

There it is, beloved. Look! *"Now we are children of God."* If you are there, we can take a step further. But if you are not there, you may hear but not cross over. There is something about the Word of God that benefits the hearer who has faith, but if the hearer does not have faith, it will not profit.

The future is what you are today, not what you are going to be tomorrow. This is the day when God makes the future possible. When God reveals something to you today, tomorrow is filled with a further illumination of God's possibility for you.

Do you dare to come into the place of omnipotence, of wonderment? Do you dare to say to God, "I am ready for all that You have for me"? It will mean living a pure and holy life. It will mean living a sanctified, a separate life. It will mean your heart is so perfect and your prospects are so divinely separated that you say to the world, "Goodbye."

INTERPRETATION OF A MESSAGE IN TONGUES:
Holiness is the habitation of Your house. Purity, righteousness, and truth are God's glorified position in the Spirit. The great desire of the Master is to make sons of God, for many sons He will gather into glory.

Listen to what God has to say. Everything must be absolutely the Word, so I only speak to you by the Word. Let us read Hebrews 2:6–10:

But one testified in a certain place, saying: "What is man that You are mindful of him, or the son of man that You take care of him? You have made him a little lower than the angels; You have crowned him with glory and honor, and set him over the works of Your hands. You have put all things in subjection under his feet." For in that He put all in subjection under him, He left nothing that is not put under him. But now we do not yet see all things put under him. But we see Jesus, who was made a little lower than the angels, for the suffering of death crowned with glory and honor, that He, by the grace of God, might taste death for everyone. For it was fitting for Him, for whom are all things and by whom are all things, in bringing many sons to glory, to make the captain of their salvation perfect through sufferings. (Heb. 2:6–10)

This second chapter of Hebrews describes the mighty, glorified position for the children of God. God wants me to announce it to every heart, like a great trumpet call. The plan is to bring you to glory as a child clothed with the power of the gifts, graces, ministries, and operations. You are to be clothed with the majesty of heaven. This is like heaven to me. My very body is filled with thoughts of heaven.

Seeing that these things are so, what manner of persons should we be? We should be keeping our eyes upon Him that we may be ready for the Rapture. Oh, brothers and sisters, what immense pleasure God has for us! There is no limit to the sobermindedness God is bringing us to so that we may be able to understand all that God has planned for us. Oh, that we may look not on the things that are, but with eyes of purity see only the invisible Son. Having our whole bodies illuminated by the power of the Holy Spirit, we grow in grace, in faith, and in Christlikeness until there is no difference between us and Him.

Let me give you the Word if you can receive it: *"As He is, so are we in this world"* (1 John 4:17). What a word! Who dares to believe it? Only God can take us to such heights, depths, lengths, and breadths in the Spirit. Are you prepared to go all the way? Are you willing for your heart to have only one attraction? Are you willing to have only one Love? Are you willing for Him to become your perfect Bridegroom?

The more bridelike we are, the more we love to hear the Bridegroom's voice; the less bridelike we are, the less we long for His Word. If you cannot rest without it, if it becomes your food day and night, if you eat and drink of it, His life will be in you, and when He appears, you will go with Him. Help us, Jesus!

How many are prepared to reveal yourself before the King? Are you prepared to yield to His call, yield to His will, yield to His desires? The Word has been preached; the Spirit has been speaking to you. How many are going to say, "At all costs I will go through!" Who says so? Who means it? Are you determined? Is your soul on the wing? Make a full consecration to God right now. It is between you and God. You are going now to enter the presence of God. Come clean with everything in the presence of God!

CHAPTER EIGHTEEN

THAT I MAY KNOW HIM

L et us pray for God to enlarge our vision. I believe that He will. By His power, He will bring us into like-minded precious faith to believe all that the Scriptures say. The Scriptures are so deep that one can never enter into their truths without being enlarged by God. Beloved, one thing is certain: God can do it. *"All things that pertain to life and godliness"* (2 Pet. 1:3) are contained in the pursuit. We seek a faith that will not have a dim sight but will clear everything and claim all that God puts before it. And so I pray that God will reveal the depths of His righteousness that we may no longer be poor but very rich in God by His Spirit. Beloved, it is God's thought to make us all very rich *"in the grace and knowledge of our Lord and Savior Jesus Christ"* (2 Pet. 3:18).

RIGHTEOUSNESS IS FROM GOD

We have before us a message that is full of height, depth, length, and width, a message that came out of brokenness of spirit and the loss and enduring of all things. It is a message where flesh and all that relates to this world had to come to nothing. God can take us into this spiritual plane with Himself where we may be grounded in all knowledge. We can become so established in spiritual matters that we will always be lifted by God. Men try to lift themselves, but there is no inspiration in that. But when you are lifted by the Spirit, things come into perfect harmony, and you go forth right on to victory. That is a grand place to come to where we *"rejoice in Christ Jesus, and have no confidence in the flesh"* (Phil. 3:3). Paul adds, *"Though I also might have confidence in the flesh"* (v. 4). Although Paul had kept the law blamelessly, it was not his own performance in which he had confidence.

Oh, that is the greatest of all, when the Lord Jesus has the reins. Then we no longer have anything to boast about because all our righteousness that is determined by how perfectly we keep the law ceases. It is beautiful as we gaze upon the perfect Jesus. Jesus so exceeds everything else. For this reason, Paul felt that whatever he was, whatever he had been, whatever he had accomplished, he considered *"rubbish"* (v. 8). He could not achieve righteousness in his own strength.

BROKENNESS PRECEDES BLESSING

We must acknowledge our helplessness and nothingness. Although laboring in the Spirit is painful, God can lift the burden from us. I have had those days when I feel burdened. I have had it this morning, but now God is lifting the heaviness. And I say, brother and sister, unless God brings us into a place of brokenness of spirit, unless God remolds us in the great plan of His will for us, the best of us will utterly fail. But when we are absolutely taken in hand by the almighty God, God turns even our weakness into strength. He makes even that barren, helpless, groaning cry come forth, so that men and women are reborn in the travail. There is a place where our helplessness is touched by the power of God and where we come out shining as *"gold refined in the fire"* (Rev. 3:18).

There is no hope for Pentecost unless we come to God in our brokenness. It was on the cross that our Lord died with a broken heart. Pentecost came out of jeering and sneering. It included being mocked and beaten and an offer of sour wine. He received an unfair judgment and a cross that He had to bear. But, glory to God, Pentecost rings out this morning for you through the words, *"It is finished!"* (John 19:30). And now because it is finished, we can take the same place that He took and rise out of that death in majestic glory with the resurrection touch of heaven. People will know that God has done something for us.

BE MADE NEW

Daily, there must be a revival touch in our hearts. He must change us after His fashion. We are to be made new all the time. There is no such thing as having all grace and knowledge. God wants us to begin with these words of power found in Philippians 3 and never stop, but go on to perfection. God wants us to reach the blessings in these verses today:

> *But what things were gain to me, these I have counted loss for Christ. Yet indeed I also count all things loss for the excellence of the knowledge of Christ Jesus my Lord, for whom I have suffered the loss of all things, and count them as rubbish, that I may gain Christ.* (Phil. 3:7–8)

Turn to Hebrews 10:32: *"But recall the former days in which, after you were illuminated, you endured a great struggle with sufferings."* I am positive that no man can attain like-mindedness except by the illumination of the Spirit.

God has been speaking to me over and over that I must urge people to receive the baptism of the Holy Spirit. In the baptism of the Holy Spirit, there is unlimited grace and endurance as the Spirit reveals Himself to us. The excellency of Christ can never be understood apart from illumination. And I find that the Holy Spirit is the great Illuminator who makes me understand all the depths of Him. I must witness about Christ. Jesus said to Thomas, *"Thomas, because you have seen Me, you have believed. Blessed are those who have not seen and yet have believed"* (John 20:29).

There is a revelation that brings us into touch with Him where we get all and see right into the fullness of Christ. As Paul saw the depths and heights of the grandeur, he longed that he might win Him. Before his conversion, in his passion and zeal, Paul would do anything to bring Christians to death. His passion raged like a mighty lion. As he was going to Damascus, he heard the voice of Jesus saying, *"Saul, Saul, why are you persecuting Me?"* (Acts 9:4). What touched him was the tenderness of God.

Friends, it is always God's tenderness that reaches us. He comes to us in spite of our weakness and depravity. If somebody came to oppose us, we would stand our ground, but when He comes to forgive us, we do not know what to do. Oh, to win Christ! A thousand things in the nucleus of a human heart need softening a thousand times a day. There are things in us that unless God shows us *"the excellence of the knowledge of Christ Jesus"* (Phil. 3:8), we will never be broken and brought to ashes. But God will do it. We will not merely be saved, but we will be saved a thousand times over! Oh, this transforming regeneration by the power of the Spirit of the living God makes me see there is a place to *"gain*

Christ" (v. 8), that I may stand complete there. As He was, so am I to be. The Scriptures declare that we can be:

Found in Him, not having [our] *own righteousness, which is from the law, but that which is through faith in Christ, the righteousness which is from God by faith.* (v. 9)

We cannot depend upon our works, but upon the faithfulness of God, being able under all circumstances to be hidden in Him, covered by the almighty presence of God. The Scriptures tell us that we are in Christ and Christ is in God. What is able to move you from this place of omnipotent power? *"Shall tribulation, or distress, or persecution, or famine, or nakedness, or peril, or sword?"* (Rom. 8:35). Oh, no! Will life, or death, or principalities, or powers? (v. 38). No, *"we are more than conquerors through Him who loved us"* (v. 37).

FOUND IN HIM

I must be *"found in Him"* (Phil. 3:9). There is a place of seclusion, a place of rest and faith in Jesus where there is nothing else like it. Jesus came to His disciples on the water, and they were terrified. But He said, *"It is I; do not be afraid"* (Matt. 14:27). My friend, He is always there. He is there in the storm as well as in the peace; He is there in adversity. When will we know He is there? When we are *"found in Him,"* not having our own work, our own plan, but resting in the omnipotent plan of God. Oh, is it possible for the child of God to fail? It is not possible, for *"He who keeps Israel shall neither slumber nor sleep"* (Ps. 121:4). He will watch over us continually, but we must be *"found in Him."*

I know there is a secret place in Jesus that is open to us today. My brother, my sister, you have been nearly weighed down with troubles. They have almost crushed you. Sometimes you thought you would never get out of this place of difficulty, but you have no idea that behind the whole thing, God has been working a plan greater than all.

Today is a resurrection day. We must know the resurrection of His power in brokenness of spirit: *"That I may know Him and the power of His resurrection"* (Phil. 3:10). Jesus said to Martha, *"I am the resurrection and the life"* (John 11:25). Oh, to know the resurrection power, to know the rest of faith. Any one of us, without exception, can reach this happiness in the Spirit. There is something different between saying you have faith and then being pressed into a tight corner and proving that you have faith. If you dare to believe, it will be done according to your faith: *"Whatever things you ask when you pray, believe that you receive them, and you will have them"* (Mark 11:24). Jesus is *"the resurrection and the life"* (John 11:25). With God's help, we must gain this life. We can reach it with the knowledge that He will make us as white as snow, as pure and holy as He, that we may go with boldness to His *"throne of grace"* (Heb. 4:16). Boldness is in His holiness. Boldness is in His righteousness. Boldness is in His truth. You cannot have the boldness of faith if you are not pure. What blessed words follow: *"the fellowship of His sufferings"* (Phil. 3:10). Remember, unless that fellowship touches us, we will never have much power.

When the Spirit of the Lord moves within you, you will be broken down and then built up. Jesus came forth in the glory of the Father, filled with all the fullness of God. It was God's plan before *"the foundation of the world"* (Matt. 25:34). God loved the fearful, helpless human race, with all its blackness and hideousness of sin, and He provided the way for redemption. May God give us such *"fellowship of His sufferings"* (Phil. 3:10) that when we see a person afflicted with cancer, we will pray right through until the disease is struck dead. When we see a bent and helpless woman or a man who is weak and sick, may God give us compassion and a fellowship with them that will lighten their heavy burdens and set them free. How often we have missed the victory because we did not have the Lord's compassion at the needed moment. We failed to pray with a broken heart.

Is there anything more? Oh, yes, we must see the next thing. We must be *"conformed to His death"* (Phil. 3:10). *"Unless a grain of wheat falls into the ground and dies, it remains alone; but if it dies, it produces much grain"* (John 12:24). God wants you to see that unless you are dead indeed, unless you come to a perfect crucifixion, unless you die with Him, you are not in the *"fellowship of His sufferings"* (Phil. 3:10). May God move upon us in this life to bring us into an absolute death, not merely to talk about it. In this way, Christ's life may be made manifest. With Paul, we can say:

> *I do not count myself to have apprehended; but one thing I do, forgetting those things which are behind and reaching*

*forward to those things which are ahead, I press toward
the goal for the prize of the upward call of God in Christ
Jesus.*   (vv. 13–14)

The Lord wants us to understand that we must come to a
place where our natural life ceases, and by the power of God, we
rise into a life where God rules and reigns. Do you long to know
Him? Do you long to be *"found in Him"* (v. 9)? Your longing will be
satisfied today. I ask you to fall in the presence of God. All you who
want to know God, yield to His mighty power, and obey the Spirit.

CHAPTER NINETEEN

OUR INHERITANCE

*His divine power has given to us all things that pertain to life
and godliness, through the knowledge of Him who called us
by glory and virtue.*
—2 Peter 1:3

Many people make wills and appoint someone to carry out
their final requests. After the person dies, very often
those people who have had property left to them never
get it because of unfaithful stewards who have been left in charge.
But there is one will that has been left, and He who made the
whole will is our Lord Jesus Christ. After dying, He rose to carry
out His own will. And now we may have all that has been left to us
by Him: all the inheritance, all the blessings, all the power, all the
life, and all the victory. All His promises are ours because He is
risen. I believe the Lord wants us to know our inheritance.

Because He is risen as a faithful High Priest, He is here to help
us understand His divine principles. May God provide us with a
clear knowledge of what He means for us in these days. He has
called us to great banquets and wants us to bring good appetites to
His table.

It is a serious thing to come to a banquet of the Lord and not
be able to eat anything. We must have very thirsty conditions and
hungry souls. Then we can have what is prepared for us. We can be
"strengthened with might through His Spirit in the inner man"
(Eph. 3:16). May the Lord take us into His treasures now.

A DIVINE MIND

We will find out that the truth is always revealed to us
through Christ. All the fullness is in Him. All the glories surround

Him. All the divine virtue flows from Him. We must understand that God is bringing us into the place where we can understand what He means by *"things that pertain to life and godliness, through the knowledge of Him."* God has brought us from one step to another. First, He gave us a glimpse of faith. Then, He gave us assurance of the faith on the principles of the groundwork of Christ being the foundation of all things. Now, the Lord wants to show us how this virtue can remain in us. We must reach to attain this virtue.

What is virtue? Oh, friends, Paul received these divine powers, which he calls *"the effective working of His power"* (Eph. 3:7). He is talking about the divine infilling, which has to fill the whole body with life, virtue, grace, power, and faith. There are no limitations. God is the Executive of the kingdom of heaven. He has power in our body as we open ourselves to Him. We recognize His immeasurable fullness as He reveals Himself to us.

So, beloved, God wants us to understand that whatever it costs, whatever it means, we must have a personal incoming of this life of God, this Holy Spirit, this divine person.

I want you to think about what it really means to receive the Holy Spirit. We are born again *"not of corruptible seed but incorruptible, through the word of God"* (1 Pet. 1:23). The Word *"lives and abides forever"* (v. 23). We are born again by the incorruptible power of God. It is His plan for us. This divine power is beyond anything that the human mind can conceive. We must have a divine mind in order to understand divine things.

Our lives must be changed by His grace. Our bodies must become a *"temple of the Holy Spirit"* (1 Cor. 6:19). We must *"have the mind of Christ"* (1 Cor. 2:16). And we must understand that God has come to change us into His image, filling us with His power.

Jesus came into this world, but He had an eternal perspective. Jesus lived in the present but often spoke of the future. Beloved, there is a future, but we must not neglect the present. Whatever God has designed for man, we must claim it now. We will always have greater demonstrations of power if we are living in the now instead of in the future. We must experience a now power, a now blessing, a now God, a now heaven, a now glory, a now virtue.

INTERPRETATION OF A MESSAGE IN TONGUES:

It is the Spirit that works in us all these divine plans so that He may build us on the foundations of the living Word, which lives, which always quickens and moves. Builds high, higher,

higher, into and with love. It is always in a higher sense be-cause God has no lower means.

He wants us to go higher and higher. Oh, for a heavenly sight and a divine touch of God today. One touch of deity, one flash of light, one moment in His presence, one touch of the infinite Trinity makes us strong; in a moment, we are able to see all things as He sees them.

INTERPRETATION OF A MESSAGE IN TONGUES:
Oh, I must never cease until I reach that which God has for me, for I must be for others what He wants me to be.

It is a divine virtue to recognize the presence of the Holy Spirit. May it be said of us as it was said of Stephen: *"A man full of faith and the Holy Spirit"* (Acts 6:5). Barnabas was also a good man filled with the Holy Spirit and faith. (See Acts 15:25–26.) There is a divine place of purity where the unclean can never put their feet. It is a holy place where the pure in heart can see God (Matt. 5:8). Only through following God's directions can you get to that place. God's way is called the *"Highway of Holiness"* (Isa. 35:8), and He longs to bring us into that place where we can hear the voice of God, see the form of God, understand the ways of God, and walk in communion with God. In this place, divine virtue flows.

Once at a very late meeting being held outdoors, I was sur-rounded by a great number of people. God was saving people, and oh, the joy I felt in pointing people to Jesus. When I went home, my family said to me, "Aunt Mary is going home, and Uncle Sam would like you to see her before she bids farewell." I went there, not knowing what to say but "Goodbye." As I came close to her bed, I was impressed to stretch out my hand. What there is in a hand! What there is in a person touched by the power of God, no one can tell. As my hand touched her hand, the divine virtue of heaven flowed through her dying body and brought her into perfect life, perfect as she ever was, instantaneously brought back from death into life, joy, and peace.

There is a virtue; there is a truth. God must manifest His power until everything we touch moves at the power of God. Paul knew it, the apostles had a clear understanding of it, and Jesus spoke about it. When the woman who touched the hem of Christ's garment was healed, she felt His power. Knowing immediately that *"power had gone out of Him,"* Jesus asked, *"Who touched My clothes?"* (Mark 5:30).

There is a power that goes through the human body to another body. I see that it is in perfect alignment with the Scriptures that we *"lay hands on the sick, and they will recover"* (Mark 16:18).

There is a truth in John's gospel that some have never understood. May God reveal it to us now:

> *Most assuredly, I say to you, We speak what We know and testify what We have seen, and you do not receive Our witness. If I have told you earthly things and you do not believe, how will you believe if I tell you heavenly things? No one has ascended to heaven but He who came down from heaven, that is, the Son of Man who is in heaven.*
>
> (John 3:11–13)

A DIVINE SOURCE

Now, look at that electric light. It is illuminating the place because of the generator. It has a receiver and a transmitter. Although the wires are important, it is the power of the generator that is sending forth the light through those wires. Likewise, every man who is born of God is receiving life from God. God is the source of power. Inside man's heart and mind is the wire that receives the revelation and transmits the illumination. In order to keep it functioning perfectly, it must always return to the source of power. And so it is with everyone who is born of God. He is kept alive by a power that he cannot see but he can feel, a power that is generated in glory, comes down into earthen vessels, and returns to the throne of God.

We are receiving and transmitting all the time. When we stop for a moment to place our hands upon a needy case, the supernatural goes through that person and brings life. God wants us to know that He is the source of divine glory, divine virtue, and perfect knowledge.

The Holy Spirit is the great Motivator of us all. He receives all, He disburses all, and He sends out the wonderful manifestations after He has had the call. So we must have life in the Spirit, united, illuminated, transformed all the time by this glorious regenerating power of the Spirit. May God reveal that it is for us all. Such a manifestation of the life and power of God will be given to us until there will be neither barrenness nor unfruitfulness, but rather a surrender to all His will. Hallelujah!

INTERPRETATION OF A MESSAGE IN TONGUES:

It is that which God has designed from the beginning. It is no new thing. It is as old as God. It lasts as long as eternity. We are, we will be, forever with Him. He has created us for this purpose: that we should be the sons of God with power, with promise, with life, for all the world.

Oh, brothers and sisters, don't tell me that we have received all the fullness of the Spirit, an immeasurable portion! Don't tell me that there are any limitations to it. It comes in floods that we cannot contain. We drink and drink and drink again, and yet, we are still dry. Saints of God, the more of this joy you get, the more you require, the more you desire. It is God in you who longs for all His fullness to come into you, praise His name. But we must be partakers of it.

A DIVINE GLORY

Two words here are closely connected. They are beautiful words, full of meaning for this moment. Let me read them: *"Through the knowledge of Him who called us by glory and virtue."*

A lot of people have a great misunderstanding about glory. Glory is always an expression. For instance, on the Day of Pentecost, it was necessary that the moving by the mighty rushing wind should be made evident in the upper room. It was also important that the disciples should be clothed with *"tongues, as of fire"* (Acts 2:3). Then it was significant that the whole group gathered there should receive not only the fire but also the rushing wind, the personality of the Spirit in the wind. The divine order is in the wind, and all the manifestation of the glory is in the wind.

Now let me express it. The inward man instantly receives the Holy Spirit with great joy and blessedness. He cannot express it. It is beyond his expression. He received the power of the Spirit, which is the Word. I want you to notice that when the Holy Spirit is in the body, this divine power, this personality, this breath of God, takes the things of Jesus and utters them by this expressive wind. Like a river, He sends forth the utterances of the Spirit.

Then again, when the body is filled with joy, sometimes it is so inexpressible. Thrown on the canvas of the mind, the mind moves the tongue to speak power, love, and joy to us from the very depths of the heart. By the same process, the Spirit, which is the breath of God, brings forth the manifestation of the glory.

When God speaks, there is always glory. Peter wrote about being on the holy mountain:

For we did not follow cunningly devised fables when we made known to you the power and coming of our Lord Jesus Christ, but were eyewitnesses of His majesty. For He received from God the Father honor and glory when such a voice came to Him from the Excellent Glory: "This is My beloved Son, in whom I am well pleased." (2 Pet. 1:16–17)

Sometimes people wonder how and why it is that the Holy Spirit is always expressing Himself in words. It cannot be otherwise. You couldn't understand it otherwise. You cannot understand God by shakings, and yet shakings may be in perfect order sometimes. There isn't any manifestation of the body—shakings, rollings, jumpings, and all kinds of things that are allowed—that is a manifestation of God. Only the utterances are manifestations of God. The others may be so mixed with the flesh and the Spirit that it would take a great deal of divine intuition and divine revelation to discriminate between the Spirit and flesh.

But you can always tell when the Spirit moves and brings forth utterances. These utterances, not waving of hands and shakings of body, magnify God. But the Holy Spirit has a perfect plan. He comes right through every man who is so filled and brings divine utterances that we may understand what the mind of the Lord is.

You notice I give all my addresses by inspiration. I dare not work things out in my mind before I come. If I did, I would get out of the plan of God. I have to come to you with the bare Word of God and expect the Holy Spirit to enlighten it. I must read into my heart the perfect law of liberty. If I came to you with a fixed arrangement of an address, the whole thing would come from my humanity. But I cannot afford to be natural. I can only afford to be supernatural now. I cannot afford to be anything less than directed entirely by the Holy Spirit. If I turn to any other plan, then I lose the unction, the power, the revelation of what God has. When I come into the presence of God, He takes the things of the Spirit and reveals them to me. Our hearts are comforted and built up. And there is no way to warm a heart more than by the heart that first touched the flame. There must be the heavenly fires burning within.

We are born of the Spirit, and nothing but the Spirit of God can feed that spiritual life. We must live in it, feed in it, walk in it, talk in it, and sleep in it. Hallelujah! We must always be in the Holy Spirit whether asleep or awake. There is a place for man in the Holy Spirit where God has him; he is lost to every man, but he is never lost to God. God can find him any time He wants him. Oh, hallelujah!

I want to turn to three Scriptures so that we may see what they say about glory and not be deceived. *"Therefore my heart is glad, and my glory rejoices; My flesh also will rest in hope"* (Ps. 16:9). The psalmist's rejoicing brings forth the glory. It was because his heart was glad. In Psalm 108, we see another side of glory: *"O God, my heart is steadfast; I will sing and give praise, even with my glory"* (v. 1). So you see, glory is a manifestation of language. It is when the body is filled with the powers of God. Then the tongue is the only thing that can express the glory. And God has given us tongues so that we can express the glory, the glory of God.

Glory is not a halo. It is a presence, and the presence always comes by the tongue bringing forth the revelations of God. In Acts, we see yet another aspect to glory:

> *For David says concerning Him: "I foresaw the LORD always before my face, for He is at my right hand, that I may not be shaken. Therefore my heart rejoiced, and my tongue was glad; moreover my flesh also will rest in hope."*
> (Acts 2:25–26)

You will always find that God works this way. First, He fills us with His power. Then He gives us verbal expressions by the same Spirit moving within us in order that the manifestation of the Spirit will be evident outwardly as well. Therefore, *"out of the abundance of the heart the mouth speaks"* (Matt. 12:34).

What is all this about? I want you to notice that virtue and glory will be inexpressible conditions sometimes. You will find out that virtue has to be transmitted, and you will find out that glory has to be expressed. And so God, by filling us with the Holy Spirit, has brought into us that which He has in the glory so that out of us may come forth His glory.

The world's needs, our manifestations, revivals, and all conditions are first settled in heaven, then worked out on earth. So we must be in touch with God Almighty to bring out on the face of the earth all the things that God has in the heavens. This is an ideal for us. May God help us not to forsake the sense of holy communion we enjoy privately so that we may manifest His glory publicly.

We must see the face of the Lord and understand His workings. There are things that God says to me that I know must take place. It doesn't matter what people say. I have been face to face with some of the most trying moments of men's lives when it meant so much to me to keep the vision and hold fast to what God had said.

A man must be in an immovable condition. The voice of God must mean to him more than what he sees, feels, or hears. He must have an originality born in heaven, transmitted by tongues, or expressed in some way. We must bring heaven to earth. That is our godly purpose.

A DIVINE NATURE

We must enter into this because we have to be partakers of His divine nature. The priceless promises that we have been given enable us to *"be partakers of the divine nature, having escaped the corruption that is in the world through lust"* (2 Pet. 1:4). Turn to Romans 8:2: *"For the law of the Spirit of life in Christ Jesus has made me free from the law of sin and death."* God wants us to see that there are two laws, but the *"law of the Spirit of life in Christ Jesus"* is different from the *"law of sin and death."* One looks on the divine principles, which make me know that I am free.

Let me turn to that law of the Spirit. This same life that is the *"law of the Spirit of life"* brings us into the same attitude of being partakers of His divine nature. You see, it is a divine life. I have two lives. I have a spiritual life and a natural life.

I hope no one will ever be so foolish as to believe that the natural life is done away with. You will always have it as long as you live. It may be there for great advantages. For instance, I thank God for my natural life this morning, which has enabled me to walk and to dress myself. I thank God for the natural life that has brought us here. It is the natural body that brought your spiritual perception into a holy meeting, and your natural body is necessary to bring you to a place where you can feed your spiritual desires.

But we must understand that the natural has only a certain part to play. It is always to advance the control the Spirit of the living God has over our bodies. The spiritual life is so powerful. It can bring to death the natural man, until the righteousness of God can so permeate the whole body that the virtues of Christ are as much in the fingers as in the hand. It is the divine life, the divine virtue of our Lord Jesus Christ.

Then while we walk about, it is absolutely true that we have no desire for the world because our desires are greater than the world. You cannot fascinate a man of God with gold, houses, or lands. We seek a country, a *"house not made with hands, eternal in the heavens"* (2 Cor. 5:1). And if this mortal body will be put off, the heavenly body will be put on. And we are waiting and longing with an expression, with an inward joy, with a great leap of life, waiting to jump into that.

INTERPRETATION OF A MESSAGE IN TONGUES:

He has designed the plan. He has the unfolding of the purpose. He is the grandeur of the principles. He lays the foundation of the spiritual life, quickened always by His own life, for He is our life, and when He will appear, we will be like Him. He will appear!

Beloved, there is a longing in the soul. There is a travail in the spirit, a yielding of the will, the blending of the life that only gives utterances as He wishes. I believe God is bringing us to a longing for these utterances in the Spirit.

Oh, this is a lovely verse. See, there is so much depth in it, but it is all real from heaven. It is as divinely appointed for this meeting as when the Holy Spirit was upon Peter, and He brings it out for us. I will read it again, for it is life, breath, and marrow. It moves me. I must live in this grace: *"As His divine power has given to us all things that pertain to life and godliness, through the knowledge of Him who called us by glory and virtue."*

You cannot get away from Him. He is the center of all things. He moves the earth, transforms beings, can live in every mind, and plans every thought. Oh, He is there all the time.

The Holy Spirit has only language. There is no language on earth that man has formed; it takes the Holy Spirit to form a language. You will find if you go to one of the epistles, when Paul has finished, he is full of the strength of the Spirit. The Spirit breathes through him, yet he comes to a place where he feels he must stop. There are greater things than even he can utter. Prayer, the breath of the Almighty, breathes through the human soul. There He breathes through Paul.

In Ephesians 3:20, you find words that no human could ever think or plan. They are so mighty, so of God: *"Now to Him who is able to do exceedingly abundantly above all that we ask or think, according to the power that works in us."* The mighty God of revelation through a man! There the Holy Spirit gave these words of grandeur to stir our hearts, to move our affections, to transform us altogether. This is ideal. This is God. Will we teach these words? Will we have them? Oh, they are ours. Will they remain ours? God has never put anything over on a pole you could not reach. God has brought His plan down to man.

Sometimes we have as much as we can digest, yet there are divine nuggets of precious truth held before our hearts. It makes you understand that there are yet heights, depths, lengths, and breadths of the knowledge of God that God has laid up for us (v. 18). We might truly say:

> My heavenly bank, my heavenly bank,
> The house of God's treasure and store.
> I have plenty in here; I'm a real millionaire.

Glory is all in here. We are never to be poverty stricken anymore. We have an inward knowledge of an unfolding of a greater bank than ever the Rothschilds or any other child ever knew about. There it is stored up, nugget upon nugget, weights of glory, expression of the countenance of the invisible Christ to be seen.

God is shaking the earth and the foundations of all nationalities. Constantly, He is helping us to understand the principle in the Scriptures that can bring man freedom from the natural order of every institution. He wants to bring man to a place of holiness, righteousness, and God's peace, which passes all human understanding (Phil. 4:7). We must touch it. We must reach it. Praise God!

One thing is certain. God has brought us in on purpose to take us on. You say, "How will I be able to get all these things that are laid up for me?" Brothers and sisters, I know of no other way but through a *"broken and a contrite heart,"* which *"God...will not despise"* (Ps. 51:17).

A man asked me last night, "Don't you think I am baptized with the Holy Spirit?"

I said, "I don't know anything about you."

"I am willing for anything," he told me.

Then I knew he was not baptized. I never saw a man "willing for anything" that got anything. The man that gets anything is the man who goes after one thing. *"One thing have I desired of the LORD, that will I seek"* (Ps. 27:4). Whatever you want, make it one thing and get it.

What do you want? Make it one thing. You know better than I do what you want, and God knows what you want. That one thing you require is for you today. May God help you to move from your seats where you are and get that one thing. Determine to know the powers of the world to come, and you will see, for truly when Daniel set his mind to get all the things which were provided, God gave an abundance of other things which have not yet been fulfilled. So I remind you of one thing:

> *Ask, and it will be given to you; seek, and you will find; knock, and it will be opened to you. For everyone who asks receives, and he who seeks finds, and to him who knocks it will be opened.* (Matt. 7:7–8)

May God help you to take your own course, to do as the Spirit leads, and to leave everything in God's hands.

CHAPTER TWENTY

A LIVING SACRIFICE

I beseech you therefore, brethren, by the mercies of God, that you present your bodies a living sacrifice, holy, acceptable to God, which is your reasonable service. And do not be conformed to this world, but be transformed by the renewing of your mind, that you may prove what is that good and acceptable and perfect will of God.
—Romans 12:1–2

Here we have the words of a man who had come right out of the ashes of broken faith, speaking to all the saints, saying: "He has brought me to the place where everything has gone on the altar. All that I have and all that I am is consecrated to God. Such a lovely place! Such a wealthy place! Such a rich place! And I want all the saints to come into the same place."

THE WEAKNESS OF THE FLESH

Flesh will interfere with us and stop our progress, but if the Spirit of the Lord is upon us, the flesh is brought to a place where we understand the truth of Romans 8:10: *"And if Christ is in you, the body is dead because of sin, but the Spirit is life because of righteousness."*

The moment flesh is dealt with and judgment comes to it, we are brought to a place of helplessness. The flesh has gone; it is dead, but the Spirit breathes life within us. The body is helpless, but it is dominated by the power of the Spirit until it longs to breathe and act in the Spirit. It is beautiful.

One of the greatest mercies that you will ever have will be a revelation to your heart of how to get rid of yourself. Boundless spiritual resources are available after the flesh no longer reigns. Bask in these words: *"Blessed are those who hunger and thirst for righteousness, for they shall be filled"* (Matt. 5:6). You cannot hunger and thirst after righteousness if you have any leanings toward the worldly life. The righteousness of God is a perfect development in your life of inward heart sanctification, where no defilement can enter, and the pure in heart always see God (v. 8). It is a deep death, and it is a great life. God makes it a holy sacrifice, and He accepts it as an offering. Then, when we have perfectly considered the whole thing, we come to the conclusion that it was a reasonable thing to do.

A SENSIBLE CHOICE

Anything less than surrendering yourself completely to God is unreasonable because God has claimed us. In every way, we belong rightfully to Him. As you sit at the table where God in His great provision has amply supplied enough to satisfy your earthly needs, remember that a man is more capable of doing the mighty works of God and the will of God with a strong body than with a weak body. The strong body is never so richly in the presence of God as it is when it knows its weakness, for then there comes a real privilege. Strong bodies, strong minds, strong physiques, and strong muscles are wonderful, but they are no good until all is on the altar. Then God can flow through the body and give that person perfect life. He receives the resurrection life of the Spirit. Then his whole body is spiritual. It is severed from the natural, and he receives the fulfillment of the promise, *"Be strong in the Lord and in the power of His might"* (Eph. 6:10). The natural body is in perfect harmony with the Spirit to show forth the glory of God.

There is a Scripture that we seldom understand. This verse has taken me a long time to grasp: *"So then death is working in us, but life in you"* (2 Cor. 4:12). Only as death was manifested in the saints could life come to them. Death to us, life to you. That means absolutely nothing less than that everything you count on in life has to go, and as it goes, you are transformed. *"Death is working in us, but life in you."*

DYING TO LIVE

In the measure that you remain dead, you live forever: *"For the law of the Spirit of life in Christ Jesus has made* [you] *free from the law of sin and death"* (Rom. 8:2). You are *"transformed by the renewing of your mind."* The mind of Christ is in you, and your mind is subservient to the mind of Christ. Submissively, Jesus offered His mind, body, and will. Wonderful Jesus. He lived as no one else ever has or will. He is beautiful. I am devoted to Him. I love the Word of God because Christ is in every verse, illuminating every chapter. The Word is the breath of God, and it is life to you. It is eternal life. May God enable us always to breathe it in.

CHAPTER TWENTY-ONE

ABOVE ALL YOU CAN ASK OR THINK

*To Him who is able to do exceedingly abundantly above all that we
ask or think...be glory.*
—Ephesians 3:20–21

R ead Ephesians 3 carefully. This is a lovely chapter on
Paul's mission to the Gentiles whom God has grafted in.
Paul wrote that previously it had not been revealed *"that
the Gentiles should be fellow heirs, of the same body, and partakers
of* [God's] *promise in Christ"* (vv. 5–6). Paul had become a *"minister according to the gift of the grace of God given to* [him] *by the effective working of His power"* (v. 7). This power in Paul resulted in
a very effective work. Although he was *"less than the least of all the
saints"* (v. 8), he was given this grace of mystery and revelation. It
came forth as a living reality of a living substance dwelling in him:
*"to the intent that now the manifold wisdom of God might be made
known by the church to the principalities and powers in the heavenly places"* (v. 10).

WISDOM

When we are completely humbled before God in a place where
the Holy Spirit has full control, the wisdom of God is revealed to
us. There alone, the vision comes to all His saints. We are now in
the process of revelation. You must let the Holy Spirit perform His
perfect function. I give myself to the leading of the manifold wisdom of God, *"in whom we have boldness and access with confidence
through faith in Him"* (v. 12).

Boldness brings us into a place of access (Heb. 4:16), a place of confidence, laying hold, taking all off the table, and making it ours. In the human body, the Holy Spirit unfolds the mystery that we might know and have the revelation according to the will of God. The flesh is brought to a place of nonexistence, and the mighty power of God is shown to us. Paul responds by saying: *"I bow my knees to the Father"* (Eph. 3:14).

PRAYER

Jude speaks of praying in the Holy Spirit. There is no natural line of thought here, not one point in particular upon which the mind can rest, but what is predicted from the throne of glory. Then the tongue and all the divine attributes are displayed above all, exceedingly above all, so that the glory of God may be revealed in the face of Jesus. God cannot display the greater glory except through those coequal in the glory, *"for we are His workmanship, created in Christ Jesus for good works"* (Eph. 2:10). The Holy Spirit is the ideal and brings out the very essence of heaven through the human soul. We need the baptism of the Holy Spirit. Here we have the greatest liberty that can come to humanity; all the liberty of heaven is open to us. Praise the Father *"from whom the whole family in heaven and earth is named"* (Eph. 3:15).

I love the thought that the veil is so thin that the tie between the family of God in heaven and the family of God on earth is closer than ever. Christ is with them, and they are with us. What loftiness, reverence, and holiness! This wedlock and fellowship in the Spirit is a wonderful thing. It results in an infinite mind of fulfillment and glory. *"Are they not all ministering spirits?"* (Heb. 1:14). Who can help us more than those who have experienced the same trials as we? As the body is so fitly joined together by the effective working of His power, we are all one. Nothing separates us, but we look for the appearing of Jesus. He is there in glory, and they are with Him:

> *For the Lord Himself will descend from heaven with a shout, with the voice of an archangel, and with the trumpet of God. And the dead in Christ will rise first. Then we who are alive and remain shall be caught up together with them in the clouds to meet the Lord in the air. And thus we shall always be with the Lord.* (1 Thess. 4:16–17)

We can pray only as the Holy Spirit gives us the ability to express our thoughts. The Holy Spirit gives the highest principles through this prayer that the purposes of salvation are a continuous working and an increasing power all the time. The day that is coming will declare all things. We will be strengthened by the Spirit according to the riches of His glory.

GLORY

What is glory? All glory that ever comes is from Him. You have glory in the measure that you have the Son of glory in you. If you are filled with Jesus, you are filled with glory. When we have *"the spirit of wisdom and revelation in the knowledge of Him"* (Eph. 1:17), there is nothing to hinder the Holy Spirit from having control of our whole beings.

"That Christ may dwell in your hearts through faith" (Eph. 3:17). Faith is the production of all things. The Holy Spirit indwells and enlarges until the whole body is filled with Christ, and we are coming there in a very remarkable way. Did the Holy Spirit ever utter a prayer that no power could answer? In John 17:21, Jesus says: *"That they all may be one, as You, Father, are in Me, and I in You; that they also may be one in Us."* What works in us through being one with Him, through *"being rooted and grounded"* (Eph. 3:17)? Perfect love, which has justice wrapped up in it. The day is coming when the saints will say "Amen" to the judgments of God. Justice will do it. All the wood, hay, and stubble must be destroyed (1 Cor. 3:12), and we must be *"rooted and grounded"* in the Word.

I am a production of what God is forming, and I can arrest the gates of hell and laugh in the face of calamity and say, *"All things work together for good to those who love God"* (Rom. 8:28). *"Rooted and grounded in love"* (Eph. 3:17). Someone may leave me, but if I am grounded, it is for my good, and nothing can be against me but myself. We live for the glory of God. It is the Lord that establishes, strengthens, and upholds the weak, enabling them to withstand difficulties and to triumph in the day of battle. God is with you *"to do exceedingly abundantly above all that* [you] *ask or think."*

FAITH

Are we children of circumstances or children of faith? In our humanity, we may be troubled by the blowing of the wind. As it

131

blows, it whispers fearfulness; but if you are *"rooted and grounded,"* you can stand the tests, and it is only then that you *"may be able to comprehend...what is the width and length and depth and height; to know the love of Christ which passes knowledge"* (Eph. 3:18–19). It is an addition sum to meet every missionary's needs, to display God's power, enlarging what needs to be quickened.

What does Paul mean by the width of Christ's love? It is recognizing that God is sufficient in every circumstance. The length of His love indicates that God is in everything. God is in the depths and the heights! God is always lifting you, and the truth in that verse is enough for anyone in any circumstance to triumph. He *"is able to do exceedingly abundantly above all that we can ask or think,"* not according to the mind of Paul, but *"according to the power that works in us"* (v. 20). Simplicity of heart can broaden one's perspective, but this fullness is an ideal power of God in the human soul, enlarging every part. God is there instead of you to make you full, and you are full as your faith reaches out to be filled with all the fullness of God.

The power of the Lord was present to heal. His fullness of power flowed out of the disciples to others. In Acts 1, we see the power of God revealed as Jesus was lifted up to where He was before—into the presence of God. Jesus Christ showed the power of God in human flesh. The fullness of the Godhead was bodily manifested in Jesus (Col. 2:9). John says that *"in Him was life, and the life was the light of men"* (John 1:4). His substance revealed the fullness of God. How can it be fulfilled in me, you ask? The Scripture provides the answer: He is *"able to do exceedingly abundantly above all that we can ask or think."* It is filled there in the glory. But it's a tremendous thing. God will have to do something. Beloved, it is not according to your mind at all but according to the mind of God, according to the revelation of the Spirit. *"Above all that we can ask or think."* The blood has been poured out.

THE HOLY SPIRIT HAS BEEN GIVEN TO US

Truly, we are not worthy, but He is worthy. He will do more than we can even ask. How can it be possible? God puts it in your heart. He can do it. We hear much about rates of interest, but if you will faithfully follow God, He will add, enlarge, and lift you all the time, adding compound interest. Five percent? No! A thousand percent, a million percent! If you are willing, if holiness is the purpose of your heart, it will be done, for God is in His place. Will you be in the plan *"according to the power that works in* [you]*"* (Eph. 3:20)? Whatever you are at any time, it will be by His effective power, lifting, controlling, and carrying you in constant rest and peace; it is *"according to the power that works in* [you]*."* Let all the people say: *"To Him be glory in the church by Christ Jesus to all generations, forever and ever. Amen"* (v. 21).

CHAPTER TWENTY-TWO

THIS GRACE

When we are filled with the joy of the Lord, there comes forth a glad "Praise the Lord!" David experienced that joy and proclaimed: *"Let everything that has breath praise the LORD"* (Ps. 150:6). It is a tragedy if there is not a divine spring within you bubbling forth with praise. God wants you to be so filled with the Spirit that your whole life is a praise. How my soul longs for you to catch fire.

Four symbols divinely ascertained or revealed by the Lord are fire, love, zeal, and faith. Fire burns intensely, making us full of activity for God. Love, where there is nothing but pure, undefiled willingness or yieldedness, knows no sacrifice. Zeal acts in full obedience to the will of God, empowered with His mighty strength until we press beyond measure into that which pleases God. Faith laughs at impossibilities and cries, "It will be done." May God make these things immediately real before our eyes and give us these emblematic displays of inward flame.

THE NATURE OF CHRIST

The following message from Romans 5 will teach us deeper insights about God. We have been talking about receiving the life of Christ and the nature of the Son of God. We have been seeing that God's nature can be conveyed to us by the Word, and His Spirit can fill our hearts. The Word is made life as the Spirit pours it into the body. Then the body is quickened by the same nature of Jesus, with the same power over all weaknesses. In other words, an incorruptible force presses through human nature, changing it to resurrection life, eternal life, which is quickened by the Spirit and changed from one state of grace to another.

These days, many people are receiving a clear knowledge of an inward working of the power of the Spirit. It not only revives their mortal bodies but also transforms the natural body into an incorruptible power, getting the body ready for the Rapture. The divine teaching of the Lord has revealed to us the transformation that takes place in the inward life. His new nature is in the old nature, His resurrection power enlivens our lifelessness, and His divinity is seen in our humanity. Believers possess the nature of the living Christ, and with it, power over death. Do not be afraid to claim it. Claim power over sin and disease. The Christlike spirit is forming, quickening, and renewing the natural life.

The former law was of the natural man. The new law of the life of the Spirit is the manifestation of the new creation, which is *"Christ in* [us], *the hope of glory"* (Col. 1:27). Glory is a manifestation of a divine nature in the human body.

THE BLESSINGS OF GRACE AND PEACE

Now I want to go on from that, reading from Romans: *"Therefore, having been justified by faith, we have peace with God through our Lord Jesus Christ"* (5:1). You are justified. You are being made at peace. And remember, the peace of God is different from any other peace. It *"surpasses all understanding"* (Phil. 4:7); it helps you keep your composure. You are not shaken by earthly things. It is a deep peace, created by the knowledge of a living faith, which is the living principle of the foundation of all truth. Christ is in us, the hope and the evidence of the glory (Col. 1:27).

See how rich you are in Christ: *"Through whom also we have access by faith into this grace in which we stand, and rejoice in hope of the glory of God"* (Rom. 5:2). This is perhaps the greatest of all thoughts we have reached. Faith has access through Jesus Christ into all the fullness of God. First, it was by grace that you were *"saved through faith"* (Eph. 2:8), but now another grace, a grace of access, is ours. It is a grace that will bring us into a deeper knowledge of God.

Peter calls it a *"precious faith"* (2 Pet. 1:1). It has passed through Abraham, Jesus, the Father, and the Holy Spirit. We have access, we have a right into, we have an open door to all that the Father has, all that Jesus has, and all that the Holy Spirit has. Nothing can keep us out of it. Jesus Christ is the *"Alpha and the Omega, the Beginning and the End"* (Rev. 1:8). Through Him, we may know grace, favor, and mercy, which will lift us and take us through into grace and peace: *"Grace and peace be multiplied to you in the knowledge of God and of Jesus our Lord"* (2 Pet. 1:2). Do you want grace and peace to be multiplied? You have it if you dare to believe. We have access to it; we have a right to it. The promise of the Scripture is for us:

> *As His divine power has given to us all things that pertain to life and godliness, through the knowledge of Him who called us by glory and virtue, by which have been given to us exceedingly great and precious promises, that through these you may be partakers of the divine nature.* (vv. 3–4)

We have access. We have the right to the promises and the right to all the inheritance of which He has made us heirs.

It is true that He came to us in grace. He met us in need and transformed us by His power. It is right to say that now we have within us an inheritance that is incorruptible and undefiled. It is filled with glory and virtue. We have a right to say we have the same nature as the Lord Jesus Christ.

Do we have the same nature of His flesh? Yes and no. It is true He was made in the likeness of our sinful flesh and condemned sin in the flesh (Rom. 8:3), but Christ also had a higher, spiritual order, a divine nature, a nature of love and faith.

The nature of faith is a divine nature, which was the same nature as He was spiritually. He has committed His faith to us. Human weaknesses can spoil the effectiveness of faith. Victories become uncertain, prayers lose the anointing, and the power to take hold is hindered. But God comes to us, breathes new life into us, and shows us *"we have access by faith into this grace in which we stand"* (Rom. 5:2). Now we may have a nature that has *"no variation or shadow of turning"* (James 1:17), but *"bears all things, believes all things, hopes all things, endures all things"* (1 Cor. 13:7).

INTERPRETATION OF A MESSAGE IN TONGUES:

It is the law of the life of the Spirit of Christ, which is the hope, which is the glory in the hope, which is the revelation in the glory of the hope, which is filled with opening of keen perception of things above where Christ is sitting at the right hand of God, and we see jointly the Father and the Son; and so filled with purity of unmixed reality, faith rises, changes its order, lays hold and believes, dethrones, and stands fast to see the kingdom of God manifested.

A LIVING FAITH

How can we describe this faith? It is genuine and pure. It never wavers. It is confident and sensitive to the breath of God. This faith, which is the very nature of the Son of God, comes from the Author of faith. It is holy in action, dares to believe, rests assured, and sees the mighty power of God evidenced in its workings. It is a living faith that allows us to claim all that He has for us. Faith sees *"the crooked places...made straight"* (Isa. 40:4). It sees *"the lame...leap like a deer"* (Isa. 35:6). It is not surprised when *"the blind see"* (Matt. 11:5). God has finished creation; it is forever completed by the perfect work of our Lord. We are *"complete in Him, who is the head of all principality and power"* (Col. 2:10). We are His righteousness and created for His purpose.

Romans 7 is one of those marvelous, masterpiece chapters. All of God's Word is encouraging. You can feel yourself lifted. Gravity is the only thing that causes you to remain. The Spirit lifts, the Word of incarnation moves, the life divine operates, the Spirit renews. You are being changed, made right, and made ready. Regeneration is one of the greatest words in the Scriptures. The Word of God is regenerating. Whatever you were this morning, you are never to be as you were again. Nothing will move you as much as knowing what you were so that you may become what you were not. Believe it. God's plan, purpose, and revelation is for us so that we may *"rejoice in that day and leap for joy!"* (Luke 6:23).

INTERPRETATION OF A MESSAGE IN TONGUES:
The Lord's life is moving; the Lord's life is flowing. Put your spirit into the joy of the breath, and let yourself rest on the bosom of His love, to be transformed by all the Spirit life from above.

THE HOPE OF GLORY

We *"rejoice in hope of the glory of God"* (Rom. 5:2). In this study, we are laying the foundation to examine the hope of the glory of all saints. The hope of glory is that you must know where you are going. The great, mighty masterpiece of all is the great plan of the Rapture. It is the hope of glory, life divine, the peace of God, and the enrichment of the soul. It is *"poured out in our hearts by the Holy Spirit"* (v. 5).

The Holy Spirit is the manifestation of God's Son. The Holy Spirit always reveals Him to us as divine. He is so uniquely divine that He has the power to overcome. His power is pure. His power must not cease to develop. The Holy Spirit is there to create development and to help us progress in our faith as the Lord would have us to.

We are saved by His life. Now that we have received salvation, He wants to open our eyes to understand what Christ really did for us. *"In due time"* (v. 6), when there was no other to save us, when there was no hope, when the law had failed, Christ took our place, delivered us from all the powers of human weaknesses and failure, and so came to us in our sins. He reached out to us in love *"while we were still sinners"* (v. 8). At just the right moment, He died for us and delivered us from the power of the Devil, delivered us from death, delivered us from sin, delivered us from the grave, and gave us a hope of immortality through His life. We are saved by His life.

Jesus is eternal. He has the power to impart eternal gifts. He is here now; He has delivered us from the curse of the law and set us free. Who loves the Gospel as much as those who have been saved? What is the Gospel? It is *"the power of God to salvation"* (Rom. 1:16). It has the power to bring immortality and life. Through His life in us, we are delivered from all things and are being prepared for the glorious hope of the coming of the Lord. That hope causes us to sing:

> Christ arose, a victor over death's domain.
> He arose, forever with His saints to reign;
> He arose! He arose!
> Hallelujah, Christ arose!

AT ONE WITH GOD

What was it that arose? Christ's life. How did He rise? Out of death, over death victorious. Are we not *"united together in the likeness of His death"* (Rom. 6:5)? Then the only thing that can happen is that we will be seated with Him. The past is under the blood; the whole thing is finished. We also have reason to be happy because *"we have now received the reconciliation"* (Rom. 5:11). He

138

has absolutely taken every trace of human deformity, depravity, lack of comprehension, and inactivity of faith. He has nailed them to the cross. You died with Him on the cross, and, if you will only believe you are dead with Him, you are dead indeed to sin and alive to righteousness.

The atonement, this wonderful regenerative power of God, makes us complete in His oneness. No shadow of human weakness remains. If I dare believe, I am so in alignment with God's Son that He makes me perfect. I am at one with Him. We can be without sin, without blemish, without failure, perfectly at one with Him.

Do you dare to believe it? It may not be easy for you, but I want to make it easy. In the Scriptures, we read that *"faith is the substance of things hoped for, the evidence of things not seen"* (Heb. 11:1). In every way that the Word of God speaks to you, faith lends its help. Faith stirs you. Faith says to you, "If you believe, you will receive. If you dare to believe, oneness, purity, power, and eternal fact are working through you." In Christ, we have oneness. We are perfectly covered, hidden, and lost in God's Son. He has made us whole through His blood. The Scripture tells us how it happens:

> *Therefore, just as through one man sin entered the world, and death through sin, and thus death spread to all men, because all sinned; (for until the law sin was in the world, but sin is not imputed when there is no law. Nevertheless death reigned from Adam to Moses, even over those who had not sinned according to the likeness of the transgression of Adam, who is a type of Him who was to come. But the free gift is not like the offense. For if by the one man's offense many died, much more the grace of God and the gift by the grace of the one Man, Jesus Christ, abounded to many.* (Rom. 5:12–15)

ABUNDANT BLESSINGS

Through one man's disobedience, through one man's sin, death came and reigned. Then Another came. Adam was the first man; Christ, the second. One was earthly; the other, heavenly. As sin and death reigned by one, so now the New Man, the Christ-man, will make us awake to righteousness, peace, and abounding in God. Just as death had its power through a man, life has to have its power and victory. Through the God-man, we come into a new divine order.

"I cannot understand this truth, Wigglesworth." No, brother, you never will. It is a thousand times bigger than your mind. But Christ's mind replanted in your natural order will give you a vision so that you may see what you cannot understand. What you will never understand, God thoroughly understands. He blesses you abundantly.

You know how sin was abounding, how we were held, how we were defeated, how we groaned and travailed. Has sin abounded? Now grace, now life, now the ministry abounds to us.

Friends, take a leap that you may never know what defeat is any more. This is a real divine healing chapter; this is a real ascension chapter; this is a powerful resurrection chapter. It looses you from your limitations. It moves you from your former place into a place of coveted grace. It takes your weaknesses and sins and abounds to you with atonement. It reveals to you all that Adam ever had that bound you and all that Christ ever had or will have that abounds toward you to liberate you from all that is human and bring you into all that is divine. This is the glorious liberty of the Gospel of Christ:

And the gift is not like that which came through the one who sinned. For the judgment which came from one offense resulted in condemnation, but the free gift which came from many offenses resulted in justification.
(Rom. 5:16)

We have been condemned and lost. How human nature destroys! We all know sin had its reign, but there is justification. God works in the lower order with His mighty higher order. He touches human weaknesses with His touch of infinite, glorious resurrection power. He transforms you:

For if by the one man's offense death reigned through the one, much more those who receive abundance of grace and of the gift of righteousness will reign in life through the One, Jesus Christ. (v. 17)

How rich we are. The death life has been replaced. Now there is a righteous life. You were in death and it was the death life, but now you have received the righteous life. How much have you acquired of it? Have you received an *"abundance of grace"* (v. 17)?

Your grace has run out years ago. My grace has been depleted years ago, but I realized by the revelation of the Spirit that His grace should take the place of my grace. His power should cover me where I cannot cover myself. He stands beside me when I am sure to go down. Where sin abounded, grace abounded, and His love abounded. He stretched out His hand in mercy; He never failed. He was there every time when I was sure to go down. Grace abounded. Oh, the mercy, the boundless mercy of the love of God to us!

I hope you are getting it, thriving in it, and triumphing in it. I hope you are coming to the place to see that you are a victor in it. God must give you these divine attributes of the Spirit so that you may come into like-mindedness with Him in this wonderful provision.

THE GIFT OF RIGHTEOUSNESS

Many people fail to access the divine personality of God's gift because of their fears. They know that they are imperfect. The Devil sets a tremendous trap trying to catch poor people who have made a little slip or just said the wrong thing. There has been nothing special, but the Devil tries to make it like a mountain when it is nothing more than a molehill. I like the thought that God's Son is so gracious toward us.

Beloved, where you fail in your righteousness, Jesus Christ has a gift of righteousness that replaces your righteousness. He takes away your *"filthy rags"* (Isa. 64:6) and clothes you with a new garment. He has the power to *"tame the tongue"* (James 3:8) and remove your evil thoughts. God wants to replace your righteousness with His righteousness. It is the righteousness of the Son of God. It has no corruption in it; it has no judgment in it. It is full of mercy and entreaty. It is the righteousness of the law of God's Spirit. Do you dare to accept it?

GOD IS NEAR

Being saved is a reality. There is a great deal of truth about having the peace of God. There is a great deal of knowledge in knowing that you are free, and there is a wonderful manifestation of power to keep you free. But I find Satan dethrones some of the loveliest people because he catches them at a time when they are unaware. I find these poor souls constantly being deceived by the power of Satan.

Hear this word: when Satan is the nearest, God is nearer with an abundant measure of His grace. When you feel almost defeated, He has a banner waving over you to cover you. He covers you with His grace; He covers you with His righteousness. It is the very nature of the Son of God.

It is impossible to remain in the natural body when you experience the life of God. When you are intoxicated with the Spirit, the Spirit life flows through the avenues of your mind and the keen perception of the heart with deep pulsations. You are filled with the passion of the grace of God until you are illuminated by the power of the new wine, the wine of the kingdom. This is rapture. No natural body will be able to stand this process. It will have to leave the body, but the body will be a preserver to it until the sons of God are marvelously manifested. Sonship is a position of rightful heirship. Sons have a right to the first claiming of the will.

I would like you to realize that redemption is so perfect that it causes you to stop judging yourself. You believe that God has a righteous judgment for you. Escape from the powers of the Devil. You can have an abundance of grace, righteousness, liberty for the soul, and transformation of the mind. You can be lifted out of your earthly place into God's power and authority.

POWER TO REIGN

This holy new life, this ability to know the Son of God in your human body, is so Christlike that you come into a deep relationship with the Father, Son, and Holy Spirit. God has been showing me that Jesus meant us when He said, *"If you forgive the sins of any, they are forgiven them; if you retain the sins of any, they are retained"* (John 20:23).

This power was evidenced in the days of the first apostles. When Elymas, the sorcerer, stood in the way of the power of the Holy Spirit, Paul said to him: *"You shall be blind, not seeing the sun for a time"* (Acts 13:11). Likewise, Peter condemned Simon, who wanted to buy the power that came when the disciples laid hands on someone. Peter said to Simon: *"I see that you are poisoned by bitterness and bound by iniquity"* (Acts 8:23).

So we have to see that God through the Holy Spirit is bringing us into like-mindedness of faith. I speak this to you because I know what the Holy Spirit is bringing this church through. She has passed through many dark days of misunderstanding, but God is showing us that we have His power to defeat the powers of the Enemy. We have power to reign in this life. God has mightily justified us with abundant grace, filled us with the Holy Spirit, and given us the hope of glory. When we were helpless, Jesus Christ came and took our place. Through Adam, we all received the carnal nature, but Jesus gives a new nature. Through His work within us, grace replaces sin, righteousness replaces unrighteousness, and we move from grace to grace, toiling in the Spirit until the whole man longs for redemption.

Bless God! It is not far off; it is very near. It will not be long before there will be a shout some day. He will be here:

> *Therefore, as through one man's offense judgment came to all men, resulting in condemnation, even so through one Man's righteous act the free gift came to all men, resulting in justification of life. For as by one man's disobedience many were made sinners, so also by one Man's obedience many will be made righteous. Moreover the law entered that the offense might abound. But where sin abounded, grace abounded much more, so that as sin reigned in death, even so grace might reign through righteousness to eternal life through Jesus Christ our Lord.* (Rom. 5:18–21)

Eternal life is resurrection. Eternal life has come into us, and as the Father is, so are we; as the Son is, so are we. This life eternal is manifested in mortal bodies so that the life of Christ will be so manifested in our mortal bodies that everything will *"be dead indeed to sin, but alive to God in Christ Jesus our Lord"* (Rom. 6:11).

We are gloriously ready. Hallelujah! Do you have eternal life, the redemption, the glorious life in the Spirit? Have you entered into it? Is it reality to you?

One day, I saw a huge magnet lowered among pieces of iron; it picked up loads of iron and carried them away. That is an earthly occurrence, but our experience is with a holy Magnet. What is in you is holy; what is in you is pure. When the Lord of righteousness will appear, who is our Life, then what is holy, what is His nature, what is His life, will go, and we will be forever with the Lord.

You have not gone yet, but you are sure to go. While we are here, comfort one another with these words: "Lord, may we please you. Father, let us become more holy; let us be more pure. Let the life of Your Son consume all mortality until there is nothing left but what is to be changed, *'in a moment, in the twinkling of an eye'* (1 Cor. 15:52)."

Do not let one thought, one action, one thing in any way interfere with the Rapture. Ask God that every moment will be a moment of purifying. Let God take you into the fullness of redemption in a wonderful way. Strive to be more holy, more separate. Desire God, the gifts of the Holy Spirit, and the graces. Earnestly follow the Beatitudes.

May God show us that divine order that will change our natures, enabling us to love as He loves, until the whole church is love. *"A new commandment I give to you, that you love one another"* (John 13:34). Breathe this holy, intense love into our hearts. Let it please You, Lord, that this bond of unity, this holy covenant with You, will be so strong that no man *"shall be able to separate us from the love of God which is in Christ Jesus our Lord"* (Rom. 8:39). May we love as God loves, and may His love take us to the peak of perfection.

Smith Wigglesworth on
POWER TO
SERVE

Contents

CHAPTER ONE

THE DISPENSATION
OF THE HOLY SPIRIT

These are the days of the dispensation of the Holy Spirit. I find in the book of Galatians that there is a very blessed way to receive the Holy Spirit:

That the blessing of Abraham might come upon the Gentiles in Christ Jesus, that we might receive the promise of the Spirit through faith. (Gal. 3:14)

When we have the right attitude, faith becomes remarkably active. But it can never be remarkably active in a dead life. When sin is out, when the body is clean, and when the life is made right, then the Holy Spirit comes, and faith brings the evidence.

Why should we tarry, or wait, for the Holy Spirit? Why should we wrestle and pray with a living faith to be made ready? In the book of John, we find the reason:

Nevertheless I tell you the truth. It is to your advantage that I go away; for if I do not go away, the Helper will not come to you; but if I depart, I will send Him to you. And when He has come, He will convict the world of sin, and of righteousness, and of judgment. (John 16:7–8)

To convict the world of sin, righteousness, and judgment—that is why the Holy Spirit is to come into your body. First of all, your sin is gone, and you can see clearly to speak to others. But Jesus does not want you to point out the speck in somebody else's eye while the plank is in your own. (See Matthew 7:3–5.) When your own sins are gone, then the Holy Spirit is to convince the world of sin, of righteousness, and of judgment.

The place of being filled with the Holy Spirit is the only place of operation where the believer binds the power of Satan. Satan thinks that he has a right, and he will have a short time to exhibit that right as the Prince of the World; but he can't be Prince as long as there is one person filled with the Holy Spirit. That is the reason that the church will go before the Tribulation.

Now, how dare you resist coming into the place of being filled with the life and power of the Holy Spirit? I call you to halt, and then to march.

Halt! Think! What is the attitude of your life? Are you thirsty? Are you longing? Are you willing to pay the price? Are you willing to forfeit in order to have? Are you willing to allow yourself to die so that He may live? Are you willing for Him to have the right-of-way in your heart, your conscience, and all you are? Are you ready to have God's deluge of blessing upon your soul?

Are you ready? "What for?" you ask. To be changed forever, to receive the Holy Spirit, to be filled with divine power forever.

RECEIVING THE HOLY SPIRIT

If you would believe half as much as you ask, you would receive. Many people do not receive the Holy Spirit because they are continually asking and never believing.

Ask, and it will be given to you; seek, and you will find; knock, and it will be opened to you. For everyone who asks receives, and he who seeks finds, and to him who knocks it will be opened. (Matt. 7:7–8)

"Everyone who asks receives." He who is asking is receiving; he who is seeking is finding. The door is being opened right now; that is God's present Word. The Bible does not say, "Ask and you will not receive." Believe that asking is receiving, seeking is finding, and to him who is knocking, the door is being opened.

Faith has its request. Faith claims it because it has it. *"Faith is the substance of things hoped for"* (Heb. 11:1). As sure as you have faith, God will give you the overflowing, and when He comes in, you will speak as the Spirit gives utterance (Acts 2:4).

CHAPTER TWO

FULL OF THE HOLY SPIRIT

J esus says, *"Do not be afraid; only believe"* (Mark 5:36). The people in whom God delights are the ones who rest upon His Word without wavering. God has nothing for the man who doubts, for *"let not that man suppose that he will receive anything from the Lord"* (James 1:7). Therefore, I would like us to get this verse deep down into our hearts, until it penetrates every fiber of our being: *"Only believe!"* We know that *"all things are possible"* (Matt. 19:26). *"Only believe."*

God has a plan for this meeting, beyond anything that we have ever known before. He has a plan for every individual life, and if we have any other plan in view, we miss the grandest plan of all! Nothing in the past is equal to the present, and nothing in the present can equal the things of tomorrow, for tomorrow should be so filled with holy expectations that we will be living flames for God. God never intended His people to be ordinary or commonplace. His intentions were that they should be on fire for Him, conscious of His divine power, realizing the glory of the Cross that foreshadows the crown.

THE STORY OF STEPHEN

God has given me a very special Scripture to share:

Now in those days, when the number of the disciples was multiplying, there arose a complaint against the Hebrews by the Hellenists, because their widows were neglected in the daily distribution. Then the twelve summoned the multitude of the disciples and said, "It is not desirable that we should leave the word of God and serve tables. Therefore,

brethren, seek out from among you seven men of good repu-
tation, full of the Holy Spirit and wisdom, whom we may
appoint over this business...." And the saying pleased the
whole multitude. And they chose Stephen, a man full of
faith and the Holy Spirit, and Philip, Prochorus, Nicanor,
Timon, Parmenas, and Nicolas, a proselyte from Antioch.

(Acts 6:1–3, 5)

During the time of the early church, the disciples were hard-pressed in all areas. The things of the natural life could not be attended to, and many were complaining about the neglect of their widows. The disciples therefore decided on a plan, which was to choose seven men to do the work—men who were *"full of the Holy Spirit."* What a divine thought! No matter what kind of work was to be done, however menial it may have been, the person chosen had to be filled with the Holy Spirit. The plan of the church was that everything, even the things of the natural life, had to be sanctified unto God, for the church had to be a Holy Spirit church.

Beloved, God has never ordained anything less! There is one thing that I want to stress in these meetings; that is, no matter what else may happen, first and foremost, I want to emphasize these questions: "Have you received the Holy Spirit since you believed?" (Acts 19:2 KJV). "Are you filled with divine power?" This is the heritage of the church, to be so clothed with power that God can lay His hand on any member at any time to do His perfect will.

There is no stopping in the Spirit-filled life. We begin at the Cross, the place of ignominy, shame, and death, and that very death brings the power of resurrection life. And, being filled with the Holy Spirit, we go on *"from glory to glory"* (2 Cor. 3:18). Let us not forget that possessing the baptism in the Holy Spirit means that there must be an ever increasing holiness in us. How the church needs divine anointing—God's presence and power so manifested that the world will know it! People know when the tide is flowing; they also know when it is ebbing.

The necessity that seven men be chosen for the position of serving tables was very evident. The disciples knew that these seven men were men ready for active service, and so they chose them. In Acts 6:5, we read, *"And the saying pleased the whole multitude. And they chose Stephen, a man full of faith and the Holy Spirit, and Philip."* There were five others listed, of course, but Stephen and Philip stand out most prominently in the Scriptures.

Philip was a man so filled with the Holy Spirit that a revival always followed wherever he went. Stephen was a man so filled with divine power that, although serving tables might have been all right in the minds of the other disciples, God had a greater vision for him— a baptism of fire, of power and divine anointing, that took him on and on to the climax of his life, until he saw right into the open heavens.

Had we been there with the disciples at that time, I believe we would have heard them saying to each other, "Look here! Neither Stephen nor Philip are doing the work we called them to. If they do not attend to business, we will have to get someone else!" That was the natural way of thinking, but divine order is far above our finite planning. When we please God in our daily activities, we will always find in operation the fact that *he who is faithful in what is least* [God will make] *faithful also in much"* (Luke 16:10). We have such an example right here—a man chosen to serve tables who had such a revelation of the mind of Christ and of the depth and height of God that there was no pause in his experience, but a going forward with leaps and bounds. Beloved, there is a race to be run; there is a crown to be won; we cannot stand still! I say unto you, *"Be vigilant"* (1 Pet. 5:8). Be vigilant! Let no one take your crown (Rev. 3:11)!

God has privileged us in Christ Jesus to live above the ordinary human plane of life. Those who want to be ordinary and live on a lower plane can do so, but as for me, I will not! For the same anointing, the same zeal, the same Holy Spirit power that was at the command of Stephen and the apostles is at our command. We have the same God that Abraham had, that Elijah had, and we do not need to come short in any gift or grace (1 Cor. 1:7). We may not possess the gifts as abiding gifts, but as we are full of the Holy Spirit and divine anointing, it is possible, when there is need, for God to manifest every gift of the Spirit through us. As I have already said, I do not mean by this that we should necessarily possess the gifts permanently, but there should be a manifestation of the gifts as God may choose to use us.

This ordinary man Stephen became mighty under the Holy Spirit's anointing, and now he stands supreme, in many ways, among the apostles. *"And Stephen, full of faith and power, did great wonders and signs among the people"* (Acts 6:8). As we go deeper in God, He enlarges our understanding and places before us a wide-open door, and I am not surprised that this man chosen to serve tables was afterward called to a higher plane. "What do you mean?" you may ask. "Did he quit this service?" No! But he was lost in the power of God. He lost sight of everything in the natural and steadfastly fixed his gaze upon Jesus, *"the author and finisher of our faith"* (Heb. 12:2), until he was transformed into a shining light in the kingdom of God.

Oh, that we might be awakened to believe His Word, to understand the mind of the Spirit, for there is an inner place of whiteness and purity where we can see God. Stephen was just as ordinary a person as you and I, but he was in the place where God could so move upon him that he, in turn, could move everything before him. He began in a most humble place and ended in a blaze of glory. Beloved, dare to believe Christ!

RESISTANCE TO THE HOLY SPIRIT

As you go on in this life of the Spirit, you will find that the Devil will begin to get restless and there will be a "stir in the synagogue," so to speak. It was so with Stephen. Any number of people may be found in the church who are very proper in a worldly sense—always properly dressed, the elite of the land, welcoming into the church everything but the power of God. Let us read what God says about them:

> *Then there arose some from what is called the Synagogue of the Freedmen (Cyrenians, Alexandrians, and those from Cilicia and Asia), disputing with Stephen. And they were not able to resist the wisdom and the Spirit by which he spoke.* (Acts 6:9–10)

The Freedmen could not stand the truth of God. With these opponents, Stephen found himself in the same predicament as the blind man whom Jesus had healed. (See John 9:1–34.) As soon as the blind man's eyes were opened, the religious leaders shut him out of the synagogue. They would not have anybody in the synagogue with his eyes open. It is the same today; as soon as you receive spiritual eyesight, out you go!

These Freedmen, Cyrenians, and Alexandrians rose up full of wrath in the very place where they should have been full of the power of God, full of divine love, and full of reverence for the Holy

Spirit. They rose up against Stephen, this man who was *"full of the Holy Spirit"* (Acts 6:3).

Beloved, if there is anything in your life that in any way resists the power of the Holy Spirit and the entrance of His Word into your heart and life, drop on your knees and cry out loud for mercy! When the Spirit of God is brooding over your heart's door, do not resist Him. Open your heart to the touch of God. There is a resisting of and a *"striving against sin"* that leads even *"to bloodshed"* (Heb. 12:4), and there is also a resisting of the Holy Spirit that will drive you into sin.

Stephen spoke with remarkable wisdom. Where he was, things began to move. You will find that there is always a moving when the Holy Spirit has control. These people were brought under conviction by the message of Stephen, but they resisted; they did anything and everything to stifle that conviction. Not only did they lie, but they got others to lie against this man, who would have laid down his life for any one of them. Stephen had been used by God to heal the sick and to perform miracles, yet they brought false accusations against him. What effect did their accusations have on Stephen? *"And all who sat in the council, looking steadfastly at him, saw his face as the face of an angel"* (Acts 6:15).

Something had happened in the life of this man chosen for menial service, and he had become mighty for God. How was it accomplished in him? It was because his aim was high. Faithful in little, Stephen was brought by God to full fruition. Under the inspiration of divine power, by which he spoke, his opponents could not help but listen. Even the angels listened, for he spoke with holy, prophetic utterance before that council. Beginning with Abraham and Moses, he continued unfolding the truth. What a marvelous exhortation! Take your Bibles and read the seventh chapter of Acts; "listen in" as the angels listened in. As light upon light, truth upon truth, revelation upon revelation found its way into his opponents' calloused hearts, they gazed at Stephen in astonishment. Perhaps their hearts became warm at times, and they may have said, "Truly, this man is sent by God." But then he hurled at them the truth:

> *You stiffnecked and uncircumcised in heart and ears! You always resist the Holy Spirit; as your fathers did, so do you. Which of the prophets did your fathers not persecute? And they killed those who foretold the coming of the Just*

One, of whom you now have become the betrayers and murderers, who have received the law by the direction of angels and have not kept it. (Acts 7:51–53)

Then what happened? These men were moved; they were *"cut to the heart, and they gnashed at him with their teeth"* (v. 54).

There are two marvelous occasions in the Scriptures where the people were *"cut to the heart."* In the second chapter of the Acts of the Apostles, in the thirty-seventh verse, after Peter had delivered that inspired sermon on the Day of Pentecost, the people were *"cut to the heart"* with conviction, and three thousand souls were added to the church.

Then, here is Stephen, speaking under the inspiration of the Holy Spirit, and the men of this council, being *"cut to the heart,"* rose up as one man to slay him. As you go down through this seventh chapter of Acts, starting with the fifty-fifth verse, what a picture you have before you! As I close my eyes, I can get a vision of this scene in every detail—the howling mob with their revengeful, murderous spirit, ready to devour this holy man, and he, *"being full of the Holy Spirit"* (v. 55), gazing steadfastly into heaven. What did he see there? From his place of helplessness, he looked up and said, *"Look! I see the heavens opened and the Son of Man **standing** at the right hand of God!"* (v. 56, emphasis added).

Is that the position that Jesus went to heaven to take? No! He went to *sit* at the right hand of the Father. But on behalf of the first martyr, on behalf of the man with that burning flame of Holy Spirit power, God's Son stood up in honorary testimony of him who was first called to serve tables and was faithful unto death.

But is that all? No! I am so glad that that is not all. As the stones came flying at Stephen, pounding his body, crashing into his bones, striking his head, mangling his beautiful face, what happened? How did this scene end? With a sublime, upward look, this man, chosen for an ordinary task but filled with the Holy Spirit, was so moved upon by God that he finished his earthly work in a blaze of glory, magnifying God with his last breath. Looking up into the face of the Master, he said, *"Lord, do not charge them with this sin"* (Acts 7:60). *"And when he had said this, he fell asleep"* (v. 60).

Friends, it is worth dying a thousand deaths to gain that spirit. What a divine ending to the life and testimony of a man who had been chosen to serve tables.

CHAPTER THREE

THE CLOTHING OF THE SPIRIT

Only believe! Only believe! God will not fail you, beloved. It is impossible for God to fail. Believe God; rest in Him. God's rest is an undisturbed place where heaven bends to meet you. The Bible is the most important book in the world. But some people have to be pressed in before they can be pressed on. Oh, this glorious inheritance of holy joy and faith, this glorious baptism in the Holy Spirit—it is a perfected place. *"All things have become new"* (2 Cor. 5:17), because *"you are Christ's, and Christ is God's"* (1 Cor. 3:23).

> *But you shall receive power when the Holy Spirit has come upon you; and you shall be witnesses to Me in Jerusalem, and in all Judea and Samaria, and to the end of the earth.*
> (Acts 1:8)

God means for us to walk in this royal way. When God opens a door, no man can shut it (Rev. 3:8). John made a royal way, and Jesus walked in it. Jesus left us the responsibility of allowing Him to bring forth through us the greater works (John 14:12). Jesus left His disciples with much and with much more to be added until God receives us in that day.

When we receive power, we must stir ourselves up with the truth that we are responsible for the need around us. God will supply all our need (Phil. 4:19) so that the need of the needy may be met through us. God has given us a great indwelling force of power. If we do not step into our privileges, it is a tragedy.

INTERPRETATION OF A MESSAGE IN TONGUES:
God, who ravishes you, brings forth within the heart new revelation. We are changed by the Spirit from vision to vision, and glory to glory.

There is no standing still. *"As He is, so are we in this world"* (1 John 4:17). *"We are the offspring of God"* (Acts 17:29), and we have divine impulses. We must get into line. The life of the Son of God is to make the whole body aflame with fire. After we have received, we will have power. God has given me a blessed ministry by helping me to stir others up. The purpose of our gathering together must be for increase. I am zealous and eager that we come into the divine plan. If we wait for power, we have mistaken the position. We have been saying, "If only I could feel the power!" We have been focusing too much on feeling the power. God is waiting for us to act. Jesus lived a life of perfect activity. He lived in the realm of divine appointment.

The pure in heart see God (Matt. 5:8). Our *"God is a consuming fire"* (Deut. 4:24). We must dare to press on until God comes forth in mighty power. May God give us the hearing of faith so that the power may come down like a cloud.

When I was at Stavanger in Norway, God told me to ask. He said, "I will give you every soul." It seemed too much! The voice came again: "Ask!" I dared to ask, and the power of God swept through the meeting like a mighty wind. We want this power in our cities. *"Go...and speak...all the words of this life"* (Acts 5:20). Press on until Jesus is glorified and multitudes are gathered in.

CHAPTER FOUR

CALLED TO SERVE

W e are a very wealthy and privileged people to be able to gather together to worship the Lord. I count it a very holy thing to gather together to think of Him, because it is impossible to think of Him and be in any way unholy. The very thought of Jesus will confirm truth and righteousness and power in your mortal body. There is something very remarkable about Him. When John saw Him, the impression that he had was that He was the *"lamb without blemish and without spot"* (1 Pet. 1:19). When God speaks about Jesus, He says, "He came forth in the brightness of the expression of the countenance of God." When revelation comes, it says, *"In Him dwells all the fullness"* (Col. 2:9).

His character is beautiful. His display of meekness is lovely. His compassion is greater than that of anyone in all of humanity. He felt infirmities. He helps those who pass through trials. And it is to be said about Him what is not said about anyone else: "[He] *was in all points tempted as we are, yet without sin"* (Heb. 4:15).

I want you, as the author of Hebrews wonderfully said, to *"consider Him who endured such hostility from sinners against Himself, lest you become weary and discouraged in your souls"* (Heb. 12:3). When you are weary and tempted and tried and all men are against you, consider Him who has passed through it all, so that He might be able to help you in the trial as you are passing through it. He will sustain you in the strife. When all things seem to indicate that you have failed, the Lord of Hosts, the God of Jacob, the salvation of our Christ will so reinforce you that you will be stronger than any concrete building that was ever made.

Your God, your Lord, in whom you trust, will make you so strong in the Lord and in the power of His might that no evil thing will befall you. As He was with Moses, He will be with you. As He stood by Daniel, He will cause the lions' mouths to close. He will shut up all that is against you; and the favor of heaven, the smile of the Most High, the kiss of His love, will make you know you are covered with the Dove.

OUR CALLING

The following Scripture is so beautiful: *"I, therefore, the prisoner of the Lord, beseech you to walk worthy of the calling with which you were called"* (Eph. 4:1).

Paul, who spoke to us in this verse, was an example for the church. He was filled with the loveliness of the character of the Master through the Spirit's power. He was zealous that we may walk worthy. This is the day of calling that he spoke about; this is the opportunity of our lifetime. This is the place where God increases strength or opens the door of a new way of ministry so that we will come into like-mindedness with this holy apostle who was a prisoner.

LOWLINESS AND MEEKNESS

The passage goes on to say, *"With all lowliness and gentleness, with longsuffering, bearing with one another in love"* (Eph. 4:2).

Jesus emphasized the new commandment when He left us: *"A new commandment I give to you, that you love one another; as I have loved you, that you also love one another"* (John 13:34). To the extent that we miss this instruction, we miss all the Master's instruction. If we miss that commandment, we miss everything. All the future summits of glory are yours in the very fact that you have been recreated in a deeper order by that commandment He gave us.

When we reach this attitude of love, then we make no mistake about lowliness. We will submit ourselves in the future in order that we may be useful to one another. The greatest plan that Jesus ever presented in His ministry was the ministry of service. He said, *"I am among you as the One who serves"* (Luke 22:27). And when we come to a place where we serve for pure love's sake, because it is the divine hand of the Master upon us, we will find out that we will never fail. Love never fails when it is divinely appointed in us. However, the so-called love in our human nature does fail and has failed from the beginning.

Suppose a man corresponds with me, seeking to learn more about me and to establish a relationship. The only thing I would have to say in answering his letters is, "Brother, all that I know about Wigglesworth is bad." There is no good thing in human nature. However, all that I know about the new creation in Wigglesworth is good. The important thing is whether we are living in the old creation or the new creation.

So I implore you to see that there is a lowliness, a humbleness, that leads you to meekness, that leads you to separate yourself from the world, that puts you so in touch with the Master that you know you are touching God. The blood of Jesus cleanses you from sin and all pollution (1 John 1:7). There is something in this holy position that makes you know you are free from the power of the Enemy.

We have yet to see the forcefulness of the Word of God. I refer to it in passing, in Hebrews 4:12:

For the word of God is living and powerful, and sharper than any two-edged sword, piercing even to the division of soul and spirit, and of joints and marrow, and is a discerner of the thoughts and intents of the heart.

The Word, the life, the presence, the power, is in your body, in the very marrow of your bones, and absolutely everything else must be discharged. Sometimes we do not fully reflect on this wonderful truth: the Word, the life, the Christ who is the Word, separates your soul from your spirit. What a wonderful work! The Spirit divides you from soul affection, from human weakness, from all depravity. The blood of Jesus can cleanse your blood until your very soul is purified and your very nature is destroyed by the nature of the living Christ.

I am speaking to you about resurrection touches. In Christ, we have encountered divine resurrection touches. In the greatest work God ever did on the face of the earth, He had to use His operation power: Christ was raised from the dead by the operation of the power of God. As the resurrection of Christ operates in our hearts,

159

it will dethrone the wrong things. And at the same time that it dethrones, it will build the right things. Callousness will have to change; hardness will have to disappear; all evil thoughts will have to go. And in the place of these will be lowliness of mind.

What beautiful cooperation with God in thought and power and holiness! The Master *"made Himself of no reputation"* (Phil. 2:7). He absolutely left the glory of heaven, with all its wonder. He left it and submitted Himself to humiliation. He went down, down, down into death for one purpose only: that He might destroy the power of death, even the Devil, and deliver those people who all their lifetime have been subject to fear—deliver them from the fear of death and the Devil (Heb. 2:14–15).

This is a wonderful plan for us. But how will it come to pass? By transformation, resurrection, thoughts of holiness, intense zeal, desire for all of God, until we live and move in the atmosphere of holiness.

If I say "holiness" or "baptism" or "resurrection" or "rapture," remember that all these words are tremendous. And there is another phrase I would like to emphasize: *"After you were illuminated"* (Heb. 10:32). Have you been to the place of illumination? What does the word mean? Illumination means this: that your very mind, which was depraved, is now the mind of Christ; the very nature that was bound now has a resurrection touch; your very body has come in contact with the life of God until you who were lost are found, and you who were dead are alive again by the resurrection power of the Word of the life of Christ. What a glorious inheritance in the Spirit!

Have you come to this place? Don't forget the ladder that Jacob saw. (See Genesis 28:10–22.) As I was nearing Jerusalem and saw the city for the first time, someone said to me, "See that place there? That is where Jacob saw the ladder that reached from earth to heaven."

Believer, if you have not reached all this, the ladder extends from heaven to earth to take you from earth to heaven. Do not be afraid of taking the steps. You will not slip back. Have faith in God. Experience divine resurrection life—more divine in thought, more wonderful in revelation. Resurrection life means living in the Spirit, wakened into all likeness, made alive by the same Spirit!

INTERPRETATION OF A MESSAGE IN TONGUES:
He rose, and in His rising, He lifted us and He placed us in the place of seating, and then gave us a holy language, and

160

then began to entertain us and show in us that now the body is His and that we become members in particular of the body. Sometimes He chastens us so that all the dross might go and all the wood and the stubble might be burned in the testing, so that He might get purer gold, purer life, purer soul, so that there should be nothing in the body that should be defiling, but He should take us out of the world and make us like a ripe shock of corn, ready for the dawning of the morning.

Are you lowly and meek in your mind? It is the divine plan of the Savior. You must be like Him. Do you desire to be like Him? There is nothing but yourself that can hinder you in this. You are the one who stops the current. You are the one who stops the life. The river and the current are coming just now; I feel them all over me.

While ministering in one place, we had a banquet for people who were distressed—people who were lame and weary, blind and diseased in every way. We had a big crowd of people, and we fed them all.

After we got them well filled with all the good things that were provided, we said, "Now we are going to give you some entertainment."

A man who had spent many years in a wheelchair but had been healed came onto the platform and told how he had been set free. A person who had suffered from a hemorrhage for many years came and testified. A blind man came and told how his eyes had been opened. For one hour, the people were entertained.

Then I said to the people, "Are you ready?"

Oh, they were all so ready! A dear man got hold of a boy who was encased in iron from top to bottom, lifted him up, and placed him onto the platform. Hands were laid upon him in the name of Jesus.

"Papa! Papa! Papa!" the boy said. "It's going all over me! Oh, Papa, come and take these irons off!" I do like to hear children speak; they say such wonderful things. The father took the irons off, and the life of God had gone all over the boy!

This is what I feel: the life of God going all over me, the power of God all over me. Don't you know this is the resurrection touch? This is the divine life; this is what God has brought us into. Let it go over us, Lord—the power of the Holy Spirit, the resurrection of heaven, the sweetness of Your blessing, the joy of the Lord!

If our fellowship below with Jesus be so sweet,
What heights of rapture shall we know
When round His throne we meet!

INTERPRETATION OF A MESSAGE IN TONGUES:

The Spirit sweetly falls like the dew, just as still on the grass,
and as it comes, it is for a purpose—God's purpose. It may be
withered grass, but God calls it to come forth again. And the
Spirit of the Lord is right in the midst of you this morning.
Though you might have been withered, dried, and barren for
a long time, the dew is falling. God is in the midst of us with
His spirit of revival, and He is saying to you, "All things are
possible; only believe," and He will change you.

THE UNITY OF THE SPIRIT

*"Endeavoring to keep the unity of the Spirit in the bond of
peace"* (Eph. 4:3).

You are bound forever out of loyalty to God to see that no division comes into the church body, to see that nothing comes into the
assembly, as it came into David's flock, to tear and rend the body.
You have to be careful. If a person comes along with a prophecy
and you find that it is tearing down and bringing trouble, denounce
it accordingly; judge it by the Word. You will find that all true
prophecy will be perfectly full of hopefulness. It will have compassion; it will have comfort; it will have edification. So if anything
comes into the church that you know is hurting the flock and dis-
turbing the assembly, you must see to it that you begin to pray so
that this thing is put to death. Bring unity in the bonds of perfection so that the church of God will receive edification. Then the
church will begin to be built up in the faith and the establishing of
truth, and believers will be one.

Do not forget that God means for us to be very faithful to the
church so that we do not allow anything to come into the church to
break up the body. You cannot find anything in the body in its rela-
tion to Christ that has schism in it. Christ's life in the body—there
is no schism in that. When Christ's life comes into the church,
there will be no discord; there will be a perfect blending of heart
and hand, and it will be lovely. Endeavor *"to keep the unity of the
Spirit in the bond of peace"* (Eph. 4:3).

ONE BODY

Now I come to a very important point: *"There is one body"* (v. 4). There is one body. Recognize that fact. When schism comes into the body, believers always act as though there were more than one. For instance, there is the Wesleyan Church, there is the Baptist Church, and there are many other churches. What do I need to notice about them? I have to see that right in that body, right in that church, God has a remnant belonging to His body. All the members of that church may not be of the body, but God has a remnant in that church. I should not go out and denounce the Baptists, the Wesleyans, or any other church. What I need to do, what I must do, is to so live in the Spirit of Christ that they will see that I am one with them. It is the Holy Spirit in the new church, in the body, the spiritual body, who is uniting, binding, and mightily moving. In every church, whether that church baptizes or not, there is a place where the Spirit is.

Now, the baptism of the Spirit is to be planted deeper and deeper in us until there is not a part that is left, and the manifestation of the power of the new creation by the Holy Spirit is right in our mortal bodies. Where we once were, He now reigns supreme, manifesting the very Christ inside of us, the Holy Spirit fulfilling all things right there.

Jesus has been wonderfully ordained; He has been incarnated by God, and God has given Him preeminence. He has to be preeminent in us. And someday we will see the preeminence of this wonderful Savior, and we will take our crowns and place them at His feet. Then He will put the Father in all preeminence and will take all our crowns and us also and present us to the Father, with Himself, so that the Father will be all in all, forever and ever.

That will take ten million years. In thinking about it, my calculation is that the Marriage and the Supper of the Lamb will take fifty million years. "What do you mean?" you ask. *"With the Lord one day is as a thousand years"* (2 Pet. 3:8). Our supernatural bodies, in the glory of their infinite relationship, will so live in the bliss of heaven that time will fly. The Supper and the Marriage will be supremely delightful and full and refreshing, pure and glorious and light. Oh, hallelujah! It is coming! It is not past; it is on the way. It is a glory we have yet to enter into.

ONE LORD AND ONE FAITH

"There is one body and one Spirit, just as you were called in one hope of your calling; one Lord, one faith, one baptism" (Eph. 4:4–5).

"One Lord." Oh, it is lovely! One Lord, one heart, one love, one association. *"One Lord, one faith, one baptism."* It is the baptism of the Spirit, the baptism of the new creation order, the baptism into divine life, the baptism with fire, the baptism with zeal, the baptism with passion, the baptism with inward travail. Oh, it is a baptism indeed! Jesus had it. He travailed; He acted with compassion.

"One Lord." We are all one, all in Christ Jesus, all one in Christ. We have *"one faith,"* which lays hold of the immensities, which dares to believe, which holds fast to what we have, so that no one may take our crowns (Rev. 3:11). For we are being quickened by this resurrection, and now faith lays hold.

Contend for eternal life. Lay hold of it—eternal life! It is something we cannot handle, something we cannot see, yet it is more real than we are. Lay hold of it. Let no man rob you of it. It is a crown; it is a position in the Holy One. It is a place of identification. It is a place of Him bringing you into order. Only He can do it—and He does it.

THE GOD WHO IS OVER ALL

Let us look at the next verse, which is very beautiful, for here is our position in this world: *"One God and Father of all, who is above all, and through all, and in you all."* (Eph. 4:6)

"Who is above all." Think of that! It does not matter what the Enemy may bring to you, or try to bring; remember, the Father, who is above all, is over you. Is there anything else? Yes, the next thought is larger still: *"Through all."* And the next: *"In you all."*

The God of power, majesty, and glory can bring you to a place of dethroning everything else! The Father of all is *"above all, and through all, and in you all."*

Do you dare to believe it? You should go away with such inspiration in the area of faith that you will never have a doubt again, and I want above all things to take you to that place.

Remember, God our Father is so intensely desirous to have all the fullness of the manifestation of His power, that we do not have to have one thing that His Son did not come to bring. We have to have perfect redemption; we have to know all the powers of righteousness; we have to understand perfectly that we are brought to the place where He is with us in all power, dethroning the power of the Enemy.

God over you—that is real. The God who is over you is more than a million times greater than the Devil, than the powers of evil, than the powers of darkness. How do I know? Hear what the Devil said to God about Job: *"Have You not made a hedge around him?"* (Job 1:10). This verse means that the Devil was unable to get near Job because there was a hedge. What was the hedge? It was the almighty power of God. It was not a thorny hedge; it was not a hedge of thistles. It was the presence of the Lord all around Job. And the presence of the Lord Almighty is so around us that the Devil cannot break through that wonderful covering.

The Devil is against the living Christ and wants to destroy Him, and if you are filled with the living Christ, the Devil is eager to get you out of the way in order to destroy Christ's power. Say this to the Lord: "Now, Lord, look after this property of yours." Then the Devil cannot get near you. When does he get near? When you dethrone Christ, ignoring His rightful position over you, in you, and through you.

You will be strong if you believe this truth. I preach faith, and I know it will carry you through if you dare to believe. Faith is the victory—always. Glory to Jesus!

THE GIFTS OF CHRIST

Notice next that the apostle Paul received revelation about Jesus. He spoke about the grace and the gifts of Christ—not the gifts of the Holy Spirit, but the gifts of Christ: *"But to each one of us grace was given according to the measure of Christ's gift"* (Eph. 4:7).

The gifts of Christ are so different from the gifts of the Holy Spirit that I want to explain this for a moment:

Therefore He says, "When He ascended on high, He led captivity captive, and gave gifts to men."...And He Himself gave some to be apostles, some prophets, some evangelists, and some pastors and teachers, for the equipping of the saints for the work of ministry, for the edifying of the body of Christ. (Eph. 4:8, 11–12)

These verses are in the Epistles. The Gospels are the Gospel of the kingdom. In the Acts of the Apostles, those who believed repented, were saved, were baptized, and became eligible to come into the Epistles, so that they might be in the body as is described in the Epistles. The body is not made up after you get into the Epistles; you are joined to the body the moment you believe.

For instance, some of you may have children, and they have different names, but the moment they appeared in the world, they were in your family. The moment they were born, they became a part of your family.

The moment you are born of God, you are in the family, and you are in the body, as He is in the body, and you are in the body collectively and particularly. After you come into the body, then the body has to receive the sealing of the promise, or the fulfillment of promise, that is, that Christ will be in you, reigning in you mightily. The Holy Spirit will come to unveil the King in all His glory so that He might reign as King there, the Holy Spirit serving in every way to make Him King.

You are in the body. The Holy Spirit gives gifts in the body. Living in this holy order, you may find that revelation comes to you and makes you a prophet. Some of you may have a clear understanding that you have been called into apostleship. Some of you may have perfect knowledge that you are to be pastors. When you come to be sealed with the Spirit of promise, then you find out that Jesus is pleased and gives gifts, in order that the church might come into a perfect position of being so blended together that there could be no division. Jesus wants His church to be a perfect body—perfect in stature, perfect in oneness in Him.

I have been speaking to this end: that you may see the calling that Paul was speaking about—humility of mind, meekness of spirit, knowing that God is in you and through you, knowing that the power of the Spirit is mightily bringing you to the place where not only the gifts of the Spirit but also the gifts of Christ have been given to you, making you eligible for the great work you have to do.

My purpose in this teaching was not to tell what God has for you in the future. Press in now, and claim your rights. Let the Lord Jesus be so glorified that He will make you fruit-bearers—strong in power, giving glory to God, having *"no confidence in the flesh"* (Phil. 3:3) but being separated from natural things, now in the Spirit, living fully in the will of God.

CHAPTER FIVE

THE CRY OF THE SPIRIT

J ohn the Baptist said, *"I am 'The voice of one crying in the wilderness: "Make straight the way of the LORD,"' as the prophet Isaiah said"* (John 1:23). He also said, *"Repent, for the kingdom of heaven is at hand!"* (Matt. 3:2). *"Then Jerusalem, all Judea, and all the region around the Jordan went out to him and were baptized by him in the Jordan, confessing their sins"* (vv. 5–6).

John's clothing was camel's hair, his belt leather, his food locusts and wild honey (v. 4). No angels or shepherds or wise men or stars heralded John's birth. But the heavenly messenger Gabriel, who had spoken to Daniel and to Mary, also spoke to John's father, Zacharias.

In the wilderness, John was without the food and clothing of his earthly father's priestly home. He had only a groan, a cry—the cry of the Spirit. Yet from John's place in the wilderness, he moved the whole land. God cried through him. It was the cry of the Spirit—oh, that awful cry. All the land was moved by that piercing cry.

Some are ashamed to cry. There is a loneliness in a cry. However, God is with a person who has only a cry.

WATER BAPTISM

So God spoke to John and told him about a new thing—water baptism.

And John bore witness, saying, "I saw the Spirit descending from heaven like a dove, and He remained upon Him. I did not know Him, but He who sent me to baptize with water said to me, 'Upon whom you see the Spirit descending,

167

and remaining on Him, this is He who baptizes with the Holy Spirit.' And I have seen and testified that this is the Son of God." (John 1:32–34)

God spoke to John in the wilderness about water baptism. It was a clean cut; it was a new way. He had been with those of the circumcision; now he was an outcast. It was the breaking down of the old plan.

REPENTANCE

The people heard his cry—oh, that cry, the awful cry of the Spirit—and the message that he gave: *"'Repent, for the kingdom of heaven is at hand!'* (Matt. 3:2). Make straight paths—no treading down of others or exacting undue rights. *'Make straight paths for your feet'* (Heb. 12:13)." All were startled! All were awakened! They thought the Messiah had come. The searching was tremendous! Is this He? Who can it be? John said, "I am a voice, crying, crying, making a way for the Messiah to come."

Now this is the testimony of John, when the Jews sent priests and Levites from Jerusalem to ask him, "Who are you?" He confessed, and did not deny, but confessed, "I am not the Christ." And they asked him, "What then? Are you Elijah?" He said, "I am not." "Are you the Prophet?" And he answered, "No."...He said: "I am 'The voice of one crying in the wilderness: "Make straight the way of the LORD,"' as the prophet Isaiah said."* (John 1:19–21, 23)

Individuals were purged; they found purpose. God pressed life through John. Through him, God moved multitudes and changed the situation. The banks of the Jordan were covered with people. The conviction was tremendous. They cried out. The prophet Isaiah had predicted, *"The rough ways* [will be made] *smooth; and all flesh shall see the salvation of God"* (Luke 3:5–6).

Then he [John] *said to the multitudes that came out to be baptized by him, "Brood of vipers! Who warned you to flee from the wrath to come? Therefore bear fruits worthy of repentance, and do not begin to say to yourselves, 'We have Abraham as our father.' For I say to you that God is able to raise up children to Abraham from these stones. And even now the ax is laid to the root of the trees. Therefore every tree which does not bear good fruit is cut down and thrown into the fire." So the people asked him, saying, "What shall we do then?" He answered and said to them, "He who has two tunics, let him give to him who has none; and he who has food, let him do likewise." Then tax collectors also came to be baptized, and said to him, "Teacher, what shall we do?" And he said to them, "Collect no more than what is appointed for you." Likewise the soldiers asked him, saying, "And what shall we do?" So he said to them, "Do not intimidate anyone or accuse falsely, and be content with your wages."* (Luke 3:7–14)

The people, the multitude, cried out and were baptized by John in the Jordan, confessing their sins.

ALONE WITH GOD

Oh, to be alone with God. God's Word came to John when he was alone.

The word of God came to John the son of Zacharias in the wilderness. And he went... preaching a baptism of repentance for the remission of sins. (Luke 3:2–3)

Alone! Alone!
Jesus bore it all alone!
He gave Himself to save His own.
He suffered—bled and died alone—alone.

Oh, to be alone with God, to get His mind, His thoughts, and His impression and revelation of the need of the people.

There was nothing ordinary about John—all was extraordinary. Herod was reproved by him because of Herodias, his brother Philip's wife, and for all the evils that Herod had done. Herodias's daughter danced before Herod, who promised her up to half his kingdom. She asked for John the Baptist's head.

This holy man was alone. God had John in such a way that he could express that cry—the burden for the whole land. He could cry for the sins of the people.

A CALL TO GOD'S PEOPLE TO CRY

God is holy. We are the children of Abraham—the children of faith. Awful judgment is coming. Cry! Cry!

John could not help but cry because of the people's sin. John had been filled with the Holy Spirit from his mother's womb (Luke 1:15). He had the burden. He was stern, but through his work, the land was open to Jesus. Jesus walked in the way; He came a new way.

"John came neither eating nor drinking" (Matt. 11:18)—John came crying. The only place he could breathe and be free was in the wilderness—the atmosphere of heaven—until he turned with a message to declare the preparation needed. Before Jesus came, repentance came to open up the place of redemption.

First, there must be a working of the Spirit in you; then God will work through you for others.

John's father and mother were left behind. His heart bled at the altar. He bore the burden, the cry, the need of the people.

INTERPRETATION OF A MESSAGE IN TONGUES:
Give way unto the Lord, even to the operation of the Spirit. A people known of God, doing exploits, gripped by God. Continue in the things revealed unto you. The enemy put to flight. Even those around you will acknowledge that the Lord has blessed.

CHAPTER SIX

EXPERIENCES WORKED OUT BY HUMILITY

W hat a privilege to care for the flock of God, to be used by God to encourage the people, to help stand against the many trials that affect the needy. What a holy calling! We each have our own work, and we must do it, so that boldness may be ours in the day of the Master's appearing, and so that no man can take our crowns (Rev. 3:11). Since the Lord is always encouraging us, we have encouragement for others. We must have a willingness, a ready mind, a yielding to the mind of the Spirit. There is no place for the child of God in God's great plan except in humility.

THE PLACE OF KNOWING OUR NEED

God can never do all He wants to do, all that He came to do through the Word, until He gets us to the place where He can trust us, and where we are in abiding fellowship with Him in His great plan for the world's redemption. We have this truth illustrated in the life of Jacob. It took God twenty-one years to bring Jacob to the place of humility, contrition of heart, and brokenness of spirit. God even gave him power to wrestle with strength, and Jacob said, "I think I can manage after all," until God touched his thigh, making him know that he was mortal and that he was dealing with immortality. As long as we think we can save ourselves, we will try to do it.

In Mark 5:25–34, we have the story of the woman who had suffered many things from many physicians and had spent all that she had. She was no better but rather grew worse. She said, *"If only I may touch His clothes, I shall be made well"* (v. 28). She came to know her need. Our full cupboard is often our greatest hindrance. It is when we are empty and undone, when we come to God in our nothingness and helplessness, that He picks us up.

PETER'S WORDS OF WISDOM

Let's take a look at the fifth chapter of 1 Peter. Peter said, *"Therefore humble yourselves under the mighty hand of God, that He may exalt you in due time"* (v. 6). Look at the Master at the Jordan River, submitting Himself to the baptism of John, then again submitting Himself to the cruel Cross. Truly, angels desire to look into these things (1 Pet. 1:12), and all heaven is waiting for the man who will burn all the bridges behind him and allow God to begin a plan in righteousness, so full, so sublime, beyond all human thought, but according to the revelation of the Spirit.

"Casting all your care upon Him, for He cares for you" (1 Pet. 5:7). He cares! We sometimes forget this. If we descend into the natural, all goes wrong, but when we trust Him and abide beneath His shadow, how blessed it is. Oh, many times I have experienced my helplessness and nothingness, and casting my care upon Him has proved that He cares.

Verse eight tells us to *"be sober, be vigilant."* What does it mean to be sober? It means to have a clear knowledge that we are powerless to manage, but also to have a rest of faith, knowing that God is close at hand to deliver all the time. The Adversary's opportunity is when we think that we are something and try to open our own door. Our thoughts, words, and deeds must all be in the power of the Holy Spirit. Oh yes, we need to be sober—not only sober, but vigilant. We need not only to be filled with the Spirit but to have a "go forth" in us, a knowledge that God's holy presence is with us. To be sober and vigilant, to have an ability to judge, discern, and balance things that differ—this is what we need.

"Your adversary the devil walks about like a roaring lion, seeking whom he may devour. Resist him, steadfast in the faith" (vv. 8–9). We must resist in the hour when Satan's schemes may bewilder us, when we are almost swept off our feet, and when darkness is upon us to such a degree that it seems as if some evil thing had overtaken us. *"Resist him, steadfast in the faith."* *"He who keeps Israel shall neither slumber nor sleep"* (Ps. 121:4). God covers us, for no human can stand against the powers of hell.

INTERPRETATION OF A MESSAGE IN TONGUES:

The strongholds of God are stronger than the strength of man, and He never fails to interpose on behalf of His own.

"After you have suffered a while" (1 Pet. 5:10). Then there is some suffering? Yes! But it is *"not worthy to be compared with the glory which shall be revealed in us"* (Rom. 8:18). The difference is so great that our suffering is not even worthy of mention. Ours is an eternal glory, from glory to glory, until we are swallowed up, until we are swallowed up in Him, the Lord of glory.

FOUR HELPS FOR THE HEART

Then, also in 1 Peter 5:10, we have four other things that enable the heart to be fixed in God: *"But may the God of all grace, who called us to His eternal glory by Christ Jesus, after you have suffered a while, perfect, establish, strengthen, and settle you."* The God of all grace wants to do the following in us: first, *"perfect"*; second, *"establish"*; third, *"strengthen"*; and fourth, *"settle."*

First is *"perfect."* In the book of Hebrews, we read,

May the God of peace...make you complete ["perfect," KJV*] in every good work to do His will, working in you what is well pleasing in His sight, through Jesus Christ.*
(Heb. 13:20–21)

Keep in mind that when perfection is spoken of in the Word, it is always through a joining up with eternal things. Perfection is a working in us of the will of God.

There are some of us who would be fainthearted if we thought we had to be perfect to receive the blessing of God. We would ask ourselves, "How is it going to happen?" However, we find as we continue to follow God that the purpose of eternal life is an advancement, for we are saved by the blood. Our actions, our minds, are covered by the blood of Jesus, and as we yield and yield, we find ourselves in possession of another mind, even the mind of Christ (1 Cor. 2:16), which causes us to understand the perfection of His will.

Someone may be saying, "I can never be perfect! It is beyond my greatest thought." You're right; it is! But as we press on, the Holy Spirit enlightens, and we enter in, as Paul said, according to the revelation of the Spirit. I am perfected as I launch out into God

173

by faith, His blood covering my sin, His righteousness covering my unrighteousness, His perfection covering my imperfection. This is a very important fact: I am holy and perfect in Him.

Second is *"establish."* You must be established in the fact that it is His life, not yours. You must have faith in His Word, faith in His life. You are supplanted by Another. You are disconnected from the earth. You are insulated by faith.

Third is *"strengthen."* You are strengthened by the fact that God is doing the business, not you. You are in the plan that God is working out.

INTERPRETATION OF A MESSAGE IN TONGUES:
There is nothing in itself that can bring out that which God designs. What God intends is always a going on to perfection until we are like unto Him. It is an establishment of righteousness on His own Word.

Fourth is *"settle."* What does it mean to be settled? It means knowing that I am in union with His will, that I am established in the knowledge of it, that day by day, I am strengthened. It is an eternal work of righteousness, until by the Spirit we are perfected. First is an enduring, then an establishing, a strengthening, and a settling. This happens according to our faith. It happens as we believe.

Now a closing word: *"To Him be the glory and the dominion forever and ever"* (1 Pet. 5:11). How can this verse be realized in my case? By living for His glory. There must be no withdrawal, no relinquishing, no looking back, but going on, on, on, for His glory now and forever. We must go on until, like Enoch, we walk with God and are not, for God has taken us (Gen. 5:24).

CHAPTER SEVEN

THE FLOOD TIDE

The body...grows with the increase that is from God.
—Colossians 2:19

Wherever Jesus went, the multitudes followed Him, because He lived, moved, breathed, was swallowed up, clothed, and filled by God. He was God; and as the Son of Man, the Spirit of God—the Spirit of creative holiness—rested upon Him. It is lovely to be holy. Jesus came to impart to us the Spirit of holiness.

We are only at the edge of things; the almighty plan for the future is marvelous. God must do something to increase. We need a revival to revive all we touch within us and outside of us. We need a flood tide with a deluge behind it. Jesus left 120 men to turn the world upside down. The Spirit is upon us to change our situation. We must move on; we must let God increase in us for the deliverance of multitudes; and we must travail until souls are born and quickened into a new relationship with heaven. Jesus had divine authority with power, and He left it for us. We must preach truth, holiness, and purity *"in the inward parts"* (Ps. 51:6).

You have loved righteousness and hated lawlessness; therefore God, Your God, has anointed You with the oil of gladness more than Your companions. (Heb. 1:9)

I am thirsty for more of God. He was not only holy, but He loved holiness.

It is the depths that God gets into that we may reflect Him and manifest a life having Christ enthroned in the heart, drinking into a new fullness, new intuition, for as He is, so are we in this world.

Jesus trod the winepress alone (Isa. 63:3), despising the cross and the shame. He bore it all alone so that we might be *"partakers of the divine nature"* (2 Pet. 1:4), sharers in the divine plan of holiness. That's revival—Jesus manifesting divine authority. He was without sin. People saw the Lamb of God in a new way. Hallelujah! Let us live in holiness, and revival will come down, and God will enable us to do the work to which we are appointed. All Jesus said came to pass: signs, wonders, mighty deeds. Only believe, and yield and yield, until all the vision is fulfilled.

A MIGHTY FAITH

God has a design, a purpose, a rest of faith. We are saved by faith and kept by faith. Faith is substance; it is also evidence (Heb. 11:1). God is! He is! And *"He is a rewarder of those who diligently seek Him"* (v. 6). We are to testify, to bear witness to what we know. To know that we know is a wonderful position to be in.

INTERPRETATION OF A MESSAGE IN TONGUES:
The Lord is the great promoter of divine possibility, pressing you into the attitude of daring to believe all that the Word says. We are to be living words, epistles of Christ, known and read of all men. The revelation of Christ, past and future; in Him all things consist. He is in us.

We are living in the inheritance of faith because of the grace of God. We are saved for eternity by the operation of the Spirit, who brings forth unto God. Heaven is brought to earth until God quickens all things into beauty, manifesting His power in living witnesses. God is in us for the world, so that the world may be blessed. We need power to lay hold of Omnipotence and to impart to others the Word of Life. This is a new epoch with new vision and new power. Christ in us is greater than we know. All things are possible if you dare to believe. The treasure is in earthen vessels so that Jesus may be glorified (2 Cor. 4:7).

Let us go forth bringing glory to God. Faith is substance, a mightiness of reality, a deposit of divine nature, the creative God within. The moment you believe, you are clothed with a new power to lay hold of possibility and make it reality. The people said to Jesus, *"Lord, give us this bread always"* (John 6:34). Jesus said, *"He who feeds on Me will live because of Me"* (v. 57).

Have the faith of God. The man who comes into great association with God needs a heavenly measure. Faith is the greatest of all. We are saved by a new life, the Word of God, an association with the living Christ. A new creation continually takes us into new revelation.

THE LIFE OF GOD WITHIN US

In the beginning was the Word, and the Word was with God, and the Word was God....All things were made through Him, and without Him nothing was made that was made. (John 1:1, 3)

All was made by the Word. I am begotten by His Word. There is a substance within me that has almighty power in it if I dare to believe. Faith goes on to be an act, a reality, a deposit of God, an almighty flame moving me to act, so that signs and wonders are manifested. I have a living faith within my earthen body.

Are you begotten? Is faith an act within you? Some need a touch; some are captives and need liberty. As many as Jesus touched were made perfectly whole. Faith takes you to the place where God reigns and you drink from God's bountiful store. Unbelief is sin, for Jesus went to death to bring us the light of life.

Jesus asked, *"Are you able to drink the cup that I am about to drink, and be baptized with the baptism that I am baptized with?"* (Matt. 20:22). The cup and the baptism are a joined position. You cannot live if you want to bring everything into life. His life is manifested power overflowing. We must decrease if the life of God is to be manifested. (See John 3:30.) There is not room for two kinds of life in one body. Death for life—that is the price to pay for the manifested power of God through you. As you die to human desire, there comes a fellowship within, perfected cooperation, you ceasing, God increasing. God in you is a living substance, a spiritual nature. You live by another life, the faith of the Son of God.

INTERPRETATION OF A MESSAGE IN TONGUES:

The Spirit, He breathed through and quickens until the body is a temple exhibiting Jesus—His life, His freshness, a new life divine. Paul said, "Christ lives in me, and the life I live in the flesh I live by faith."

As the Holy Spirit reveals Jesus, He is real—the living Word, effective, acting, speaking, thinking, praying, singing. Oh, it is a wonderful life, this substance of the Word of God, which includes possibility and opportunity, which confronts you, bringing you to a place undaunted. *"Greater is he that is in you"* (1 John 4:4 KJV). Paul said, *"When I am weak, then I am strong"* (2 Cor. 12:10).

Jesus walked in supremacy; He lived in the kingdom. And God will take us through because of Calvary. He has given us power over all the power of the Enemy (Luke 10:19). He won it for us at Calvary. All must be subject to His power. What should we do to work the works? *"This is the work of God, that you believe"* (John 6:29). Whatsoever He says will come to pass. That is God's Word.

A frail, weak man with sunken cheeks said to me, "Can you help me?" Beloved, there is not one who cannot be helped. God has opened the doors for us to let Him manifest signs and wonders. The authority is inside, not outside.

Could I help him? He had been fed liquid food through a tube for three months. I said, "Go home and eat a good supper." He did, and woke up to find the tube hole closed up. God knew he did not need two holes to eat by.

We must remain in a strong, resolute resting on the authority of God's Word. We must have one great desire and purpose: to do what He says. We must live in this holy Word, rejoicing in the manifestation of the life of God on behalf of the sick and perishing multitudes.

CHAPTER EIGHT

CHANGING STRENGTHS
TO SAVE ANOTHER

P*aul, an apostle of Jesus Christ by the will of God"* (2 Cor. 1:1). What a beautiful thought: we are here by the will of God. By the will of God, we are saved, we are sanctified, and we are baptized in the Holy Spirit.

THE HOLY SPIRIT IS OUR COMFORTER

"Blessed be the God and Father of our Lord Jesus Christ, the Father of mercies and God of all comfort" (v. 3). Jesus could not have breathed any greater words than John 14:16: *"I will pray the Father, and He will give you another Helper* ['Comforter,' KJV]*, that He may abide with you forever."*

"The Father of mercies and God of all comfort." We need a revelation of a greater power, an abiding presence sustaining and comforting us in the hour of trial, ready at a moment's notice, an inbreathing of God in the human life. What more do we need in these last days when perilous times are upon us than to be filled, saturated, baptized with the Holy Spirit? Baptized. Baptized into Him, never to come out. How comforting! Exhilarating! Joyful! May it please the Lord to establish us in this state of grace. May we know nothing among men except Jesus Christ and Him crucified (1 Cor. 2:2). May we be clothed with His Spirit—nothing outside of the blessed Holy Spirit. This, beloved, is God's ideal for us.

COMFORT IN THE MIDST OF TRIBULATION

[God] *comforts us in all our tribulation, that we may be able to comfort those who are in any trouble, with the comfort with which we ourselves are comforted by God.*

(2 Cor. 1:4)

Are we here in this experience?

> Where He may lead me I will go,
> For I have learned to trust Him so,
> And I remember it was for me,
> That He was slain on Calvary.

"[God] *comforts us in all our tribulation!*" God has chosen me to go through certain experiences to profit others. In all ages, God has had His witnesses, and He is teaching, chastening, correcting, and moving me just up to the point that I am able to bear it, in order to meet a needy soul who would otherwise go down without such comfort. All the chastening and the hardship is because we are able to bear it. No, we are not able, but we yield to Another—even the Holy Spirit. We are strengthened so that we may endure and so that we may comfort others *"with the comfort with which we ourselves are comforted by God."*

Why do we need brokenness and travail? The reason can be found in the book of Psalms: *"Before I was afflicted I went astray, but now I keep Your word"* (Ps. 119:67). Another passage in Psalms says,

> *Fools, because of their transgression, and because of their iniquities, were afflicted. Their soul abhorred all manner of food, and they drew near to the gates of death. Then they cried out to the LORD in their trouble, and He saved them out of their distresses.* (Ps. 107:17–19)

He saves them? What does the word *fool* mean? One who knows better than to do what he is doing. *"The fool has said in his heart, 'There is no God'"* (Ps. 53:1). But he knows better. It is only the hardened heart and the stiff neck that are destroyed without remedy (Prov. 29:1).

YIELDING TO GOD'S PLAN

> *Now no chastening seems to be joyful for the present, but painful; nevertheless, afterward it yields the peaceable fruit of righteousness to those who have been trained by it.* (Heb. 12:11)

It works out that chastening provokes or bestows upon us fruits unto holiness. It is in the hard places where we see no help that we cry out to God. He delivers us. What for? So that we can help the tempted. It was said of Jesus that He was *"in all points tempted as we are"* (Heb. 4:15). Where did He receive strength to comfort us? It was at the end of *"strong crying and tears"* (Heb. 5:7), when the angel came just in time and ministered and saved Him from death. Is He not able? Oh, God highly exalted Him. Now He can send angels to us. When? Just when we are about to go straight down. At such times in the past, did He not stretch out to us a helping hand?

INTERPRETATION OF A MESSAGE IN TONGUES:
It is God who sees into the depths of the human heart. He sees and saves those in trouble. There is in it a plan and a purpose for others. How is it worked out? On the line of submission and yielding and a yielding to the unfolding of God's plan. Then we will be able to save others.

[God] *comforts us in all our tribulation, that we may be able to comfort those who are in any trouble, with the comfort with which we ourselves are comforted by God.*

(2 Cor. 1:4)

There is a sense of the power of God in humanity bringing you through necessities, never touching the mortal body, only the mind. We must have *"the mind of Christ"* (1 Cor. 2:16).

CONSOLATION ABOUNDING

"For as the sufferings of Christ abound in us, so our consolation also abounds through Christ" (v. 5). God takes us to a place of need, and before we are barely aware of it, we are full of consolation toward the needy. How? The sufferings of Christ abound! The ministry of the Spirit abounds so often. It is a great blessing. We do not know our calling in the Spirit. It is so much greater than our appreciation of it. Then we speak a word in season (Isa. 50:4); here and there we minister, sowing beside all waters as the Holy Spirit directs our paths.

DIVINE COOPERATION

Now if we are afflicted, it is for your consolation and salvation, which is effective for enduring the same sufferings

which we also suffer. Or if we are comforted, it is for your
consolation and salvation. (2 Cor. 1:6)

Paul and the people he ministered to cooperated with one another. Here is the value of testing: it results in a great flow of life
from one to another. John Wesley woke up one day and became
conscious of the need of one establishing another. In this way, he
bore witness to the ministry of the Spirit, and multitudes were
born again in his meetings when they heard the wonderful works
of God. They heard stories and had consolation poured out to them
by the revelation of the Spirit.

We are members of one another. When God's breath is upon
us and we are quickened by the Holy Spirit, we can pour into each
other wonderful ministries of grace and helpfulness. We need a
strong ministry of consolation, not deterioration or living below our
privileges.

CONSOLATION RESULTING FROM DEPRIVATION

These consolations come out of deprivation, affliction, and endurance. *"Yes, we had the sentence of death in ourselves, that we*
should not trust in ourselves but in God who raises the dead" (2
Cor. 1:9).

Have we gone as far as Paul? Not one of us has. Can you see
how Paul could help and comfort and sustain because he yielded to
God all his trust as Jesus did? Because he was yielded to the Holy
Spirit to work out the sentence of death, he could help others.

I pray to God that He may never find us *"kick*[ing] *against the*
goads" (Acts 9:5). We may have to go through the testing; the
truths you stand for, you are tried for. Divine healing, purity of
heart, baptism in the Holy Spirit and in fire—we are tested for
these truths. We cannot get out of this testing. But in every meeting, the glory rises. We descend down into trials also to be sustained and brought out for the glory of God. *"If God is for us, who*
can be against us?" (Rom. 8:31). *"For our light affliction, which is*
but for a moment, is working for us a far more exceeding and eter-
nal weight of glory" (2 Cor. 4:17). Oh, the joy of being worthy of
suffering! How will I stand the glory that will be after?

There are many of God's people who are victorious in suffering
but fail or back out when things are going fine. Deprivation is often

easier than success. We need a sound mind all the time to balance us so that we do not trade our liberty for something less.

We get glimpses of the glory all the time. To Paul in the glory, the presence of the Lord was so wonderful. But he said, *"Lest I should be exalted...a thorn in the flesh was given to me"* (2 Cor. 12:7). That was the mercy of God. *"The Lord knows how to deliver the godly out of temptations"* (2 Pet. 2:9) and *"saves such as have a contrite spirit"* (Ps. 34:18). What a revelation for the time to come! If Satan had his way, we would be devoured.

GOD'S GREAT DELIVERANCE

"[God] *delivered us from so great a death, and does deliver us; in whom we trust that He will still deliver us"* (2 Cor. 1:10).

Hebrews 11:6 tells us that God is! He will never fail us. He has been faithful until this moment, and He will keep us to the end.

[God] *delivered us from so great a death, and does deliver us; in whom we trust that He will still deliver us, you also helping together in prayer for us, that thanks may be given by many persons on our behalf for the gift granted to us through many.* (2 Cor. 1:10–11)

"[God] *delivered us from so great a death, and does deliver us; in whom we trust that He will still deliver us."*

CHAPTER NINE

REVIVAL—IT'S COMING, AND THE PRICE IS MARTYRDOM

Revival is coming. God's heart is in the place of intense passion. Let us bend or break, for God is determined to bless us. Oh, the joy of service and the joy of suffering! Oh, to be utterly cast upon Jesus! God is coming forth with power. The latter rain is appearing (James 5:7). There must be no coming down from the cross but a going on from faith to faith and from glory to glory, with an increasing diligence so that we may be found in Him without spot and blameless (2 Pet. 3:14).

GOD IS WAITING

A divine plan is working. *"See how the farmer waits for the precious fruit of the earth...until it receives the early and latter rain"* (James 5:7). Jesus is waiting to do all.

Worship is higher than fellowship. Oh, the calmness of meeting with Jesus! All fears are gone. His tender mercy and indescribable peace are ours. I have all if I have Jesus.

God is pruning the tree. The goal of all God's plans for us is a yielded will. God is waiting for the precious fruit of the earth, for the outcome of a sown life, which is to be diviner, lovelier. But first, the seed has to die.

"Great will be the day of Jezreel [which means 'whom God sows' or 'the seed of God']*"* (Hos. 1:11). *"I will break the bow of Israel in the Valley of Jezreel"* (v. 5).

Bow and sword of battle I will shatter from the earth....I will betroth you to Me forever...in righteousness and justice, in lovingkindness and mercy; I will betroth you to Me in faithfulness, and you shall know the LORD....I will answer the heavens, and they shall answer the earth. The earth shall answer with grain, with new wine, and with oil; they shall answer Jezreel [the seed of God].

(Hos. 2:18–22)

Amen. Let them answer. Let God do it—He commands it. God says, *"'Let there be light!' (Gen. 1:3). Let your light shine!"*

God awaits the death of the seed. How do you know the seed is dead? Why, the green shoots appear. It springs into life. God awaits the evidence of death; He waits for Isaiah 11 to appear—a place of profound rest. Jesus said, *"I will pray the Father, and He will give you another Helper"* (John 14:16).

Allow me to read the eleventh chapter of Isaiah:

There shall come forth a Rod from the stem of Jesse, and a Branch shall grow out of his roots. The Spirit of the LORD shall rest upon Him, the Spirit of wisdom and understanding, the Spirit of counsel and might, the Spirit of knowledge and of the fear of the LORD. His delight is in the fear of the LORD, and He shall not judge by the sight of His eyes, nor decide by the hearing of His ears; but with righteousness He shall judge the poor, and decide with equity for the meek of the earth; He shall strike the earth with the rod of His mouth, and with the breath of His lips He shall slay the wicked. Righteousness shall be the belt of His loins, and faithfulness the belt of His waist. "The wolf also shall dwell with the lamb, the leopard shall lie down with the young goat, the calf and the young lion and the fatling together; and a little child shall lead them. The cow and the bear shall graze; their young ones shall lie down together; and the lion shall eat straw like the ox. The nursing child shall play by the cobra's hole, and the weaned child shall put his hand in the viper's den. They shall not hurt nor destroy in all My holy mountain, for the earth shall be full of the knowledge of the LORD as the waters cover the sea. And in that day there shall be a Root of Jesse, who shall stand as a banner to the people; for the Gentiles shall seek Him, and His resting place shall be glorious." It shall come to pass in that day that the LORD shall set His hand again the second time to recover the remnant of His people who are left, from Assyria and Egypt, from

185

Pathros and Cush, from Elam and Shinar, from Hamath and the islands of the sea. He will set up a banner for the nations, and will assemble the outcasts of Israel, and gather together the dispersed of Judah from the four corners of the earth. Also the envy of Ephraim shall depart, and the adversaries of Judah shall be cut off; Ephraim shall not envy Judah, and Judah shall not harass Ephraim. But they shall fly down upon the shoulder of the Philistines toward the west; together they shall plunder the people of the East; they shall lay their hand on Edom and Moab; and the people of Ammon shall obey them. The LORD will utterly destroy the tongue of the Sea of Egypt; with His mighty wind He will shake His fist over the River, and strike it in the seven streams, and make men cross over dry-shod. There will be a highway for the remnant of His people who will be left from Assyria, as it was for Israel in the day that he came up from the land of Egypt. (Isa. 11:1–16)

Not a sound invades the stillness,
Not a form invades the scene,
Save the voice of my Beloved
And the person of my King.

Precious, gentle, holy Jesus,
Blessed Bridegroom of my heart,
In Thy secret inner chamber
Thou wilt whisper what Thou art.

And within those heavenly places,
Calmly hushed in sweet repose,
There I drink with joy absorbing
All the love Thou wouldst disclose.

Wrapt in deep adoring silence,
Jesus, Lord, I dare not move,
Lest I lose the smallest saying
Meant to catch the ear of love.

Rest then, oh my soul, contented,
Thou hast reached that happy place
In the bosom of thy Savior,
Gazing up in His dear face.

THE EARLY RAIN AND THE LATTER RAIN

The early and the latter rain appear. The early rain is to make the seed die, come to an end, come to ashes. And out of the ashes will come the great fire of consummation, which will burn in the hearts of the people, the Word of the living God producing Christ by the breath of the Spirit.

First ashes, then the latter rain gives a surging of life. The old is finished; now a surging life and the effects of the latter rain will come forth on those who know the Father. A universal outpouring of the Holy Spirit will come. The coming of the Lord is at hand.

The Judge is standing at the door. Has He come? *"When He has come, He will convict the world of sin"* (John 16:8). He has come! *"He will convict the world...of judgment, because the ruler of this world is judged"* (vv. 8, 11). Jesus said, *"If I depart, I will send Him* [the Helper] *to you"* (v. 7). He has come!

God waits to move and shake all that can be shaken. Mark 16:17–18 describes the signs following those who believe—an outpouring, mighty and glorious. The early rain gets us ready for that which is to come. Be killed. Be prepared—a vessel ready to pour out torrents.

The baptism of the Holy Spirit is for the death of the seed. The Holy Spirit wakes up every passion, permits every trial. His purpose is to make the vessel pure.

All must die before we see a manifestation of God that is unthought of, undreamed of. It is a call to martyrdom, to death—a call to death! The choice is before you. Decide. Accept the path of death to life. Absolute abandonment is required for a divine equipping. The early and the latter rain appear.

Isaiah 11 is God's equipment for understanding the worldwide purposes of God, the loveliness of Jesus, and the glory of God.

We need revelation for a perishing world. *"Where there is no vision, the people perish"* (Prov. 29:18 KJV). Wake up! The air is full of revival, but we look for a mighty outpouring that will shake all that can be shaken. Take everything else, but give me vision and revelation of the purposes of God and a wonderful burning love. It is difficult to tell of the freedom of the Holy Spirit in revealing the love of Jesus. *"David spoke to the LORD the words of this song.... And he said...my cry entered His ears"* (2 Sam. 22:1–2, 7).

Oh yes, it must come, this surging life—this uttermost death for uttermost life. The early and the latter rain appear. *"We count them blessed who endure"* (James 5:11). *"Beloved, do not think it strange"* (1 Pet. 4:12), for the fiery breath of revival is coming. There is a ripple on the lake, a murmur in the air. The price is tremendous: it is martyrdom. We must seal the testimony with our blood. We must die to ourselves. Dying, searching, crucifixions—no resistance. Trust me, it is finished. Yes, be sown first; then comes the revelation of God with eternal issues for multitudes. The latter rain appears. Everything moves before the men whom God has moved, and millions are gathered in, and the heart of God is satisfied.

God says to us,

> Since thou art come to that holy room
> Where with the choirs of saints forevermore
> Thou art made My music,
> Tune the instrument here at the door,
> And what thou must do then think here before.

CHAPTER TEN

THE SPIRIT OF THE LORD
IS UPON ME

J esus picked up the book of Isaiah in the temple and read the wonderful words also found in Luke 4:18–19. He further emphasized these words by the work He was doing:

The Spirit of the LORD is upon Me, because He has anointed Me to preach the gospel to the poor; He has sent Me to heal the brokenhearted, to proclaim liberty to the captives and recovery of sight to the blind, to set at liberty those who are oppressed; to proclaim the acceptable year of the LORD.

THE IMPORTANCE OF HAVING THE SPIRIT UPON US

I believe God is bringing us to a place where we know the Spirit of the Lord is upon us. If we have not gotten to that place, God wants to bring us to the fact of what Jesus said in John 14: *"I will pray the Father, and He will give you another Helper ['Comforter,' KJV], that He may abide with you forever"* (v. 16). Because the Spirit of the Lord came upon Him who is our Head, we must see to it that we receive the same anointing, and that the same Spirit is upon us. The Devil will cause us to lose the victory if we allow ourselves to be defeated by him. But it is a fact that the Spirit of the Lord is upon us, and as for me, I have no message apart from the message He will give, and I believe that the signs He speaks of will follow.

I believe that Jesus was the One sent forth from God, and the propitiation for the sins of the whole world (1 John 2:2). We see the

189

manifestation of the Spirit resting upon Him so that His ministry was with power. May God awaken us to the fact that this is the only place where there is any ministry of power.

In asking the Lord what to say to you, it came to me to arouse you to the fact that the Comforter has come. He has come, and He has come to abide forever. Are you going to be defeated by the Devil? No, for the Comforter has come so that we may receive and give forth the signs that must follow, so that we may not by any means be deceived by the schemes of the Devil. There is no limit to what we may become if we dwell and live in the Spirit. In the Spirit of prayer, we are taken right away from earth into heaven. In the Spirit, the Word of God seems to unfold in a wonderful way, and it is only in the Spirit that the love of God is poured out in us (Rom. 5:5).

As we speak in the Spirit, we feel that the fire that burned in the hearts of the two men on their way to Emmaus, when Jesus walked with them, is burning in our hearts. (See Luke 24:13–32.) It is sure to come to pass that when we walk with Him, our hearts will burn; the same power of the Spirit is present to make it happen. The two men on their way to Emmaus could not understand what was happening on the road, but a few hours later, they saw Jesus break the bread, and their eyes were opened.

But, beloved, our hearts ought to always burn. There is a place where we can live in the anointing and the clothing of the Spirit, where our words will be clothed with power. *"Do not be drunk with wine...but be filled with the Spirit"* (Eph. 5:18). Being filled with the Spirit is a wonderful privilege.

I see that it was necessary for John to be in the Spirit on the Isle of Patmos for the revelation to be made clear to him (Rev. 1:9–10). What does it mean to this generation for us to be kept in the Spirit? All human reasoning and all human knowledge cannot be compared with the power of the life that is lived in the Spirit. In the Spirit, we have power to loose and power to bind (Matt. 16:19). There is a place where the Holy Spirit can put us where we cannot be anywhere else but in the Spirit. If we breathe the Holy Spirit's thoughts into our thoughts, and live in the anointing of the Holy Spirit as Jesus lived, then there will be evidences that we are in the Holy Spirit, and we will do His works. But it is only in the Spirit.

Now, I read in Matthew 16:19 that Jesus says, in essence, "I will give you power to bind, and I will give you power to loose." This is a power that we have not yet claimed, and we will not be able to claim this manifestation of the Spirit unless we live in the Spirit. When are you able to bind and loose? It is only in the Spirit. You cannot bind things in human strength or with the natural mind. This power was never lacking in Jesus, but I feel as I preach to you tonight that there is a great lack of it in most of us. God help us!

"The Spirit of the LORD is upon Me" (Luke 4:18). Beloved, there was a great purpose in this Spirit being on Jesus, and there is a special purpose in your being baptized in the Spirit. We must not forget that we are members of His body, and by this wonderful baptismal power, we are partakers of His divine nature (2 Pet. 1:4).

The revelation came this way: I saw Adam and Eve driven out of the Garden and a flaming sword at every side to keep them from entering into the Garden. But I saw that all around me was a flaming sword keeping me from evil, and it seemed this would be true if I would claim it, and I said, "Lord, I will." The flaming sword was around me, delivering me from the power of hell. In this way, we are preserved from evil. God is like a wall of fire around us (Zech. 2:5); why should we fear? What a wonderful salvation! What a wonderful Deliverer!

Notice Ezekiel 37. The only need of Ezekiel was to be in the Spirit, and while he was in the Spirit, it came to him to prophesy to the dry bones and say, *"O dry bones, hear the word of the LORD"* (v. 4). And as he prophesied according to the Lord's command, he saw an *"exceedingly great army"* (v. 10) rising up about him. The prophet obeyed God's command, and all we have to do is exactly this: obey God. What is impossible with man is possible with God (Luke 18:27).

I pray to God that your spirit, soul, and body may be preserved holy (1 Thess. 5:23), and that you may be always on fire, always ready with the anointing on you. If this is not so, we are out of divine order, and we ought to cry to Him until the glory comes back upon us.

SPIRIT-FILLED MISSIONARY WORK

"The Spirit of the LORD is upon Me" (Luke 4:18). There must have been a reason that the Spirit was upon Jesus. First of all, it says here,

> *Because He has anointed Me to preach the gospel to the poor; He has sent Me to heal the brokenhearted* [what a

Gospel!], *to proclaim liberty to the captives* [what a wonderful Spirit was upon Him!] *and recovery of sight to the blind, to set at liberty those who are oppressed; to proclaim the acceptable year of the LORD.*   (Luke 4:18–19)

You missionaries who are going to India and Africa and China and other places have a wonderful Gospel to take to these people who know nothing about God—a Gospel of salvation and healing and deliverance. If you want to know how missionaries are to work, look at Paul among the natives on the island of Malta. When the viper came out of the fire and fastened onto Paul's hand, they watched to see him swell up and die. When he neither swelled up nor died, they said, "He is a god." (See Acts 28:3–6.)

When you go forth to these dark lands where the Holy Spirit has sent you to preach the unsearchable riches of Christ, to loose the bands of Satan, and to set the captives free, be sure you can say, *"The Spirit of the LORD is upon Me"* (Luke 4:18). Remember that Christ is made unto us not only salvation, but also wisdom and redemption (1 Cor. 1:30).

"Filled with God, yes, filled with God, pardoned and cleansed and filled with God." Being filled with God leaves no room for doubting or fearing. We have no idea of all that this means—to be filled with God. It means emptied of self. Do you know what it means to be filled with God? It means that you have no fear, for when you are filled with God, you are filled with love, and *"perfect love casts out fear"* (1 John 4:18).

I want to know more about this manifestation of the power of the Holy Spirit. Let us follow Paul further. Next in the twenty-eighth chapter of Acts, we find that the chief of the island had a fever and dysentery. When Paul ministered to him, he was healed, and the people gave Paul things to take with him. (See Acts 28:8–10.)

When we think that the church is poor and needy, we forget that the spirit of intercession can unlock every safe in the world. What did God do for the children of Israel? He took them to vineyards and lands flowing with milk and honey, and all they did was walk in and take possession. If we will only live in the Spirit and the anointing of the Spirit, there will be no lack. There is only lack where faith is not substance, but the Word says faith is the substance (Heb. 11:1), and whatsoever is not of faith is sin (Rom. 14:23). Things will surely come to pass if you will believe this. You do not have to try to bring Christ down; He is down (Rom. 10:6–8). You do not have to try to bring Him here; He is here. If we will obey the Lord, there is nothing He will not give us since He has given us Jesus. The Spirit will have to reveal to us the fact that, because the Lord has given us Jesus, He has given us all things.

"The Spirit of the LORD is upon Me" (Luke 4:18). It is true that we must be filled with the Spirit. Father, teach us what this means! It was only because Jesus had an understanding of what it means to be filled with the Spirit that He could stand before those men and say to the demon, "Come out of him." Who is the man who is willing to lay down everything so that he may have God's all? Begin to seek, and don't stop seeking until you know that the Spirit of the Lord is upon you.

"I thank You, Father...that You have hidden these things from the wise and prudent and have revealed them to babes" (Matt. 11:25). If you are in the infant class tonight, the Spirit must have revealed to you your lack. We need to seek with all our hearts. We need to be made flames of fire.

CHAPTER ELEVEN

A DOOR OF UTTERANCE

[Pray] *also for us, that God would open unto us a door of utterance, to speak the mystery of Christ, for which I am also in bonds: that I may make it manifest, as I ought to speak.*
—Colossians 4:3–4 KJV

P aul felt, as we do, the need of utterance. He had plenty of language, but he wanted utterance. We can have inspiration, operation, tongue, mind, heart—we need all these. God works through these in this divine order to give forth the truth most needed for the time. But the supreme need of the hour is prayer for utterance. "[Pray] *also for us, that God would open unto us a door of utterance...that I may* [speak]*...as I ought.*"

Paul and his helpers were men sent forth by the power of the Holy Spirit. But without anointing, they could not open the door or give forth the right word for the hour. Paul and his helpers were unequal to the need. Was this an indication that something was out of order? No! For *"unless the LORD guards the city, the watchman stays awake in vain"* (Ps. 127:1). We are dependent on the Holy Spirit to breathe through us. Apart from this living breath of the Spirit, the message is ordinary and not extraordinary.

The question is, How can we live in this place, thrown on omnipotent power? It is by the Spirit of the Lord giving vent, speaking through us. It is not an easy thing. God said to David, "It is good that the desire is in your heart." (See 2 Chronicles 6:8.) But that will not do for us who live in the latter days when God is pouring

194

forth His Spirit, and rivers are at our word. We need to live by Mark 11:22–23: *"Have faith in God....Whoever...believes...will have whatever he says."* In Genesis 1:3, God said, *"Let there be light."* Let God arise. Let God breathe His Holy Spirit through your nature, through your eyes and tongue—the supernatural in the natural for the glory of God. God raised Paul for this ministry,

> *To open their eyes, in order to turn them from darkness to light, and from the power of Satan to God, that they may receive forgiveness of sins and an inheritance among those who are sanctified by faith in Me.* (Acts 26:18)

What was the means? Jesus said, *"By faith in Me."* The faith of God.

SPEECH INSPIRED BY THE SPIRIT

> *The Lord GOD has given Me the tongue of the learned, that I should know how to speak a word in season to him who is weary. He awakens Me morning by morning, He awakens My ear to hear as the learned. The Lord GOD has opened My ear; and I was not rebellious.* (Isa. 50:4–5)

Do you believe it? Oh, for more to believe God that *"the tongue of the dumb* [might] *sing"* (Isa. 35:6). When will they? When they believe and fulfill the conditions. Oh, beloved, it is not easy. But Jesus died and rose again for the possibility. *"Have faith in God"* (Mark 11:22). Be able to say, *"My tongue is the pen of a ready writer"* (Ps. 45:1). The whole man needs to be immersed in God so that the Holy Spirit may operate and the dying world may have the ministry of life for which it is famishing.

> *But if the Spirit of Him who raised Jesus from the dead dwells in you, He who raised Christ from the dead will also give life to your mortal bodies through His Spirit who dwells in you.* (Rom. 8:11)

As the dead body of Christ was given life and brought out by the Holy Spirit, may we be given eyes to see and ears to hear and a tongue to speak as the oracles of God. *"If anyone speaks, let him speak as the oracles of God"* (1 Pet. 4:11). Those are our orders:

speaking what no one knows except the Holy Spirit, as the Spirit gives divine utterance—a language that would never come at all unless the Holy Spirit gave utterance and took the things of Christ and revealed them. I am talking about *"the mystery of Christ."* *"[Pray] also for us, that God would open unto us a door of utterance, to speak the mystery of Christ, for which I am also in bonds: that I may make it manifest, as I ought to speak."* Did God answer these prayers? Yes! *"In mighty signs and wonders, by the power of the Spirit of God...from Jerusalem and round about to Illyricum I have fully preached the gospel of Christ"* (Rom. 15:19).

It was the grace of our Lord Jesus Christ, that great Shepherd of the sheep, that brought to us redemption. It was by the grace of God—His favor and mercy, a lavished love and an undeserved favor—that God brought salvation. We did not deserve it.

SEASONED WITH SALT

"Let your speech always be with grace, seasoned with salt" (Col. 4:6). Salt has three properties: first, it stings; second, it heals; and third, it preserves. In the same way, your words by the Spirit are filled with grace, yet they cut to the heart, and they bring preservation. We must be very careful to be salty. God's Word will not return void; it will accomplish, and it will prosper (Isa. 55:11)—but our mouths must be clean and our desire wholly for God.

Jesus' words were straightforward. To the elite of the holiness movement of His day, He said, *"Woe to you...hypocrites! For you are like whitewashed tombs"* (Matt. 23:27). To others He said, "You are deceived; you have the idea that you are the children of Abraham, but you are the children of the Devil, and you do his works." (See John 8:39, 44.) His mouth was full of meekness and gentleness and yet was so salty because of their corruption. Unless you know the charm of Christ, you might think you are out of the working of His eternal power. However, hear what the prophet Isaiah said: *"A bruised reed He will not break"* (Isa. 42:3). To those for whom there is no lifting up, He comes as the healing Balm of Gilead.

"Know how you ought to answer each one" (Col. 4:6). This is not easy to learn. It is only learned in the place of being absorbed by God. When we are in that place, we seek to glorify God and can give a chastening word full of power to awaken and to save. Use the salt! Use conviction; use the healing for their preservation.

How true we have to be! You are seasoned with salt. I love it! It is inspiring! It is conviction! Thus the Holy Spirit writes on the fleshly tablets of the temple of the Spirit (2 Cor. 3:3). O Lord, enlarge our sense of Your presence in the temple so that we may discern the Lord's body in our midst.

FULL OF THE LIFE OF OUR PRECIOUS LORD

For He is so precious to me,
For He is so precious to me;
'Tis heaven below
My Redeemer to know,
For He is so precious to me.

We want our whole being to be so full of the life of our Lord that the Holy Spirit can speak and act through us. We want to live always in Him. Oh, the charm of His divine plan. We cry out for the inspiration of the God of power. We want to act in the Holy Spirit. We want to breathe out life divine. We want the glory, miracles, and wonders that work out the plan of the Most High God. We want to be absorbed by God, and we want to know nothing among men except Jesus and Him crucified (1 Cor. 2:2). Unto You, O God, be the glory and the honor and the power (Rev. 5:13)!

Yes, filled with God,
Yes, filled with God,
Emptied of self and filled with God.
Yes, filled with God,
Yes, filled with God,
Emptied of self and filled with God.

Can you wonder why I love Him so? May there be a cry until we witness Acts 11:15: *"And as I began to speak, the Holy Spirit fell upon them."*

Oh, be on fire, oh, be on fire,
Oh, be on fire for God.
Oh, be on fire, be all on fire,
Be all on fire for God.

CHAPTER TWELVE

WAY, MANIFESTATION, AND MINISTRY

I will be referring throughout this message to the third chapter of 2 Corinthians. Three things have been pressing through this morning: first, the way of faith; second, the manifestation of the power of the Spirit; and third, the ministry of the Spirit.

THE MINISTRY OF THE SPIRIT

Now, the ministry of the Spirit has been entrusted to us. The word may be in letter or in power. (See 1 Corinthians 4:20.) We must be in the place of edifying the church. Law is not liberty, but if there is a move of God within you, God has written His laws in your heart so that you may delight in Him. God desires to set forth in us a perfect blending of His life and our life so that we may have abounding inward joy—a place of reigning over all things, not a place of endeavor. Ours is not an endeavor society, but a delight to run in the will of God. There is a great difference between an endeavor and a delight.

God says to us, *"Be holy, for I am holy"* (1 Pet. 1:16). Trying will never cause us to reach a place of holiness, but there is a place, or an attitude, where God gives us faith to rest upon His Word, and we delight inwardly over everything. *"I delight to do Your will, O my God"* (Ps. 40:8). There is a place of great joy. Do we want condemnation?

We know there is something within that has been accomplished by the power of God, something greater than there could be in the natural order of the flesh. We are the representatives of Jesus. He was eaten up with zeal. This intense zeal changes us by the

198

operation of the Word; we do not rest in the letter, but we allow the blessed Holy Spirit to lift us by His power.

"You are our epistle" (2 Cor. 3:2). Such a beautiful order prevailed in the Corinthian church; it was a place of holiness and power in Christ, perfect love, and the sweetness of association with Christ.

The disciples were with Jesus three years. He spoke out of the abundance of His heart toward them. John said, "We have touched Him; our eyes have gazed into His eyes." (See 1 John 1:1). Did Jesus know about Judas? Yes. Did He ever tell? No. When Jesus told the disciples that one of them would betray Him, they said, *"Lord, is it I?"* (Matt. 26:22). And Peter said to John, who was close to Jesus, "Find out who it is." The essence of divine order is to bring the church together, so that there is no schism in the body, but a perfect blending of heart to heart.

"The letter kills, but the Spirit gives life" (2 Cor. 3:6). The sword cut off Malchus's ear, but the Spirit healed it again. (See Luke 22:50–51.) Our ministry has to be in the Spirit, *"free from the law of sin and death"* (Rom. 8:2). When we live in the ministry of the Spirit, we are free; in the letter we are bound. If it is *"an eye for an eye"* (Matt. 5:38), we have lost the principle. If we are to come to a place of great liberty, the law must be at an end. Yet we love the law of God; we love to do it and not put one thing aside.

INTERPRETATION OF A MESSAGE IN TONGUES:
The way is made into the treasure house of the Most High. As God unfolds the Word, hearts are blended. An incision is being made by the Spirit of the living God, so that we may move, live, act, think, and pray in the Holy Spirit—a new order, life in the Holy Spirit, ministry in the Spirit.

"Clearly you are an epistle of Christ, ministered...by the Spirit of the living God...on tablets of flesh, that is, of the heart" (2 Cor. 3:3). It's heart worship when God has made the incision; the Spirit has come to blend with humanity.

BABIES ARE PRECIOUS

There is something beautiful about a baby. Jesus said, *"Therefore whoever humbles himself as this little child is the greatest in the kingdom of heaven"* (Matt. 18:4).

There was a house with ten children and only ten chairs. What was to happen with the baby? When the baby came, every chair was a seat for the baby.

It is a great joy to me to dedicate children, but I believe that when they are old enough, they should be buried in water baptism (Rom. 6:4). *"Of such is the kingdom of heaven"* (Matt. 19:14). A baby is a beautiful thing, and God looks on His people at the possibility. The child is lent to us to be brought up in the fear of God.

HAVING GOD'S WORD IN OUR HEARTS

> I know He's mine, this Friend so dear;
> He lives in me, He's always near.

I want to refer to the word *incision*. God's Word, our life, is written on the fleshly tablets of the heart.

I was in Rome, where I saw thousands of pilgrims kissing the steps there. It made me sorrowful. How I thank God for His Word! There are many Pentecostal assemblies in Italy, and I saw on the people there a great hunger and thirst after God. God moved mightily among them, and people were saved and baptized in the Holy Spirit in the same meeting.

We must keep in the spiritual tide—God supreme, the altar within the body. Faith is the evidence, the power, the principle, keeping us in rest. We must have the Spirit in anointing, intercession, revelation, and great power of ministry. To be baptized in the Holy Spirit is to be in God's plan—the Spirit preeminent, revealing the Christ of God, making the Word of God alive—something divine. *"Our sufficiency is from God, who also made us sufficient as ministers of the...Spirit; for the...Spirit gives life"* (2 Cor. 3:5–6).

I knew a believer whose job was to carry bags of coal. He had been in bed three weeks away from his work. I showed him Romans 7:25: *"I thank God; through Jesus Christ our Lord! So then, with the mind I myself serve the law of God, but with the flesh the law of sin."* I said, "Keep your mind on God and go to work, shouting victory." He did, and the first day he was able to carry a hundred bags, his mind stayed on God and kept in peace.

If your peace is disturbed, there is something wrong. If you are not free in the Spirit, your mind is in the wrong place. Apply the blood of Jesus, and keep your mind stayed upon Jehovah, where "hearts are fully blessed, finding as He promised, perfect peace and rest." Keep your mind on God, gaining strength in Him day by day.

"The law was given through Moses, but grace and truth came through Jesus Christ" (John 1:17). This is a new dispensation, this divine place: Christ in you, the hope and evidence of glory (Col. 1:27).

INTERPRETATION OF A MESSAGE IN TONGUES:
Let your eyes be stayed upon Him, your heart moved by the Spirit, your whole being in a place of refining to come forth as gold. Behold; see the glory. God covers you with a mantle of power.

INTERPRETATION OF A MESSAGE IN TONGUES:
For the Lord delights in you, to serve Him with all your heart and strength. Take in all the land, worldwide. Oh, the rest of faith! Ask largely of Him. Until now you have asked nothing (John 16:24).

May God gird you with truth (Eph. 6:14). I commend you to Him in the name of Jesus.

CHAPTER THIRTEEN

WHAT DO YOU WANT ME TO DO?

As soon as Paul saw the light from heaven brighter than the sun, he said, *"Lord, what do You want me to do?"* (Acts 9:6). And as soon as he was willing to yield, he was in a condition where God could meet his need, where God could display His power, where God could have the man.

Are you saying today, *"What do You want me to do?"* The place of yieldedness is where God wants us. People are saying, "I want the baptism of the Holy Spirit. I want to be healed. I would like to know that I am a child of God," and I see nothing, absolutely nothing, in the way, except that they have not yielded to the plan of God.

In Acts 19:6, the condition was met that Paul demanded, and when he laid his hands on the Ephesian disciples, they were instantly filled with the Spirit and spoke in other tongues and prophesied. The only thing they needed was just to be in the condition where God could come in.

The main thing today that God wants is obedience. When you begin yielding and yielding to God, He has a plan for your life, and you come in to that wonderful place where all you have to do is eat the fruits of Canaan. I am convinced that Paul must have been in divine order, as well as those men, and Paul had a mission right away to all of Asia.

It is the call of God that counts. Paul was in the call of God. I believe God wants to stir somebody's heart to obedience; God may want him to go to China or India or Africa, but the thing God is looking for is obedience. Our words should be, *"Lord, what do You want me to do?"* (Acts 9:6).

UNUSUAL MIRACLES

Now God worked unusual miracles by the hands of Paul, so that even handkerchiefs or aprons were brought from his body to the sick, and the diseases left them and the evil spirits went out of them. (Acts 19:11–12)

If God can have His way today, the ministry of somebody will begin. It always begins as soon as a person yields. Paul had been putting many believers in prison, but God brought Paul to such a place of yieldedness and brokenness that he cried out, *"What do You want me to do?"* (Acts 9:6). Paul's choice was to be a bondservant for Jesus Christ.

Beloved, are you willing for God to have His way today? God said about Paul, *"I will show him how many things he must suffer for My name's sake"* (Acts 9:16). But Paul saw that these things were working out *"a far more exceeding and eternal weight of glory"* (2 Cor. 4:17). You people who have come for a touch from God, are you willing to follow Him? Will you obey Him?

When the Prodigal Son had returned and the father had killed the fatted calf and made a feast for him, the elder brother was angry and said, *"You never gave me a young goat, that I might make merry with my friends"* (Luke 15:29). But the father said to him, *"All that I have is yours"* (v. 31). He could kill a fatted calf at any time. Beloved, everything in the Father's house is ours, but it will come only through obedience. And when He can trust us, we will not come short in anything.

"God worked unusual miracles by the hands of Paul" (Acts 19:11). Let us notice the handkerchiefs that went from his body. This passage indicates that when Paul touched handkerchiefs and sent them forth, God worked special miracles through them, and diseases departed from the sick, and evil spirits went out of them. Isn't this lovely? I believe that after we lay hands on these handkerchiefs and pray over them, they should be handled very sacredly. Even as we carry them, they will bring life, if we carry them in faith to the suffering ones. The very effect, if you would only believe, would be to change your own body as you carry the handkerchief.

A woman came to me one day and said, "My husband is such a trial to me. The first salary he gets, he spends on drink. Then he cannot do his work and comes home. I love him very much. What can be done?" I said, "If I were you, I would take a handkerchief and would place it under his head when he goes to sleep at night, saying nothing to him but having a living faith." We anointed a handkerchief in the name of Jesus, and she put it under his head.

Oh, beloved, there is a way to reach these wayward ones. The next morning on his way to work, he ordered a glass of beer. He lifted it to his lips, but he thought there was something wrong with it, and he put it down and left. He went to another saloon, and another, and did the same thing. He came home sober. His wife was gladly surprised, and he told her the story of how he had been affected. That was the turning point in his life; it meant not only giving up drink, but it meant his salvation.

God wants to change our faith today. He wants us to see that it is not obtained by struggling and working and longing. *"The Father Himself loves you"* (John 16:27). *"He Himself took our infirmities and bore our sicknesses"* (Matt. 8:17). *"Come to Me, all you who labor and are heavy laden, and I will give you rest"* (Matt. 11:28). Who is the man who will take the place of Paul and yield and yield and yield until God possesses him in such a way that power will flow from his body to the sick and suffering? It will have to be the power of Christ that flows. Don't think there is some magic power in the handkerchief, or you will miss the power. It is the living faith within the man who lays the handkerchief on his body, and the power of God through that faith. Praise God, we may lay hold of this living faith today. The blood has never lost its power. As we get in touch with Jesus, wonderful things will take place. And what else? We will get nearer and nearer to Him.

THE SECRET OF POWER

There is another side to it:

Then some of the itinerant Jewish exorcists took it upon themselves to call the name of the Lord Jesus over those who had evil spirits, saying, "We exorcise you by the Jesus whom Paul preaches."...And the evil spirit answered and said, "Jesus I know, and Paul I know; but who are you?"
(Acts 19:13, 15)

I implore you in the name of Jesus, especially those of you who are baptized, to wake up to the fact that you have power if God is with you. But there must be a resemblance between you and Jesus. The evil spirit said, *"Jesus I know, and Paul I know; but who are you?"* Paul had the resemblance. You are not going to get this resemblance without having His presence; His presence changes you.

204

You are not going to be able to get the results without the marks of the Lord Jesus. The man must have the divine power within himself; devils will take no notice of any power if they do not see Christ. *"Jesus I know, and Paul I know; but who are you?"* The difference in these exorcists was that they did not have the marks of Christ, so the manifestation of the power of Christ was not seen.

If you want power, don't make any mistake about it. If you speak in tongues, don't mistake that for the power. If God has given you revelations along certain lines, don't mistake that for the power. Or if you have even laid hands on the sick and they have been healed, don't mistake that for the power. *"The Spirit of the LORD is upon Me"* (Luke 4:18)—that alone is the power. Don't be deceived. There is a place to be reached where you know the Spirit is upon you so that you will be able to do the works that are accomplished by this blessed Spirit of God in you. Then the manifestation of His power will be seen, and people will believe in the Lord.

What will make men believe the divine promises of God? Beloved, let me say to you today that God wants you to be ministering spirits, and this means being clothed with another power. You know when this divine power is there, and you know when it goes forth. The baptism of Jesus must bring us to the place of having our focus centered on the glory of God; everything else is wasted time and wasted energy. Beloved, we can reach it; it is a high mark, but we can get to it. Do you ask how? Say to God, *"What do You want me to do?"* (Acts 9:6). That is the plan. It means a perfect surrender to the call of God, and perfect obedience.

EXAMPLES OF GOD'S WONDER-WORKING POWER

A dear young Russian came to England. He did not know the language but learned it quickly and was very much used and blessed by God. As the wonderful manifestations of the power of God were seen, people pressed him to find out the secret of his power, but he felt it was so sacred between him and God that he should not tell it. But they pressed him so much that he finally said to them, "First, God called me, and His presence was so precious that I said to God at every call that I would obey Him. I yielded and yielded and yielded until I realized that I was simply clothed with another power altogether, and I realized that God had taken me—tongue, thoughts, and everything—and I was not myself, but it was Christ working through me."

How many of you today have known that God has called you over and over and has put His hand upon you, but you have not yielded? How many of you have had the breathing of His power within you, calling you to prayer, and you have to confess that you have failed?

I went to a house one afternoon where I had been called, and I met a man at the door. He said, "My wife has not been out of bed for eight months; she is paralyzed. She has been looking forward so much to your coming. She is hoping God will raise her up." I went in and rebuked the Devil's power. She said, "I know I am healed; if you leave, I will get up." I left the house and went away, not hearing anything more about her. I went to a meeting that night, and a man jumped up and said he had something he wanted to say; he had to go to catch a train but wanted to talk first. He said, "I come to this city once a week, and I visit the sick all over the city. There is a woman I have been visiting, and I was very much distressed about her. She was paralyzed and lay on her bed many months. However, when I went there today, she was up doing her work." I tell this story because I want you to see Jesus.

A letter came to our house that said that a young man was very ill. He had been to our mission a few years before with a very bad foot; he had worn no shoe but had fastened a piece of leather around his foot. God had healed him that day. Three years afterward, something else came upon him. What it was I don't know, but his heart failed, and he was helpless. He could not get up or dress or do anything for himself, and in that condition, he called his sister and told her to write to me and see if I would pray. My wife said to go, and she believed that God would give me that life. I went, and when I got to this place, I found that the whole country was expecting me. They had said that when I came, this man would be healed.

I said to the woman when I arrived, "I have come." "Yes," she said, "but it is too late." "Is he alive?" I asked. "Yes, barely alive," she said. I went in and put my hands on him and said, "Martin." He just breathed slightly and whispered, "The doctor said that if I move from this position, I will never move again." I said, "Do you know that the Scripture says, 'God is the strength of my heart and my portion forever' (Ps. 73:26)"? He said, "Should I get up?" I said, "No."

That day was spent in prayer and ministering the Word. I found a great state of unbelief in that house, but I saw that Martin had faith to be healed. His sister was home from an asylum. God kept me there to pray for that place. I said to the family, "Get Martin's clothes ready; I believe he is to be raised up." I felt the unbelief.

I went to the chapel and had prayer with a number of people around there, and before noon they, too, believed that Martin would be healed. When I returned, I said, "Are his clothes ready?" They said, "No." I said, "Oh, will you hinder God's work in this house?" I went into Martin's room all alone. I said, "I believe God will do a new thing today. I believe that when I lay hands on you, the glory of heaven will fill this place." I laid my hands on him in the name of the Father, Son, and Holy Spirit, and immediately the glory of the Lord filled the room, and I fell at once to the floor. I did not see what took place on the bed or in the room, but this young man began to shout out, "Glory, glory!" and I heard him say, "For Your glory, Lord," and he stood before me perfectly healed. He went to the door and opened it, and his father stood there. He said, "Father, the Lord has raised me up," and the father fell to the floor and cried for salvation. The young woman brought out of the asylum was perfectly healed at that moment by the power of God in that house.

God wants us to see that the power of God coming upon people has something more in it than we have yet known. The power to heal and to baptize is in this place, but you must say, *"Lord, what do You want me to do?"* (Acts 9:6). You say it is four months before the harvest. If you had the eyes of Jesus, you would see that the harvest is already here (John 4:35). The Devil will say you can't have faith. Tell him he is a liar. The Holy Spirit wants you for the purpose of manifesting Jesus through you. Oh, may you never be the same again! The Holy Spirit moving upon us will make us to be like Him, and we will truly say, *"Lord, what do You want me to do?"*

Chapter Fourteen

Workers Together with God

Interpretation of a Message in Tongues:
God has come to visit us, and He has revealed Himself unto us, but He wants you to be so ready that nothing that He says will miss. He wants to build you on the foundation truth.

Are you ready? "Why?" you ask. Because God has something even better than what He gave us yesterday. He wants to give us higher ground, holier thoughts, and a more concentrated, clearer ministry. God wants us to be in a rising tide every day. This rising tide is a changing of faith; it is an attitude of the spirit; it is where God rises higher and higher.

God wants us to come to the place where we will never look back. God has no room for the person who looks back, thinks back, or acts back.

The Holy Spirit wants to get you ready to stretch yourself out to God and to believe that *"He is a rewarder of those who diligently seek Him"* (Heb. 11:6). You do not need to use vain repetitions when you pray (Matt. 6:7). Simply ask and believe. Do more believing and less begging.

People come with their needs, they ask, and then they leave with their needs because they do not faithfully wait to receive what God has promised them. If they ask for it, they will get it.

Many people are missing the highest order. I went to a person who was full of the Spirit but was constantly saying, "Glory! Glory! Glory!" I said, "You are full of the Holy Spirit, but the Spirit cannot speak because you continually speak." He kept still then, and the Spirit began to speak through him. This story illustrates the fact that often we are altogether in God's way.

208

I want to so change your operation in God that you will know that God is operating through you for this time and forevermore. May the Spirit awaken us to deep things today.

Are you ready? "What for?" you ask. To move and be moved by the mighty power of God that cannot be moved, and to be so chastened and built up that you are in the place where it doesn't matter where the wind blows or what difficulty comes because you are fixed in God.

Are you ready? "What for?" you ask. To come into the plan of the Most High God, believing what the Scriptures say and holding fast to what is good, believing so that no one will take your crown (Rev. 3:11).

THE WORD CHANGES THE BELIEVER

God can so change us by His Word day by day that we are altogether different. David knew this. He said, *"Your word has given me life"* (Ps. 119:50). *"He sent His word and healed them"* (Ps. 107:20). How beautiful that God can make His Word abound! *"Your word I have hidden in my heart, that I might not sin against You!"* (Ps. 119:11).

It is absolute disloyalty and unbelief to pray about anything in the Word of God. The Word of God does not need to be prayed about: the Word of God needs to be received. If you will receive the Word of God, you will always be in a big place. If you pray about the Word of God, the Devil will be behind the whole thing. Never pray about anything concerning which it can be said, "Thus says the Lord." You need to receive God's words so that they will build you on a new foundation of truth.

Let us look at a very important verse in the book of Romans:

I beseech you therefore, brethren, by the mercies of God, that you present your bodies a living sacrifice, holy, acceptable to God, which is your reasonable service.

(Rom. 12:1)

We see in this verse that Paul had been operated on. He had undergone a mighty operation on more than just a surgical table. He had been cut to the very depths of his being, until he had absolutely reached a place on the altar of full surrender. When he came to this place, out of the depths of this experience, he gave his whole life, as it were, in a nutshell.

Now, I want to turn your attention to the sixth chapter of 2 Corinthians, which was also written by Paul. This is a summit position for us, although there are many lines to be examined to see if we are rising to the summit of these glorious experiences. This passage is also the groundwork of deep heart searching. It is divine revelation of the spiritual character to us. Paul must have been immersed in this holy place.

Here in this sixth chapter of 2 Corinthians, we have again a beautiful word that ought to bring us to a very great place of hearing by the hearing of faith: *"We then, as workers together with Him"* (v. 1).

This verse is a collective thought; it preaches to the whole church in Christ Jesus. Paul had the Corinthians in mind because the Corinthian church was the first church among the Gentiles, and he was the Apostle to the Gentiles.

Do Not Receive God's Grace in Vain

"We then, as workers together with Him also plead with you not to receive the grace of God in vain" (v. 1). This is one of the mightiest verses in the Scriptures. People are getting blessed all the time and are receiving revelation all the time, and they go from one point to another, but they do not establish themselves in the thing that God has brought to them.

If you do not let your heart be examined when the Lord comes with blessing or with correction, if you do not make the blessing or the correction a stepping-stone, or if you do not make it a rising place, then you are receiving the grace of God in vain. People could be built up much more in the Lord and be more wonderfully established if they would step out sometimes and think over the graces of the Lord.

Grace will be multiplied on certain conditions. How? In the first chapter of 2 Timothy, we have these words: *"The genuine faith that is in you"* (v. 5). Everyone in the entire church of God has the same precious faith within him. If you allow this same precious faith to be foremost, utmost in everything, you will find that grace and peace are multiplied.

Just the same, the Lord comes to us with His mercy, and if we do not see that the God of grace and mercy is opening to us the door of mercy and utterances, we are receiving His grace in vain.

I thank God for every meeting. I thank God for every blessing. I thank God every time a person says to me, "God bless you, brother!" I say, "Thank you, brother. The Lord bless you!" We are in a very great place when people desire for us to be blessed.

If we want strength in building our spiritual character, we should never forget our blessings. When you are in prayer, remember how near you are to the Lord. Prayer is a time during which God wants you to be strengthened, and He wants you to remember that He is with you.

When you open the sacred pages and the light comes right through and you say, "Oh, isn't that wonderful!" thank God, for it is the grace of God that has opened your understanding. When you go to a church meeting and the revelation comes forth and you feel that it is what you needed, receive it as the grace of the Lord. God has brought you to a place where He might make you a greater blessing.

CONSTANT SALVATION

For He says: "In an acceptable time I have heard you, and in the day of salvation I have helped you." Behold, now is the accepted time; behold, now is the day of salvation.
(2 Cor. 6:2)

There are two processes of salvation. First, God helped you when the Spirit was moving you and when the Adversary was against you, when your neighbors and friends did not want you to be saved, and when everybody rose up in accusation against you. When you knew there was fighting on the outside and fighting within, He helped you; He covered you until you came into salvation. And then, second, He keeps you in the plan of His salvation.

This is the day of salvation. The fact that you are being saved does not mean that you were not saved, but it means that you are being continually changed. In the process of regeneration, you are being made like God; you are being brought into the operation of the Spirit's power; you are being made like Him.

This is the day of salvation. He has helped you in a time when Satan would destroy you, and He is with you now.

This is the day of salvation. If we remain stationary, God has nothing for us. We must see that we must progress. Yesterday will not do for today. I must thank God for yesterday. However, tomorrow is affected by what I am today.

Today is a day of inspiration and divine intuition, a day in which God is enrapturing the heart, breaking all shorelines, getting my heart to the place where it is responsive only to His cry, where I live and move honoring and glorifying God in the Spirit. This is the day of the visitation of the Lord. This is the great day of salvation, a day of moving on for God.

INTERPRETATION OF A MESSAGE IN TONGUES:
It is the Lord. Let Him do what seems good to Him. It may be death, but He has life in the midst of death.

We will praise and magnify the Lord, for He is worthy to be praised! He has helped us, and now He is building us; now He is changing us; now we are in the operation of the Holy Spirit. Every day you must climb to higher ground. You must deny yourself in order to go forward with God. You must refuse everything that is not pure and holy and separate. God wants you to be pure in heart. He wants your intense desire after holiness.

"Seek first the kingdom of God and His righteousness, and all these things shall be added to you" (Matt. 6:33).

IN PERFECT HARMONY

"Give no offense in anything, that our ministry may not be blamed" (2 Cor. 6:3). That is lovely. Oh, the church can be built! God will break down opposing things.

If you, being a member of a certain church, are in a place where you would rather see one person saved at your church than two people saved at another church, then you are altogether wrong, and you need to be saved. You are still out of the order of the Spirit of God, and you are a stranger to true, holy life with God.

If your ministry is not to be blamed, how can you help to prevent it from being blamed? You have to live in love. See to it that you never say or do anything that would interfere with the work of the Lord; rather, live in the place where you are helping everybody, lifting everybody, and causing everybody to come into perfect harmony. Remember, there is always a blessing where there is harmony. "One accord" is the keynote of the victory that is going to come to us all the time.

There are thousands and thousands of different churches, but they are all one in the Spirit to the extent that they receive the life of Christ. If there is any division, it is always outside of the Spirit. The spiritual life in the believer never has known dissension, because where the Spirit has perfect liberty, there is total agreement, and there is no schism in the body.

"The letter kills, but the Spirit gives life" (2 Cor. 3:6). When there is division, it is only because people choose the letter instead of the Spirit. If we are in the Spirit, we will have life. If we are in the Spirit, we will love everybody. If we are in the Spirit, there will be no division; there will be perfect harmony.

God wants to show us that we must so live in the Spirit that the ministry is not blamed.

It is a wonderful ministry God has given to us because it is a life ministry. Pentecostal positions are spiritual positions. We recognize the Holy Spirit, but we recognize first the Spirit giving us life, saving us from every form of evil power, transforming our human nature until it is in divine order. Then, in that divine order, we see that the Lord of Hosts can very beautifully arrange the life until we live in the Spirit and are not fulfilling the lusts of the flesh (Gal. 5:16). I like that because I see that when the Holy Spirit is perfectly in charge, He lifts and lightens and unveils the truth in a new way until we grasp it.

INTERPRETATION OF A MESSAGE IN TONGUES:
Do not let your good be spoken of as evil, but so live in the spiritual life with Christ that He is being glorified over your body, your soul, and your spirit, until your very life becomes emblematic and God reigns over you in love and peace.

Oh, how wonderful it would be if every one of us would possess this word in our hearts: *"Do not let your good be spoken of as evil"* (Rom. 14:16). I know we all want to be good. It is not a wrong thing to desire that our goodness be appreciated. But we must watch ourselves because it is an evil day (although it is the day of salvation), and we must understand these days that the Lord wants to chasten and bring a people right into a full-tide position.

I believe that it is just as possible for God to sweep a group of believers right into glory before the Rapture as during the Rapture. It is possible for you to be taken even if others are left. May God give us a very keen inward discerning of our hearts' purity. We want to go to heaven—it is far better for us to go—but it is far better for the church that we stay (Phil. 1:23–24).

Paul realized the following truth: *"To depart* [to] *be with Christ...is far better"* (v. 23). Then there is another side to it. Believing that God made us for the proclamation of the Gospel, for the building of the church, we would say, "Lord, for the purpose of being a further blessing for Your sake and for the sake of the church, just keep us full of life to stay." We do not want to be full of disease, but we want to be full of life.

May the Lord grant to us right now a living faith to believe.

IN AFFLICTION FOR THE CHURCH

"But in all things we commend ourselves as ministers of God: in much patience, in tribulations, in needs, in distresses" (2 Cor. 6:4). Now, these tribulations are not the tribulations of various diseases. Paul is very definite along these lines. He suffered tribulations with the people. Jesus suffered tribulations with the people. There can be many tribulations within our human frame along the lines of feeling that our spiritual influence is not bearing fruit in the lives of others.

You have to so live in the Spirit that when you see the church not rising into its glory, you suffer tribulation for the church. You are very sorry and deeply distressed because the church is not capturing the vision, and there is tribulation in your sorrow.

God wants us to be so spiritual that we have perfect discernment of the spirit of the people. However, if I can in a moment discern the spirit in a meeting, whether it is life-giving, whether the whole church is receiving it, whether my heart is moved by this power, then I can also see faith waning, and that will bring tribulation and trouble to my life.

May God give us the realization that we are so joined to the church that we may labor to bring the church up. Paul said that he labored in birth in order that Christ might be formed in the people again (Gal. 4:19). He was not laboring so that they could be saved again. No, but they had lacked perception; they had missed fellowship of the divine order; so he labored again so that they might be brought into this deep fellowship in the Spirit.

May God help us to see that we can labor for the church. Blessed is the person who can weep between the church door and the altar. Blessed are the people of God who can take someone else's church on their hearts and weep and cry through until the church is formed again, until she rises in glory, until the power of heaven is over her, until the spiritual acquaintance rises higher and higher, until a song lifts her to the heights.

This is the order of the church of God: the ministry not being blamed, but the church rising to a higher height, a glorious truth, a blessed faithfulness, higher and higher.

POSSESS YOUR SOUL IN PEACE

"In much patience" (2 Cor. 6:4). That is an important message for these days. I know I am speaking to people who have churches and who have a lot of responsibilities in churches. Remember this: you never lose as much as when you lose your peace. If the people see that you have lost your groundwork of peace, they know that you have gotten outside of the position of victory. You have to possess your soul in peace.

Strange things will happen in the church. All circumstances will appear to be against the church, and you will feel that the Enemy is busy. At that time, possess your soul in peace. Let the people know that you are acquainted with One *"who, when He was reviled, did not revile in return"* (1 Pet. 2:23).

Possess patience to such an extent that you can suffer anything for the church, for your friends, for your neighbors, or for anyone. Remember this: we build character in others as our character is built. As we are pure in our thoughts, are tender and gracious to other people, and possess our souls in patience (Luke 21:19), then people have a great desire for our fellowship in the Holy Spirit.

Now, Jesus is an example to us along these lines. The people saw Him undisturbed. I love to think about Him. He helps me so much because He is the very essence of help.

DO NOT GIVE OFFENSE OR CAUSE DISTRESS

"In needs, in distresses" (2 Cor. 6:4). This verse is referring to spiritual distresses that are a result of acquaintance with the church. It is the church we are dealing with here. Paul was in a place where he was speaking by divine appointment to the church.

The purpose of these meetings is to gather the church together along the lines of faithfulness, because if ten people could have saved Sodom and Gomorrah, ten holy people in a church can hold the power of the Spirit until light reigns. We do not want to seek to save ourselves; on the contrary, we want to lose ourselves so that we may save the church (Matt. 16:25). You cannot stop distresses from coming; they will come, and offenses will come. But woe to those who cause offenses (Matt. 18:7). See that you do not cause offense. See that you live on a higher plane. See that your tongue does not speak evil of others.

I wonder if you have ever fully seen the picture presented in the twenty-sixth chapter of Matthew. Jesus said, *"One of you will betray Me"* (v. 21). The disciples asked, *"Lord, is it I?"* (v. 22). Every one of them was so conscious of his human weaknesses that not a single one of them could say that it would not be he.

John was leaning on the Lord, and Peter motioned to him and said, "Please find out who it is." He knew that if anybody could find out, it would be John.

How long do you think Jesus had known? He had known for at least close to three years. Jesus had been with them, He had been feeding them, He had been walking up and down with them, and He had never told any of them it was Judas.

Those who follow Jesus should be so sober and sensitive that they would not speak against someone else, whether the words were true or not.

Jesus is the great Personality. In every way, I need to listen to Him and also be motivated by His holy inward generosity, His purity, and His acquaintance with love.

If Jesus had told the disciples that Judas would one day betray Him, what would have been the result? Everyone would have been bitter against Judas. So He saved all His disciples from being bitter against Judas for three years.

What love! Can't you see that holy, divine Savior? If we saw Him clearly, every one of us would throw ourselves at His feet. If we had a crown worth millions of dollars, we would cast it at His feet and say, "You alone are worthy." O God, give us such a holy, intense, divine acquaintance with You that we would rather die than grieve You! Oh, for inward character that will make us say, "A thousand deaths rather than sinning once." O Jesus, we worship You! You are worthy!

INTERPRETATION OF A MESSAGE IN TONGUES:
Into the very depths have I gone to help you. And in the very depths I called you my own, and I delivered you when you

were oppressed and in oppression, and I brought you out when you were sure to sink below the waves, and I lifted you and brought you into the banqueting house.

It is the mercy of the Lord. It is the love of the Lord. It is the grace of the Lord. It is the Spirit of the Lord. It is the will of the Lord.

Be ready and alert for God. Live in the Holy Spirit. Oh, I can understand the Scripture that says,

> *I wish you all spoke with tongues, but even more that you prophesied; for he who prophesies is greater than he who speaks with tongues, unless indeed he interprets, that the church may receive edification.* (1 Cor. 14:5)

I pray to God that we may learn the lesson of how to keep ourselves so that the Spirit will blend us, making the harmony beautiful. There is not a person in this place who is not feeling the breath of the Almighty over us. This is one of those moments when the Spirit is coming to us and saying, "Don't forget, this is the receiving of the grace of God." You are not to go away and forget; you are to go away and be what God intends for you to be.

ARRESTED IN SWEDEN

"In stripes, in imprisonments, in tumults, in labors, in sleeplessness, in fastings" (2 Cor. 6:5). How those first apostles did suffer! And how we do suffer together with them.

Sweden is a most remarkable place in many ways. When I was in Sweden, the power of God was upon me, and it was there that I was arrested for preaching these wonderful truths, for talking about the deep things of God, and for being used by God to heal all kinds of people.

A certain denomination, along with a group of doctors, rose up like an army against me and had special meetings with the king to try to get me out of the country. At last they succeeded. It was in Sweden that I was escorted out by two detectives and two policemen because of the mighty power of God moving among the people in Stockholm. But, beloved, it was very lovely!

One of the nurses in the king's household came to a meeting, and she was healed of leg trouble—I forget whether it was a broken thighbone or a dislocated joint. She went to the king and said, "I have been so wonderfully healed by this man. You know I am walking all right now."

"Yes," he said, "I know everything about him. Tell him to go. I do not want him to be turned out. If he leaves, he can come back; but if he is turned out, he cannot come back."

I thank God I was not turned out—I was escorted out.

Some of the people went to see the police to see if I could have a big meeting in the park on the following Monday. The policemen joined together and said, "There is only one reason that we could refuse him, and it is this: if that man puts his hands on the sick in the great park, it would take thirty more policemen to guard the situation. But if he will promise us that he will not lay his hands on the people, then we will allow him to use the park."

The people came and asked me if I would agree to the police's stipulation, and I said, "Promise them. I know God is not subject to my laying hands on the people. When the presence of the Lord is there to heal, it does not require hands. Faith is the great operation position. When we believe God, all things are easy."

So they built a platform where I could speak to thousands of people.

I prayed, "Lord, You know. You have never yet been powerless in any place. You know all things; show me how these people can be healed today without having hands laid on them. Show me."

To the people I said, "All of you who would like the power of God to go through you today, healing everything, put your hands up."

There was a great crowd of hands; thousands of hands went up.

"Lord, show me."

And He told me as clearly as anything to pick a person out who stood on a rock. So I told them all to put their hands down except that person. To her I said, "Tell all the people your troubles."

She began to relate her troubles. From her head to her feet she was in so much pain that she felt that if she did not sit down or lie down she would never be able to go on.

"Lift your hands high," I said. Then, "In the name of Jesus, I rebuke from your head to your feet the Evil One, and I believe that God has loosed you."

Oh, how she danced and how she jumped and how she shouted!

That was the first time that God revealed to me that He could heal without the laying on of hands. We had hundreds healed without touching them and hundreds saved without touching them. Our God is a God of mighty power.

IN PRISON IN SWITZERLAND

"In imprisonments" (2 Cor. 6:5). In Switzerland, I have been put into prison twice for this wonderful work. But, praise God, I was brought out all right!

The officers said to me, "We find no fault. We are so pleased. We have found no fault because you are such a great blessing to us in Switzerland." And in the middle of the night, they said, "You can go."

I said, "No. I will only go on one condition—that is, that every officer in the place gets down on his knees and I pray with all of you."

Glory to God!

A HIGH TIDE

Are you ready? "What for?" you ask. To believe the Scriptures. That is necessary. The Scriptures are the foundation that we must have in order to build properly. Christ is the cornerstone; we are all in the building.

Oh, if I could let you see that wonderful city coming down out of heaven! It is made up of millions, trillions, countless numbers of people. It is a city of people coming down out of heaven to be married (Rev. 21:2).

Get ready for that. Claim your rights in God's order. Do not give way. Have faith in God. Believe the Scriptures are for you. If you want a high tide that is rising in the power of God, say, "Lord, give me what I need so that I will be lacking in nothing." Have a real faith. Believe that love covers you, that His life flows through you, that His life-giving Spirit lifts you. This is my prayer:

O God, take these people into Your great pavilion. Lead them, direct them, preserve them, strengthen them, uphold them by Your mighty power. Let the peace that passes understanding, the joy of the Lord, the comfort of the Holy Spirit, be with them. Amen.

219

CHAPTER FIFTEEN

QUESTIONS ANSWERED

Q: What should be our attitude toward the coming of the Lord? Should we be enjoying His personal presence now, disregarding the time of His coming, or should we wait for and anticipate His coming?

A: Do what Peter did: he hastened toward Christ's coming (2 Pet. 3:12), and he left everything behind him to catch a glimpse of it. You have to keep your mind on it, looking toward and hastening it. Christ's coming is a joy to the church; it is that *"blessed hope"*; it is that *"glorious appearing"* (Titus 2:13). Keeping your mind on it will save you from a number of troubles, for he who looks for it purifies himself (1 John 3:2–3).

Q: Does the wrestling referred to in the following passage mean wrestling in prayer?

> *For we do not wrestle against flesh and blood, but against principalities, against powers, against the rulers of the darkness of this age, against spiritual hosts of wickedness in the heavenly places.* (Eph. 6:12)

A: According to 2 Corinthians 10:5, we are able to strike the Enemy and bring every thought into perfect obedience to the law of Christ:

> *Casting down arguments ["imaginations," KJV] and every high thing that exalts itself against the knowledge of God, bringing every thought into captivity to the obedience of Christ.*

Now, are we able to do this through prayer or through something else? It is quite clear to me that faith inspires us to pray, but faith will command us to command. If we are in the place of real faith, when opposition comes against us, we will say, "Get behind me" (Matt. 16:23), no matter what it is.

Prayer is without accomplishment unless it is accompanied by faith. Jude said we can pray in the Holy Spirit (Jude 20). Be sure that you are filled with the Spirit, that it is not you who is praying but Another. Be sure that you are filled with the life of Christ until faith rises, claims, destroys, and brings down imaginations and everything that opposes Christ.

Q: Which is the right way to baptize—in the name of Jesus, or in the name of the Father, Son, and Holy Spirit?

A: Water baptism in the name of Jesus causes more trouble than anything else, and we should never have trouble in the church; we should be at peace. The Lord said that we are to baptize in the name of the Father, Son, and Holy Spirit (Matt. 28:19), and when we stay in the right order, as He said, then there is no schism in the body.

When we do things our own way and set out on a new path, we cause dissension and trouble. Baptizing in the name of Jesus has caused more trouble than anything else because people have not been satisfied to stop there; they have gone further and said that Jesus is the Father, Jesus is the Son, and Jesus is the Holy Spirit. If we do not keep on the right track, adhering to the words that Jesus spoke, we will be toppled over in awful distress and darkness. Stay on the high road.

Q: Does a person have to go to school in order to save souls?

A: I think a believer will save more souls outside of school. What we have to understand is that soul-saving work is never made in schools. Soul-saving work is the regeneration of the spirit, of the life; it causes a believer to be eaten up with the zeal of the Lord. Soul saving is the best thing; it is the sure place, the right place, and I hope we are doing it when Christ comes.

Q: What is meant when it is said that Jesus *"did not consider it robbery to be equal with God"* (Phil. 2:6)?

A: It means that Jesus was equal with God in power, in authority, and in glory. He was perfectly one with the Father (John 10:30). What His Father was, He was; they were perfectly joined. Yet in order to act in perfect obedience, so that all people could learn obedience, He left heaven, left everything behind, to save us. He had the right to stop and say, "Father, You go," but He was willing to go. He left heaven even though He had the right not to leave.

Q: Suppose that a contract is entered into by two people and is then broken by one party. Should damages be collected by law by the other party?

A: Yes, if you live in the law. But if you live in the Spirit, then you will not go to law with your brother. So, the answer depends on whether you live in law or live in grace. If you live in grace, you will never go into law.

I thank God that although I was in business for twenty-five years and might have picked up a lot of money, it is still there because I would not go to law. I do not believe in it.

But I am not a law to you people. I tell you what law is and what grace is.

Q: What is the seal put upon God's people?

A: The seal is the Holy Spirit. It is different from anything else. It is upon you, and the Devil knows it; all the evil powers of the earth know it. You are sealed with the Holy Spirit of promise until the day of redemption (Eph. 1:13–14). You are also baptized in the same Spirit, and that truth is in the Epistles.

All who are in Christ will be *"caught up"* (1 Thess. 4:17) at His coming. The twenty-second chapter of Luke distinctly says that Jesus will not sit down again to break bread until the kingdom has come (vv. 15–16). Now, the kingdom is in every believer, and Jesus will not sit down until every believer is there. The kingdom is in the believer, and the kingdom will come, and I am sure millions and millions of people will be there who were never baptized with the Holy Spirit but had the life of Christ inside. It is not the Holy Spirit who is the life: Christ is the life (Col. 3:4). When Christ comes, who is our life, we will go to Him.

Q: Is it every Christian's privilege to have his eyes so preserved that he never needs to wear glasses?

A: The aging process affects every person. There are many people who have been praying ever since they were ten years old, and if praying and the life within them could have altered the situation, it would have been altered. But I see that many are here today with gray hair and white hair; this shows that the natural man decays, and you cannot do what you like with it. But the supernatural man may so abound in the natural man that it never decays; it can be replaced by divine life.

There comes a time in life when at age fifty or so, all eyes, without exception, begin to grow dim. However, although the natural man has had a change, I believe and affirm that the supernatural power can be so ministered to us that even our eyesight can be preserved right through. But I say this: any person who professes to have faith and then gets a large print Bible so that he will not need glasses is a fool. It presents a false impression before the people. He must see that if he wants to carry a Bible that is not huge, his eyesight may require some help, or he may not be able to read correctly.

I have been preaching faith to my people for thirty years. When my daughter came back from Africa and saw her mother and me with glasses, she was amazed. When our people saw us put glasses on the first time, they were very troubled. They were no more troubled than we were. But I found it was far better to be honest with the people and acknowledge my condition than get a Bible with large print and deceive the people and say that my eyesight was all right. I like to be honest.

My eyesight gave way at about age fifty-three, and somehow God is doing something. I am now sixty-eight, and I do not need a stronger prescription than I needed then, and I am satisfied that God is restoring me.

When I was seeking this way of divine healing, I was baffled because all the people who had mighty testimonies of divine healing were wearing glasses. I said, "I cannot go on with this thing. I am baffled every time I see the people preaching divine healing wearing glasses." And I got such a bitterness in my spirit that God had to settle me along that line—and I believe that I have not yet fully paid the price.

My eyes will be restored, but until then, I will not deceive anybody. I will wear glasses until I can see perfectly.

A woman came up to me one day, and I noticed that she had no teeth. "Why," I said, "your mouth is very uneven. Your gums have dropped in some places, and they are very uneven."

"Yes," she said, "I am trusting the Lord for a new set of teeth."

"That is very good," I said. "How long have you been trusting Him for them?"

"Three years."

"Look here," I said, "I would be like Gideon. I would put the fleece out, and I would tell the Lord that I would trust Him to send me teeth in ten days or money to buy a set in ten days. Whichever came first, I would believe it was from Him."

In eight days, fifty dollars came to her from a person whom she had never been acquainted with in any way, and it bought her a beautiful set of teeth—and she looked nice in them.

Often I pray for a person's eyesight, and as soon as he is prayed for, he believes, and God stimulates his faith, but his eyesight is about the same. "What should I do?" he asks. "Should I go away without my glasses?"

"Can you see perfectly?" I ask. "Do you need any help?"

"Yes. If I were to go without my glasses, I would stumble."

"Put your glasses on," I say, "for when your faith is perfected, you will no longer need your glasses. When God perfects your faith, your glasses will drop off. But as long as you need them, use them."

You can take that for what you like, but I believe in common sense.

Chapter Twelve

Our Calling
Part One

Beloved, I believe that the Lord would have us this morning to consider the gifts. I will more or less be speaking to preachers and to those who desire to be preachers. I want to speak to you from the fourth chapter of Ephesians. We will begin with the first verse:

I, therefore, the prisoner of the Lord, beseech you to walk worthy of the calling with which you were called, with all lowliness and gentleness, with longsuffering, bearing with one another in love, endeavoring to keep the unity of the Spirit in the bond of peace. There is one body and one Spirit, just as you were called in one hope of your calling; one Lord, one faith, one baptism; one God and Father of all, who is above all, and through all, and in you all. But to each one of us grace was given according to the measure of Christ's gift. Therefore He says: "When He ascended on high, He led captivity captive, and gave gifts to men." (Now this, "He ascended"; what does it mean but that He also first descended into the lower parts of the earth? He who descended is also the One who ascended far above all the heavens, that He might fill all things.) And He Himself gave some to be apostles, some prophets, some evangelists, and some pastors and teachers, for the equipping of the saints for the work of ministry, for the edifying of the body of Christ, till we all come to the unity of the faith and of the knowledge of the Son of God, to a perfect man, to the measure of the stature of the fullness of Christ.

(Eph. 4:1–13)

CALLED BY GOD TO PREACH THE GOSPEL

I would like to utter those same words that Paul uttered in 1 Corinthians 14:5: *"I wish you all spoke with tongues, but even more that you prophesied."* I believe that there is no way to make proclamation but by the Spirit. And I believe that those who are sent are chosen and called by God to be sent. And so, as we study this passage from Ephesians, I trust that everyone will understand what his calling is in the Spirit, and what the Lord demands of us as preachers.

In the face of God and in the presence of His people, we should be able to behave ourselves in a way that is so appropriate and pleasing to the Lord that we always leave behind us a life of blessing and power without creating strife.

It is a great choice to become a preacher of the Gospel, to handle the Word of Life. We who handle the Word of Life ought to be well equipped in the areas of common sense and judgment, and we must not be given to anything that is contrary to the Word of God. There should always be in us such deep reverence toward God and His Word that under all circumstances we would not forfeit our principles along the lines of the faith that God has revealed to us by the truth.

Today I believe God will show us how wonderful we may be in the order of the Spirit, for God wants us to be always in the Spirit. He wants us to rightly divide the Word of Truth (2 Tim. 2:15) so that it will give strength to weakness in all who hear it. It will bring oil to the troubled heart. It will bring rest. The Word of God will make us know that, having done all, we may stand in the trial (Eph. 6:13).

God wants us to know that there is strength by the power of the Spirit. There is an equipping of character to bring us into likemindedness with the Lord. We must know that to be baptized in the Holy Spirit is to leave our own lives, as it were, out of all questioning, to leave ourselves out of all pleasing, and in the name of Jesus to come into like-mindedness with Him.

How Jesus pleased God! How He brought heaven to earth, and all earth moved at the mightiness of the presence of heaven in the midst! We must see our calling in the Spirit, for God has chosen us. We must remember that it is a great choice.

Turning to the tenth chapter of Romans, we read,

And how shall they preach unless they are sent? As it is
written: "How beautiful are the feet of those who preach the
gospel of peace, who bring glad tidings of good things!"
(Rom. 10:15)

We want to be sent. It is a great thing to be called by God to preach
"the unsearchable riches of Christ" (Eph. 3:8).

You have in this land, and we have in our land, men of note
and of authority, who are looked to for answers to social problems.
I often think that a statesman has a wonderful time, but not a time
like a preacher. He only preaches about natural things, but the
man who handles the Word of God preaches supernatural life and
immortality that swallows up the natural life. When we come into
this blessed life, we know that we are teaching principles and ideals
that are for life eternal.

God has given to us in the Spirit. Behold, we are spiritual children today, and we must know that we have to be spiritual all the
time. God forbid that we should ever be like the Galatian church in
that after we have been in the Spirit, we come into the flesh (Gal.
3:3). We are allowed to go into the Spirit, but we are never allowed
to go into the flesh after we have been in the Spirit. And so, God
gives such an idea of this high order in the Spirit so that we may be
moved by its power to see how we may be strengthened and come
into full faith in the Lord.

Let me turn to the first verse of this wonderful fourth chapter of
Ephesians: *"I, therefore, the prisoner of the Lord, beseech you to walk*
worthy of the calling with which you were called." When Paul wrote
this, he was in prison. If I can take a word from anyone, I can take
it from anyone who is in prison for taking a stand for the Word of
God. I have never completely read a book except the Bible, but
there are some things I have read in *The Pilgrim's Progress* that
have helped me very much. It was when John Bunyan was in
prison that God awakened him on so many wonderful lines of
thought. How Paul must have read the Word right into the hearts
of those who came and went when he was bound with chains for
two full years. He could speak about a fullness, freedom, power,
and joy although he was bound with chains.

Fellow believers, there is something in the Gospel that is different from anything else. These early believers could go through
such hardships. Read the first epistle of Peter, and you will see how
the early Christians were scattered. God says that the world wasn't

227

worthy of the people He was filling with His power and that they were in dens and caves of the earth (Heb. 11:38).

Oh, brothers and sisters, there have been some wonderful gems that have passed through the world that have been touched by the Master's hand. There have been some wonderful men in the world who have caught the glory as the rays have shone from the Lord's lips by the power of His expression. As they beheld Him, they were fascinated with Him. And I can almost see, as Peter drew near the time of his departure, just what Jesus had said to him:

> *Most assuredly, I say to you, when you were younger, you girded yourself and walked where you wished; but when you are old, you will stretch out your hands, and another will gird you and carry you where you do not wish.*
>
> (John 21:18)

And as Peter drew near to the portals of glory, he wished to be crucified upside down. My word! What grace incarnated in a human body that it should have such ideals of worship!

Oh, beloved, God is the essence of joy to us in a time when all seems barren, when it seems that nothing can help us but the light from heaven that is far brighter than the sun. Then that touches you, then that changes you, and you realize nothing is worthwhile but that.

LOWLINESS AND MEEKNESS

How Paul spoke to us from prison about *"the calling with which you were called, with all lowliness and gentleness"* (Eph. 4:1–2). He spoke to the preacher. Let no person in this place think that he cannot become a preacher. Let none think he cannot reach this ideal of lowliness and meekness. God can bring us all to that place.

Some preachers get the idea that nobody ought to say a word until he is established. I, however, like to hear the bleating of the lambs. I like to hear the life of the young believers. I like to hear something coming right from heaven into the soul as they rise the first time with tears streaming from their eyes, telling of the love of Jesus.

The Holy Spirit fell upon a young man outside a church. He went into the church, where they were all very sedate. If anything were to move in that church out of the ordinary, my word, it would be extraordinary! And this young man, with his fullness of life and zeal for the Master, started shouting and praising the Lord and manifesting the joy of the Lord, and he disturbed the old saints.

In this church, an old man was reading the Psalms quietly one day. It touched the young Spirit-filled man who was sitting behind him. And the young man shouted, "Glory!" Said the old man, "Do you call that religion?"

The father of the young man was one of the deacons of the church. The other deacons gathered around him and said, "You must talk to your boy and make him understand that he has to wait until he is established before he manifests those things."

So the father had a long talk with the boy and told him what the deacons had said. "You know," he said, "I must respect the deacons, and they have told me they won't have this thing. You have to wait until you are established."

As they neared their home, their horse made a sudden and complete stop. The father tried to make it go forward or backward, but the horse would not move for anything.

"What is up with the horse?" asked the father of the boy. "Father," replied the boy, "this horse has gotten established."

I pray God the Holy Spirit that we will not get established in that way. God, loose us from these old, critical, long-faced, poisoned countenances, which haven't seen daylight for many days. Some come into the sanctuary and act in a terrible way. May the Lord save Pentecost from going to dry rot. Yes, deliver us from any line of sentimentality, anything that is not reality. For remember, we must have the reality of supernatural quickening until we are sane and active and not in any way dormant, but filled with life, God working in us mightily by His Spirit.

We must always be in a transforming position, not in a conforming condition, always renewing the mind, always being renovated by the mighty thoughts of God, always being brought into line with what God has said to us by the Spirit. *"This is the way, walk in it"* (Isa. 30:21). *"Walk in the Spirit, and you shall not fulfill the lust of the flesh"* (Gal. 5:16).

Lord, how will we do it? Can a man be meek and lowly and filled with joy? Do these things work together? *"Out of the abundance of the heart the mouth speaks"* (Matt. 12:34). The depths of

God come in with lowliness and meekness and cause the heart to love. There is no heart that can love like the heart that God has touched.

Oh, the love that is made to love the sinner! There is no love like it. I always feel I can spend any amount of time with the sinner. Oh, brother, there is a love that is God's love! There is a love that only comes by the principles of the Word of God. He loved us and gave Himself for us (Gal. 2:20).

When that meekness and lowliness of mind take hold, the preacher is moved by his Creator to speak from heart to heart and move the people. We must be moved by an inward power and an inward ideal of principles. We must have ideals that come from the throne of God. We must live in the throne, live on the throne, and let Him be enthroned, and then He will lift us to the throne.

INTERPRETATION OF A MESSAGE IN TONGUES:
Out of the depths He has called us; into the heights He has brought us; unto the uttermost He has saved us, to make us kings and priests unto God. For we are His property, His own, His loved ones. Therefore, He wants to clothe us with the gifts of the Spirit and make us worthy for His ministry.

Glory to God! Thank the Lord!

A LOVE THAT BEARS WITH OTHERS

"With all lowliness and gentleness, with longsuffering, bearing with one another in love" (Eph. 4:2).

Oh, how we need to bear *"with one another in love."* Oh, how this is contrary to hardness of heart, contrary to the evil powers, contrary to the natural mind. It is a divine revelation, and you cannot bear with others until you know how God has borne with you. It is God's love toward you that gives you tender, compassionate love toward one another.

It is only the broken, contrite heart that has received the mark of God. And it is only in that secluded place, where He speaks to you alone and encourages you when you are down and out. When no hand is stretched out to you, He stretches out His hand with mercy and brings you into a place of compassion. And then you cannot think evil; then you cannot in any way act harshly. God has brought you into longsuffering, with tenderness and with love.

Oh, this love! Many times my two brothers have been under conviction and have wept under conviction as I have tried to bring them into the light. But up until now, neither of them is in the light. I believe that God will bring them.

In the church of God, where a soul is on fire, kindled with the love of God, there is a deeper love between me and that brother than there is between me and my earthly brother. Oh, this love that I am speaking about is divine love; it is not human love. It is higher than human love; it is more devoted to God. It will not betray. It is true in everything. You can depend on it. It won't change its character. In divine love, you will act exactly as He would act, for you will act with the same spirit. *"As He is, so are we in this world"* (1 John 4:17).

As you rise into association with Him in the Spirit, as you walk with Him *"in the light as He is in the light"* (1 John 1:7), then the fellowship becomes unique in all its plan. I pray that God will help us to understand it so that we will be able to be clothed upon as we have never been, with another majestic touch, with another ideal of heaven.

No one can love like God. And when He takes us into this divine love, we will precisely understand this word, this verse, for it is full of entreaty; it is full of passion and compassion; it has every touch of Jesus right in it. It is so lovely: *"With all lowliness and gentleness, with longsuffering, bearing with one another in love"* (Eph. 4:2).

Isn't it glorious? You cannot find it anywhere else. You cannot get these pictures in any place you go. I challenge you to go into any library in the world and find words coined or brought forth like these words, unless they are copied from this Word. They aren't in nature's garden; they are in God's. It is the Spirit explaining, for He alone can explain this ideal of beatitudes. These words are marvelous; they are beautiful; they are full of grandeur; they are God's. Hallelujah!

I hope you are having a good time, for I am just being filled with new wine this morning. Oh, it is lovely!

KEEPING OUR EYES ON GOD

"Endeavoring to keep the unity of the Spirit in the bond of peace" (Eph. 4:3). This is one of the main principles of this chapter in Ephesians. Beloved, let us keep in mind this very thought today.

I am speaking this morning, by the grace of God, to the preacher. It should never be known that any preacher caused any distraction or detraction, or any split or disunion in a meeting. The preacher has lost his anointing and his glory if he ever stoops to anything that would weaken the assembly in any way.

The greatest weakness of any preacher is to draw men to himself. It is a fascinating point, but you must stay away from fascination. If you don't crucify your *"old man"* (Rom. 6:6) in every area, you are not going into divine lines with God. When the people wanted to make Jesus king, He withdrew Himself to pray. Why? It was a human desire of the people. What did He want? His kingdom was a spiritual kingdom. He was to reign over demon powers. He was to have power over the passions of human life. He was to reign supremely over everything that is earthly, so that all the people might know that He was divine.

He is our pattern, beloved. When the people want to make anything of you, He will give you grace to refuse. The way to get out of it is to find that there is nothing in the earth that is worthy of Him, that there is no one in the world who is able to understand except Him, that everything will crumble to the dust and become worthless. Only that which is divine will last.

Every time you draw anyone to yourself, this action has a touch of earth. It does not speak of the highest realm of the thoughts of God. There is something about it that cannot bear the light of the Word of God. Keep men's eyes off you, but get their eyes on the Lord. Live in the world without a touch or taint of any natural thing moving you. Live high in the order and authority of God, and see that everything is bearing you on to greater heights and depths and greater knowledge of the love of God.

When you are living this way, you will help any assembly you go to, and everybody will get a blessing and will see how much richer they are because you brought them Jesus. Only Jesus! He is too big for any assembly, and He is little enough to fill every heart. We will always go on to learn of Him. Whatever we know, the knowledge is so small compared with what He has to give us. And so, God's plan for us in giving us Jesus is all things, for all things consist in Him. *"All things were made through Him, and without Him nothing was made that was made"* (John 1:3). *"In Him we live and move and have our being"* (Acts 17:28). And when it is a spiritual being and an activity of holiness, see how wonderfully we grow in the Lord. Oh, it is just lovely!

INTERPRETATION OF A MESSAGE IN TONGUES:

Yes, it is the Lord Himself. He comes forth, clothed upon, to clothe you in your weakness, to strengthen you in your helplessness, to uphold you in the limitation of your knowledge, to unfold the mysteries of the kingdom in the dire straits where two ways meet and you do not know where to go. He says, "This is the way." When you are in such a distressing place that no hand but God is able to lead you out, then He comes to you and says, "Be strong and fear not, for I am with you."

Hallelujah! Praise the Lord of glory! He is the everlasting King and will reign forever and ever and ever. Glory! Glory! Amen!

INTERPRETATION OF A MESSAGE IN TONGUES:

God has spoken, and He will make it clear, for He is in the midst of you to open your mind and reveal unto you all the mysteries of the kingdom, for the God of grace is with you. For God is greater than all unto you. He is making your way straight before you, for the Lord is He who comforts you as He comforted Israel, and He will lead you into His power. His right hand is with you to keep you in all your ways lest you should dash your foot against a stone, for the Lord will uphold you.

How beautiful is the Scripture coming to us this morning! How lively it appears to us! And now we can understand something about the fourteenth chapter of 1 Corinthians:

> *I will pray with the spirit, and I will also pray with the understanding. I will sing with the spirit, and I will also sing with the understanding.* (1 Cor. 14:15)

So God is bringing us right into the fullness of the Pentecostal power as it was given in the first days. God wants us to know that after we have been brought into this divine life with Christ, we are able to speak in the Spirit, and we are able to sing in the Spirit. We are also able to speak with the understanding and sing with the understanding. Ah, hallelujah! This is a good day!

KEEPING THE BODY IN PERFECT UNITY

I think I ought to say a few more words concerning Ephesians 4:3: *"Endeavoring to keep the unity of the Spirit in the bond of peace.*" Beloved, I want you, above all things, to remember that the church is one body. She has many members, and we are all members of that one body. At any cost, we must not break up the body, but rather keep the body in perfect unity. Never try to get the applause of the people by any natural thing. Yours is a spiritual work. Yours has to be a spiritual breath. Your word has to be the Word of God. Your counsel to the church has to be such that it cannot be declared untrue. You have to have such solid, holy reverence in every area so that every time you handle anybody, you handle them for God, and you handle the church as the church of God. By that means, you keep the church bound together.

As the people of the church are bound together in one Spirit, they grow into that temple in the Lord (Eph. 2:21), and they all have one voice, one desire, and one plan. And when they want souls saved, they are all of one mind. I am speaking now about spiritual power. If you get the people into the mind of the Spirit with Christ, all their desires will be the same as the desires of Christ the Head. And so nothing can break the church along those lines.

As a preacher, you must never try to save yourself along any line. You must always be above mentioning a financial matter on your side. Always mention your need before God in the secret place, but never bring it to an assembly. If you do, you drop in the estimation of the assembly. You are allowed to tell any need belonging to the assembly or the church management, but never refer to your personal need on the platform.

If a man preaches faith, he must live it, and a man is not supposed to preach unless he preaches a living faith. And he must so impress it upon the people that they will always know that God has taken him on for a special plan, and that he is not an ordinary man. After we are called by God and chosen for Him, we are not supposed to have ordinary men's plans. We ought to have God's ideals only.

Here is another thing that I think is perhaps more essential to you than anything else: you preachers, never drop into an assembly and say the Lord sent you, because sometimes the assembly has as much going on as she can manage. But it is right for you to get your orders from heaven. Never go unless you are really sent. Be sure you are sent by God.

Brothers and sisters, can you be out of God's will when you hear His voice? *"My sheep hear My voice...and they follow Me"* (John 10:27). Oh, that God today will help us by the mind of the

Spirit to understand. I believe God has a message on fire. He has men clothed by Him. He has men sent by Him. Will you be the men? Will you be the women?

You ask, "Can I be the man? Can I be the woman?" Yes. God says, *"Many are called, but few are chosen"* (Matt. 22:14). Are you the chosen ones? Those who desire to be chosen, will you allow God to choose you? Then He will put His hand upon you. And in the choice, He will give you wisdom; He will lead you forth; He will stand by you in the narrow place; He will lead you every step of the way, for the Lord's anointed will go forth and bring forth fruit, and their fruit will remain (John 15:16).

INTERPRETATION OF A MESSAGE IN TONGUES:
Behold, now is the day of decision. Yield now while the moment of pressure by the presence of God comes. Yield now and make your consecration to God.

The altar is ready now for all who will obey.

CHAPTER SEVENTEEN

OUR CALLING
PART TWO

INTERPRETATION OF A MESSAGE IN TONGUES:
The Lord is that Spirit that moves in the regenerated and brings us to the place where fire can begin and burn and separate and transform and make us all know that God has made an inroad into every order. We have to be divine, spiritual, changed, and on fire to catch all the rays of His life. First, burning out; second, transforming; and third, making us fit to live or die.

Oh, thank God for that interpretation. To continue our subject of the last meeting, I want to turn your attention again to the fourth chapter of Ephesians. I will start with the first verse:

I, therefore, the prisoner of the Lord, beseech you to walk worthy of the calling with which you were called, with all lowliness and gentleness, with longsuffering, bearing with one another in love, endeavoring to keep the unity of the Spirit in the bond of peace. There is one body and one Spirit, just as you were called in one hope of your calling; one Lord, one faith, one baptism; one God and Father of all, who is above all, and through all, and in you all. But to each one of us grace was given according to the measure of Christ's gift. Therefore He says: "When He ascended on high, He led captivity captive, and gave gifts to men." (Now this, "He ascended"; what does it mean but that He also first descended into the lower parts of the earth? He

*who descended is also the One who ascended far above all
the heavens, that He might fill all things.) And He Himself
gave some to be apostles, some prophets, some evangelists,
and some pastors and teachers, for the equipping of the
saints for the work of ministry, for the edifying of the body
of Christ, till we all come to the unity of the faith and of
the knowledge of the Son of God, to a perfect man, to the
measure of the stature of the fullness of Christ.*

(Eph. 4:1–13)

PASS IT ON

This morning, as on the previous morning, I believe that the
Lord especially wants me to emphasize facts that will bless and
strengthen preachers. If there is anything of importance, it is for
preachers, because God must have preachers in the place of building and edifying the church. And preachers must be in that order
of the Spirit in which God can work through them for the needs of
the church.

As it was only out of the brokenness of Paul's life that blessing
came forth, so it is out of the emptiness and brokenness and yieldedness of our lives that God can bring forth all His glories through
us to others. And as one man said earlier in today's service, unless
we pass on what we receive, we will lose it. If we didn't lose it, it
would become stagnant.

Virtue is always manifested through blessings that you have
passed on. Nothing will be of any importance to you except what
you pass on to others. God wants us to be so in the order of the
Spirit that when He breaks upon us the alabaster box of ointments,
which represents the precious anointing that He has for every child
of His, we will be filled with perfumes of holy incense for the sake
of others. Then we may be poured out for others, others may receive the graces of the Spirit, and the entire church may be edified.
And this church will never know one dry day, but there will always
be freshness and life that make all of your hearts burn together as
you know that the Lord has talked with you once more.

We must have this inward burning desire for more of God. We
must not be at any stationary point. We must always have the most
powerful telescopes, looking at and hurrying toward what God has
called us to, so that He may perfect that forever.

Oh, what a blessed inheritance of the Spirit God has for us in these days, so that we should no longer be barren or unfruitful, but rather filled with all fullness, increasing with all increasings, having a measureless measure of the might of the Spirit in the inner man, so that we are always like a great river that presses on and heals everything that it touches. Oh, let it be so today!

INTERPRETATION OF A MESSAGE IN TONGUES:

The Lord has awakened in us the divine touches of His spiritual favor to make us know that He is here with all that you require if you are ready to take it.

But are we ready to take it? If we are, God can give us wonderful things. We must be always hungry, always ready for every touch of God.

WHAT IT MEANS TO BE A PEACEMAKER

In the first part of this sermon, if you remember, we were dwelling upon Ephesians 4:3: *"Endeavoring to keep the unity of the Spirit in the bond of peace."* It was a very precious word to us because it meant that under any circumstances we would not have our own way but God's way. We have God's way for the person and for the church.

Of all the things God intends for us to be, He intends for us to be peacemakers. Yes, He wants us to have a pure love, a love that always helps someone else at its own expense. I won't find a Scripture to help me in this area as much as Matthew 5:23–24:

Therefore if you bring your gift to the altar, and there remember that your brother has something against you, leave your gift there before the altar, and go your way. First be reconciled to your brother, and then come and offer your gift.

Most Christians are satisfied with the first meaning of this passage, but the second meaning is deeper. Most people believe it is perfectly right, if you have offended another, to go to that person and say, "Please forgive me," and you win your brother when you take that part. But this is the deeper sense: *"If you...remember that your brother has something against you,"* go and forgive him his transgressions. It is so much deeper than getting your own side right to go and get his side right by forgiving him of all that he has done.

That will be a stepping stone to very rich grace in the area of keeping *"the unity of the Spirit in the bond of peace"* (Eph. 4:3). Someone may say, "I cannot forgive them because she did that and he said that. You know, he didn't recognize me at all. And he hasn't smiled at me for at least six months." Poor thing! May God help you through evil report and good report (2 Cor. 6:4, 8). God can take us right through if we get to the right side of grace.

My brother, when you get to the place of forgiving your brother who has something against you, you will find that that is the greatest ideal of going on to perfection, and the Lord will help us *"to keep the unity of the Spirit in the bond of peace"* (Eph. 4:3).

I like that *"bond of peace."* It is an inward bond between you and another child of God. *"Bond of peace."* Hallelujah! Oh, glory to God!

ONE BODY

"There is one body and one Spirit, just as you were called in one hope of your calling" (Eph. 4:4). We must recognize that there is only one body. It seems to me that at one time God would have made such an inroad of truth into all nations through the Plymouth Brethren, if they had only recognized that there were more people in the body than just the Plymouth Brethren. You will never gain interest unless you see that in every church there is a nucleus that has as real a God as you have.

It is only along these lines, I believe, that the longsuffering of God waits for the precious fruit (James 5:7). The longsuffering of God is with the believers who have the idea that only those in their church are right, or those in their city, or those in their country. It is all foolishness.

It is foolishness for fancy people to sit around their table and think that their table is the only table. What about the hundreds of people I know who are sitting around their tables every day and are partaking of the bread and the wine? Brother, the body of Christ consists of all who are in Christ.

While we know the Holy Spirit is the only power that can take the church up, we also know that the Holy Spirit will go with the church. The Scriptures are very definite in saying that all who are Christ's at His coming will be changed. It seems that we cannot be all Christ's unless something is done, and God will sweep away so many things that are spoiling things. We must reach the place of perfect love, and we will see that God can make even those in Caesar's household a part of His family (Phil. 4:22). Glory to God!

INTERPRETATION OF A MESSAGE IN TONGUES:
It is the Spirit that joins us and makes us one. It is the health of the Spirit that goes through the body, that quickens the body and makes it appear as one.

Oh, the body appearing as one body! Oh, the entire body possessing the same joy, the same peace, the same hope! No division, all one in Christ! What a body! Who can make a body like that? It seems to me that this body is made deep in the Cross. Hundreds of people are carrying a cross around their necks. I could never carry a cross. Christ has carried the cross; He has borne the shame. I find that right there in that atoning blood is cleansing and purifying. The blood takes away all impurities and everything that will mar the vessel. God is making a vessel for honor, fit for the Master's use (2 Tim. 2:21), joined with that body—one body.

Let us be careful that we do not in any way defile the body, because God is chastening the body and fitting it together and bringing it together. The body of Christ will rise. You ask, "How will it rise?" It will rise in millions and billions and trillions, more than any man can number. It will be a perfect body.

Oh, there is one body! It is a lovely body. I look at you; I see you. I look in your faces, and I know there is a closer association than one can tell or speak about. Oh, beloved, there is something deeper down in the spirit of the regenerated person when the impurities of life and of the flesh fall off. Oh, there is a resemblance, a likeness, a perfection of holiness, of love! O God, take away the weaknesses and all the depravities.

"Now you are the body of Christ, and members individually ["in particular," KJV]" (1 Cor. 12:27). I like the word "particular"; it tells us that there is just the right place for us. God sees us in that place. He is making us fit in that place so that for all time we will have a wonderful place in that body. Ah, it is so lovely!

Oh, these exhaustless things! Brothers, sisters, it isn't the message; it is the heart. It isn't the heart; it is the Christ. It isn't the Christ; it is the God. It isn't the God; it is the whole body. This is deeper and more precious than we have any conception of!

THE CALLING

"There is one body and one Spirit, just as you were called in one hope of your calling" (Eph. 4:4). I feel that God would have me say a word about the calling. Many people who are called miss the call because they are dull of hearing. There is something in the call, beloved. *"Many are called, but few are chosen"* (Matt. 22:14). I want a big heart this morning to believe that all will be chosen. You ask, "Can it be so?" Yes, beloved, it can—not a few chosen, but many chosen.

And how will the choice be made? The choice is always your choice first. You will find that gifts are your choice first. You will find that salvation is your choice. God has made it all, but you have to choose. And so God wants you especially this morning to make an inward call, to be in a great intercessory condition of imploring the Holy One to prepare you for that wonderful spiritual body.

Called! Beloved, I know that some people have the idea (and it is a great mistake) that because they are not successful in everything they touch, because they have failed in so many things that they desire to go forward in, because they don't seem to aspire in prayer as some do and perhaps don't enter into the fullness of tongues, there is no hope for them in this calling. Satan comes and says, "Look at that black list of your weaknesses and infirmities! You can never expect to be in that calling!"

Yes, you can, beloved! God says it in the Scriptures. Oh, beloved, it is the weakness that is made strong! It is the last who can be made first (Matt. 19:30). What will make the whole situation different? Confessing our helplessness. God says that He feeds the hungry with good things, but the satisfied He sends away empty (Luke 1:53). If you want to grow in grace and in the knowledge of the grace of God, get hungry enough to be fed; get thirsty enough to cry out; be broken enough that you do not want anything in the world unless He comes Himself.

I was reading last night in my Bible—it was so lovely—that *"God will wipe away every tear from their eyes"* (Rev. 21:4). Ah, you say, that will be in heaven. Thank God that it will also be here. Hallelujah! Let God do it this morning. Let Him wipe away all tears. Let Him comfort your heart. Let Him strengthen your weakness. Let Him cause you to come into the place of profit. Let Him help you into the place He has chosen for you, for *"many are called, but few are chosen"* (Matt. 22:14). But God has a big choice.

Our Jesus is a big Jesus! If I could measure Him, He would be very small. But I cannot measure Him, and I know He is very large. I am glad I cannot measure Jesus, but I am glad I can touch Him all the same.

ONE BAPTISM

Ephesians 4:5 says, *"One Lord, one faith, one baptism."* I must touch on the thought of baptism this morning. We must get away from the thought of water baptism when we are in the Epistles. If water baptism is at all mentioned in any way in the Epistles, it is always mentioned in the past tense.

We must always remember this, beloved, that while water baptism, in my opinion, is essential—*"He who believes and is baptized will be saved"* (Mark 16:16)—I wouldn't say for a moment that a man could not be saved unless he was baptized in water, because that statement would be contrary to Scripture.

I see there is a blending. If we turn to the third chapter of John's gospel, we find that *"unless one is born of water and the Spirit, he cannot enter the kingdom of God"* (v. 5). I believe God would have us know that we never ought to put aside water baptism. On the contrary, we ought to believe it is in perfect conjunction and in operation with the working of the Spirit so that we may be buried with Christ (Rom. 6:4).

But, oh, the baptism in the Holy Spirit! The baptism of fire! The baptism of power! The baptism of oneness! The baptism of association! The baptism of communion! This is the baptism of the Spirit of life that takes the man, shakes him up, builds him up, and makes him know he is a new creature in the Spirit, worshiping God in the Spirit.

If my preaching and the preaching of those who come on this platform emphasize the baptism with the Holy Spirit, and you have only touches of it, if you stop at that, it will be almost as though you are missing the calling.

John said by the Spirit, *"He who comes after me is preferred before me"* (John 1:15). He also said, *"I indeed baptize you with water unto repentance, but He who is coming after me is mightier than I....He will baptize you with the Holy Spirit and fire"* (Matt. 3:11).

By all means, if you can tarry, you ought to tarry (Luke 24:49). If you have the Spirit's power upon you, go into that room or somewhere else and never cease until God finishes the work.

Churches outside the Pentecostal church that don't have a revival spirit, that don't have people being born again, become dead, dry, barren, and helpless. They enter into entertainment and all kinds of social functions. They live on a natural association and lose their grand, glorious hope.

Now I want to talk about the Pentecostal church. Unless the Pentecostal church is having an increase along the lines of salvation, unless it is continually having baptisms in the Holy Spirit, the Pentecostal church will become dry, lukewarm, and helpless, and you will wonder what church it is.

But if every night somebody stands up to testify that he has received the Holy Spirit, and if others say, "Oh, last night I was saved," that church is ripening. She will not flounder. She is ripening for greater things, for God will take that church.

Beloved, you are responsible for this; the platform is not responsible. The whole church is responsible to keep this place on fire. If you are baptized with the Holy Spirit and you have come into this meeting without an anointing upon you, without being so ready that you feel like bursting into tongues, without having a psalm, hymn, or some spiritual song—unless you have a tongue or interpretation, or unless something is taking place along these lines—you have fallen from the grace of the Pentecostal position.

You talk about a message. God has given us a message this morning if you dare to hear it. We dare to say in the open air and everywhere that we are Pentecostal. If we are Pentecostal, we will be biblical Pentecostals. What is the definition of "biblical Pentecostals"? It is found in 1 Corinthians 14:26:

> *How is it then, brethren? Whenever you come together, each of you has a psalm, has a teaching, has a tongue, has a revelation, has an interpretation. Let all things be done for edification.*

This verse was instruction for a Pentecostal continuance in the Corinthian church. Suppose that what was happening in the Corinthian church was the case of our own Pentecostal church. It would not be possible for sinners to come in without being saved, or for people not having the baptism to come in without becoming hungry and thirsty to come into that fullness. It must be so. God must bring us to a place where we do not have merely a name, but where we have the position that brings the name.

How many of you felt like speaking in tongues as you came into the room this morning? Praise God, there are some. How many of you have a psalm burning in you and feel like singing it in the streets? Praise God, that is very good. How many of you sang a hymn as you came in? Praise the Lord, glory to God! You are doing very well. But don't you see that this is what we have to continue? There has to be a continuance of such things.

INTERPRETATION OF A MESSAGE IN TONGUES:
The hope of the church is springing up by the Spirit through the Word. Therefore, as many of you as are living in the Spirit are putting to death the flesh. You are quickened by the Spirit and live in the realms of His grace.

Praise the Lord, it is the grace of our Lord Jesus. Hallelujah! We can sing, "I will never be cross anymore." Beloved, it is the most wonderful thing on earth when God touches you with this new life in the Spirit. Then, whether you are in a car, a ship, or train, it doesn't matter where you are because you are in the Spirit; you are ready to be caught up.

Oh, beloved, here we are this morning, *"one body"* (Eph. 4:4). Praise the Lord! There is *"one Spirit"* (v. 4). There is *"one baptism"* (v. 5). I am crying to God for these meetings because I believe God can do a great thing in a moment when we are all brought into the line of the Spirit. I wouldn't be surprised no matter what happened.

I was in ten days of meetings in which the attention was on the gifts, and the people got so worked up, as it were, in the Spirit that they felt something new had to happen or else they couldn't live. And it happened. I believe these and other meetings are bringing us to a place of great expectancy.

ONE FAITH

"One Lord, one faith, one baptism" (Eph. 4:5). Just in the proportion that you have the Spirit unfolding to you *"one Lord, one faith, one baptism,"* you have the Holy Spirit incarnated in you, bringing into you a revelation of the Word. Nothing else can reveal the Word, for the Spirit gave the Word through Jesus. Jesus spoke by the Spirit that was in Him, He being the Word. The Spirit brought out all the Word of this life. We must have the

Spirit. If you look in John's gospel, you will find that when the Spirit came, He didn't come to speak about Himself but to bring forth all Jesus said (John 16:13–14).

Just as we have the measure of the Spirit, there will be no measure of unbelief. We will have faith. The church will rise to the highest position when there is no schism in the body along the lines of unbelief. When we all, with one heart and one faith, believe the Word as it is spoken, then signs and wonders and various miracles will be manifested everywhere. This is one accord: *"One Lord, one faith, one baptism"* (Eph. 4:5). Hallelujah!

ABOVE ALL, THROUGH ALL, AND IN YOU ALL

I think that the next verse is probably one of the primary verses of all: *"One God and Father of all, who is above all, and through all, and in you all"* (v. 6). If this spiritual life is in us, we will find that we have no fear. We will have no nervous condition; it will vanish. Every time you have fear, it is imperfect love. Every time you have nervous weaknesses, you will find it is a departure from an inner circle of true faith in God. We read in 1 John 4:18, *"There is no fear in love; but perfect love casts out fear, because fear involves torment. But he who fears has not been made perfect in love."*

There is also a very good word in the sixteenth verse of the same chapter: *"God is love, and he who abides in love abides in God, and God in him."* Where is the man who abides in God? He is swallowed up in God. And when God takes hold of us along these lines, it is remarkable to see that we are encircled and overshadowed by Him.

INTERPRETATION OF A MESSAGE IN TONGUES:
I feel we must magnify the Lord in the Spirit.

"One God and Father of all, who is above all, and through all, and in you all" (Eph. 4:6). God is over all. Take a long look at that. Think about God being through all. See if any satanic powers can work against you. But just think about another fact: He is in you all. How can the Devil have a chance with the body when God is in you all? Hallelujah! Glory!

Don't you see the groundwork, the great base, the rock of the principles of these Scriptures, how they make us know that we are not barren, that we cannot be unfruitful, but that we must always be abounding in the joy of the Lord? We lack because we are short of truth.

When this truth of God lays hold of a man, he is no longer a man. What is he? He is a divine construction. He has a new perception of the ideals of God. He has a new measurement. Now he sees that God is over all things. Now he sees that God is through all things. The whole world can join in a league of nations—they can do as they like—but the Word of God abides forever.

"In you all" (Eph. 4:6). Think of that. God is in you all. Who is God? Who is the Holy Spirit? Who is Jesus? Is it possible to have any conception of the mightiness of the power of God? And yet you take the thoughts of Jesus and see that all the embodiment of the fullness was right in Him. And I have Him. I have the Holy Spirit also, who is as great in equality, for those three are one and are joined equally in power. They are perfectly one.

When the Spirit comes in the body, how many are in the body? You have Jesus, the Holy Spirit, and God. Hallelujah! Talk about Samson carrying the gates (Judg. 16:3)! If you know your position, you will take both the gates and the city. Go in and possess every part of the land, for surely there is a land of gladness, a land of pleasure, a land of peace.

And remember, brothers and sisters, when the Holy Spirit gets an end of us, and we just operate by the Spirit's power and utter the Spirit's words, we find out it is always more and more and more. Oh yes, we will magnify the Lord on all these lines. If we don't, the stones will begin to cry out against us (Luke 19:40).

THE MEASURE OF CHRIST'S GIFT

"But to each one of us grace was given according to the measure of Christ's gift" (Eph. 4:7). This is a great summing up. Oh, beloved, I wish you to see Jesus this morning, because if we don't see Him, we miss a great deal. Grace and gifts are equally abounding in Him. It is as you set your strength on Jesus, it is as you allow the Holy Spirit to penetrate every thought, always bringing on the canvas of the mind a perfect picture of holiness, purity, and righteousness, that you enter into Him and become entitled to all the riches of God.

How do you measure up this morning? God gives a measure. Oh, this is a lovely word: *"But to each one of us grace was given according to the measure of Christ's gift."*

I know that salvation, while it is a perfect work, is an insulation that may have any number of volts behind it. In the days when bare wires were laid, when electric power was obtained from Niagara, I am told that there was a city whose lights suddenly went out. Following the wires, the repairmen came to a place where a cat had gotten on the wires, and the lights had been stopped.

I find that the dynamo of heaven can be stopped with a smaller thing than a cat. An impure thought stops the circulation. An act can stop the growth of the believer. I like Hebrews 4:12:

For the word of God is living and powerful, and sharper than any two-edged sword, piercing even to the division of soul and spirit, and of joints and marrow, and is a discerner of the thoughts and intents of the heart.

Then I find in 2 Corinthians 10:5 these words:

Casting down arguments and every high thing that exalts itself against the knowledge of God, bringing every thought into captivity to the obedience of Christ.

So I find that if I am going to have all the revelations of Jesus brought to me, I am going to attain to all that God has for me through a pure and clean heart, right thoughts, and an inward affection toward Him. Then heaven bursts through my human frame, and all the rays of heaven flow through my body. Hallelujah! It is lovely!

The measure of the gift of Christ remains with you. I cannot go on with inspiration unless I am going on with God in perfection. I cannot know the mind of the natural and the mysteries of the hidden things with God unless I have power to penetrate everything between me and heaven. Nothing goes through but a pure heart, for the pure in heart will see God (Matt. 5:8).

Oh, it is lovely! And I see that the pure heart can come into such closeness with God that the graces are so enriched and the measure of Christ so increased that one knows that he is going on to possess all things.

Nothing comes to my mind that is as beautiful as a soul just developing in his first love and wanting to preach to all people. In Revelation, one church is reproved for having lost its first love. (See

Revelation 2:1–7.) And I believe that God would have us to know that this first love, the great love that Jesus gives us with which to love others, is the primary stepping stone to all these things that we have looked at this morning. I don't know whether there is anyone here who has never lost that first love.

I love the preacher. I love the young man. Oh, how I love the youth who is developing in his character and longing to become a preacher. If you ask me whether I have a preference, I will say, "Yes, I have a preference for a young preacher." I love them. God has perfect positions of development for the preacher.

The young preacher may have greater inward longings to get people saved than he has power over his depravities. And he is hindered in his pursuit into this grandeur of God. I want to take you to a place where there is wonderful safety and security.

God will take into captivity the young life—or the old life—that is longing to preach the glories of Christ but is captive to weaknesses, to failures, and to the power of Satan that has interfered with him. God will take him into captivity if he will let Him, for God has gifts for him. He takes the captive into captivity and surrounds him, keeps him, chastens him, purifies him, cleanses him, washes him. And He is making prophets, apostles, and evangelists of such.

God has never been able to make goodness except out of helplessness, lest we should glory in the flesh. God destroys every bit of flesh so that no flesh can glory in His sight (1 Cor. 1:29). If we have any glory, we will glory in the Lord (v. 31).

Do you want to be preachers? Truly, I know you do. There isn't a child in this place who does not want to bear glad tidings. *"How beautiful are the feet of those who preach the gospel of peace, who bring glad tidings of good things!"* (Rom. 10:15). Oh, glad tidings! What does it mean? Eternal salvation. You talk about gold mines and diamonds and precious stones! Oh, my brother, to save one soul from death! Oh, to be the means of saving many! God has for us a richer treasure than we have any idea of. Don't say you cannot reach it, brother or sister. Never look at yourself; get a great vision of the Master. Let His love so penetrate you that you will absolutely make everything death but Him. And as you see Him in His glory, you will see how God can take you.

I believe that there are many in this place whom God is taking hold of this morning. My brother, don't fail God, but by the measure of faith in Christ, let your hand be outstretched; let your eye be fixed with an eternal fixedness; let an inward passion grip you with the same zeal that gripped the Lord. Let your mind forget all the past. Come into like-mindedness with Jesus, and let Him clothe you.

GOD PERFECTS HIS PEOPLE

"Therefore He says: 'When He ascended on high, He led captivity captive, and gave gifts to men'" (Eph. 4:8). He has gifts for men. You ask, "What kind of men?" Even for rebels. Did they desire to be rebels? No. Sometimes there are transgressions that break our hearts and make us groan and travail. Was it our desire to sin? No. God looks right at the very canvas of your whole life history, and He has set His mind upon you.

I would like you preachers to know that *"eye has not seen, nor ear heard, nor have entered into the heart of man the things which God has prepared for those who love Him"* (1 Cor. 2:9). Your weakness has to be sifted like the chaff before the wind, and every corn will bring forth pure grain after God's mind. The fire will burn like an oven to burn up the stubble (Mal. 4:1), but the wheat will be gathered into the granary, the treasury of the Most High God, and He Himself will lay hold of us.

What is this process for? The perfecting of the saints. Oh, just think—that brokenness of yours is to be made whole like Him; that weakness of yours is to be made strong like Him! You have to bear the image of the Lord in every detail. You have to have the mind of Christ (Phil. 2:5) in perfection, in beauty.

Beloved, don't fail and shrivel because of the hand of God upon you, but think that God must purify you for the perfecting of the saints. Oh, Jesus will help us. Oh, beloved, what are you going to do with this golden opportunity, with this inward pressure of a cry of God in your soul? Are you going to let others be crowned while you lose the crown? Are you willing to be brought into captivity today for God?

Truly, this morning must decide some things. If you are not baptized, you must seek the baptism of the Spirit of God. And if there is anything that has marred the fruit or interfered with all of His plan, I implore you this morning to let the blood so cover, let the anointing of Christ so come, let the vision of Christ be so seen, that you will have a measure that will take all that God has for you.

CHAPTER EIGHTEEN

YOU ARE OUR EPISTLE
PART ONE

G od's Word is very beautiful and very expressive. I want to read to you this morning the entire third chapter of 2 Corinthians:

Do we begin again to commend ourselves? Or do we need, as some others, epistles of commendation to you or letters of commendation from you? You are our epistle written in our hearts, known and read by all men; clearly you are an epistle of Christ, ministered by us, written not with ink but by the Spirit of the living God, not on tablets of stone but on tablets of flesh, that is, of the heart. And we have such trust through Christ toward God. Not that we are suffi-cient of ourselves to think of anything as being from our-selves, but our sufficiency is from God, who also made us sufficient as ministers of the new covenant, not of the letter but of the Spirit; for the letter kills, but the Spirit gives life. But if the ministry of death, written and engraved on stones, was glorious, so that the children of Israel could not look steadily at the face of Moses because of the glory of his countenance, which glory was passing away, how will the ministry of the Spirit not be more glorious? For if the ministry of condemnation had glory, the ministry of right-eousness exceeds much more in glory. For even what was made glorious had no glory in this respect, because of the glory that excels. For if what is passing away was glorious, what remains is much more glorious. Therefore, since we have such hope, we use great boldness of speech; unlike Moses, who put a veil over his face so that the children of

Israel could not look steadily at the end of what was pass-ing away. But their minds were blinded. For until this day the same veil remains unlifted in the reading of the Old Testament, because the veil is taken away in Christ. But even to this day, when Moses is read, a veil lies on their heart. Nevertheless when one turns to the Lord, the veil is taken away. Now the Lord is the Spirit; and where the Spirit of the Lord is, there is liberty. But we all, with un-veiled face, beholding as in a mirror the glory of the Lord, are being transformed into the same image from glory to glory, just as by the Spirit of the Lord. (2 Cor. 3:1–18)

We have this morning one of those high-water marks of very deep things of God in the Spirit. I believe the Lord will reveal to us these truths as our hearts are open and responsive to the Spirit's leadings.

Do not think that you will receive anything from the Lord ex-cept along the lines of a spiritual revelation, for there is nothing that will profit you, or bring you to a place of blessing, except that which denounces or brings to death the natural order so that the supernatural plan of God may be in perfect order in you.

The Lord of Hosts encamps all around us with songs of deliv-erance (Ps. 34:7) so that we may see face to face the glories of His grace in a new way. For God has not brought us into *"cunningly devised fables"* (2 Pet. 1:16), but in these days He is rolling away the mists and clouds and every difficulty so that we may under-stand the mind and will of God.

If we are going to catch the best of God, there must be in this meeting a spiritual desire, an open ear, an understanding heart. The veil must be lifted. We must see the Lord in that perfection of being glorified in the midst of us. As we enter into these things of the Spirit, we must clearly see that we are not going to be able to understand these mysteries that God is unfolding to us unless we are filled with the Spirit.

Even when these special meetings close, the pastor and every-body else will find that we must grow in grace all the time. We must see that God has nothing for us along the old lines. The new plan, the new revelation, the new victories are before us. The ground must be gained; supernatural things must be attained. All carnal things, evil powers, and spiritual wickedness in high places (Eph. 6:12) must be dethroned. We must come into the line of the Spirit by the will of God in these days.

THE WORD OF GOD IN US

Let us turn to the Word, which is very beautiful and expressive in so many ways.

Do we begin again to commend ourselves? Or do we need, as some others, epistles of commendation to you or letters of commendation from you? You are our epistle written in our hearts, known and read by all men; clearly you are an epistle of Christ, ministered by us, written not with ink but by the Spirit of the living God, not on tablets of stone but on tablets of flesh, that is, of the heart. And we have such trust through Christ toward God. (2 Cor. 3:1–4)

This morning I want to dwell upon these words for a short time: *"Clearly you are an epistle of Christ."*

What an ideal position that now the sons of God are being manifested; now the glory is being seen; now the Word of God is becoming an expressed purpose in life until the life has ceased and the Word has begun to live in God's children.

This position was truly in the life of Paul when he came to a climax and said,

I have been crucified with Christ; it is no longer I who live, but Christ lives in me; and the life which I now live in the flesh I live by faith in the Son of God, who loved me and gave Himself for me. (Gal. 2:20)

How can Christ live in you? There is no way for Christ to live in you except by the manifested Word in you, through you, manifestly declaring every day that you are a living epistle of the Word of God. Beloved, God would have us see that no man is perfected or equipped in any area except as the living Word abides in him.

It is the living Christ; it is the divine likeness to God; it is the express image of Him. The Word is the only factor that works out and brings forth in you these glories of identification between you and Christ. It is the Word richly dwelling in your hearts by faith (Col. 3:16).

We may begin at Genesis and go right through the Scriptures and be able to rehearse them, but unless they are a living power within us, they will be a dead letter. Everything that comes to us must be quickened by the Spirit. *"The letter kills, but the Spirit gives life"* (2 Cor. 3:6).

We must have life in everything. Who knows how to pray except as the Spirit prays (Rom. 8:26)? What kind of prayer does the Spirit pray? The Spirit always brings to your remembrance the Scriptures, and He brings forth all your cries and your needs better than your words. The Spirit always takes the Word of God and brings your heart, mind, soul, cry, and need into the presence of God.

So we are not able to pray except as the Spirit prays, and the Spirit only prays according to the will of God (Rom. 8:27), and the will of God is all in the Word of God. No man is able to speak according to the mind of God and bring forth the deep things of God by his own mind. The following Scripture rightly divides the Word of Truth:

> *Clearly you are an epistle of Christ, ministered by us, written not with ink but by the Spirit of the living God, not on tablets of stone but on tablets of flesh, that is, of the heart.*
> (2 Cor. 3:3)

God, help us to understand this, for it is out of the heart that all things proceed (Matt. 12:34). When we have entered in with God into the mind of the Spirit, we will find that God enraptures our hearts.

"Or do you think that the Scripture says in vain, 'The Spirit who dwells in us yearns jealously'?" (James 4:5). I have been pondering over that for years, but now I can see that the Holy Spirit very graciously, very extravagantly, puts everything to one side so that He may enrapture our hearts with a great inward cry for Jesus. The Holy Spirit *"yearns jealously"* for us to have all the divine will of God in Christ Jesus right in our hearts.

When I speak about the *"tablets of flesh, that is, of the heart"* (2 Cor. 3:3), I mean the inward love. Nothing is as sweet to me as to know that the heart yearns with compassion. Eyes may see, ears may hear, but you may be immovable on those two lines unless you have an inward cry where *"deep calls unto deep"* (Ps. 42:7).

When God gets into the depths of our hearts, He purifies every intention of the thoughts and the joys. We are told in the Word that it is *"joy inexpressible and full of glory"* (1 Pet. 1:8).

Beloved, it is true that the commandments were written on tablets of stone. Moses, like a great big loving father over Israel, had a heart full of joy because God had shown him a plan by which Israel could partake of great things through these commandments. But God says that now the epistle of Christ is *"not on tablets of stone"* (2 Cor. 3:3), which made the face of Moses shine with great joy. It is deeper than that, more wonderful than that: the commandments are in our hearts; the deep love of God is in our hearts; the deep movings of eternity are rolling in and bringing God in. Hallelujah!

Oh, beloved, let God the Holy Spirit have His way today in unfolding to us all the grandeurs of His glory.

INTERPRETATION OF A MESSAGE IN TONGUES:

The Spirit, He Himself, it is He who wakes you morning by morning and unfolds to you in your heart, tenderness, compassion, and love toward your Maker until you weep before Him and say to Him in the Spirit, "You are mine! You are mine!"

Yes, He is mine! Beloved, He is mine!

OUR TRUST MUST BE IN GOD

And we have such trust through Christ toward God. Not that we are sufficient of ourselves to think of anything as being from ourselves, but our sufficiency is from God.

(2 Cor. 3:4–5)

Ah, those verses are lovely! We should keep them in mind and read them again later. Beloved, that is a climax of divine exaltation that is very different from human exaltation.

The end is not yet, praise the Lord!
The end is not yet, praise the Lord!
Your blessings He is bestowing,
And my cup is overflowing,
And the end is not yet, praise the Lord!

We need to get to a place where we are beyond trusting in ourselves. Beloved, there is so much failure in self-assurances. It is not bad to have good things along the lines of satisfaction, but we must never rest upon anything in the human. There is only one sure place to rest upon, and our trust is in God.

In His name we go. In Him we trust. And God brings us the victory. When we have no confidence in ourselves, when we do not trust in ourselves, but when our whole trust rests upon the authority of the mighty God, He has promised to be with us at all times, and to make the path straight, and to make a way through all the mountains. Then we understand how it was that David could say, *"Your gentleness has made me great"* (2 Sam. 22:36).

Ah, God is the lover of souls! We have no confidence in the flesh. Our confidence can only be placed in and rest upon the One who never fails, the One who knows the end from the beginning, the One who is able to come in at the midnight hour as easily as at midday. In fact, God makes the night and the day alike to the man who rests completely in His will with the knowledge that *"all things work together for good to those who love God"* (Rom. 8:28) and trust in Him. And we have such trust in Him.

This is the worthy position; this is where God wants all souls to be. We would find that we would not run His errands and make mistakes; we would not be settling down in the wrong place. We would find that our lives were as surely in agreement with the thoughts of God as the leading of the children of Israel through the wilderness. And we would be able to say, "Not one good thing has the Lord withheld from me" (Ps. 84:11), and, *"All the promises of God in Him are Yes, and in Him Amen, to the glory of God through us"* (2 Cor. 1:20).

The Lord has helped me to have no confidence in myself, but to wholly trust in Him. Bless His name!

LIVING IN THE SPIRIT

[God] *also made us sufficient as ministers of the new covenant, not of the letter but of the Spirit; for the letter kills, but the Spirit gives life. But if the ministry of death, written and engraved on stones, was glorious, so that the children of Israel could not look steadily at the face of Moses because of the glory of his countenance, which glory was passing away, how will the ministry of the Spirit not be more glorious? For if the ministry of condemnation had glory, the ministry of righteousness exceeds much more in glory.* (2 Cor. 3:6–9)

Let us reverently think on these great words. If I go on with God, He wants me to understand all His deep things. He doesn't want anybody in the Pentecostal church to be a novice or to deal with the Word of God on natural grounds. We can understand the Word of God only by the Spirit of God.

We cannot define, separate, or deeply investigate and unfold this holy plan of God unless we have the life of God, the thought of God, the Spirit of God, and the revelation of God. The Word of Truth is pure, spiritual, and divine. If you try to discern it on natural grounds, you will only finish up on natural lines for natural man, but you will never satisfy a Pentecostal assembly.

The people who are spiritual can only be fed with spiritual material. So if you are expecting your message to catch fire during the meeting, you will have to bring it on fire to the meeting. You won't have to light up the message during the meeting; you will have to bring the message red-hot, burning, living. The message must be directly from heaven. It must be as truly "Thus says the Lord" as the Scriptures that are "Thus says the Lord," because then you will speak only as the Spirit gives utterance, and you will always be giving fresh revelation. You will never be stale; whatever you say will be fruitful, elevating the mind, lifting the people, and all the people will want more.

To come into this, we must see that we not only need the baptism of the Spirit, but we also need to come to a place where there is only the baptism of the Spirit left. Look at the first verse of the fourth chapter of Luke, and you will catch this beautiful truth: *"Then Jesus, being filled with the Holy Spirit, returned from the Jordan and was led by the Spirit into the wilderness."* But look at Mark 1:12, and you will find that He was *driven* by the Spirit into the wilderness: *"Immediately the Spirit drove Him into the wilderness."*

In John's gospel, Jesus says He does not speak or act of Himself: *"The words that I speak to you I do not speak on My own authority; but the Father who dwells in Me does the works"* (John 14:10).

We must know that the baptism of the Spirit immerses us into an intensity of zeal, into a likeness to Jesus; it makes us into pure, liquid metal so hot for God that it travels like oil from vessel to vessel. This divine line of the Spirit will let us see that we have ceased and we have begun. We are at the end for a beginning.

There isn't a thing in the world that can help us in this meeting. There isn't a natural thought that can be of any use here. There isn't a thing that is carnal, earthly, or natural that can ever live in these meetings. There is only one pronouncement for carnal things: they have to die eternally. There is no other plan for a baptized soul.

God, help us to see that we may be filled with the letter without being filled with the Spirit. We may be filled with knowledge without having divine knowledge. And we may be filled with wonderful natural things and still remain natural men. But we cannot remain natural men in this truth that I am dealing with this morning. No man is able to walk this way unless he is in the Spirit. He must live in the Spirit, and he must realize all the time that he is growing in that same ideal of his Master, in season and out of season, always beholding the face of the Master, Jesus.

David said, *"I foresaw the LORD always before my face, for He is at my right hand, that I may not be shaken. Therefore...my tongue was glad"* (Acts 2:25–26). Praise the Lord!

OLD THINGS HAVE PASSED AWAY

For even what was made glorious had no glory in this respect, because of the glory that excels. For if what is passing away was glorious, what remains is much more glorious.　　　　　　　　　　(2 Cor. 3:10–11)

I notice here that the one has to pass away, and the other has to increase.

One day I was having a good time speaking about this third chapter of 2 Corinthians. I was speaking to a lot of people who were living on the Thirty-nine Articles (doctrinal statements of the Church of England) and infant baptism and all kinds of things. The Lord showed me that all these things had to pass away. I find there is no way into the further plan of God unless you absolutely put them to one side. *"Passing away."*

Is it possible to do away with the commandments? Yes and no. If they have not so passed away with you that you have no consciousness of keeping commandments, then they have not passed away. If you know that you are living in holiness, you don't know what holiness is. If you know that you are keeping commandments, you don't know what keeping commandments is.

These things have passed away. God has brought us in to be holy without knowing it, and to keep the whole truth without knowing it—living in it, moving in it, acting in it—a new creation in the Spirit. The old things have passed away. If there is any trouble in you at all, it shows that you have not come to the place where you are at rest.

"Passing away." God, help us to see it. If the teaching is a bit too high for you, ask the Lord to open your eyes so that you can come into it. For there is no man here who has power in prayer, or has power in life with God, if he is trying to keep the commandments. They have passed away, brother. And thank God, the very doing away with them is fixing them deeper in our hearts than ever before. For out of the depths we cry unto God (Ps. 130:1), and in the depths He has turned righteousness in and uncleanness out. It is out of the depths that we cry unto God in these things. May God lead all of us every step of the way in His divine leading.

CHAPTER NINETEEN

YOU ARE OUR EPISTLE
PART TWO

This is a continuation of my previous sermon by the same title. I am going to commence with the sixth verse of the third chapter of 2 Corinthians:

[God] *also made us sufficient as ministers of the new covenant, not of the letter but of the Spirit; for the letter kills, but the Spirit gives life. But if the ministry of death, written and engraved on stones, was glorious, so that the children of Israel could not look steadily at the face of Moses because of the glory of his countenance, which glory was passing away, how will the ministry of the Spirit not be more glorious? For if the ministry of condemnation had glory, the ministry of righteousness exceeds much more in glory. For even what was made glorious had no glory in this respect, because of the glory that excels. For if what is passing away was glorious, what remains is much more glorious. Therefore, since we have such hope, we use great boldness of speech; unlike Moses, who put a veil over his face so that the children of Israel could not look steadily at the end of what was passing away. But their minds were blinded. For until this day the same veil remains unlifted in the reading of the Old Testament, because the veil is taken away in Christ. But even to this day, when Moses is read, a veil lies on their heart. Nevertheless when one turns to the Lord, the veil is taken away. Now the Lord is the Spirit; and where the Spirit of the Lord is, there is liberty. But we all, with unveiled face, beholding as in a mirror the glory of the Lord, are being transformed into the*

*same image from glory to glory, just as by the Spirit of the
Lord.* (2 Cor. 3:6–18)

Think about that: even the glory that was on the face of Moses
had to pass away. For what? For something that had greater glory.
I am positive we have no conception of the depths and heights of
the liberties and blessings and incarnations of the Spirit. We must
attain to these positions of godliness, and we must be partakers of
His divine nature (2 Pet. 1:4). Praise the Lord!

WE DELIGHT TO DO GOD'S WILL

*How will the ministry of the Spirit not be more glorious?
For if the ministry of condemnation had glory, the ministry of righteousness exceeds much more in glory.*

(2 Cor. 3:8–9)

May the Lord help us now in this. I see the truth as it was
brought to the Israelites in the law. Paul had something to glory
in when he kept the law and was blameless, but he said he threw
that to one side to win Him who is even greater than that (Phil.
3:8).

Now we come to the truth of this: what is in the law that isn't
glorious? Nothing. It was so glorious that Moses was filled with joy
in the expectation of what it was. But what is ours in the excellence
of glory? It is this: we live, we move, we reign over all things. It
isn't "Do, do, do"; it is "Will, will, will." I rejoice to do. It is no
longer "Thou shalt not"; it is "I will." *"I delight to do Your will, O
my God"* (Ps. 40:8)! So the glory is far exceeding. And, beloved, in
our hearts there is exceeding glory. Oh, the joy of this celestial
touch this morning!

INTERPRETATION OF A MESSAGE IN TONGUES:
The living God, who is chastening us after this manner, is always building us after His manner so that there may be no
spot in us. For the Lord Himself has designed the plan, is
working out in us His divine mind, and is taking the man and
transforming him in this plan until he loses his identity in
the mighty God of possibilities.

Hallelujah! We praise You, O God. And we will praise You forever.

Far above all,
Far above all,
God hath exalted Him,
Far above all.

Amen! Glory to God! Thank God for that interpretation. I will be glad to read that, for I don't know what I said. I only know the joy of it.

Oh yes, the glory is exceeding. The glory is excellent. When Peter was describing that wonderful day on the Mount of Transfiguration, he said, *"Such a voice came to Him [Christ] from the Excellent Glory"* (2 Pet. 1:17). And so we are hearing this morning from the Excellent Glory. It is so lovely.

If I were to come to you this morning and say, "Whatever you do, you must try to be holy," I would miss it. I would be altogether outside of this plan. But this morning by the Holy Spirit, I take the words of the epistle that says, *"Be holy"* (1 Pet. 1:16).

It is as easy as possible to be holy, but you can never be holy by trying to be. But when you lose your heart and Another takes your heart, and you lose your desires and He takes the desires, then you live in that sunshine of bliss that no mortal can ever touch.

Divine immortality swallows up all natural mortality. And God wants us to see that we have to be entirely eaten up by His holy zeal so that every day we walk in the Spirit. It is lovely to walk in the Spirit; then we will not fulfill any part of the law without the Spirit causing us to dwell in safety, rejoice inwardly, praise God reverently, and know that we are an increasing force of immortality swallowing up life. Hallelujah!

Ah, it is lovely! As the song says, "I will never be cross anymore." Beloved, it is impossible to go on with God and have the old life reappearing. Glory to God!

BEAUTIFUL RIGHTEOUSNESS

"For if the ministry of condemnation had glory, the ministry of righteousness exceeds much more in glory" (2 Cor. 3:9). This is a beautiful verse. I want to speak about *"righteousness"* now. There is nothing as beautiful as righteousness. You cannot touch these beatitudes we are dwelling upon this morning without seeing that the excellent glory exists right in Christ. All the excellent glory is in Him. All righteousness is in Him.

Everything that pertains to holiness and godliness, everything that denounces and brings to death the natural, everything that makes you know you have ceased to be forever, is always in the knowledge of an endless power in the risen Christ. And we have come into an endless power of the risen Christ.

I want you to notice that there is an excellent glory about Christ's power. Whenever you look at Jesus, you can look at so many different facts of His life. I see Him in those forty days with wonderful truth, which was an infallible proof of His ministry. What was the ministry of Christ? When you come to the very essence of His ministry, it was the righteousness of His purpose. The excellence of His ministry was the glory that covered Him. His Word was convincing, inflexible, divine, with a personality of an eternal endurance. It never failed.

Oh, the righteousness of God. If Christ said it, it was there. He said it, and it stood fast (Ps. 33:9). It was an unchangeable condition with Him. When God spoke, it was done (v. 9). And His righteousness abides. God must have us in this place of righteousness. We must be people of our word. People ought to be able to depend on our word.

If there were only five saved in a meeting, we should never say there were six. If there were five baptized, we should never say there were seven. If the building holds five hundred people, we should never say it was packed and had a thousand in it. God is establishing righteousness in our hearts so that we will not exaggerate about anything.

Jesus was true inwardly and outwardly. He is *"the way, the truth, and the life"* (John 14:6), and on these things we can build; on these things we can pray; on these things we can live. When we know that our own hearts do not condemn us, we can say to the mountain, *"Be removed"* (Matt. 21:21). (See 1 John 3:21–22.) But when our own hearts condemn us, there is no power in prayer, no power in preaching, no power in anything. We are just sounding brass and clanging cymbals (1 Cor. 13:1).

May God the Holy Spirit show us there must be a ministry of righteousness. We ought to stand by our word and abide by it. If we were cut in two, our persecutors should find pure gold right through us. That is what I call righteousness. Jesus was righteousness through and through. He is lovely! Oh, truly, He is beautiful!

One thing God wants to fix in our hearts is to be like Him. Be like Him in character. Don't be troubled so much about your faces, but be more concerned about your hearts. Makeup won't change the heart. All the adorning of silks and satins won't create purity. Beloved, if I was going down a road and I saw a foxtail sticking out of a hole, I wouldn't ask anybody what was inside. And if there is anything hanging outside of us, we know what is inside. God wants righteousness in the inward parts, purity through and through.

Listen! There is an excellent glory attached to the ministry of righteousness. We read, *"For if the ministry of condemnation had glory, the ministry of righteousness exceeds much more in glory"* (2 Cor. 3:9).

The Bible is the plumb line of everything. And unless we are lined right up with the Word of God, we will fail in the measure in which we are not righteous. And so, may God the Holy Spirit bring us this morning into that blessed ministry of righteousness. Amen! Glory to God!

A Heavenly Citizenship

"For even what was made glorious had no glory in this respect, because of the glory that excels" (v. 10). Ah, brother, this verse is truly of God! You couldn't say anything else. You have to get right behind this blessed Word and say it is of God. Just for a moment let us glance at this, for it is a beautiful word: *"For even what was made glorious had no glory in this respect, because of the glory that excels."*

Come again right to the law. I see that it was truly a schoolmaster that brought us to Christ (Gal. 3:24). I like the thought that law is beautiful, that law is established in the earth. As far as possible, in every country and town, you will find that the law has something to do with keeping things in order. And to a certain degree, the city has some kind of sobriety because of the law.

But, beloved, we belong to a higher, nobler citizenship, and it isn't an earthly citizenship, for *"our citizenship is in heaven"* (Phil. 3:20). So we must see that there is an excellent glory about this position we are holding this morning. For if the natural law will keep an earthly city in somewhat moderate conditions, what will the excellent glory be in the divine relationship of the citizenship to which we belong?

I call it an excellent glory because it outshines. It makes all the people feel a longing to go. What there is about the excellent glory is this: the earth is filled with broken hearts, but the excellent glory is filled with redeemed men and women, filled with the excellency of the graces of the glory of God. Oh, the excellent glory is marvelous! Ah, praise the Lord, O my soul! Hallelujah!

PLAIN PREACHING

For if what is passing away was glorious, what remains is much more glorious. Therefore, since we have such hope, we use great boldness ["plainness," KJV] of speech; unlike Moses, who put a veil over his face so that the children of Israel could not look steadily at the end of what was passing away. (2 Cor. 3:11–13)

Yesterday morning I was preaching to preachers, but we can see that this message is for the perfecting of preachers. The man who is going on with God will have no mix-up in his oratory. He will be so plain and precise and so divine in his leadings that everything will lift toward the glory. And his hearers will always realize that he will not play around to satisfy human curiosity. He must have his mind upon higher things altogether, and he must see that God would not have him loiter about. He must *"use great plainness of speech"* (v. 12 KJV). He must be a man who knows his message. He must know what God has in His mind in the Spirit, not in the letter, because no man who is going to speak by the Spirit of God knows what God is going to say in the meeting.

The preacher is a vessel for honor, God's mouthpiece. And therefore, he stands in the presence of God, and God speaks and uses him. But listen! God is a Spirit who works within the human life with thought, might, truth, and life. The Spirit transfers power from the great treasury of His mightiness to the human life, to the heart, and sends His might right through onto the canvas of the mind, and the language comes out according to the operation of the Spirit of God.

Beloved, should we any longer try any lines but the divine? Every man is not in the same order, but I could say to the man with faith that, as a spiritual orator, there is a touch of faith for that man to come into. He has to forget all he has written in his notes because of a higher order of notes.

I always say that you cannot sing the song of victory in a minor key. And you never can have a spiritual horizon on a low note. If your life isn't at a constant pitch, you will never ring the bells of heaven. You must always be in tune with God, and then the music will come out as sweetly as possible.

Let us get away from going into libraries and filling our minds with human theology. We have the Bible, which is better than any book in any library.

I am not here for any other purpose than for the glory of God. God forbid! I have known so many people who have been barren and helpless, and they have used other people's material on the platform. If you ever turn to another man's material, you have dropped from the higher sense of an orator from heaven.

We must now be the mouthpieces of God, not by letter, but by Spirit. And we must be so in the will of God that God rejoices over us with singing (Zeph. 3:17). Isn't it lovely? We are going forward a little.

A GREAT DAY FOR THE JEWS

Let us look again at the third chapter of 2 Corinthians:

Moses...put a veil over his face so that the children of Israel could not look steadily at the end of what was passing away. But their minds were blinded. For until this day the same veil remains unlifted in the reading of the Old Testament, because the veil is taken away in Christ.
(2 Cor. 3:13–14)

I have nothing to say about the Jew except this: I know I am saved by the blood of a Jew. I owe my Bible to the Jews, for the Jews have kept it for us. We have a Savior who was a Jew. The first proclamation of the Gospel was by the Jews. I know that I owe everything to the Jew today, but I see that the Jew will never have the key to unlock the Scriptures until he sees Jesus. The moment he does, he will see this truth that Jesus gave to Peter: *"And I also say to you that you are Peter, and on this rock I will build my church....And I will give you the keys of the kingdom of heaven"* (Matt. 16:18–19).

Jesus was saying, "I will give you the key of truth, the key to unveil." The key was brought in the moment Peter saw the Lord (see verse 16). The moment the Jews see Christ, the whole of the Scriptures will be opened to them. It will be a great day when the Jews see the Lord. They will see Him!

TOUCHING THE HEART

But their minds were blinded. For until this day the same veil remains unlifted in the reading of the Old Testament, because the veil is taken away in Christ. But even to this day, when Moses is read, a veil lies on their heart.

(2 Cor. 3:14–15)

God doesn't say that the veil is upon their mind, but upon their heart. And, beloved, God can never save a man through his mind. He saves him through his heart. God can never bring all the glories into a man's life by his mind. He must touch the deep things of his heart.

THE PROPER USE OF LIBERTY

Nevertheless when one turns to the Lord, the veil is taken away. Now the Lord is the Spirit; and where the Spirit of the Lord is, there is liberty. But we all, with unveiled face, beholding as in a mirror the glory of the Lord, are being transformed into the same image from glory to glory, just as by the Spirit of the Lord. (2 Cor. 3:16–18)

I must speak about liberty first. We must never use liberty, but we must be in the place where liberty can use us. If we use liberty, we will be as dead as possible, and our efforts will all end with a fizzle. But if we are in the Spirit, the Lord of Life is the same Spirit. I believe it is right to jump for joy, but don't jump until the joy makes you jump, because if you do, you will jump flat. If you jump as the joy makes you jump, you will bounce up again.

In the Spirit, I know there is any amount of divine plan. If the Pentecostal people had only come into this plan in meekness and in the true knowledge of God, it would all be so manifest that every heart in the meeting would be moved by the Spirit.

"Now the Lord is the Spirit; and where the Spirit of the Lord is, there is liberty" (v. 17). Liberty has a thousand sides to it, but there is no liberty that is going to help the people as much as testimony. I find people who don't know how to testify properly. We must testify only as the Spirit gives utterance. We find in the book of Revelation that *"the testimony of Jesus is the spirit of prophecy"* (Rev. 19:10).

Sometimes our flesh keeps us down, but our hearts are so full that they lift us up. Have you ever been like that? The flesh is fastening you to your seat, but your heart is bubbling over. At last the heart has more power, and you stand up. And then in that heart affection for Jesus, in the Spirit of love and in the knowledge of truth, you begin to testify, and when you are done, you sit down. Liberty used wrongly goes on after you have finished saying what God wants you to say, and it spoils the meeting. You are not to use your liberty except for the glory of God.

So many churches are spoiled by long prayers and long testimonies. The speaker can tell, if he stays in the Spirit, when he should sit down. When you begin to speak your own words, the people get tired and wish that you would sit down. The anointing ceases, and you sit down worse than when you rose up.

It is nice for a man to begin cold and warm up as he goes on. When he catches fire and sits down in the midst of it, he will keep the fire afterward. Look! It is lovely to pray, and it is a joy to hear you pray, but when you go on and on after you are truly done, all the people get tired of it.

So God wants us to know that we are not to use liberty because we have it to use, but we are to let the liberty use us, and we should know when to end.

This excellent glory should go on to a liberality to everybody, and this would prove that all the church is in liberty. The church ought to be free so that the people always go away feeling, "Oh, I wish the meeting had gone on for another hour," or, "What a glorious time we had at that prayer meeting!" or, "Wasn't that testimony meeting a revelation!" That is the way to finish up. Never finish up with something too long; finish up with something too short. Then everybody comes again to pick up where they left off.

FROM GLORY TO GLORY

The last verse of our text is the most glorious of all for us:

But we all, with unveiled face, beholding as in a mirror the glory of the Lord, are being transformed into the same image from glory to glory, just as by the Spirit of the Lord.
(2 Cor. 3:18)

So there are glories upon glories, and joys upon joys, exceeding joys and an abundance of joys, and a measureless measure. When we get the Word so wonderfully into our hearts, it absolutely changes us in everything. And we so feast on the Word of the Lord, so eat and digest the truth, so inwardly eat of Him, until we are absolutely changed every day from one state to another.

As we look into the perfect mirror of the face of the Lord, we are changed from one state of grace to another, *"from glory to glory."* You will never find anything else except the Word of God to take you there. So you cannot afford to put aside the Word.

I implore you, beloved, that you do not come short in your own lives of any of these blessed teachings we have been speaking of. These grand truths of the Word of God must be your testimony, must be your life, must be your pattern. You must be in the Word; in fact, you are of the Word. God says to you by the Spirit that *"you are an epistle of Christ"* (2 Cor. 3:3). Let us see to it that we put off everything so that by the grace of God we may put on everything.

Where there is a standard that hasn't been reached in your life, God, in His grace, by His mercy and your yieldedness, can equip you for that place. He can prepare you for that place that you can never be prepared for except by a broken heart and a contrite spirit, except by yielding to the will of God. If you will come with a whole heart to the throne of grace, God will meet you and build you on His spiritual plane.

Experiencing God's Power Today

Contents

CHAPTER ONE

FAITH'S LAUGHTER

"My faith pure, my joy sure."

G od told Abraham, *"In Isaac* ["laughter," Hebrew] *your seed shall be called"* (Gen. 21:12). Faith is the great inheritance, for *"the just shall live by faith"* (Rom. 1:17). For twenty-five years, Abraham waited for God to fulfill His promise to give him a son. He looked to God, who never fails, and believed His Word. As we live in the Spirit, we live in the process of God's mind, and act according to His will.

Could a child be born? Yes! According to the law of faith in God who had promised. There is no limitation when you place your faith in God. *"Therefore it is of faith that it might be according to grace"* (Rom. 4:16). Grace is God's inheritance in the soul that believes.

Faith always brings a fact, and a fact brings joy. Faith! Faith! Making us know that God exists, *"and that He is a rewarder of those who diligently seek Him"* (Heb. 11:6). *"God, who gives life to the dead and calls those things which do not exist as though they did"* (Rom. 4:17)! Those who trust God lack nothing. He gives life to the dead. The more Abraham was pressed, the more he rejoiced.

> *Not being weak in faith, he did not consider his own body, already dead (since he was about a hundred years old), and the deadness of Sarah's womb. He did not waver at the promise of God through unbelief, but was strengthened in faith, giving glory to God, and being fully convinced that what He had promised He was also able to perform.*
>
> (Rom. 4:19–21)

Abraham became *"heir of the world...through the righteousness of faith"* (v. 13). God gave life to what was dead. The more there was no hope, the more Abraham believed in hope (v. 18). If we knew the value of our trials, we would praise God for them. It is in the furnace of affliction that God gets us to the place where He can use us. Paul said concerning difficulty, "I do and will rejoice." (See Philippians 1:18.) *"For I know that this will turn out for my deliverance through your prayer and the supply of the Spirit of Jesus Christ...[that] Christ will be magnified in my body"* (vv. 19–20). Before God puts you in the furnace, He knows that you will make it through it. He never gives us anything that is above what we are able to bear. (See 1 Corinthians 10:13.)

If you know that the baptism of the Holy Spirit is taught in the Scriptures, never rest until God gives it to you. If you know that it is scriptural to be healed of every weakness—to be holy and pure, to overcome in the midst of all conditions—never rest until you are an overcomer.

If you have seen the face of God, and have had vision and revelation, never rest until you attain to it.

> *That the God of our Lord Jesus Christ, the Father of glory, may give to you the spirit of wisdom and revelation in the knowledge of Him, the eyes of your understanding being enlightened; that you may know what is the hope of His calling, what are the riches of the glory of His inheritance in the saints, and what is the exceeding greatness of His power toward us who believe.* (Eph. 1:17–19)

Holy men spoke as God gave them power and utterance. (See 2 Peter 1:21.) We must be blameless amid the crooked attitudes and behavior of the world. (See Philippians 2:15.) Jesus is the type of Sonship that we are to attain to. He was God's pattern, the *"firstfruits"* (1 Cor. 15:20), clothed with power. You must go in His name, so that when you lay hands on the sick, Satan has no power, and when you command in Jesus' name, the Enemy has to go.

> The walls are falling down,
> The walls are falling down;
> Oh, praise the Lord, praise His name,
> The walls are falling down.

Let us take God's Word and stand upon it as our strength to resist the Devil, until he is forced to flee. (See James 4:7.)

Chapter Two

The rock Faith

Let us hear and believe the Word of God by the Spirit's power. Let us be changed by the grace of God, changed by the revelation of God. *"Only believe"* (Mark 5:36). I have no other refuge than this command of Jesus.

"If you can believe" (Mark 9:23). We should be awake to the fact that we must believe; we must know the Scriptures and rest unconditionally, absolutely, upon the Word of God. God has never failed anyone who relied on His Word. Some human plan or your mind may come between you and God's Word, but rest upon what God's Word says. *"Only believe."* Oh, the charm of that truth, making you rich forever, taking away all weariness.

Those who put their trust in God are like Mount Zion; they cannot be moved (Ps. 125:1). "Rock of Ages, cleft for me." Oh, the almightiness of God's plan for us; it is tremendous. We are only weak and helpless when we forget the visitation of the Lord. From the uttermost to the uttermost. (See Mark 13:27 KJV.) *"Ask, and it will be given to you; seek, and you will find; knock, and it will be opened to you"* (Matt. 7:7).

On This Rock

When Jesus came into the region of Caesarea Philippi, He asked His disciples, saying, "Who do men say that I, the Son of Man, am?"...Simon Peter answered and said, "You are the Christ, the Son of the living God." Jesus answered and said to him, "Blessed are you, Simon Bar-Jonah, for flesh and blood has not revealed this to you, but My Father who is in heaven. And I also say to you that you are Peter, and on this rock I will build My church, and the gates of

273

Hades shall not prevail against it. And I will give you the keys of the kingdom of heaven, and whatever you bind on earth will be bound in heaven, and whatever you loose on earth will be loosed in heaven."   (Matt. 16:13, 16–19)

Jesus was full of ideals, perfect in those He was dealing with. Jesus came with a perfect purpose, so that many might hear and live and come into apostolic conditions, into divine life. Jesus was the *"firstfruits"* (1 Cor. 15:20) in order to bring to the disciples the knowledge that they were in a divine act to supersede every last power in the world. Holiness is the keynote. Saving grace is a revelation from heaven. Christ within sets up the heavenly standard, the heavenly mind, so that we live, act, and think in a new world.

Jesus asked His disciples, *"Who do men say that I, the Son of Man, am?"* (Matt. 16:13). Then Peter, with eyes and heart aflame, said, *"You are the Christ, the Son of the living God"* (v. 16). Jesus, perceiving in a moment that the revelation had come from heaven, said, *"Blessed are you, Simon Bar-Jonah, for flesh and blood has not revealed this to you, but My Father who is in heaven"* (v. 17).

God's great plan is that His children should be salt for a world that is diseased. *"You are the salt of the earth....You are the light of the world"* (Matt. 5:13–14). To be saved is to have the revelation of the glory of Christ. It is our inheritance to have the evidence of the Holy Spirit upon us. We are to be sons with power (see Romans 1:4), manifestations of the Son, built upon *"the faith of the Son of God"* (Gal. 2:20 KJV). *"On this rock I will build My church, and the gates of Hades shall not prevail against it"* (Matt. 16:18).

INTERPRETATION OF A MESSAGE IN TONGUES:
God is visiting the earth with His resplendent glory. His coming is to revive, to heal, to deliver from the power of the pit. The ransom is the Lord, and He comes to save the oppressed, whose eyes, ears, and heart will see, hear, and feel with a new beauty.

UNCONQUERABLE FAITH

The Holy Spirit abides in power in the innermost soul, for the King has come to fill and rule the body, and to transform the life. A new creature is formed who is pure and holy, a perfect preservation and manifestation over all the powers of evil. Jesus is so sweet; He is the most lovely of all. (See Song 5:16.) *"A bruised reed He will not break, and smoking flax He will not quench"* (Isa. 42:3).

God has designed, by the Holy Spirit, to bring forth divine character in us. *"As He is, so are we in this world"* (1 John 4:17). God has saved and chosen and equipped us so that those bound by Satan may go free. Jesus was speaking to the disciples about a plan of ministry. He said, *"Most assuredly, I say to you, he who believes in Me, the works that I do he will do also; and greater works than these he will do, because I go to My Father"* (John 14:12). This truth, faith, and Christ's rock are one and the same structure: rock! *"On this rock I will build My church, and the gates of Hades shall not prevail against it"* (Matt. 16:18).

Rock! It is emblematic of a living faith, a divine principle—what God the Holy Spirit has to create and bring forth within us. No devil or evil power should be allowed to remain where we are. Jesus was teaching His disciples that, as they believed, greater things would be accomplished because He was going to the Father. *"On this rock,"* on this living faith, *"I will build My church."*

"Whatever you bind on earth will be bound in heaven, and whatever you loose on earth will be loosed in heaven" (v. 19). Keep this truth in mind, for Satan has tremendous power in the world, and people suffer as they never would if they only knew the truth, which cannot be denied. *"On this rock I will build My church"*: on this rock, this living faith, the kingdom, the new birth that has come with power (1 Thess. 1:5).

I have an awful responsibility, because unless I believe and act on this truth, it will not be operative in others. More than ninety percent of all diseases are caused by satanic power. How many here received a touch from Jesus this afternoon and were loosed from their pains? How was this accomplished? By binding and destroying the evil power in the name of Jesus. Jesus said that not only are we given power to loose and bind, but also that the gates of hell will not prevail against His church.

However, when we are ministering to others, we must know the fellowship of Christ's sufferings (Phil. 3:10). He has suffered for the people, and there also must be an entering in, a compassion, on our part. We are to be moved in union with needy sufferers. Jesus was *"moved with compassion."* (See, for example, Matthew 9:36.) Oh, the compassion of Jesus! We must be moved, the compassion taking us to the place of delivering the people.

God knows all about this meeting, and we have power to bind or loose in the name of Jesus. Who will believe? *"Have ye received the Holy Ghost since ye believed?"* (Acts 19:2 KJV). After God has saved you by His power, He wants you to be illuminators of the King, new creations. The King is already on the throne, and the Holy Spirit has come to reveal the fullness of the power of His ministry.

To be filled with the Holy Spirit is to be filled with prophetic illumination. The baptism in the Holy Spirit brings divine utterance, the divine bringing out pure prophecy. Then it becomes a state of being. God is our foundation; the Word of God is our standing. We are here to glorify God. I know how weak I am. Are we to struggle? No, no! We are to believe what God has said. We must be in our place, ready for the opportunity. God wants to give us divine life from heaven. The gates of hell will not prevail against it. The rock of deliverance comes by the key of faith. You will open the kingdom of heaven and shut the gates of hell. You will bind and loose in Jesus' name.

INTERPRETATION OF A MESSAGE IN TONGUES:

He comes with the truth. Know His strength for the broken and the helpless. He reveals His strength. A great tide of revival spirit. Clothed with His Spirit, the Lord will give you light. Fall down and worship Him.

Ask what you will (John 15:7). *"Whatever things you ask when you pray, believe"* (Mark 11:24). Believe! *"You will have them"* (v. 24)!

CHAPTER THREE

A NEW EPOCH—
A DIVINE VOCATION

F aith is an action, a changing. If we dare to believe God's Word, He moves and changes situations. Our purpose is to let the Holy Spirit glorify God through us. *"Only believe!"* (Mark 5:36). It will be to you as you believe (Matt. 9:29).

Hebrews 11 is called the Faith Chapter. A bundle of treasure of divine purpose, God unfolds His truth to us, and through us to others. Dare to believe God; He will not fail. Faith is the greatest subject; in it is power to lay hold of the Word of God.

It is God who brings us into victory through the blood of the slain Lamb (Rev. 12:11). Faith quickens us into a divine order, a living new source, a holy nature, having divine rights through Jesus. It is a new epoch, a new vocation; it is white hot!

> *As it is written: "Eye has not seen, nor ear heard, nor have entered into the heart of man the things which God has prepared for those who love Him." But God has revealed them to us through His Spirit.* (1 Cor. 2:9–10)

We must be ablaze with passion for souls, so that someone may catch a new ray to bring in a new day, for the end is not yet. Praise the Lord! Glory!

JESUS IS THE AUTHOR AND FINISHER OF OUR FAITH

"Faith is the substance" (Heb. 11:1); it is bigger than we know. It has power to express the new creation and bring forth the glory of God. Faith is always at peace, undisturbed no matter what happens. The waves may be terrible, the wind blowing hard, as when

Jesus and His disciples were on the boat in the storm. (See Mark 4:36–41.) Jesus was asleep during the storm, and the disciples cried out to him, *"Teacher, do You not care that we are perishing?"* (v. 38). He spoke, and there was a great calm! Then He said to His disciples, *"Why are you so fearful? How is it that you have no faith?"* (v. 40). Jesus Christ is *"the author and finisher of our faith"* (Heb. 12:2), the divine authority with inspiration. We preach this word of faith to bring forth to the world the touch of heaven.

The Lord is in this place. He is here to revive, to fill, to change, to express, to give power *"over all the power of the enemy"* (Luke 10:19).

There is therefore now no condemnation to those who are in Christ Jesus, who do not walk according to the flesh, but according to the Spirit. For the law of the Spirit of life in Christ Jesus has made me free from the law of sin and death.　　　　　　　　　　　　　　　　(Rom. 8:1–2)

Life came out of death because of the Cross, and then came resurrection, a manifestation of the operation of God. I was dead in trespasses and sins, and now I am alive unto God (Eph. 2:1). I have eternal life.

He opens the prison doors to all who believe, and by faith we enter in. He *"became for us…righteousness"* (1 Cor. 1:30), and we are one with Him forever. Heirship and joint heirship have been made possible for us by His death, resurrection, and ascension (Rom. 8:17).

"There is therefore now no condemnation to those who are in Christ Jesus" (v. 1). There is no cloud, nothing between us and God. Oh, the thrill of it! We are *"hidden with Christ in God"* (Col. 3:3)—immersed, covered—and nothing can break through. It is by the grace of God that we are here, and as sure as we are here, we will be there, *"receiving a kingdom which cannot be shaken"* (Heb. 12:28), *"for our God is a consuming fire"* (v. 29). There is something very beautiful about being in Christ in God, ready for everything—ready!

God *"has begotten us again to a living hope"* (1 Pet. 1:3) in order to make us like Himself. The radiance of the divine makes a new creation. *"The law of the Spirit of life in Christ Jesus [makes us] free from the law of sin and death"* (Rom. 8:2). The quickening

Spirit, fellow-heirs, a divine flow—white heat, full, holy, inflammable, causing others to catch fire—quickening, no condemnation. Do you know these things? Glory! This is a magnificent conception of our eternal relationship: catching the rays of divine glory, a changing all the time. We are ready because of the intensity of the fire within! Jesus is manifested in our flesh (2 Cor. 4:11), ruling and reigning until the rivers flow and the floodtide is here, bringing life, life to all.

> Filled with the Holy Spirit,
> Has He come?
> Does He abide?
>
> I know the Lord's laid His hand on me,
> I know the Lord's laid His hand on me.
> He fills me with the Holy Spirit,
> I know the Lord's laid His hand on me.

Filled! A flowing, quickening, moving flame of God.

We are *"not drunk with wine,...but...filled with the Spirit"* (Eph. 5:18 KJV), more and more filled with this life, this great expansiveness of God's gifts, graces, and beatitudes, which is changing us all the time, moving us on to greater enlargement in the Spirit.

God is with you. The Spirit of the Lord is upon you. Count on Him. Be a chosen vessel in fellowship with God for this day. If you in any way fail to be filled, some need will be unmet. God makes the opportunity for the person who is ready. The Bible is our all. There God reveals His plan and feeds us. Those who trust in Him will never be put to shame (Ps. 22:5; 1 Pet. 2:6).

We cannot be ordinary people; God must be glorified in us. Some say, "If I could only feel the power!" Do not pay any attention to what you feel if you are moved to act in a situation of need. Act in the authority of the power. God makes the opportunity when we are in the place of being hidden in God, of being *"hidden with Christ in God"* (Col. 3:3). *"The law of the Spirit of life"* (Rom. 8:2) is opposed to death and disease; it is the opposite of what is earthly, for within us is a heavenly production. Fresh desire for God's glory makes us ready for the place of opportunity. *"Our God is a consuming fire"* (Heb. 12:29). The cross is empty and Jesus is glorified through us. He is risen, and rivers of white heat are flowing.

"Multitudes, multitudes in the valley of decision! For the day of the LORD is near in the valley of decision" (Joel 3:14). Decide, and the floods will appear. Faith is the victory, for faith is substance and evidence (Heb. 11:1).

CHAPTER FOUR

THE HEARING OF FAITH

P raise the Lord; praise the Lord. *"Only believe"* (Mark 5:36). All things are possible, only believe (Mark 9:23). We are to be absolutely dependent on God alone, on His grand will. *"Only believe."*

"What then shall we say that Abraham our father has found according to the flesh?" (Rom. 4:1). He found something wonderful through God the Holy Spirit. Also, considering the fact that all flesh is like grass (Isa. 40:6), and that *"in me (that is, in my flesh) nothing good dwells"* (Rom. 7:18), what has Abraham, our father, found? Only this: that, for the believer, God has One who can live in the flesh, who can hold the flesh, by the power of God, above sin and judgment.

Jesus Christ is the center of the life where the body, the flesh, has come to the place of being inhabited by God, where God, dwelling in these earthly temples, can live and reign supreme. He has made alive what was dead, bringing *"life and immortality to light through the gospel"* (2 Tim. 1:10), and the Son of God is manifested there.

God has wonderful things for us. Many days in the past have been wonderful, but no day is like the present—the Holy Spirit lifting us into His presence, the power flowing, our whole being flaming with the glory of God. This is God's divine plan for humanity when the Holy Spirit has come. Today, we are nearer to the goal; the vision is clearer, the Holy Spirit bringing us into the treasure of the Most High. What did our father Abraham have? I depend upon the Holy Spirit to bring us into revelation concerning this. There is no room for weakness if we see this mighty incoming life through the Spirit.

OBEYING GOD

"What then shall we say that Abraham our father has found according to the flesh?" (Rom. 4:1). He found that, as he heard the voice of God and obeyed it, it did not only judge him, but wonderful things were also manifested. One day, long ago, God said to Abraham, "Come out." (See Genesis 12:1–4.) God has wonderful things to say to you if you come to the hearing of faith, not to the hearing of the natural order, taste, desire, or affection. Oh yes, if God gets your ear, you will come out.

One day, God said to me, also, "Come out." I was in the Wesleyan Church; I had not been in it for long. Was there anything wrong with the Wesleyan Church? No. Only, God said, "Come out." He had something further for me. The Salvation Army was in full swing at that time. I was very anxious to get the best. Revival was in full swing there, but then the Salvation Army turned to other things. So God again said to me, "Come out." We need to have the hearing of faith, always soaring higher, understanding the leading of the Spirit. Oh, the Breath of God! Then I went to the Brethren. They had the Word, but they had so much of the letter of the law with it (see Romans 7:6; 2 Corinthians 3:6); they split hairs over too many things. And God again said to me, "Come out." "Oh," people said, "he has gone again; there is no satisfying him." Then came the baptism of the Holy Spirit, *"with signs following"* (Mark 16:20 KJV), according to Acts 2—God alone speaking, faith bringing us to a place of revelation to cover us, God coming in and manifesting His power.

BELIEVING AND ACTING ON THE WORD

"What then shall we say that Abraham our father has found according to the flesh?" (Rom. 4:1). He found two things: first, a righteousness by law; second, a righteousness by faith. That is, believing what God says, and daring to act on the authority of God's Word. God will meet us there, within that blessed place, making opportunities of blessing for us—love, truth, revelation, manifestation—God and us in activity, bringing divine ability and activity into action.

> Oh, it's all right now,
> It's all right now,
> For Jesus is my Savior,
> So it's all right now.

The way into the treasure-house of the Most High is the authority of the living Word. The kingdom of heaven is open to all believers. God has called us, bringing us into divine association with heaven, if we will dare to believe, for *"all things are possible to him who believes"* (Mark 9:23).

When we believe, we will find, like Abraham who believed God, tremendous ability—weakness changed into strength, character, power, association within; *"all things* [made] *new"* (Rev. 21:5). We will find a life yielded, absorbed by divine authority, standing on the principles of God.

In Wellington, New Zealand, a crowd of needy people had come for help at one of my meetings, and among them was a heavyset woman. God revealed to me the presence of the Enemy within her body. She cried out, "You are killing me," and fell down in the aisle. I said, "Lift her up. God has not finished yet." The onlookers who were judging us over this case didn't know, but just three yards from them, she was loosed from a cancer.

It is wise to believe God. God has a place for the man or woman who dares to believe. The one whom God has His hand on is not subject to the opinions of others. Our father Abraham discovered this. May God increase the number who dare to believe under all circumstances, who dare to believe God on the authority of the Word.

I once came across a peculiar case. A man was bent double; he was in agony, having cancer of the bladder, and he cried and cried. I said, "Do you believe God?" He said, "No, I have nothing in common with God." I tried to bring him to the place of believing, but his mental capacity was affected. I said, "I see that you don't understand; it may be that God wants me to help you." I said, "What is the name of Jesus? It is the name of the One who met us at Calvary, who has come with new life divine."

Believe all the message; God intends us to be an extraordinary people with this wonderful life of faith in the body. Abraham found, when he believed God, that by faith he was bound to almighty power, equipped for service.

Laying my hands on the sick man in the name of Jesus, I didn't have to say, "Are you whole?" He knew he was whole. He couldn't tell what he had received. This man had been interested in yachts; he was a member of a yacht club. His friends went as usual to see him and began talking about yachts. He said, "Yachts! Yachts! Talk to me about Jesus!"

Oh, yes, there is something in the name of Jesus. Our father Abraham found it. The Word of God is the link, the key, the personality of divine equipping. There is something mighty in believing God. Have you found it? Have you found a faith that believes God, that apprehends what God has said? What did God say? God said that because Abraham believed Him, He would cover him with His righteousness, holiness, integrity of faith. (See Genesis 15:6.) God loves to see His children when they believe Him. He covers them. It is a lovely covering, the covering of the Almighty. Blessed is the man to whom God imputes righteousness (Rom. 4:6). Is it to be so in your life?

God has a perfect work for us, a hearing of faith. When we have the hearing of faith, we are within the sound of His voice, and when we hear Him speak, we find that our own speech betrays us. With this hearing of faith, we are epistles of the divine character (see 2 Corinthians 3:2–3), having His life, passion, and compassion. Beloved, there must be this divine fellowship between us and God.

The people asked Jesus, *"What shall we do, that we may work the works of God?"* (John 6:28). Jesus answered, *"This is the work of God, that you believe in Him whom He sent"* (v. 29).

CHRIST DWELLING WITHIN BY FAITH

This is what our father Abraham found: he became a written epistle, *"known and read by all men"* (2 Cor. 3:2). Paul was delighted with being an epistle of Christ; he followed this divine fire with all *"those who are of the faith of Abraham"* (Rom. 4:16). When we read what Paul wrote in Ephesians and Colossians, we see what he, with Abraham, had received: *"Christ in you, the hope of glory"* (Col. 1:27). Everything we need is embedded within us; we are *"filled with all the fullness of God"* (Eph. 3:19).

The baptism in the Holy Spirit crowns Jesus King in His royal palace within us. When the King is crowned, what tremendous things we find pertaining to our flesh: perpetual divine motion, the power of God sweeping through the regions of weakness. What have we received pertaining to our flesh? New life flowing through it. All the Word of God is *"Yes, and...Amen"* (2 Cor. 1:20) to faith. We receive mighty, divine actions in the human frame, which are so full of divine operation that we see God working. I see such possibilities for young men and women who come into line with God; nothing can interfere with the progress of God, the Author of Life (see Hebrews 5:9) and the Finisher of Faith (Heb. 12:2). Never be afraid of your voice when the Spirit is upon you, nor of how you live your life when you are operating in the ministry of freedom.

"No one can say that Jesus is Lord except by the Holy Spirit" (1 Cor. 12:3). In the truth of this verse, I see the dew of the Spirit (see Psalm 133:3), the order of blessing, the ability to crown Jesus King, being set apart for God.

Then there is the sealing of the Spirit (2 Cor. 1:22; Eph. 1:13), the great adjusting, giving us knowledge in the revelation of Jesus as King over all; all our affections, desires, and wishes are His.

We receive His compassion, His meekness, His dynamic, the power to move the Devil away. We live in a big plan, a force of unity, a divine capacity, making things move.

A man and his wife came to me troubled about things that were taking place in the meetings they were holding. I said, "You two can be so perfectly joined in unity that you can take the victory in every meeting. Not a thing can stand against you; you can have a perfect fellowship in Christ, which the Devil is not able to break. *'If two of you agree on earth concerning anything that they ask, it will be done for them by My Father in heaven'* (Matt. 18:19). Dare, on the authority of God's Word, to bind every evil spirit in the meeting."

We have a faith manifested in our human bodies, a *"circumcision of Christ"* (Col. 2:11; see also Romans 2:29; Philippians 3:3) for our home life, financial difficulties, and the like. We are *"more than conquerors"* (Rom. 8:37) in this operation of faith.

> *It is of faith that it might be according to grace, so that the promise might be sure to all the seed, not only to those who are of the law, but also to those who are of the faith of Abraham, who is the father of us all.* (Rom. 4:16)

Nothing is as large, inhabited by this operation of faith, that is brought to us through Calvary. I feel mighty revival coming; my whole being moves toward it. I dare to believe in simplicity of faith.

Once, in Norway, the halls were packed, and people thronged the streets wanting to hear God's Word. We want the same thing to happen in London. God has given us a divine plan to operate with Him. The deluge can come—a Pentecostal outpouring for the glory of God.

There is now a way into the kingdom of heaven by faith. God is not holding back; we only have to believe in order to see the mighty power of God fall, and I am here to awaken you to this.

THE TESTING OF OUR FAITH

Abraham was tested. Yet God is greater than our testing, and He opens a door of deliverance. Faith! God never changes. What had Abraham received? Testing. But he was called, chosen, and faithful. He was faithful to God in the trial. For twenty-five years, Abraham waited for the promise of a son to be fulfilled. He believed *"contrary to hope"* (Rom. 4:18), *"giving glory to God"* (v. 20). Not one thing will fail if you dare to believe. All fullness in manifestation will arise through faith; all needs of the body will be met in a moment on the word of faith. Give God the glory. Stuttering, tuberculosis, neurasthenia, need of salvation—all needs will be met if we dare to believe. We are in the place of receiving all that our father Abraham received. Let us put in our claim, letting the deluge come, which God wants to send.

WHAT GOD HAS PROMISED, HE IS ABLE TO PERFORM

Let us be *"strengthened in faith, giving glory to God, and being fully convinced that what He* [has] *promised He* [is] *also able to perform"* (Rom. 4:20–21). Then God will be glorified in us and we in Him (2 Thess. 1:12), because we will have found, as Abraham did, the hearing of faith, the righteousness that is ours through faith.

CHAPTER FIVE

FAITH: THE SUBSTANCE

L et us read from Hebrews 11. This chapter contains one of the greatest subjects there is from Genesis to Revelation. It is impossible to bring to you anything greater than the nature of God. We have now entered into not the covenant but the very nature of God, the divine nature, through faith. God has all thoughts and all knowledge, and we may have glimpses of His divine life. The Word of God is life. Jesus, the Word, became flesh (John 1:14); He came in the flesh for the very purpose of moving people. Yes, beloved, the Creator was in the midst of creation. He opened blind eyes, unstopped deaf ears, and made the lame walk; but He had all knowledge.

We experience the new birth as much as we allow natural things to cease; then He comes in, in all His fullness. If He comes in, the *"old man"* (Rom. 6:6) goes out. Now, I believe this morning's plan is for us all, but we must get into the real spirit of it. Beloved, do not stumble if you cannot move mountains; oh, no, there may be some molehills that need moving first. *"He who is in you is greater than he who is in the world"* (1 John 4:4). God has no need of a person who is hot today and cold tomorrow; He needs people who are hot today and hotter tomorrow and still hotter the next day, for they are the ones who are going to touch the glory. The Lord never changes; He is always the same (Heb. 13:8). If you change, it does not mean that God has changed. I am amazed all the time at what God is doing—it is *"from glory to glory"* (2 Cor. 3:18).

THE FOUNDATION OF THE WORD OF GOD

It is no good unless we have a foundation, but, glory to God, our foundation is the most powerful and unmovable foundation; it is the very Word of God. When we are born again, we are born of a *"substance"* (Heb. 11:1), the Word of God; there is no corruption in it. It is the incorruptible Word of God (1 Pet. 1:23). I believe that when a person is born again, he receives knowledge with respect to how to sow the Word of God so that it will bring another into the same knowledge. Everyone who is born again can sow.

When Jesus said, *"God so loved the world that He gave His only begotten Son, that whoever believes in Him should not perish but have everlasting life"* (John 3:16), it was an immeasurable sowing. It's a fact that is worked within us and has to come out; but it is the plan of God, and you are all in it. I believe that there can be an enlargement in us such as will swallow us up, and if you are not in that place, then you must take a back seat. But remember this, we all have more than we are using.

We must build ourselves up in our *"most holy faith"* (Jude 20). Do not stop running in the race of faith; it is an awful thing for a person to run and then stop, and for someone else to get the prize. Paul spoke about this in 1 Corinthians 9:24: *"Do you not know that those who run in a race all run, but one receives the prize? Run in such a way that you may obtain it."* He also said, in Philippians 3:12, *"Not that I have already attained, or am already perfected; but I press on, that I may lay hold of that for which Christ Jesus has also laid hold of me."* Therefore, Paul cried out, *"I **press** toward the goal"* (v. 14, emphasis added). It is a disgrace to God for a person just to keep pace. We must press on. If you are making no headway, you must be a backslider, because you have had such opportunities.

"THE EVIDENCE OF THINGS NOT SEEN"

Now I want to dwell a little on the word *"substance."* *"Substance"* is *"the evidence of things not seen"* (Heb. 11:1). In every born-again person, there is a power that is greater than the natural force. God says twice in one chapter, *"Lay hold on eternal life"* (1 Tim. 6:12, 19). Eternal life is something we cannot see, and yet we have to lay hold of it.

Now, beloved, we must proceed farther than we ever have before. I really mean all I say. I am not speaking from the abundance of my mind, but of my heart. The abundance of the mind makes for swelled heads, but we want swelled hearts. I want to make you all drunk with *"new wine"* (Matt. 9:17). We can *"have this treasure in earthen vessels"* (2 Cor. 4:7). God does not want you to be natural people. He wants you to be people who will cut through anything. He wants you to be born into His life. The new birth is life, the life of God. *"Christ in you, the hope of glory"* (Col. 1:27). No person can go on in this way and stand still. Love the Word of God. *"In the beginning was the Word, and the Word was with God, and the Word was God"* (John 1:1). Jesus was *"the only begotten of the Father, full of grace and truth"* (v. 14).

Perhaps you have never before known what God wants you to possess. Now take these words: *"By faith we understand that the worlds were framed by the word of God, so that the things which are seen were not made of things which are visible"* (Heb. 11:3). My word, if you do not all become "big" today—I do not mean in your own estimation!

Now, when you first came into the world, you were made, but when you were born again, you were *"begotten"* (1 Pet. 1:3). Read John 1:1–3:

> *In the beginning was the Word, and the Word was with God, and the Word was God. He was in the beginning with God. All things were made through Him, and without Him nothing was made that was made.*

So you see, all things were made by Him. Oh, beloved, He will act if you will let Him have a chance. What do I mean? Well, listen! A man came to me and said, "Can you help me? I cannot sleep, and my nerves are in terrible shape."

Now, Jesus put a principle in the Word of God. He said, "Ask anything in My name, and I will do it." (See John 14:13–14.) So I prayed for the man, and said, "Now go home and sleep in the name of Jesus." He protested, "But I can't sleep," and I said, "Go home and sleep," and I gave him a push. So he left, and according to the Word of God, he went home and slept. He slept for so long that his wife went to wake him up, but, thinking he was tired, let him sleep on. But he slept all of Saturday, and his poor wife did not know what to do. However, the man awoke, and he was so changed that he got up and went about shouting, "I am a new man; praise the Lord!"

What had done it? Why, it was the Word of God, and we have the Word in us, *"the faith of the Son of God"* (Gal. 2:20 KJV). Now, we can all have from God what we believe for. If you want any-thing, put your hand up. If you are in earnest, walk down to the front. And if you are really desperate, run down.

CHAPTER SIX

AMBITION REALIZED— DESIRE FULFILLED

L*ike precious faith"* (2 Pet. 1:1). What would happen to us and to the needs of the world if we would get to the place where we could believe God? May God give us the desire. Faith is a tremendous power, an inward mover. We have not yet seen all that God has for us.

When I was a little boy, I remember at times asking my father for a penny's worth of something. He would not give it to me at first. So I would sit down by his side, and every now and then I would touch him ever so gently, saying, "Father, Father." My mother would say to my father, "Why don't you answer the child?" My father would reply, "I have done so." But still I would remain seated next to him, saying, "Father, Father, Father," ever so quietly. Then, if he went into the garden, I would follow him. I would just touch his sleeve and say, "Father, Father!" Did I ever go away without the accomplishment of my desire? No, not once. In a similar way, let God have His way with us. Let God fulfill His great desire for purity of heart within us, so *"that Christ may dwell in* [our] *hearts through faith"* (Eph. 3:17), and so that the might of God's Spirit may accompany our ministry. Let us be filled with divine enthusiasm, with rivers flowing.

PRECIOUS FAITH

"To those who have obtained like precious faith" (2 Pet. 1:1)—a faith of divine origin, springing up in our hearts. Our foundation is tested in a time of strain, for the outside must be as the inside. It is good to have the Holy Spirit, but the sun inside must give a brilliancy outside. Faith! *"Like precious faith"* is greater than the mind

291

or body or any activity. Faith is a living power revealed in you. The moment you believe, you have that for which you are believing. For faith is *"substance"* and *"evidence"* (Heb. 11:1).

You were not saved by feelings or experiences. You were saved by the power of God the moment you believed the Word of God. God came in by His Word and laid the foundation. Faith shattered the old life-nature by the power of God; it shattered the old life by the Word of God.

We must come to God's Book. His Word is our foundation. When we speak of the Word, we speak of almighty power, a substance of rich dynamite diffusing through the human, displaying its might, and bringing everything else into insignificance. The Word of God is formed within our bodies—*"the temple of the Holy Spirit"* (1 Cor. 6:19)—a living principle laid down of rock. The Word of the living God is formed in us—mighty in thought, language, activity, movement, and anointing, a fire mightier than dynamite and able to resist the mightiest pressure the Devil can bring against it.

In these eventful days, we must have nothing that is ordinary. We must have what is extraordinary, allowing God, by His wonderful revelations, to display His gifts and graces in our hearts for the deliverance of others. Peter said, *"To those who have obtained like precious faith"* (2 Pet. 1:1); it was the same kind of faith that Abraham had. Have the faith of God. Because we are born again, a supernatural power works within us. We have the unique peace of God, and are working with a changed vision; we are more wonderful than we know.

Peter said to the lame man, *"Silver and gold I do not have, but what I do have I give you: in the name of Jesus Christ of Nazareth, rise up and walk"* (Acts 3:6). There was operation and manifestation, and the man was healed. Faith! *"Like precious faith."* It is all of the same material: belief in God's Word. Noah had faith that was tested. Abraham had faith, and all the prophets had one fact working: faith!

GOD HAS NO LIMITATION

The patriarchs and prophets had limitations, but God has come to us with no limitation, *"exceedingly abundantly above all that we ask or think"* (Eph. 3:20). There have been memorable days when the Holy Spirit has come. When I was twenty-one years old, God flooded my life with His power, and there has not been a day since without wonderful things happening.

God, by His divine power, is flooding human vessels. God is being made manifest in the flesh, in our flesh. Christ is being made manifest by the power of God. God has chosen a new way for us. He Himself has made us *"kings and priests"* (Rev. 1:6; 5:10), and the day is not far distant when we will be with Him forever.

The Holy Spirit could not have come unless Jesus came first. The Holy Spirit crowns Him King, and all of His power is to be manifested through us. How?

INTERPRETATION OF A MESSAGE IN TONGUES:
Rivers of living water. The man divinely operated, discerning the mind of Christ without measure. To live, to drink, to sup, to walk, to talk with Him.

> Oh, 'tis all right now,
> Oh, 'tis all right now,
> For Jesus is a friend of mine
> And 'tis all right now.

FAITH AND THE WORD

But Jesus must come in first; all God's fullness is in Him (Col. 2:9). All God's revelation is in Him. The life of God comes into us by faith. *"Precious faith"* is an eternal process of working; it has no end, but it has a beginning: *"faith comes by hearing, and hearing by the word of God"* (Rom. 10:17). Faith forms things of eternal forces in our human nature. Faith, God's embrace, is the grip of almightiness. What is faith? It is the eternal nature of God; it can never decay or fade away; it is with you all the way of your spiritual journey, and will end in eternal day.

Faith is the Word (Rom. 10:8). *"There are three that bear witness in heaven: the Father, the Word, and the Holy Spirit; and these three are one"* (1 John 5:7). Faith has so many springs. *"Forever, O LORD, Your word is settled in heaven"* (Ps. 119:89). We have only *"a shadow of things to come"* (Col. 2:17).

Be a person of desire, hungry and thirsty. Don't be satisfied. I cannot move on faith unless it is better than my mind, greater than I am. No one is made on "trailing clouds of glory"; we are made in hard places, at Wits' End Corner, with no way out. A man is made in adversity. David said, "In my distress, God brought me to an enlarged place; I was set free, and He helped me." (See Psalm 4:1; 18:36 KJV.)

Eight years ago, after a distressing voyage, I went straight from the ship to a meeting. As I entered the building, a man fell down across the doorway in a fit. The Spirit of the Lord was upon me, and I commanded the evil spirit to leave. In my visit this year, I ventured to ask, "Does anyone remember that incident?" I spoke in English. The man did not know a word of English; however, he stood up. I told him to come to the platform. He said he knew the binding power of the name of Jesus, and that he had not had a fit since the "stranger" had come. That healing occurred because I knew Acts 1:1: *"Jesus began both to do and teach."* I began to do, the man was healed, and then I could teach the people. Oh, my God, keep me there!

In Palestine, at the Damascus Gate, and on the Mount of Olives, I saw men baptized with the Holy Spirit as in Acts 2. Begin to do, and then to preach. God is always waiting to manifest His divine power. God intends us to begin.

BE A COMMUNICATOR OF DIVINE LIFE

Be a communicator of divine life for others. His divine power has called us to glory and virtue. (See 2 Peter 1:3 KJV.) My wife used to say, "He giveth grace and glory, too." Oh, beloved, receive power! Believe for the power of the Lord to be so manifested through your body that, as people touch you, they are healed. Then there will be the illumination of the power of the Life! Believe for the current to go through you to others. It is amazing what can happen when there is an urgent need; and God can arrange for an urgent need, where there is no time to pray, only to act. The person who is filled with the Holy Spirit lives in an act. I come with the life of the risen Christ, my mouth under the anointing of the Holy Spirit, my mind operative to live and act in the power of the Spirit. We must so live in God that we claim an enlarging in the wisdom of God.

At one place where I ministered, there were six thousand people outside the building, poor things in wheelchairs, and as I went laying my hands on them, they were healed; as they were touched, they were made whole. This faith means an increase in the knowledge of God and the righteousness of Christ, a life filled with God, His mantle upon you with grace multiplied. God did this for Abraham, and added blessing onto blessing. *"Blessed are those who hear the word of God and keep it!"* (Luke 11:28).

The people asked Jesus, *"What shall we do, that we may work the works of God?"* (John 6:28). Jesus answered, *"Believe in Him whom He sent"* (v. 29). Jesus also said, *"He who believes in Me, the works that I do he will do also; and greater works than these he will do, because I go to My Father"* (John 14:12). Faith sees the glory of Another, and it is revealed *"from faith to faith"* (Rom. 1:17). You may increase wonderfully before I see you again.

When I was in Örebro, Sweden, eight years ago, I ministered to a twelve-year-old blind girl; when I visited this time, they told me she has had perfect sight from that day. I never knew it; it is after I leave that testimonies come.

> *Whoever says to this mountain, "Be removed and be cast into the sea," and does not doubt in his heart, but believes that those things he says will be done, he will have whatever he says. Therefore I say to you, whatever things you ask when you pray, believe that you receive them, and you will have them.* (Mark 11:23–24)

Have faith in God! If I believe, then what? I receive what I wish, as I begin to speak. God brings it to pass—not just with a fig tree, but even with a mountain (see Matthew 21:19–22)—whatever you say.

Let me repeat a testimony to illustrate a point. In one place where I was ministering, a man said, "You have helped everyone but me." I said, "What is the trouble?" He answered, "I cannot sleep; I am losing my reason!" He had not slept much for three years, until he got in such a state that when he was shaving, an evil spirit would say, "Life is not worth living," and at times the man had almost killed himself. Whenever he was near the water, the evil spirit would say, "Jump in; jump in, and end it; it is not worth it." Then he came to one of my meetings and heard that he could be delivered. He came up to me and said, "I cannot sleep." So I said, "There is no need to go anywhere else for help; believe! According to the Word of God, go home and sleep in the name of Jesus." He returned and testified, "I can sleep anywhere. I sleep, sleep, sleep, and God has saved me."

There are nine fruits of the Spirit (Gal. 5:22–23) and nine gifts of the Spirit (1 Cor. 12:7–10). Wisdom is coupled with love, knowledge with joy, and faith with peace. Examine yourselves—are you in peace? God is delighted when we are in peace, so I said to the brother, "Go home and sleep, and I will believe God." This man went home, and his wife said, "Well, did you see him?" He said, "He helped everyone but me." However, he fell asleep. Later, his wife said, "I wonder if he is all right," for morning, noon, and night, he was still asleep. Then he awoke bright and happy, rested and restored.

What did it? Belief in God—then speaking. *"He will have whatever he says"* (Mark 11:23). Do you have this *"like precious faith"* (2 Pet. 1:1)? Deal bountifully with the oppressed. *"Everyone who asks receives"* (Matt. 7:8). Ask, and it is done. Live for God. Keep clean and holy. Live in God's anointing, in God's desires and plans. Glorify Him in the establishment of blessing for the people— seeing God's glory manifested in the midst.

CHAPTER SEVEN

BE WIDE AWAKE

*Now it came to pass, when Jesus finished commanding His twelve
disciples, that He departed from there to teach and to preach in
their cities. And when John had heard in prison about the works of
Christ, he sent two of his disciples and said to Him, "Are You the
Coming One, or do we look for another?" Jesus answered and said to
them, "Go and tell John the things which you hear and see: the
blind see and the lame walk; the lepers are cleansed and the deaf
hear; the dead are raised up and the poor have the gospel preached
to them. And blessed is he who is not offended because of Me." As
they departed, Jesus began to say to the multitudes concerning
John: "What did you go out into the wilderness to see? A reed
shaken by the wind? But what did you go out to see? A man clothed
in soft garments? Indeed, those who wear soft clothing are in kings'
houses. But what did you go out to see? A prophet? Yes, I say to you,
and more than a prophet. For this is he of whom it is written:
"Behold, I send My messenger before Your face, who will prepare
Your way before You." Assuredly, I say to you, among those born of
women there has not risen one greater than John the Baptist; but he
who is least in the kingdom of heaven is greater than he. And from
the days of John the Baptist until now the kingdom of heaven
suffers violence, and the violent take it by force.*
—Matthew 11:1–12

F aith brings into action a principle within our hearts, so that
Christ can dethrone every power of Satan. God's accomplishment for us can be proved in our experience. We are
not in a dormant position, but we have a power, a revelation, a life.
Oh, the greatness of it! How great are the possibilities of man in the
hand of God, brought out in revelation and force!

John the Baptist had a wonderful revelation, a mighty anointing. How the power of God rested upon him! All Israel was moved. Jesus said, *"There has not risen one greater than John the Baptist; but he who is least in the kingdom of heaven is greater than he."*

In this passage, we see how satanic power can blind our minds unless we are filled or insulated by the power of God. Satan suggests to John, "Don't you think you have made a mistake? Is Jesus really the Messiah?" I find that men who might be used by God to subdue kingdoms are defeated by allowing the suggestions of Satan to dethrone their better knowledge of the power of God. So John sent two of his disciples to Jesus, asking, *"Are You the Coming One, or do we look for another?"* Jesus said, *"Go and tell John the things which you hear and see."* And when they saw the miracles and wonders, they were ready.

Jesus asked the multitudes who were with him, *"What did you go out into the wilderness to see? A reed shaken by the wind?"* No; God wants men to be flames of fire (Ps. 104:4), *"strong in the Lord and in the power of His might"* (Eph. 6:10). Let us live as those who have seen the King, having a resurrection touch. We know we are sons of God as we believe His Word and stand in the truth of it. (See John 1:12; Philippians 2:15–16.)

INTERPRETATION OF A MESSAGE IN TONGUES:
The Spirit of the Lord breathes upon the bones and upon the "things that are not," and changes them in a moment, making the weak strong, quickening what is dead into life.

THE KINGDOM OF HEAVEN

The kingdom of heaven is within us; it is the Christ, the Word of God. *"The kingdom of heaven suffers violence."* How does the kingdom suffer violence? Whenever anyone is suffering, whenever someone has paralysis, if you feel distress in any way, it means that the kingdom is suffering violence at the hands of the Adversary. Could the kingdom of heaven bring weakness, disease, tuberculosis, cancers, tumors? The kingdom of God is within you; it is the life of Jesus, the power of the Highest. It is pure, holy; it has no disease or imperfection. But Satan comes *"to steal, and to kill, and to destroy"* (John 10:10).

I know of a beautiful nine-year-old girl who was possessed by an evil spirit; she screamed and moaned for years. The neighbors complained, but the father said, "These hands will work, but my child will never go to an asylum."

One day, I went to this home, and the Spirit of the Lord came upon me. I took hold of the child, looked right into her eyes, and said, "You evil spirit, come out, in the name of Jesus." She went to a couch and fell asleep, and from that day, she was perfect. I know deliverance came, but I want you to see the wiles of Satan and the reality of dethroning evil powers in the name of Jesus—the almightiness of God against the might of Satan.

Do Not Be Asleep!

Oh, do not be asleep concerning the deep things of God! Have a flaming indignation against the power of Satan. Lot had a righteous indignation, but too late (see 2 Peter 2:7–8); he should have had it when he went into Sodom in the first place. Be thankful that you are alive to hear, and that God can change situations. We all have a greater audacity of faith and fact to reach.

Fools, because of their iniquity, are afflicted; they draw near to death, and then they cry to the Lord in their trouble, and He heals them and delivers them out of their distresses. (See Psalm 107:17–20.) Catch faith by the grace of God, and be delivered. Anything that takes me from an attitude of worship, peace, and joy, of consciousness of God's presence, has a satanic source. *"He who is in you is greater than he who is in the world"* (1 John 4:4).

Is there anyone here suffering? (A young man steps out into the aisle.) Are you saved? "I am." Do you believe that the kingdom of God is within you? "I do." Now, young man, say, "In Jesus' name, come out of my leg, you evil power!" Are you free? "Yes."

Oh, people, put the Bible into practice and claim your blood-bought rights! Every step of my way since I received the baptism of the Holy Spirit, I have paid the price for others, letting God take me through, so that I might show people how to become free. Some say, "I am seeking the baptism, and I am having such a struggle; is it not strange?" No; God is preparing you to help somebody else.

The reason I am so rigid on the necessity of receiving the baptism of the Spirit is that I fought it out myself. I could have asked anybody, but God was preparing me to help others. The power of God fell on me. I could not satisfy or express the joy within as the

Spirit spoke through me in tongues. I had had anointings before, but when the fullness came with a high tide, I knew it was the baptism; but God had to show me.

There is a difference between having the gift of tongues (see 1 Corinthians 12:7–11) and speaking as the Spirit gives utterance (Acts 2:4); the Holy Spirit uses the gift. If I could make every person who has a bad leg so annoyed with the Devil that he would kick the other leg, we could accomplish something. When I say this, I am only exaggerating to wake you up.

Many times I have been shut in with insane people, praying for their deliverance. The demon power would come and bite, but I never gave in. It would dethrone a higher principle if I gave in. It is the inward presence of God that suffers violence at the hands of Satan, *"and the violent take it by force."* By the grace of God, we are to understand that we are to keep authority over our bodies, making them subject to the higher power—to God's mighty provision for sinful humanity.

> Jesus paid it all,
> All to Him I owe;
> Sin had left a crimson stain,
> He washed it white as snow.

CHAPTER EIGHT

FAITH: A LIVING POWER

But without faith it is impossible to please Him, for he who comes
to God must believe that He is, and that He is a rewarder
of those who diligently seek Him.
—Hebrews 11:6

T he substance of all things is in this verse, I think—no, I am
sure, because a preacher should preach only what he is sure
of. Anybody can think, but a preacher should say what he
knows, and I am going to preach what I know. That is a wonderful
position to be in, so we have a great subject this morning. We must
understand nothing less than this: we have to be the *"epistle of*
Christ" (2 Cor. 3:3), a living word, a living faith, equipped with the
revelation of the plan of the future. *"In Him all things consist"* (Col.
1:17).

Faith is a reality. It is not something that you can handle, but
something that handles you to handle others. I am living in the inheritance of it because of the faith of God. It is a gift of God (Eph.
2:8).

Through faith, the eternal Word brings forth life in our hearts
by the operation of His Spirit, and we realize we are living in a divine order, where God is manifesting His power and living with us.
This is the plan of God for us, our inheritance, that the world
should receive a blessing through us.

God has come within us, living in us with a divine life. Everyone, without exception, will go away from here with a new vision, a
new Book, so that we may go forth because of the Word.

The Lord has one great plan, and that is to reveal to us that we
are so much greater than we know; you are a thousand times greater

than you have any idea of. The Word of the Lord will reveal that all things are possible if you will dare to believe (Mark 9:23), and that signs and wonders are within reach of all of us. The Lord wishes me to make it known that you do not have to go up or down to find Him. He, the Word of Life, is in your hearts. (See Romans 10:6–10.) I perceive that the Lord has this treasure within us so *"that the excellence of the power"* will bring glory to God (2 Cor. 4:7).

We have become *"partakers of the divine nature"* (2 Pet. 1:4). The moment you believe, you are *"begotten...[with] a living hope"* (1 Pet. 1:3), a new power, the power to lay hold of impossibilities and to make them possible. Do you want this? The people said to Jesus, *"Give us this bread always"* (John 6:34). They were enamored with Him. Life forever, real life, eternal life—for the person who comes into this association with the Lord, this is beyond all his earthly measurement. You will need a heavenly measure to measure this.

I am very hungry for your sake today. I have seen the possibilities of every person in Christ. I must show you that, by the grace of God, it is impossible to fail, no matter what the circumstances. This knowledge of the truth that you have within you is so remarkable that it will put you in a place where failure cannot exist. You will see the power of God manifest in your midst. If I were to speak with any less truth than this, it would be of no value, for this is the greatest truth of all: I am saved by a new life, by the Word of the Lord, by the living Christ. I become associated with *"a new creation"* (2 Cor. 5:17), and He continually takes me into new revelations.

FAITH AND THE WORD OF GOD

Let us compare two passages of Scripture:

By faith we understand that the worlds were framed by the word of God, so that the things which are seen were not made of things which are visible.　　　　(Heb. 11:3)

In the beginning was the Word, and the Word was with God, and the Word was God. He was in the beginning with God. All things were made through Him, and without Him nothing was made that was made.　　　　(John 1:1–3)

Nothing is made without the Word of God. Peter said, "I am begotten with this Word." (See 1 Peter 1:3.) There is something

302

within me that has almighty power within it, if I dare to believe it. It is heavenly treasure (Matt. 13:44), and it is called the substance of faith. (See Hebrews 11:1.)

Praise the Lord, you must realize that God is within you as a mighty power, enabling you to act so that signs and wonders may be made manifest; this is the great purpose. Have we believed just in order to get to heaven? No, we must also be in the world for the manifestation of signs and wonders, for the manifestation of the mighty power of God.

It's all right now,
It's all right now,
For Jesus is my Savior,
And it's all right now.

The great secret of everything is this: have you been *"begotten"* (1 Pet. 1:3)? If so, it is all right. It is an act within you. There are people here who are in need of a touch. The well is beside you this morning, offering life and liberty for captives. God can make this manifest. You must understand this: while faith is a great assurance and takes in God's bountiful provision, unbelief is sin. You have to see the contrast.

I am positive that there is the possibility of divine life coming to dwell within human life, but there first has to be a death. From my real knowledge of truth, I can tell you that it is the depth of death—that is, association with Jesus—that brings life. With Jesus, it was a real death. He asked His disciples, *"Are you able to drink the cup that I am about to drink, and be baptized with the baptism that I am baptized with?"* (Matt. 20:22). And they said, *"We are able"* (v. 22). He replied, *"You will indeed drink My cup, and be baptized with the baptism that I am baptized with"* (v. 23). The cup and the baptism perfectly join together. "You" cannot live if you want to bring everything into life; it is only His life that brings forth manifestations of His power. It is not within the human capacity; it is foreign to the human. The human must decrease if the power of the life of God is to be made manifest by His Spirit.

There is not room for two lives in one body. Death to self is the way for the life of the Christ of God to be manifested through you. Your human desires—human supremacy, wanting to be someone, wanting to do something special—are a tremendous hindrance and curse to your life. Not until you cease can God increase. Unbelief would then be foreign to your spiritual nature, for you would then say, *"I live by the faith of the Son of God"* (Gal. 2:20 KJV).

The Holy Spirit is the only One who can reveal Jesus, and the revelation He gives makes Jesus so real. I want to prove to you that this Word is so effective that we think it, we speak it, we act on it, and we live it. Do you find Him everywhere—in the streets, at home? Are you occupied with thinking and speaking in the Holy Spirit, praying and singing in the Holy Spirit? It is the most wonderful thing in life. It is wonderful how God works along these lines. Character is what is within you. Realize the importance of that truth; it will be helpful for all time. Paul said, *"When I am weak, then I am strong"* (2 Cor. 12:10), and, *"Who is weak, and I am not weak?"* (2 Cor. 11:29). The measure to which you are weak is the measure of your strength.

FAITH, KNOWLEDGE, SUPREMACY

When you have nothing, you can possess all things. (See 2 Corinthians 6:10.) If you rely on anything other than God, you cannot possess the greater things. The infinite God is behind the person who has no trust in earthly things; he is in a place where he is trusting in nothing but God. I have never yet condemned anyone for using methods and resources in their Christian lives and ministries, but I see the difference between having a whole Bible, a rich inheritance in God, and only a part. I see that the plan of God is so much greater than everything else. If I have Him, I have life in me; I have an abundance of this life.

Jesus walked in the knowledge that He had supreme authority and power in the Father. He was living so completely in the knowledge of the fullness of God in Him that when He met people, they were bound to believe that He was in the place where He was in the supremacy. It is wonderful that God the Holy Spirit can take us to where we know we have the supremacy in the power of the name of Jesus. This is a great truth: at every moment, you are so safe that you receive nothing less than the divine life of Him who has *"all power"* (Matt. 28:18 KJV).

I am saved by the living Word, which is Christ. Christ is the living *"substance"* (Heb. 11:1) within me. As everything was subject to Him, everything really must be subject to me, because I know that He has manifested His divine authority within me.

How can I know this? On the authority of the Word. Now, what are we to do? Jesus tells us to believe (Mark 11:23). God wants to bring us to the place of believing. He intends us to know this truth: *"He will have whatever he says"* (v. 23). On the authority of the Word of God, let me prove it.

A MAN WITH CANCER HEALED

There was a certain man who was very weak and frail in every way; his eyes were sunken, his cheekbones were sticking out, and his neck was shrunken. He came to me and said, "Can you help me?"

Could I help him? You will find that there is not a person in this place who cannot be helped. Whatever you are suffering from can be cured, and your pain can cease. If there are any persons suffering, they may be healed at once; when God is manifesting His power, there must be signs and wonders. This man told me that he had cancer, and that the physician, in removing some of the cancerous matter, had taken away his ability to swallow, and now he could not swallow. When he spoke to me, he spoke only in something like a whisper.

He pulled out a tubing, and showed me a piece about nine inches long. This left an opening in his stomach, through which he had been feeding himself with liquid for three months. He was a living skeleton, but I could help him according to the Word of God. If a person *"does not doubt in his heart, but believes that those things he says will be done, he will have whatever he says"* (v. 23). In the name of the Lord, I said to him, "Go home and eat a good supper." He went home and told his wife that the preacher said he had to have a good supper. She prepared a supper, and when it was ready, he began chewing his food over and over. But the Word of God must come to pass. I said he should have a good supper, and he was able to swallow his food; he ate until he was full, and he went to bed full. He had a new experience; life had come. But this joy was not all that he would experience. When he awoke the next morning, knowing what had happened, out of curiosity, he looked down at his stomach, and he found that God had healed him; the opening in his stomach had been closed.

All this is divine revelation. We must not measure ourselves by ourselves. If we do, we will always be small. Measure yourself by the Word of God, the great measurement that God brings to you.

Don't be fearful; He wants to make us strong, powerful, stalwart, resolute, resting upon the authority of God. I can only speak along these lines, and shall we not *"be brave"* (1 Cor. 16:13)? We are those who have seen the King. We have been made alive from the dead. God has worked special miracles in us all; we have been made with one great design and purpose.

LIVING ON THE WORD

This healing was according to the Word of God. I must live on nothing else than the Word—it must mean more than my food, more than my associations, to live in this holy Word. I have been preaching faith, and I want you who are suffering from bodily pain to stand. I must deal with someone who is conspicuous. I must deal with you according to the Word of God. No one here will be overlooked. We have come here for the purpose of meeting your need; nobody will be overlooked.

Only believe, only believe,
All things are possible, only believe.

CHAPTER NINE

THE COMPASSION OF FAITH

Beloved, I believe that God would be pleased for me to read to you a passage from the fifth chapter of Mark's gospel. This is a wonderful passage; in fact, all of God's Word is wonderful. It is the Word of Life, and it is the impartation of the life of the Savior.

Now when Jesus had crossed over again by boat to the other side, a great multitude gathered to Him; and He was by the sea. And behold, one of the rulers of the synagogue came, Jairus by name. And when he saw Him, he fell at His feet and begged Him earnestly, saying, "My little daughter lies at the point of death. Come and lay Your hands on her, that she may be healed, and she will live." So Jesus went with him, and a great multitude followed Him and thronged Him. Now a certain woman had a flow of blood for twelve years, and had suffered many things from many physicians. She had spent all that she had and was no better, but rather grew worse. When she heard about Jesus, she came behind Him in the crowd and touched His garment. For she said, "If only I may touch His clothes, I shall be made well." Immediately the fountain of her blood was dried up, and she felt in her body that she was healed of the affliction. And Jesus, immediately knowing in Himself that power had gone out of Him, turned around in the crowd and said, "Who touched My clothes?" But His disciples said to Him, "You see the multitude thronging You, and You say, 'Who touched Me?'" And He looked around to see her who had done this thing. But the woman, fearing and trembling, knowing what had happened to her, came and fell down before Him and told Him the whole truth. And He said to her, "Daughter, your faith has made you well. Go in peace, and be healed of your affliction." While He was still speaking, some came from the ruler of the synagogue's house who said, "Your daughter is dead. Why trouble the Teacher any further?" As soon as Jesus heard the word that was spoken, He said to the ruler of the synagogue, "Do not be afraid; only believe." And He permitted no one to follow Him except Peter, James, and John the brother of James. Then He came to the house of the ruler of the synagogue, and saw a tumult and those who wept and wailed loudly. When He came in, He said to them, "Why make this commotion and weep? The child is not dead, but sleeping." And they ridiculed Him. But when He had put them all outside, He took the father and the mother of the child, and those who were with Him, and entered where the child was lying. Then He took the child by the hand, and said to her, "Talitha, cumi," which is translated, "Little girl, I say to you, arise." Immediately the girl arose and walked, for she was twelve years of age. And they were overcome with great amazement. But He commanded them strictly that no one should know it, and said that something should be given her to eat. (Mark 5:21–43)

Jesus came to give eternal life, and He also came to make our bodies whole. I believe that God, the Holy Spirit, wants to reveal the fullness of redemption through the power of Christ's atonement on Calvary until every soul receives a new sight of Jesus, the Lamb of God. He is lovely. *"He is altogether lovely"* (Song 5:16). Oh, He is so beautiful! You talk about being arrayed with the rarest garments, but oh, Jesus could *"weep with those who weep"* (Rom. 12:15). He could have compassion on all. (See, for example, Matthew 9:36.) There were none in need whom He did not see.

When Jesus was at the pool of Bethesda, He knew all about the sick man who lay there, and understood his situation altogether. (See John 5:2–9.) Yes, and when He was at Nain, the compassion of the Master was so manifested that it was victorious over death. (See Luke 7:11–15.) Do you know that love and compassion are stronger than death? If we touch God, the Holy Spirit, He is the ideal principle of divine life for weaknesses. He is health. He is joy.

God wants us to know that He is waiting to impart life. Oh, if you would only believe! You do not need to wait another moment. Right now, as I preach, receive the impartation of life by the power of the Word. Do you not know that the Holy Spirit is the breath of heaven, the breath of God, the divine impartation of power that moves in the human, raises from the dead, and makes all things alive?

One of the things that happened on the Day of Pentecost in the manifestation of the Spirit was a *"rushing mighty wind"* (Acts 2:2). The third person of the Trinity was manifested in wind, power, might, revelation, glory, and emancipation. Glory to God! I am preaching here today because of this holy, divine Person who is breath, life, revelation. His power moved me, transformed me, sent me, and revised my entire position. This *"wind"* in Acts 2:2 was the life of God coming and filling the whole place where Jesus' followers were sitting. Therefore, when I say to you, "Breathe in," I do not mean to merely breathe; I mean to breathe in God's life, God's power, the personality of God. Hallelujah!

The Scripture passage from Mark 5 that we read earlier tells of a father and mother who are in great trouble. Imagine what they are facing. They have a little daughter who is lying at the point of death. Everything else has failed, but they know that if they can find Jesus, she will be made whole. Is it possible to seek Jesus and not find Him? Never! There is not one person in this place who has truly sought Jesus and not found Him. As you seek, you will find; as you knock, the door will swing open; as you ask, you will receive (Matt. 7:7). Yes, if they can find Jesus, they know their little daughter will live.

As the father walks along the road, he notices a great commotion. He sees the dust rising a long time before he reaches the great company of people who surround Jesus. Imagine the children's voices and the people shouting. All are delighted because Jesus is in their company. Oh, this camp meeting will rise to a tremendous pitch as we look for Jesus.

Yes, the father of this little girl met Jesus; glory to God! He *"begged Him earnestly, saying, 'My little daughter lies at the point of death. Come and lay Your hands on her, that she may be healed, and she will live.' So Jesus went with him"* (Mark 5:23–24). I want you to know that this same Jesus is in the midst of His people today. He is right here with His ministry of power and blessing.

Now, as Jesus went with the man, something happened. *"A certain woman [who] had a flow of blood for twelve years...came behind Him in the crowd and touched His garment"* (vv. 25, 27). This poor woman was in an awful state. She had spent all her money on physicians and *"was no better, but rather grew worse"* (v. 26). This poor woman said, *"If only I may touch His clothes, I shall be made well"* (v. 28). No doubt, she thought of her weakness, but faith is never weak. She may have been very weary, but faith is never weary. The opportunity came for her to touch Him, and *"immediately the fountain of her blood was dried up, and she felt in her body that she was healed of the affliction"* (v. 29).

The opportunity comes to you now to be healed. Will you believe? Will you touch Him? There is something in a living faith that is different from anything else. I have seen marvelous things accomplished just because people have said, "Lord, I believe."

Jesus knew that power had gone out of Him, and He said, *"Who touched My clothes?"* (v. 30). The woman was fearful and trembling, but she

> *fell down before Him and told Him the whole truth. And He said to her, "Daughter, your faith has made you well. Go in peace, and be healed of your affliction." While He was still speaking, some came from the ruler of the synagogue's house who said, "Your daughter is dead. Why trouble the Teacher any further?"* (Mark 5:33–35)

But Jesus encouraged the ruler of the synagogue, and said, *"Do not be afraid; only believe"* (v. 36). When He reached the ruler's house,

> *He took the child by the hand, and said to her, 'Talitha, cumi,' which is translated, 'Little girl, I say to you, arise.' Immediately the girl arose and walked, for she was twelve years of age. And they were overcome with great amazement.* (Mark 5:41–42)

Ah, what things God does for us when we only believe! He is *"rich to all who call upon Him"* (Rom. 10:12). What possibilities there are in this meeting—if we would only believe in the divine presence, for God is here. The power of the Spirit is here. How many

310

of you dare to rise and claim your healing? Who will dare to rise and claim his rights of perfect health? *"All things are possible to him who believes"* (Mark 9:23). Jesus is the living *"substance"* of faith. (See Hebrews 11:1.) You can be made perfectly whole by the blood of Jesus. We must believe in the revelation of the Spirit's power, and see our blessed position in the risen Christ.

Only believe! Only believe!
All things are possible, only believe!

CHAPTER TEN

OVERCOMING THE WORLD

I think it will please God if I read to you the fifth chapter of the first epistle of John. It contains one of those wonderful and divine truths of God that brings the love of God into our lives, and this verifies, in every situation of life, that we are of God. There is an essential truth in this chapter that will give us a clear discernment of our position in Christ.

Whoever believes that Jesus is the Christ is born of God, and everyone who loves Him who begot also loves him who is begotten of Him. By this we know that we love the children of God, when we love God and keep His commandments. For this is the love of God, that we keep His commandments. And His commandments are not burdensome. For whatever is born of God overcomes the world. And this is the victory that has overcome the world; our faith. Who is he who overcomes the world, but he who believes that Jesus is the Son of God? This is He who came by water and blood; Jesus Christ; not only by water, but by water and blood. And it is the Spirit who bears witness, because the Spirit is truth. For there are three that bear witness in heaven: the Father, the Word, and the Holy Spirit; and these three are one. And there are three that bear witness on earth: the Spirit, the water, and the blood; and these three agree as one. If we receive the witness of men, the witness of God is greater; for this is the witness of God which He has testified of His Son. He who believes in the Son of God has the witness in himself; he who does not believe God has made Him a liar, because he has not believed the testimony that God has given of His Son. And this is the testimony: that God has given us eternal life, and this life is in His Son. He who has the Son has life; he who does not have the Son of God does not have life. These things I have written to you who believe in the name of the Son of God, that you may know that you have eternal life, and that you may continue to believe in the name of the Son of God. Now this is the confidence that we have in Him, that if we ask anything according to His will, He hears us. And if we know that He hears us, whatever we ask, we know that we have the petitions that we have asked of Him. If anyone sees his brother sinning a sin which does not lead to death, he will ask, and He will give him life for those who commit sin not leading to death. There is sin leading to death. I do not say that he should pray about that. All unrighteousness is sin, and there is sin not leading to death. We know that whoever is born of God does not sin; but he who has been born of God keeps himself, and the wicked one does not touch him. We know that we are of God, and the whole world lies under the sway of the wicked one. And we know that the Son of God has come and has given us an understanding, that we may know Him who is true; and we are in Him who is true, in His Son Jesus Christ. This is the true God and eternal life. Little children, keep yourselves from idols. Amen.

God wants us all to be so built up in truth, righteousness, and the life of God that every person we come in contact with may truly know that we are of God. And we who are of God can *"assure our hearts before Him"* (1 John 3:19), and we can have perfect *"confidence toward God"* (v. 21).

THE LIVING WORD

There is something more in the believer than words. Words are of little effect unless they have a personal manifestation of God. We must not look at the Word as only a written Word. The Word is a living fact that works living truths in the human body—changing it, moving it, until a person is a living fact of God's inheritance, until God is reigning in his body, reigning in the world and over it. In conversation or activity, the person is a production of God. It is truly a human plan first, but it is covered with God's inheritance.

I now want to come to the Word itself, and, by the grace of God, to bring us into a place where it will be impossible, whatever happens, to move us from our plan. Let us look at the first verse: *"Whoever believes that Jesus is the Christ is born of God, and everyone who loves Him who begot also loves him who is begotten of Him* (1 John 5:1).

There are hundreds of so-called religions everywhere. But look! All these differences of opinions will wither away, and there will be a perfect oneness and divine union of belief in Christ, and it will surely have to come to pass. You ask, "How is this possible?" The Bible is truth; it is the Word of God; it is God Himself portrayed in Word. You see God in the Word. God can manifest Himself through that Word until we become a living factor of that truth because *"God is light and in Him is no darkness"* (1 John 1:5). God is life. God is revelation. God is manifestation. God is operation. So God wants to truly bring us into a place where we have the clearest revelation— even though there may be much conviction through it—the clearest revelation of where we stand.

WHAT IT MEANS TO HAVE THE NEW BIRTH

"Whoever believes that Jesus is the Christ is born of God" (1 John 5:1). What is the outcome of being born of God? It is God's life, God's truth, God's walk. It is communion, fellowship, oneness, and like-mindedness with God. All that pertains to holiness, righteousness, and truth comes forth out of this new birth unto righteousness. And in it, through it, and by it we are in a perfect, regenerated position, even as we have come into light through it.

Again, it is an impartation of love, and an expression of Himself, for *"God is love"* (1 John 4:8, 16). The first breathing or revelation of light of the new creation within the soul is so pure, so unadulterated, so perfect, and so righteous that, if you go back to when you were first enlightened and had the revelation, when you first believed in your heart, you will remember that you felt so holy, that you had so much love, that you were in a paradise of wonderment. You had no desire for sin; sin had lost its appeal.

There you were with a new birth unto righteousness, filled with the first love of purity and truth. You felt as if everybody was going to be saved, and that the world was going to be turned upside down, because you had received the new birth. That was the first touch. It was a remarkable revelation to me when I first saw that God had purposed that every newborn babe in Christ is called to be a saint (Rom. 1:7; 1 Cor. 1:2); called *"from darkness to light"* (Acts 26:18; see 1 Peter 2:9), *"from the power of Satan to God"* (Acts 26:18)— separated to God at the revelation that Jesus is the Son of God.

Another result of the new birth, which I just mentioned, was that for days and days something so remarkable came over your life that you neither had a desire to sin nor did sin. How many have a recollection of those moments? Praise God! God had designed the plan for you before the world began (2 Tim. 1:9). I believe that God wants to open your heart and mind to why you are here, to a purpose of being that He predestined for you.

We need to be so established with facts that there won't be anything in the world that is able to move us from our perfect position. How many people are there who, though sin is striving with them, though evil forces are around them, still never remember a day when God did not also strive with them, drawing them back to Him? It is impossible to be in the world without satanic forces trying to bid very loudly for our lives, but how many are there who, from their very infancy, have always remembered that the good hand of God was with them? If you knew the Scriptures, you could say, like Paul, that, from your mother's womb, God had called you (Gal. 1:15–16).

God Has Great Purposes for Us

Beloved, God has predestined us. Two great truths in the Scriptures are these: *"He who believes in Him is not condemned,"* and *"He who does not believe is condemned already"* (John 3:18). God has covered the world with the blood of Jesus, and every man has the offer of redemption through Christ, whether he will receive it or not. (See 1 John 2:2; Col. 1:19–23.) But there are some people whom God has wonderfully chosen *"before the foundation of the world"* (Eph. 1:4). And as surely as we are alive, we can say that God has predestined us, even to this day. Although you have had times of defeat, the tendency, the longings, the cries, and the desires of your whole life have been that you have wanted God.

See how much God has for you in the Word! God wants people who are mighty in the Spirit, who are full of power. God has no such thing as small measures for man. God has great purposes for man. God has determined, by His power and His grace, through the Son, to bring *"many sons to glory"* (Heb. 2:10), clothed with the Holy One from heaven.

INTERPRETATION OF A MESSAGE IN TONGUES:

The Lord of life and glory, who has "begotten us to a living hope," has "chosen us before the foundation of the world" so that He may manifest His Son in us, and get the glory over the powers of darkness and the Devil and every evil thing, so that we may reign over the powers of the Devil.

The Holy Spirit is jealous over us. How He longs for us to catch the breath of His Spirit! How He longs for us to be moved in union with Himself, so that He could breathe any thought from heaven through the natural, and thereby chasten the natural by His divine plan, so that you would have a new faith or a revelation of God. You would be so perfect before Him that there would not be a thing that Satan could say contrary to God's child.

Hear what Satan said to God about Job: *"Have You not made a hedge around him?"* (Job 1:10). God said, *"All that he has is in your power; only do not lay a hand on his person"* (Job 1:12). We see that God put a hedge around His child. Oh, that we would believe! Listen to what Jesus said:

Do you not yet understand, or remember the five loaves of the five thousand and how many baskets you took up? Nor the seven loaves of the four thousand and how many large baskets you took up? How is it you do not understand?

(Matt. 16:9–11)

Oh, if we only had not forgotten the blessings and the *"pressed down"* measures (Luke 6:38), everything would be moved by the manifestation of the children of God, who would stand by the power of the righteousness of heaven and move the world.

"Who is he who overcomes the world, but he who believes that Jesus is the Son of God?" (1 John 5:5). That is a very beautiful truth! *"For whatever is born of God overcomes the world. And this is the victory that has overcome the world; our faith"* (v. 4). We will have to come into divine measurement, divine revelation. The possibilities are ours.

BELIEVING AND RECEIVING

One day, I was in Belfast, Ireland. I had a friend there named Morris. He had been with us at my hometown of Bradford, England, and I wanted to see him, so I went to his house and said, "Is

Brother Morris here?" The woman there answered, "It is not Morris you want. God sent you for me. I am a brokenhearted woman. I am going through death, having the greatest trial of my life. Come in." I went in, and she continued, "My husband is a deacon in the Presbyterian Church, and you know that when you were here, God filled me with the Holy Spirit. As a deacon's wife, I sat in a prominent place in the church. The Spirit of the Lord came upon me, and I was so filled with joy that I broke out in tongues. The whole church turned around to look at me for making such a disturbance."

At the close of the meeting, the deacons and the pastor came to her husband, saying, "You cannot be a deacon in this church because of your wife's behavior." It nearly broke his heart. When he saw that he was going to lose all his influence, he came home in bitterness. He and his wife had lived together for many years and had never known a disagreement. After causing much trouble, he left his wife with the words, "I will never come near you again as long as I live."

After she told me the story, we prayed, and the power of God shook her. God showed me that He would give to her all she required. "Madam, wake up!" I exclaimed. "Look, the situation is yours. God has given you the situation. It is according to the Word of God: *'For the unbelieving husband is sanctified by the wife, and the unbelieving wife is sanctified by the husband....For how do you know, O wife, whether you will save your husband? Or how do you know, O husband, whether you will save your wife?'* (1 Cor. 7:14, 16). You will be the means of your husband's being saved and baptized." "Yes," she replied, "if I could believe he would ever come back, but he will never come back."

"Look," I said, "the Word of God says, *'If two of you agree on earth concerning anything that they ask, it will be done for them by My Father in heaven'* (Matt. 18:19). We will agree that he will come home tonight."

INTERPRETATION OF A MESSAGE IN TONGUES:
God has designed a purpose for His people. And the word of truth comes to us by interpretation: "Whatever you bind on earth will be bound in heaven. And whatever you loose on earth will be loosed in heaven."

I advised her, "When he comes home, show him that you love him. It is possible that he won't accept your love. As soon as he goes to bed, you get down before God and get filled, just as you were here. Then touch him in God."

Her husband was obliged to come home. If you believe God, whatever you desire comes to pass. He marched up and down in the house as though he never saw her, and then he retired to his room. Then she got down before God. Oh, the place of all places where God comes to the soul! The Spirit came upon her until her whole being was filled with the flame of heaven. Then she touched him. He screamed, rolled off onto the floor, and cried for mercy. She never left him until he was filled with the Holy Spirit.

Nothing happens to the believer except what is good for him. *"All things work together for good to those who love God"* (Rom. 8:28). But we must not forget this additional injunction, *"To those who are the called according to His purpose"* (v. 28). Remember, you are called *"according to His purpose"* in the working out of the power of God within you for the salvation of others. God has you for a purpose.

BEING A CHILD OF GOD

Look, beloved, *"I want you to be without care"* (1 Cor. 7:32). How many people are bound and helpless and have no testimony because of their anxiety! Hear what the Scripture says: *"You have hidden these things from the wise and prudent and have revealed them to babes. Even so, Father, for so it seemed good in Your sight"* (Matt. 11:25–26). We have to become trusting children of our heavenly Father.

The first thing that God truly does with a newborn child of God is to keep him as a child. There are wonderful things for children. The difference between a child and the *"wise and prudent"* is this: the wise man knows too much, and the prudent man is too careful. But babies are different! They eagerly receive. When our children were babies, they were sometimes so ravenous that we had to pull the bottle back from them, lest they swallow the bottle with the milk! A child cannot dress himself, but needs his parents to dress him. In a similar way, God clothes His children. He has a special garment for His children, white and beautiful. God says there is no spot on His children (Eph. 5:27), telling them, "You are pure, *'altogether lovely'* (Song 5:16)." A baby cannot talk. Likewise, it is lovely for the child of God to know that he does not have to think about what he will say, that the Holy Spirit will speak

318

through him. (See Matthew 10:19–20.) If you are a child, if you give everything over to God, He can speak through you. He loves His children. Oh, how beautifully He sees to His children! How kind and good He is!

OVERCOMING THROUGH BELIEF IN JESUS

"Who is he who overcomes the world, but he who believes that Jesus is the Son of God?" (1 John 5:5). That pure, that holy, that devoted Person who made the world submits His will to Almighty God, and God uses His will and dwells in Him in fullness. He meets the world's need. He comes in at the dry time when there is no wine, and He makes the wine. (See John 2:1–10.) Glory to God. When there is no bread, He comes and makes the bread. (See, for example, Matthew 14:15–21.)

He who believes that Jesus is the Son of God overcomes the world (1 John 5:5). You may ask, "How can a person overcome the world just because he believes that Jesus is the Son of God?" It is because Jesus is so holy, and you become His *"habitation"* (Eph. 2:22 KJV). Jesus is so sweet; His love surpasses all understanding. His wisdom surpasses all knowledge (Rom. 11:33); therefore, He comes to you with the wisdom of God and not the wisdom of this world. (See 1 Corinthians 2:6–7.) He comes to you with peace, but not as this world gives (John 14:27). He comes to you with boundless blessing, with a measure *"pressed down...and running over"* (Luke 6:38). You do not require the world, for you have food to eat that the world does not know of. (See John 4:32.) God is a *"rewarder of those who diligently seek Him"* (Heb. 11:6), for those who seek Him *"shall not lack any good thing"* (Ps. 34:10).

Beloved, where are your boundaries? There are heights and depths and lengths and breadths to the love of God (Eph. 3:17–19). The Word of God contains the principles of life. "I" no longer live, but Another mightier than I lives (Gal. 2:20). My desires have gone into the desires of God. This is lovely! This life is so perfected in the Holy Spirit that God is continually bringing forth *"things new and old"* (Matt. 13:52).

"Who is he who overcomes the world, but he who believes that Jesus is the Son of God?" (1 John 5:5). How do we overcome? We come into this great inheritance of the Spirit. We make it our earnest desire that there will not be anything in us that Satan could use in overcoming us. Remember the words of Jesus, *"The ruler of*

this world is coming, and he has nothing in Me" (John 14:30). We desire to reach such a place as this. Is it possible? Brothers and sisters, it is the design of the Master. Without holiness, no one will see the Lord (Heb. 12:14). *"He who has been born of God keeps himself, and the wicked one does not touch him"* (1 John 5:18).

Surely the Lord is not going to send you away empty. He wants to satisfy your longing soul with good things. *"Whatever is born of God overcomes the world. And this is the victory that has overcome the world; our faith"* (v. 4).

THREE KINDS OF FAITH

Let me speak about three kinds of faith. There is a good, there is a better, and there is a best. God has the best. In this Pentecostal outpouring, I find that some people are satisfied with "tongues." That would never satisfy me. I want the Person who gives them. I am the hungriest man that you have ever seen. I want all He has. Unless God gives to me, I am a perfectly spoiled baby. "Father," I say, "You will have to give to me."

When I was a little boy, I would go to my father and say, "Father, will you give me some birdlime?" "No, no," he would answer. I knew just what he meant from the way he said it. I would plead, "Father, father, father, father." I would follow him as he walked out. "Father, father, father." Mother would ask, "Why don't you give the lad what he wants?"

I got to the place where I believed my father liked to hear me say his name. If you only knew how God likes to hear us say, "Father, my Father!" Oh, how He loves His children! I will never forget when my wife and I had our first baby. He was asleep in the cradle. We both went to him, and my wife said, "I cannot bear to have him sleep any longer. I want him!" And I remember waking the baby because she wanted him. *"If you then, being evil, know how to give good gifts to your children, how much more will your heavenly Father give the Holy Spirit to those who ask Him!"* (Luke 11:13). Ah, He is such a lovely Father!

"But," you say, "sometimes I give in to temptation." Never mind; I am going to bring you to a point where you never need to give in. Praise God! If I did not know the almighty power of God, I would jump off this platform. Because we are quickened, made alive, we move into the new spirit, the spirit of fellowship with God that was lost in the Garden of Eden. Oh, hallelujah; new birth, new life, new person!

Human faith works, and then waits for its wages. That is not saving faith. Then there is the gift of faith. *"For by grace you have been saved through faith, and that not of yourselves; it is the gift of God"* (Eph. 2:8). Faith is what God gave you in order to believe. *"Whoever believes that Jesus is the Christ is born of God"* (1 John 5:1). The sacrifice of redemption is complete, and God has kept you because you could not keep yourself (John 17:12; 1 Pet. 1:3–5).

I want to tell you of something that does not fail. Let us read Acts 26:16–18. The Lord Jesus said to Saul,

> *But rise and stand on your feet; for I have appeared to you for this purpose, to make you a minister and a witness both of the things which you have seen and of the things which I will yet reveal to you. I will deliver you from the Jewish people, as well as from the Gentiles, to whom I now send you, to open their eyes, in order to turn them from darkness to light, and from the power of Satan to God, that they may receive forgiveness of sins and an inheritance among those who are sanctified by faith in Me.*

That is faith from God, saving faith—not human faith. In 1 Corinthians 12:9, we read, *"To another* [is given] *faith by the same Spirit."* When my faith fails, then another faith lays hold of me.

AN INSANE WOMAN HEALED THROUGH FAITH

One day, I called at a home where a woman had not slept for seven weeks. She was rolling from one side of the bed to the other. In came a young man with a baby in his arms. He stooped down over the mother to try to kiss her. Instantly she rolled to the other side of the bed. Going around to her, the young man touched the lips of the mother with the baby, in order to try to bring her to consciousness again. But she switched to the other side. I could see that the young man was brokenhearted.

"What have you done for this woman?" I asked. "Everything," they replied. "We have had doctors here, we have injected morphine, and so forth." The sister said, "We must put her in an asylum. I am tired and worn out." I asked, "Have you tried God?" The husband answered, "Do you think we believe in God here? We have no confidence in anything. If you call anything like this God, we have no fellowship with it."

321

Oh, I was done, then! A young woman grinned in my face and slammed the door. The compassion in me was so moved that I did not know what to do. I began to cry, and my faith lifted me right up. Thank God for faith that lifted. I felt Another *"like the Son of God"* (Heb. 7:3) grip me. The Spirit of the Lord came upon me, and I said, "In the name of Jesus, come out of her!" She fell asleep and did not awaken for fourteen hours. She awakened perfectly sane. Beloved, there is a place in which we know the Son of God that absolutely overcomes the world.

At one time, I thought that I had the Holy Spirit. Now I know that the Holy Spirit has me. There is a difference between our hanging onto God and God lifting us up. There is a difference between my having a desire and God's desire filling my soul. There is a difference between natural compassion and the compassion of Jesus, which never fails. Human faith fails, but the faith of Jesus never fails.

Oh, beloved, I see a new dawning through these glorious truths: assemblies loving one another, being all of one accord. Until that time comes, there will be deficiencies. Hear what the Scripture says: *"Everyone who loves Him who begot also loves him who is begotten of Him"* (1 John 5:1), and *"By this all will know that you are My disciples, if you have love for one another"* (John 13:35). Love is the secret and center of the divine position. Build upon God.

You may be asking, "What is the gift of faith?" It is where God moves you to pray. In the Bible, we read about a man named Elijah who had *"a nature like ours"* (James 5:17). The sins of the people were grieving the heart of God, and the whole house of Ahab was in an evil state. But God moved upon Elijah and gave him an inward cry, and he said, *"There shall not be dew nor rain these years, except at my word"* (1 Kings 17:1). The result was that *"it did not rain on the land for three years and six months"* (James 5:17). Oh, if we only dared to believe God! *"A man with a nature like ours"* (v. 17) was stirred with almightiness! *"And he prayed again, and the heaven gave rain, and the earth produced its fruit"* (v. 18).

Brother, sister, you are now in the robing room. God is giving you another day to come into line, for you to lay aside everything that has hindered you, for you to forget the past. And I ask you, How many of you want to receive from God a faith that cannot be denied? I have learned that if I dare to lift up my hands in faith, God will fill them. Come on, beloved, seek God, and let us get a real touch of heaven. God is moving.

This day is the beginning of days, a day when the Lord will not forsake His own but will meet us. Come near to God! Jesus, Jesus, bless us! We are so needy, Lord. Jesus, my Lord! Oh, Jesus, Jesus, Jesus! Oh, my Savior, my Savior! Oh, such love! Mighty God! Oh, loving Master! Blessed, blessed Jesus! There is none like Jesus! There is none as good as He! There is none as sweet as He! Oh, blessed Christ of reality, come! Hallelujah!

CHAPTER ELEVEN

"THE SECRET PLACE"

*He who dwells in the secret place of the Most High shall abide
under the shadow of the Almighty. I will say of the LORD, "He is my
refuge and my fortress; my God, in Him I will trust." Surely He
shall deliver you from the snare of the fowler and from the perilous
pestilence. He shall cover you with His feathers, and under His
wings you shall take refuge; His truth shall be your shield and
buckler. You shall not be afraid of the terror by night, nor of the
arrow that flies by day, nor of the pestilence that walks in darkness,
nor of the destruction that lays waste at noonday. A thousand may
fall at your side, and ten thousand at your right hand; but it shall
not come near you. Only with your eyes shall you look, and see the
reward of the wicked. Because you have made the LORD, who is my
refuge, even the Most High, your dwelling place, no evil shall befall
you, nor shall any plague come near your dwelling; for He shall
give His angels charge over you, to keep you in all your ways. In
their hands they shall bear you up, lest you dash your foot against a
stone. You shall tread upon the lion and the cobra, the young lion
and the serpent you shall trample underfoot. "Because he has set his
love upon Me, therefore I will deliver him; I will set him on high,
because he has known My name. He shall call upon Me, and I will
answer him; I will be with him in trouble; I will deliver him and
honor him. With long life I will satisfy him, and show him
My salvation."*
—Psalm 91

The *"crown of life"* (James 1:12; Rev. 2:10–11) is for the overcomer; it is not for those *"at ease* [smug] *in Zion"* (Amos 6:1). We must be in the place where God can depend on us, never giving in, knowing no defeat, always making our stand by a living faith and gaining the victory. Faith is the victory. *"This is the work of God, that you believe in Him whom He sent"* (John 6:29).

England once had a war with France. The French took some prisoners, among them a drummer boy. Napoleon ordered him to sound a retreat, but he said no, he had never learned one! God never wants you to retreat in the face of the Enemy, but to learn the victory song, and to overcome. Praise the Lord. There are two kinds of shouts: a shout that is made and a shout that makes you. There are men of God, but many men are God's men. There is a place where you take hold of God, but there is a better place where God takes hold of you. *"He who dwells in the secret place of the Most High shall abide under the shadow of the Almighty."*

Do you know the presence of the Almighty? It is wonderful; it is a surety. There is no wavering, no unbelief there. There is no unrest there; it is perfect.

My great desire is to see believers *"strong in the Lord"* (Eph. 6:10) by dwelling in *"the secret place"* that is known to all who fear Him. There are two kinds of fear of God: one is to have a reverential awe of Him, and the other is to be afraid of Him. I hope none of you are afraid of God. Unbelievers are afraid of God, but believers may have a fear of God, a reverence for Him, in which they would rather die than grieve Him. They may have peace, power, and fellowship with God.

This is the will of God for all; it is His will for the world. No price is too great to pay to enter into this peace, power, and fellowship. It is our inheritance; Christ purchased it. It is the covering of the presence of the Almighty. What a covering the unfolding of His will is! *"The secret of the LORD is with those who fear Him"* (Ps. 25:14).

THE PRESENCE OF THE ALMIGHTY

Moses knew something about the presence of the Almighty: *"If Your Presence does not go with us, do not bring us up from here"* (Exod. 33:15). *"[Those] who [dwell] in the secret place."* What does being in God's presence do? It dares me to believe all that God says; it assists me in laying hold of the promises. God so indwells us that we become a force, a power, of God's abiding, until *"death is swallowed up in victory"* (1 Cor. 15:54).

We have a great salvation, filled with inspiration, with no limitation, making known the wonders of God. Psalm 91:2 says, *"I will say of the LORD, 'He is my refuge and my fortress; my God, in Him I will trust.'"* If you are dwelling *"in the secret place of the Most High,"* as it says in verse one, then you will experience what it says in verse two—a substance of faith, the fact of God's presence worked out in your lives. You must have an inward fact. You are always beyond argument when you deal in facts. We must have facts, not fears or feelings.

"I will say of the LORD, 'He is my refuge.'" Who will say this? He who abides. There is no complaining there, no bad temper, no irritability; all is swept away when we dwell in the presence of the Almighty, the covering of God.

Even the best of humanity is not good (Isa. 64:6; Rom. 7:18). Jesus was manifested to *"destroy the works of the devil"* (1 John 3:8).

> *For what the law could not do in that it was weak through the flesh, God did by sending His own Son in the likeness of sinful flesh, on account of sin: He condemned sin in the flesh.* (Rom. 8:3)

God sent forth Jesus *"in the likeness of sinful flesh,"* in the mightiness of His power; and, in the midst of flesh, He condemned it. *"The law of the Spirit of life"* (v. 2) destroys all that must be destroyed. When we are *"dead indeed to sin, but alive to God"* (Rom. 6:11), then we are above everything in Him, *"who is above all, and through all, and in you all"* (Eph. 4:6). This existence in God is not found in our sinful human nature, nor does it grow in Eden's garden; it is the gift of God from heaven. We belong to the *"new creation"* (2 Cor. 5:17); it is a wonderful place of life. It is life that is *"free from the law of sin and death"* (Rom. 8:2). Can we remain there?

GOD WILL KEEP US IN HIMSELF

> He never forgets to keep me,
> He never forgets to keep me;
> My Father has many dear children,
> But He never forgets to keep me.

Has He forgotten to keep you? No! He cannot forget. God has much in store for you. There was a time when the children of Israel hung their harps on the willows when they were in captivity (see Psalm 137:1–4), and sometimes the believer does the same. I have seen thousands of people delivered from evil power since I last saw you. However, there is a great weakness in the land; it is lack of knowledge. People "[hew] *themselves cisterns; broken cisterns that can hold no water*" (Jer. 2:13). But those who know the Word of God have no fear. God's Word is the great antidote to evil. *"There is no fear in love; but perfect love casts out fear"* (1 John 4:18).

Where is God? He is in the Word. He has embodied Himself in the Word. The Word spells destruction to all evil. He who dwells in love is the master of situations. There is no fear, no sickness, a perfect redemption. Some say, "Does it last? Does the healing hold?" What God does, He does forever. Thirty-five years ago, God healed me. My whole body was weak. My teeth were decayed, but God healed them. At sixty-two, I am as fresh as a boy. Now, Devil, take that! It is God's plan, which is better than any other plan. The Bible has so many precious promises, wealth beyond all price.

Some people exchange God's plan for fear; they abandon God's wonderful plan for a feeling! Be real, in accordance with God's plan. The waverer gets nothing (James 1:5–6 KJV). Real faith is establishment. How can I get it? *"Abide under the shadow of the Almighty."* Don't change. Remain in the presence of God, the glory of God. Pay any price to abide under that covering. The secret of victory is to abide where victory abides.

> Higher, higher, nothing dreading;
> Never, never let me stop;
> In Your footsteps keep me treading;
> Give me strength to reach the top.

INTERPRETATION OF A MESSAGE IN TONGUES:
Jesus has become the "author and the finisher of faith." "Your life is hid with Christ in God." There is no limitation where the Holy Breath blows an inward cry after Him, "for with the heart man believes unto righteousness; and with the mouth confession is made unto salvation."

"Because he has set his love upon Me, therefore I will deliver him; I will set him on high, because he has known My name." Do you know His name? If so, *"you will ask what you desire, and it shall be done for you"* (John 15:7). You will have communion with

327

Jesus, fellowship divine; you will not whisper the name of Jesus, but will have a knowledge of the name. *"He shall call upon Me, and I will answer him."* Feed upon the Word. *"With long life I will satisfy him, and show him My salvation."*

CHAPTER TWELVE

CHILDREN OF GOD

This is a banquet of love, where Jesus is looking upon us from heaven and making Himself known to us. It is surely the manifestation of God's love when we read in His Word, *"For as the heavens are high above the earth, so great is His mercy* [loving-kindness] *toward those who fear Him"* (Ps. 103:11). Surely, beloved, God intends to strengthen us through our coming near to Him, so that we may believe that our weaknesses will be turned into strength, and that our unbelief will be made into living faith. The dew of His presence, the power of His love, will be so active upon us that we will be changed by His wonderful Word.

I want to lift you to a place where you will dare to believe that God is waiting to bless you abundantly, beyond all that you can *"ask or think"* (Eph. 3:20).

Are you ready? "What for?" you ask. To get before God today with such living faith that you will dare to believe that all things are possible concerning you. (See Mark 9:23.)

Are you ready? What for? To know today that God's mercy never fails. Though you fail, He is still full of mercy.

Are you ready? You are? Then God will surely grant you a very rich blessing, so that you will forget all your poverty and come into a bountiful place of supply. You will never have—understand this, for God means it—you will never have any barrenness, but you will be brought into His treasures; He will cover you with His bountifulness, and you will know that the God of the Most High reigns.

WHAT MANNER OF LOVE

The Lord has given me the privilege of bringing before you another message, which I trust will stir you all and change you in a very remarkable way.

The Lord is still leading me along the line of the gifts of the Spirit, but I want to take a little break from talking about them because we have had so much teaching on the gifts, and I now want to put you in the position where you are worthy of receiving and operating in these divine appointments with God.

To this end, let us consider 1 John 3:1–10:

Behold what manner of love the Father has bestowed on us, that we should be called children of God! Therefore the world does not know us, because it did not know Him. Beloved, now we are children of God; and it has not yet been revealed what we shall be, but we know that when He is revealed, we shall be like Him, for we shall see Him as He is. And everyone who has this hope in Him purifies himself, just as He is pure. Whoever commits sin also commits lawlessness, and sin is lawlessness. And you know that He was manifested to take away our sins, and in Him there is no sin. Whoever abides in Him does not sin. Whoever sins has neither seen Him nor known Him. Little children, let no one deceive you. He who practices righteousness is righteous, just as He is righteous. He who sins is of the devil, for the devil has sinned from the beginning. For this purpose the Son of God was manifested, that He might destroy the works of the devil. Whoever has been born of God does not sin, for His seed remains in him; and he cannot sin, because he has been born of God. In this the children of God and the children of the devil are manifest: Whoever does not practice righteousness is not of God, nor is he who does not love his brother.

This passage is one of the pinnacles of truth. A pinnacle of truth is something that leads you to a place of sovereignty, of purity, a place where you cannot be moved by any situation. You have a fixed position. You take the position clearly on the authority of the Word of Jesus.

God intends to let the following truths ring through our hearts distinctly, clearly, marvelously: We are free from sin. We are children of God. We are heirs of the kingdom of His righteousness.

The opening word of 1 John 3 is one of those words in which we find stimulation: *"Behold."* (The Bible uses certain words to draw our attention to what precedes or follows. For example, in Hebrews, you will find the frequent occurrence of a word that has a lot to do with opening our understanding of the Scriptures: *"therefore."*) This beautiful word *"behold"* means, "Awake; open; listen, for God is speaking." What is He saying? *"Behold what manner of love the Father has bestowed on us, that we should be called children of God!"* (1 John 3:1).

"What manner of love"! God's love is manifold, and much more. It is full of expression. It was God who looked past your weaknesses, your human depravities, every part of your nature and character, which you knew were absolutely out of order. He has washed you; He has cleansed you; He has beautified you; and He looks at you and says, "You are lovely! I see no spot of sin upon you; there is no spot. (See Song 4:7.) You are now my children."

INTERPRETATION OF A MESSAGE IN TONGUES:

For the Lord is "gentle, easy to be entreated, without partiality," full of goodness and faith. He sees beyond all weakness, looks at the "Son of His love" because of the shed blood, opens unto us the treasures of His great love, and says to us, "'You are fair, my love, you are fair; I have called you into my banqueting house; I have decked you with the rarest jewels'; for you will have gifts, and the beatitudes will cover you, and my grace will follow you, and I will give you to understand the mysteries of the hidden things."

THE ORDER OF SONSHIP

"That we should be called children of God! Therefore the world does not know us, because it did not know Him" (1 John 3:1). The world does not know us in our sonship. We have to be strangers to the world's knowledge. We have to surpass all that the world knows, even as we are in the midst of the world.

I want us to examine ourselves to see if this sonship is ours, to see if we are in the order of perfect sonship. After you have confirmed this, you may strengthen yourself in God and believe for anything to come to pass. But you must examine yourself to see if you are in the Father. (See 2 Corinthians 13:5.)

The greatest blessing that will come to you will be that the Word of Life, in going forth, will create in you a deeper desire for God. If you are in the Father, as the Spirit is giving the Word, you will have a greater longing for God, for the holiness of God, for the righteousness of God; for He has to make you know today that, as He is pure, you have to be pure. (See 1 John 3:3.)

Don't stumble at the Word. If Jesus says anything, if the Word conveys anything to your mind, don't stumble at the Word. Believe that God is greater than you are, greater than your heart (1 John 3:20), greater than your mind, and can establish you in righteousness even when your thoughts and your knowledge are absolutely against it.

God blots out our transgressions in a thick cloud; and our sins, our iniquities, He will never remember. (See Isaiah 43:25.) I often find that people misunderstand God's Word because they bring only their minds to the Word, and when the Word does not exactly fit what their minds expected, they do not get liberty. They want the Word to come to their minds. It will never happen. You have to be submissive to God.

The Word of God is true. If you understand what is true and right, you can always be on the line of gaining strength, overcoming situations, living in the world but over it, making everything subject to you in Christ.

DO ALL TO THE GLORY OF GOD

One day, after I held a meeting, a man came to me and said, "Your ministry makes me feel that there is something radically wrong with me. I am a strong man, to look at; there is apparently no weakness about me. But I am ashamed of myself. I have three big lads, and they are doing the work of men, and I know it is not right. Here I am, a big man, and if I do any work for my business, I become incapacitated. I have just had three weeks of bed rest from working one day."

He had a business of carrying coal from house to house in bags that weighed 112 pounds. Every time he picked up a bag and carried it to a house, his whole frame gave way and he had to go to bed.

"Why, brother," I said, "you have never come into the line of truth. You are stranger to the truth of the Word of God."

There are any number of people who have not learned yet how they are the masters of their own bodies, masters of all kinds of work, masters of everything. You have to be a child of God in the earth—over your work, over your mind, over your body, over your life.

INTERPRETATION OF A MESSAGE IN TONGUES:

It is God who opens the heart and gives us understanding, for unless the Spirit gives life to the world, you will still be held; but let the Spirit lift you by the Word, and you will find you will come into perfect freedom today, for God takes the Word, pours it into your heart, and opens your understanding. And you are in liberty because the Word of God makes everybody free, and "the Word of God is not bound."

From Romans 7:25, we see how we can be masters over every manual labor in God: "So then, with the mind I myself serve the law of God, but with the flesh the law of sin." The result of being controlled by "the flesh" is serving "the law of sin." We need to serve "the law of God."

"My brother," I said to the man with the coal business, "you have carried those bags of coal with your body, and you have allowed your flesh to control your body, and you have become incapacitated."

People do this all the time.

Now, what is "the law of sin"? Every kind of toilsome work is the result of the law of sin. Is work sin? No, it is not sin. It is what the law brought. There was no toilsome work before the Fall; it came through sin. Because of sin, you have to eat your bread by the sweat of your brow (Gen. 3:19); sweat is a symbol of sin.

The law of sin has brought sweat, disease, weakness, calamity, and all kinds of depression. Is it sin, then, to work? No, it is not sin to work.

I went to an insane asylum one day, and I said to the man there, "What is the first indication that a man has gotten back his reason and now has clear understanding?"

"Oh," he said. "Are you a stranger here?"

"Yes."

"Well, what makes you so intense about this thing?"

"I have someone in mind. Tell me, what is the first indication?"

"Why, it is marvelous that you should ask. See that man over there? That man became perfect in a moment, and we had had six men in charge of him. In a moment, he came to his senses. We had agreed together to pray at a certain time, and that man became as free as possible."

"What is the first indication?" I asked again.

333

"The first indication is that when a man is becoming sound in his mind, he wants to work."

And the first indication that you are becoming unsound is when you will not work! There is nothing wrong in work, but there is something wrong when we do not know how to live in it and over it.

When I finished talking with the coal carrier, he said, "I see!" What did he see? He saw that he could go on to his work, take hold of those bags of coal, put them on his back, and keep his mind on the Lord. When he did so, he became stronger every hour, and he carried a hundred bags out and finished promptly.

This is what God wants us to learn: *"Whatever you do, do all to the glory of God"* (1 Cor. 10:31). If you listen to the Word of God, it will make you strong. You will find out that whatever work you have to do will be made easier if you keep your mind *"stayed"* on the Lord (Isa. 26:3). Blessed is the one who has his mind focused on the Lord! We must see to it that in the world we are not moved.

KEPT IN PERFECT PEACE

One day, God revealed to me that if I had any trouble in my heart, I had missed His will. He showed me that if I had trouble in my heart, I had taken on something that did not belong to me, and I was out of the will of God. So I investigated it and found that it was true, according to His Word: *"You will keep him in perfect peace, whose mind is stayed on You, because he trusts in You"* (Isa. 26:3).

INTERPRETATION OF A MESSAGE IN TONGUES:
God, in His great love toward us, has so distributed the power of His righteousness through our human bodies that the very activity now within us is a lift of praise. We adore Him, we thank Him, we praise Him, because he has "delivered us from the power of evil" and surrounded us by the power of light.

ATTRIBUTES OF SONSHIP

"That we should be called children of God!" (1 John 3:1). How are you to live? You are to live like a child of God. A child of God must have power over the power of the Devil (Luke 10:19). A child of God must behave in a fitting way. (See Ephesians 5:1–4.) A child

of God must be *"temperate in all things"* (1 Cor. 9:25). A child of God must have the expression of the Master. He should be filled with tenderness and compassion. He should be filled with *"tender mercies"* (Col. 3:12). A child of God must excel in every way. God says to you more than you dare to say about yourself: "Behold, you are children of God." (See 1 John 3:3.) So do not be afraid. Take your stand, come into line, and say, "I will be a child of God."

God spoke, and the heavens yielded to His voice. He cried, *"This is My beloved Son, in whom I am well pleased. Hear Him!"* (Matt. 17:5). Afterward, Jesus always said, "I am the Son of God." Now, God comes to you and says, "Behold, you are the children of God!" Oh, that we could have a regiment of believers who would rise, claim their rights, stand erect with a holy vision, and be full of inward power, saying, "I am, by the grace of God, a child of God"!

"Wisdom is justified by her children" (Matt. 11:19). The man or woman who calls out to God does not need to fear. I stretch out my hand to you; you may, in many ways, have felt that you were never worthy; but God makes you worthy, and who can say that you are not worthy?

INTERPRETATION OF A MESSAGE IN TONGUES:
It is the will of God to choose you. It is not your choice; it is the Lord's choice. Hear what He says: "I have chosen you, I have ordained you, that you should go forth bearing much fruit, and that your fruit should remain; for herein is your Father glorified, when you bring forth much fruit; so you will be my disciples."

SONS OF GOD NOW

*Beloved, **now** we are children of God; and it has not yet been revealed what we shall be, but we know that when He is revealed, we shall be like Him, for we shall see Him as He is.* (1 John 3:2, emphasis added)

I am not talking about what we will be like after the second coming of Christ. I am dealing with the life that is in the believer now. I am dealing with our sonship in the earth. I am dealing with sonship; Son-likeness; what we are to be like in this world and what will take place when we live as children of God; how we can overcome the world; and what there is in our life in Christ that causes us to overcome the world.

"Everyone who has this hope in Him"—this hope of sonship; this hope of ministry; this hope of life-giving, of transmitting life— *"purifies himself, just as He is pure"* (1 John 3:3). One thing that believers need to get to know is not how to quote Scripture but how the Scripture may be made effective by the Spirit, so that the Spirit may impart life as the Word is given. Jesus said, "My word brings life." (See John 5:24.) We need the Spirit to bring life into the believer, to impart life to him.

There is a deep secret concerning the imparting of life that involves the believer: *"Everyone who has this hope in Him **purifies himself, just as He is pure"*** (1 John 3:3, emphasis added). There is a lovely passage along this line in 1 Corinthians 11:31–32: *"If we would judge ourselves, we would not be judged. But when we are judged, we are chastened by the Lord, that we may not be condemned with the world."*

PEACE: NOT HYSTERIA OR NERVOUSNESS

This morning, a young woman asked a very important question about dealing with evil thoughts. I hope someday to specifically teach on how to discern evil spirits and how to deal with voices, because many people today are troubled by voices, and some people run here and there through the influence of voices. Certain people are so unsettled by voices that, instead of being the children of God, they seem to be gripped with a condition of hysteria or nervous breakdown.

Beloved, God wants to make you sound. God wants to make you restful. God wants to give you peace; He wants to cause you to live in the world with peace (John 14:27). The very first message the angels gave when they announced the birth of Christ was, *"On earth peace, goodwill toward men!"* (Luke 2:14). Jesus came to bring peace on earth and goodwill to men.

If you are not at peace, something is wrong. If you are not at rest, something has taken place that has robbed you of your rest. You must know that God desires you to be as much at peace as if you were in heaven.

The following statement is true; God hears me say it: I am as much at peace as if I were in the glory. I also declare to you that, according to the fact of *"the faith of the Son of God"* (Gal. 2:20 KJV) in me, I am not troubled by any pain or sickness in my body. I am free from everything that means weakness.

There is a redemption in Christ, a fullness of redemption, that will make us free from the power of sin and from the powers of evil and evil thoughts, so that we will reign in the world over demonic powers, not being subject to them, but making everything subject to us. (See Luke 10:17.)

I want you to come into a royal place, to be purified *"just as He is pure"* (1 John 3:3). Most people fail to come into perfect line with God because they allow their own reasoning or their own troubled thoughts to nullify the power that God has.

Why do we always bring up the past? Why, no one can forgive himself. The best people in the world would give anything if they could forgive themselves for what they have done. You would give the world if you could forgive yourself, but you cannot; you feel ashamed.

One thing is sure: you cannot forget the evil things that you have done. Another thing is also sure: the Devil will not let you forget. But there is a third thing that is true: God has forgotten our sins (Isa. 43:25; Jer. 31:34), and we have to decide whether we will believe ourselves, the Devil, or God. Which are you going to believe? "When He forgives, He forgets." On the authority of your believing God's Word, I can bring you into a new place. There are wonderful things to achieve along the line of faith that dares to believe God. *"Only believe"* (Mark 5:36)! *"According to your faith let it be to you"* (Matt. 9:29).

MASTER OVER EVIL THOUGHTS

The question the young woman asked this morning was this: "What is the condition of a person who is always troubled with evil thoughts? How is he going to stand? What position is he in when these evil thoughts are always following him?"

Evil thoughts are from Satan. Satan does not know your thoughts. Satan does not know your desires. God hides these things from him. God can *"search the heart"* and *"test the mind"* (Jer. 17:10), but a stranger never interferes with them. Nobody knows you but God. The Devil never has a chance of knowing you.

So what does the Devil do? First, let us see that he came to Jesus, and when he came, all the evil things he suggested could not arouse a single thing in our Lord. (See, for example, Matthew 4:1–11.) So when does the Devil find anything in you? When he suggests a thought in order to bring some thought out of you, and he gets you the moment he does. But if you are delivered by the blood and made holy, the Devil cannot arouse you. Nevertheless, if you are troubled when he suggests an evil thought, you are in a good place; but if you are not troubled, you are in a bad place.

Suppose he is continually attacking you in this manner. Is there a way to overcome it? Of course there is. How can you deal with it? Say to him, "Did Jesus come in the flesh?" And the Evil One will say, "No." No demon power out of hell or in hell has ever been willing to say that Jesus came in the flesh. So when he says "No," you can say, "Get behind me, Satan! I rebuke you in the name of Jesus." (See 1 John 4:2–4.) Oh, it is wonderful for the child of God to be brought into liberty, power, blessing, and strength, until he lives on the earth purified like the Lord.

Do you believe you can ever be like Him? Cheer up, now. Don't measure yourself by yourself, or you will be defeated. Measure yourself by the life of the Lord at work within you, and put your hope in Him. *"Everyone who has this hope in Him purifies himself, just as He is pure"* (1 John 3:3). Then you will be in a wonderful place of dominion over sin and evil.

A Dance Turned into a Prayer Meeting

There are wonderful things about this life in Christ. I would like to bring you to a place where it is so easy to triumph over the powers of the Devil, even when you are right in the midst of them.

I was traveling on a ship between England and Australia, and about the third day out, they were asking me, along with everybody else, to join with them in an entertainment. We were then running a mission according to holiness principles, and we would not allow a teacher in our Sunday school who went to questionable amusements, so we never participated in what they call entertainment. But these people came to me and said, "We want to know if you will join us in an entertainment."

So I had to go quietly to the Lord. "Can I?" I asked Him. I had the sweetest rest about it; it was all right. So I said, "Yes, I will be in the entertainment." They said, "What can you do? "I can sing," I answered. Then they said to me, "Well, we have a very large program, and we would like to put you down, and we would like to give you the song." "Oh!" I said. "My song will be given just before I sing. So you cannot put it down until I am to sing."

They did not care for that very much, but they allowed it. Then they came to me again and said, "We are very anxious to know what place in the program you would like to appear." "What are you going to have?" I asked. "How are you going to finish up?" "Oh," they said, "we have all kinds of things." There wasn't a thing the Devil could arrange that wasn't there. "Well, how are you going to finish up?" I asked again. "We are going to finish up with a dance," they replied. "Put me down just before the dance," I said.

Some ministers were attending the entertainment, and when I went there, I felt so sorry to find these clergymen trying to satisfy a giddy, godless lot of people, and trying to fit in. My turn came. A young woman who was scantily dressed came up to play the piano for me. I gave her the music. "Oh!" she said. "I never—I never could play that kind of music." "Now, don't you be troubled," I said. "I have both music and words." And I sang,

> If I could only tell it as I know it,
> My Redeemer who has done so much for me;
> If I could only tell you how He loves you,
> I am sure that you would make Him yours today.
>
> Could I tell it? Could I tell it?

I never could tell it. All around the room, people were weeping. The dance was put off; they couldn't have a dance. But we had lots of prayer meetings, and some fine young men gave themselves to Jesus.

Beloved, we must be in the world, not of it (John 17:11, 14). What a lovely thing Jesus said to the Father: *"I do not pray that You should take them out of the world, but that You should keep them from the evil one"* (v. 15). Can He do it? He can do it; He has a way to do it. You say, How does He do it?

> Let the waves wash me,
> Let the waves cleanse me,
> Lord, in Your power
> Let them roll over me.

How the blood of Jesus can cleanse! How He can make us clean! How He can stimulate faith and change our powerless condition!

SIN DETHRONED

Now I want to put before you some very difficult things. There are some things that are so difficult and yet so easy. Their difficulty rises and brings perplexity because we do not see that the Lord is greater than everything. We have to see that the Master's hand is so much greater than our hand, and that His ways over us are so much greater than our ways.

"Whoever commits sin also commits lawlessness, and sin is lawlessness. And you know that He was manifested to take away our sins, and in Him there is no sin" (1 John 3:4–5). There is to be no sin in us. We are to purify ourselves as He is pure (1 John 3:3). Sin has been destroyed. Do not be afraid to claim your position in Christ. *"Sin shall not have dominion over you"* (Rom. 6:14). Do not be afraid to see the Word of God. It is true. You are *"dead indeed to sin, but alive to God"* (v. 11). Being dead to sin and being alive to God are the same thing.

As sin had *"reigned unto death"* (Rom. 5:21 KJV), so now Christ comes and reigns over you in life, and you reign in life over sin, disease, and the Devil; you reign over *"principalities and powers"* (Col. 2:15); you reign in Christ.

Where is Christ manifested? He is manifested in our flesh, to destroy the sinful passions of our bodies, to bring carnality to an end (Gal. 5:24), to bring everything of human depravity to a place of defeat. When Christ is in the body, sin is dethroned. Sin shall not reign over you (Rom. 6:14).

Believe that God is bringing you to the place where Christ is manifested in you. This place is a dethronement of human helplessness; it is an enthronement of Christ's righteousness in us. Christ comes in and begins to rule over our human bodies according to His plan. What is His plan? *"Everyone who has this hope in Him purifies himself, just as He is pure"* (1 John 3:3).

Why is this so? There are several steps on the ladder: *"Whoever abides in Him does not sin"* (v. 6). Get that established in your heart as one of the steps. Now let's go a little farther by taking the next step: *"Whoever sins has neither seen Him nor known Him. Little children, let no one deceive you. He who practices righteousness is righteous, just as He is righteous"* (1 John 3:6–7). The third step is found in verse 8: *"He who sins is of the devil, for the devil has sinned from the beginning. For this purpose the Son of God was manifested, that He might destroy the works of the devil."*

340

Where was Christ manifested? In your flesh, *"that He might destroy the works of the devil."* Where? Outside of you? No, in your flesh, where there was *"nothing good"* (Rom. 7:18). He destroyed everything that was not good, came and ruled there, and is there now.

Now I give you one of the hardest problems of the Scriptures, and yet the most beautiful position of the Scriptures. It is a keynote of possibility. It is like being on Mount Pisgah and looking over into the Promised Land, with all the fruits of Canaan at your feet. (See Deuteronomy 34:1–4 KJV.) God will make the grapes of Eshcol very beautiful as you enter into this sublime position of faith. (See Numbers 13:23.)

OUR CONQUERING POSITION

"And everyone who has this hope in Him purifies himself, just as He is pure" (1 John 3:3). *"Whoever has been born of God does not sin, for His seed remains in him; and he cannot sin, because he has been born of God"* (v. 9). I want to explain these verses to you in order to help you. Through these truths, many people, on the authority of God's Word, will be made strong over the power of sin. Sin will not meet you any longer as a master (Rom. 6:14); you will meet it as a conqueror, dethroning it. Here is your conquering position: *"Everyone who has this hope in Him purifies himself, just as He is pure."*

This is the seed; this is the seed of life, the seed of the Son of God. This is the nature of the Son of God. The nature of the Son of God is purity, and for him who *"purifies himself,"* who has obtained this possession of the life of the Son of God—the eternal seed, the purifying position, the incorruptible power—this seed remains in him, and he cannot sin. The purifying seed makes you hate sin. One of the purposes of the salvation of the world is that people would hate sin.

Look at the Master. Have you ever really seen Jesus? God highly exalted Him and gave Him a name above every name (Phil. 2:9). Why? Jesus hated iniquity. What is the difference between hating sin, and knowing that sin is there but passing it by without seeing it or speaking to it? The latter position will never save you. You have to have a righteous indignation against the powers of evil and the Devil; you need to be continually purified, and then you will get to the place where you cannot sin.

This is a glorious position of arrival. This is a blessed place of exit. This is a glorious place of overcoming. This is a place of rest for your feet. This is a great place for endowment of power, for holiness is power, and sin is weakness and defeat.

GOD CLAIMS YOU AS HIS OWN

You are so intense. Your hearts are longing, and your souls are thirsty. You are waking up to the fact that God has chosen you to be His children, to be pure, to have power, to have righteousness. *"Sin shall not have dominion"* (Rom. 6:14); disease will be dethroned; God will claim you as His own. You will be the sons of God with power. (See Romans 1:4.) Who says so? Your Father in heaven. You will be the sons of God, with your sins dethroned and your hearts aflame! Look where God is bringing you. I will read these words to you to strengthen your hearts to enter a new place. This is the place, a wonderful place of covenant and blessing:

> *And by this we know that we are of the truth, and shall assure our hearts before Him. For if our heart condemns us, God is greater than our heart, and knows all things. Beloved, if our heart does not condemn us, we have confidence toward God. And whatever we ask we receive from Him, because we keep His commandments and do those things that are pleasing in His sight.* (1 John 3:19–22)

CHAPTER THIRTEEN

"DO NOT BE AFRAID; ONLY BELIEVE"

I believe that it is in the purpose and will of God that we look at a passage from the fifth chapter of Mark's gospel. My message is based on the words, *"Do not be afraid; only believe"* (Mark 5:36).

HEAR IN FAITH

This is one of those marvelous, glorious truths of Scripture that is written to help us. It enables us to believe, as we see the almightiness of God and also our own possibilities—not only of entering in by faith, but also of becoming partakers of the blessing God wants to give us. My message is about faith. Because some do not hear in faith, they do not profit at all from what they hear. There is a hearing of faith and a hearing that means nothing more than listening to words.

I implore you to see to it that everything that is done may bring not only blessing to you, but also strength and character. I want you to see the wonderfulness and goodness of God. I want to impress upon you the importance of believing what the Scripture says, and I may have many things to relate about people who dared to believe God until His Word came to pass.

This passage from Mark 5 is a wonderful Scripture passage. In fact, all of the Word of God is wonderful. It is an everlasting Word, a Word of power, a Word of health, a Word of substance, a Word of life. It gives life to the very nature of the one who lays hold of it, if he believes. I want you to understand that there is a need for the Word of God. But many times it is a need that brings us the blessing.

ON THE VERGE OF DEATH

Why am I here tonight? Because God delivered me when no other hand could do it. I stand before you as one who was given up by everybody, one whom no one could help.

Let me give you a little background to my story. I was earnest and zealous for the salvation of souls. If you had been in Bradford, England, the town where I lived, you would know. Our ministry had police protection for nearly twenty years in the best thoroughfare in the city, and in my humble way, with my dear wife, who was all on fire for God, I was ministering in the open air. Was I full of zeal? Yes. But one night, about thirty years ago, I was carried home helpless. My wife and I knew very little about divine healing, but we prayed through. It has been more than thirty years since God healed me. I am sixty-five years old, and I am fresher, in better health, and more fit for work than I was in my thirties. It is a most wonderful experience when the life of God becomes the life of man. The divine power that sweeps through the organism, cleansing the blood, makes the man fresh every day. The life of God is resurrection power.

Let me tell you exactly how my healing occurred. When I was brought home helpless, we prayed all night. We did all we knew to do. At ten o'clock the next morning, I said to my wife, "This must be my last roll call." We had five children around us. I tell you, it was not an easy thing to face our circumstances. I told my wife to do as she thought best, but the poor thing didn't know what to do. She called a physician, who examined me, shook his head, and said, "It is impossible for anything to be done for your husband; I am absolutely helpless. He has appendicitis, and you have waited too long. His system will not stand an operation. A few hours, at best, will finish him."

What the doctor said to my wife was true. He left her and said that he would come back again, but that he couldn't give her any hope. When he was nicely out of the house, an old lady and a young man came in who knew how to pray. The young man put his knees on the bed and said, "Come out, you devil, in the name of Jesus." It was a good job. I had no time to argue, and instantly I was free. Oh, hallelujah! I was as free as I am now.

I have never believed that any person ought to be in bed in the daytime, so I jumped up and went downstairs. My wife said, "Oh, are you up?" "I am all right, wife; it is all right now," I said. I had some men working for me, and she said none of them had shown up that morning. So I picked up my tools and went to work. Then the doctor came. He walked up the stairs, and my wife called, "Doctor, doctor, he is out!" "What?" he said. "Yes," she answered, "he went to work." "Oh," he said, "you will never see him alive again. They will bring him home a corpse." But as you can see, I am not a corpse!

Oh, when God does anything, it is done forever! And God wants you to know that He wants to do something in you forever. There are people in this place who have been delivered from appendicitis in these meetings. I have laid my hands on people with appendicitis when doctors were in the place, and God has healed them.

GOD CAN USE YOU

I will tell you one more incident before I move on. It will stir up your faith. I am not here to be on exhibition; I am here to impart divine truth to you concerning the Word of God, so that, after I leave, you can do the same things that I have done. I went to Switzerland, and after I had been there for some weeks, a brother said, "Aren't you going to the meeting tonight?" "No," I said, "I have been at it all this time; you can take charge tonight." "What shall we do?" he asked. "Do?" I said; "Paul the apostle left people to do the work and went on to another place. I have been here long enough now. You do the work." So he went to the meeting. When he came back, he said, "We had a wonderful time." "What happened?" I asked. He said, "I invited them all up, took off my coat, rolled up my sleeves, and prayed. They were all healed. I did just as you did."

Jesus said, *"I give you the authority...over all the power of the enemy"* (Luke 10:19). Jesus' disciples entered into people's houses and healed the sick who were there. The ministry of divine operation in us is wonderful, but who would take it upon himself to say, "I can do this or that"? If it is God, it is all right, but if it is you, it is all wrong. When you are weak, then you are strong. (See 2 Corinthians 12:9–10.) When you are strong in your own strength, you are weak. You must realize this and live only in the place where the power of God rests upon you, and where the Spirit moves within you. Then God will mightily manifest His power, and you will say, as Jesus said, *"The Spirit of the Lord is upon me"* (Luke 4:18 KJV).

345

DESPERATE PARENTS

God brings a remarkable, glorious fact to my mind tonight: the healing of a helpless little girl, recorded in the fifth chapter of Mark. The physicians had failed. I imagine the girl's mother said to the father, "There is only one hope—if you can see Jesus! If you can meet Jesus, our daughter will live." Do you think it is possible for anybody in this city of Washington, D.C., to go looking for Jesus without seeing Him? Is it possible to think about Jesus without Jesus drawing near? No.

This father knew the power there is in the name of Jesus: *"In My name they will cast out demons"* (Mark 16:17). But we must be sure that we truly know that name, for in Acts 19, the seven sons of Sceva said to the man who was possessed with a devil, *"We exorcise you by the Jesus whom Paul preaches"* (v. 13). The evil spirit said, *"Jesus I know, and Paul I know; but who are you?"* (v. 15). Yes, the Devil knows every believer—and the seven sons of Sceva nearly lost their lives. The evil power came upon them, and they barely escaped.

There is more to casting out demons than repeating the name of Jesus; there is the nature of that name within you. Even more than that, there is the Divine Personality within the human life who has come to take up His abode. When Christ becomes all in all in you, then God works through you. The key is the life and the power of God. God works through the life.

The Lord is that life. By the Holy Spirit, the ministry of that life and the power in the ministry bring every believer into such a place of divine relationship that He mightily lives in us and enables us to overcome the powers of the Enemy. The Lord healed that child as the parents got a vision of Jesus. The word of the Lord "[did] *not come with observation"* (Luke 17:20), but with divine, mighty power. As an oracle by the power of the Spirit, it worked in men and women until they were created anew by this new life divine. We have to see that when this divine word comes to us by the power of the Holy Spirit, we speak according to the will of God—not with man's wisdom, but with divine minds operated by the word of God; not as channels only, but as oracles of the Spirit.

THE SYNAGOGUE RULER AND THE BELIEVING WOMAN

Let us now read the passage of Scripture from which this remarkable account of the healing of the helpless little girl comes:

And behold, one of the rulers of the synagogue came, Jairus by name. And when he saw Him, he fell at His feet and begged Him earnestly, saying, "My little daughter lies at the point of death. Come and lay Your hands on her, that she may be healed, and she will live." So Jesus went with him, and a great multitude followed Him and thronged Him. Now a certain woman had a flow of blood for twelve years, and had suffered many things from many physicians. She had spent all that she had and was no better, but rather grew worse. When she heard about Jesus, she came behind Him in the crowd and touched His garment. For she said, "If only I may touch His clothes, I shall be made well." Immediately the fountain of her blood was dried up, and she felt in her body that she was healed of the affliction. And Jesus, immediately knowing in Himself that power had gone out of Him, turned around in the crowd and said, "Who touched My clothes?" But His disciples said to Him, "You see the multitude thronging You, and You say, 'Who touched Me?'" And He looked around to see her who had done this thing. But the woman, fearing and trembling, knowing what had happened to her, came and fell down before Him and told Him the whole truth. And He said to her, "Daughter, your faith has made you well. Go in peace, and be healed of your affliction." While He was still speaking, some came from the ruler of the synagogue's house who said, "Your daughter is dead. Why trouble the Teacher any further?" As soon as Jesus heard the word that was spoken, He said to the ruler of the synagogue, "Do not be afraid; only believe." And He permitted no one to follow Him except Peter, James, and John the brother of James. Then He came to the house of the ruler of the synagogue, and saw a tumult and those who wept and wailed loudly. When He came in, He said to them, "Why make this commotion and weep? The child is not dead, but sleeping." And they ridiculed Him. But when He had put them all outside, He took the father and the mother of the child, and those who were with Him, and entered where the child was lying. Then He took the child by the hand, and said to her, "Talitha, cumi," which is translated, "Little girl, I say to you, arise." Immediately the girl

*arose and walked, for she was twelve years of age. And
they were overcome with great amazement. But He commanded them strictly that no one should know it, and said
that something should be given her to eat.* (Mark 5:22–43)

As the ruler of the synagogue sought Jesus, he worshiped Him
(v. 22). How the people gathered around Him! How everybody listened to what He had to say! He spoke with authority and power,
"not as the scribes" (Matt. 7:29), and He was clothed with divine
glory.

Let me tell you another incident to emphasize what I want you
to understand about the ruler of the synagogue and his daughter. A
young man was preaching in a marketplace. At the close of the address, an atheist came and said, "There have been five Jesuses.
Tell us which one it is that you preach." He answered, *"Him who
was raised from the dead"* (Rom. 7:4). There is only One who rose
from the dead. There is only one Jesus who lives. And as He lives,
we live also. Glory to God! We are risen with Him, we are living
with Him, and we will reign with Him.

As this synagogue ruler drew near the crowd, he went up to
Jesus and said, *"My little daughter lies at the point of death. Come
and lay Your hands on her, that she may be healed, and she will
live"* (Mark 5:23). "I will come," Jesus said. (See verse 24.) What a
beautiful assurance. But as they were going along the road, they
were met by a woman who had had a flow of blood for twelve years.
When this trouble had started, she had sought help from many
physicians. She had had some money, but the physicians had taken
it all and left her worse off than when they had found her (v. 26).

Do you have any doctors around here who do the same thing?
When I was a plumber, I had to finish my work before I got the
money, and I didn't always get it then. I think that if there were an
arrangement whereby no doctor would get his fee until he cured
the patient, not as many people would die.

This woman had had twelve years of sickness. She needed
someone now who could heal without money, for she was bankrupt
and helpless.

Jesus comes to people who are withered up, diseased, lame, or
crippled in all kinds of ways. When He comes, there is liberty for
the captive, opening of eyes for the blind, and opening of ears for
the deaf. I imagine that many people had said to this woman, "If

you had only been with us today! We saw the most marvelous things—the crooked made straight, the lame made to walk, the blind made to see." And the woman who had been sick for twelve years said, "Oh, you make me feel that if I could only see Him, I would be healed." Their words strengthened her faith, and it became firm. She had a purpose within her.

Faith is a mighty power. Faith will reach at everything. When real faith comes into operation, you will not say, "I don't feel much better." Faith says, "I am whole." Faith doesn't say, "I have a lame leg." Faith says, "My leg is all right."

SEEING THROUGH THE EYES OF FAITH

A young woman with a goiter came to one of my meetings to be prayed for. In a testimony meeting, she said, "I do praise the Lord for healing my goiter." She went home and said to her mother, "Oh, Mother, when the man prayed for me, God healed my goiter." For twelve months, she went around telling everybody how God had healed her goiter. Then I came to minister there again, and people said, "How big that lady's goiter is!" There came a time for testimonies. She jumped up and said, "I was here twelve months ago, and God healed me of my goiter. It has been such a marvelous twelve months!" When she went home, her family said, "You should have seen the people today when you testified that God had healed your goiter. They think there is something wrong with you. If you will go upstairs and look in the mirror, you will see that the goiter is bigger than it ever was." She went upstairs, but she didn't look in the mirror. She got down on her knees and said, "Oh, Lord, let all the people know, just as You have let me know, how wonderfully You have healed me." The next morning, her neck was as perfect as any neck you ever saw. Faith never looks. Faith praises God, saying, "It is done!"

JESUS HEALS THE BELIEVING WOMAN
AND THE RULER'S DAUGHTER

Let us continue with the biblical account of these healings. The poor, helpless woman who had been growing weaker and weaker for twelve years pushed into the crowded thoroughfare when she knew that Jesus was in the midst. Stirred to the depths, she pushed through and touched Him. If you will believe God and touch Him, you will go out of this place as well as can be. Jesus is the Healer!

Now, listen! Some people substitute touching the Lord for faith. The Lord did not want that woman to believe that the touch had done it. As soon as she touched Him, she felt that power had gone through her, which was true. When the Israelites were bitten by fiery serpents in the wilderness, God's Word said through Moses, "He who looks at the bronze serpent on the pole will be healed." (See Numbers 21:8.) The look made it possible for God to do it. But the people who looked had to have faith that God's Word was true. Now, did the touch heal the woman? No, the touch meant something more—it was evidence of a living faith. Jesus said, *"Your **faith** has made you well"* (Mark 5:34, emphasis added).

As soon as this woman, who was in the street with the whole crowd around her, began to testify, the Devil came. The Devil is always in a testimony meeting. Even when the *"sons of God"* gathered together before the Lord in the time of Job, Satan was there (Job 1:6). So how did the Enemy come into this situation with the believing woman and the synagogue ruler? While the woman was speaking with Jesus, some people came rushing from the house of Jairus and said, "It is no use now; your daughter is dead. This Jesus can do nothing for a dead daughter. Your wife needs you at home." (See Mark 5:35.) But Jesus said, *"Do not be afraid; only believe"* (v. 36).

He spoke the word just in time! Jesus is never late. When the tumult is the worst, the pain most severe, the cancer gripping the body, then come the words, *"Only believe."* When everything seems as though it will fail, when everything is practically hopeless, the Word of God comes to us: *"Only believe."*

When Jesus came to the ruler's house, He found a lot of people weeping and wailing. People mourn for the dead, but as for me, I have taken my last wreath to the cemetery. *"To be absent from the body* [is] *to be present with the Lord"* (2 Cor. 5:8), and if you believe that, you will never need to take another wreath to the cemetery. It is unbelief that mourns. If you have faith that your departed loved ones are with the Lord, you will never need to take another flower to the grave. They are not there. Hallelujah!

These people were standing around weeping, wailing, and howling. Jesus said, *"Why make this commotion and weep? The child is not dead, but sleeping"* (Mark 5:39).

There is a wonderful word that God wants you to hear. Jesus said, *"I am the resurrection and the life"* (John 11:25). The believer may fall asleep in Christ, but the believer doesn't die. Oh, that people would understand the deep things of God; the whole situation would be changed! Then they would look with a glorious hope to the day when the Lord will return. What does the Bible say? *"God will bring with Him those who sleep in Jesus"* (1 Thess. 4:14). Jesus knew that. *"He said to them, '...The child is not dead, but sleeping.' And they ridiculed Him ["laughed Him to scorn,"* KJV]*"* (Mark 5:39–40). These wailers showed their insincerity in that they could turn from wailing to mocking.

But Jesus took the father and mother of the girl, and, going into the room where she was, took her hand and said, *"Little girl, I say to you, arise"* (v. 41). And the child sat up. Praise the Lord! And Jesus said, "Give her something to eat." (See verse 43.)

You Can Know That You Are Saved

Oh, the remarkableness of our Lord Jesus! I want to impress upon you tonight the importance of realizing that He is in the midst of us. No person needs to go away without knowing not only that he is saved, but also that God can live in these bodies of ours. You are begotten, the moment you believe, unto *"a living hope"* (1 Pet. 1:3).

I wonder if anyone in this place is a stranger to this new birth into life. Jesus said, *"He who believes in Me **has** everlasting life"* (John 6:47, emphasis added). You have eternal life the moment you believe. The first life is temporal, natural, material, but in the new birth, you exist as long as God exists—forever! We are begotten by an incorruptible power, by the Word of God (1 Pet. 1:23). The new birth is unto righteousness. You are begotten by God the moment that you believe.

We are talking about divine things tonight. Oh, the wonderful adaptability of God, for Him to come right into this place! Those of you who have not been satisfied, who have sought salvation and have had good impressions, perhaps, but have never known the reality and joy of the new birth, let me enlist you. The Word of God says, *"Before they call, I will answer"* (Isa. 65:24). The raising of your hand is a sign of your heart's desire. God always saves through the heart. He who believes in his heart and confesses with his mouth will be saved (Rom. 10:9).

Jesus is here tonight to loose those who are bound. If you are suffering in your body, He will heal you now as we pray. He is saying to every sin-sick soul, to every disease-stricken one, *"Do not be afraid; only believe"* (Mark 5:36).

CHAPTER FOURTEEN

WE MEAN BUSINESS WITH GOD

There is a power in God's Word that brings life where death is. *"Only believe"* (Mark 5:36). *"Only believe."* Jesus said that the time will come when *"the dead will hear the voice of the Son of God; and those who hear will live"* (John 5:25). For he who believes this Word, *"all things are possible to him who believes"* (Mark 9:23). The life of the Son is in the Word, and all who are saved can preach this Word. This Word frees us from death and corruption; it is life in the nature. Jesus *"brought life and immortality to light through the gospel"* (2 Tim. 1:10).

We can never exhaust the Word; it is so abundant. *"There is a river whose streams...make glad the city of God"* (Ps. 46:4); its source is in the glory. The essence of its life is God. The life of Jesus embodied is its manifested power.

> **INTERPRETATION OF A MESSAGE IN TONGUES:**
> Jesus Himself has come into death and has given us the victory; the victorious Son of God in humanity overcomes, He who succors the needy. Immortality produced in mortality has changed the situation for us. This is life indeed and the end of death, Christ having "brought life and immortality to life through the Gospel."

THE NEW CHURCH ESTABLISHED

We have a wonderful subject because of its manifestation of the nature of the church, for in God's first church, no lie could live. The new church that the Holy Spirit is building has no lie, but purity and *"holiness to the LORD"* (Jer. 2:3). I see the new church established in the breath of the Lord. God is working in a supernatural way, making faces shine with His glory, creating

353

people so in likeness with Him that they love what is right, hate iniquity and evil, and deeply reverence Him, so that a lie is unable to remain in their midst.

"There is therefore now no condemnation to those who are in Christ Jesus, who do not walk according to the flesh, but according to the Spirit" (Rom. 8:1). No one can condemn you. Many may try, but God's Word says,

> *Who shall bring a charge against God's elect? It is God who justifies. Who is he who condemns? It is Christ who died, and furthermore is also risen, who is even at the right hand of God, who also makes intercession for us.*
>
> (Rom. 8:33–34)

Will Jesus condemn the sheep for whom He died? He died to save men, and He saves all who believe.

God is purifying our hearts by faith. God has come forth, clothing us with His Spirit's might, living in the blaze of this glorious day—for there is nothing greater than the Gospel.

In Acts 5, we read that Ananias and Sapphira were moved to bring an offering (v. 1). The day will come when we will consider nothing as our own, because we will be so taken up with the Lord. The church will ripen into coming glory. The first day was a measure; the latter day was to be more generous.

Ananias and Sapphira sold a possession; it was their own, but when it was sold, it looked like so much money. They reasoned, "The Pentecostal order is new; it might dry up." So they agreed to give a part and reserve the other (v. 2). Satan is very subtle. Many people miss the greatest things by drawing aside. Let us pay our vows to the Lord (Ps. 116:14, 18).

"But Peter said, 'Ananias, why has Satan filled your heart to lie to the Holy Spirit and keep back part of the price of the land for yourself?'" (Acts 5:3). The moment Ananias and Sapphira lied to the Holy Spirit by presenting only a portion of the money to the apostles, they were struck down (vv. 2–11).

God has shown us a new order of the Spirit in this Holy Spirit baptism. One day, when I came into my house, my wife said, "Did you come in at the front door?" I said, "No, I came in at the back." "Oh," she said. "At the front you would have seen a crowd and a man with little clothing on, crying out, 'I have committed the unpardonable sin!'"

As I went to the door, God whispered to me, "This is what I baptized you in the Spirit for." The man came in crying, "I have committed the unpardonable sin!" I said, "You lying devil, come out, in Jesus' name." The man said, "What is it? I am free. Thank God, I never committed the unpardonable sin." The moment the lying spirit was gone, he was able to speak the truth. I realized then the power in the baptism of the Holy Spirit. It was the Spirit who said, "This is what I baptized you for," and I believe we ought to be in the place where we will always be able to understand the mind of the Spirit amid all the other voices in the world.

Purity of Life before God

When Ananias and Sapphira died, great fear came upon the church (Acts 5:5, 11). It demonstrated the believers' love for God in that they feared to grieve Him. Why, they could ask and receive anything from God.

The church is to be of one accord, with perfect faithfulness, love, oneness, and consolation. God can lift the church into a place of manifested reconciliation and oneness, until the Devil has no power in our midst, and God is smiling on us all the time.

"And through the hands of the apostles many signs and wonders were done among the people" (v. 12). A purity of life before God means a manifested power among men, with multitudes gathered into the kingdom of God. God has mightily blessed the work at Elim Tabernacle, where this meeting is taking place. Those of you who are still lingering outside the kingdom, yield to God. Get *"clean hands"* and a right purpose (Ps. 24:4), join what is holy and on fire, and mean business for God.

"And believers were increasingly added to the Lord, multitudes of both men and women" (Acts 5:14). Oh, for this kind of revival, God breaking forth everywhere and London swept by the power of God! There must be a great moving among us, a oneness of heart and soul, and revival is sure to come as God moves upon the people.

> *They brought the sick out into the streets and laid them on beds and couches, that at least the shadow of Peter passing by might fall on some of them. Also a multitude gathered from the surrounding cities to Jerusalem, bringing sick people and those who were tormented by unclean spirits, and they were all healed.* (Acts 5:15–16)

Unity has the effect of manifesting the work of God every time. Glory to God, it is so lovely. The people had such a living faith; they were of one heart, one mind. They thought, "Oh, if only Peter's shadow passes over our sick ones, God will heal them."

Have faith. God will heal the land. Oneness of heart and mind on the part of the church means signs and wonders in all lands. *"Whatever things you ask when you pray, believe that you receive them, and you will have them"* (Mark 11:24). *"Only believe"* (Mark 5:36). I see, beloved, that we need to get more love, and the Lord will do it. How the Master can move among the needy and perishing when He has the right of way in the church!

The finest thing is persecution. We must have a ministry that makes the people glad and the Devil mad. Never mind if the people run away, for conviction is within, and God has them. And if the people are glad, the Lord also has them, so it works both ways. Don't be disturbed at anything. Remember that it was written of the Master, *"Zeal for Your house has eaten Me up"* (John 2:17). We need to have a melting, moving, broken condition—*"as poor, yet making many rich; as having nothing, and yet possessing all things"* (2 Cor. 6:10). Let us be in harmony with the divine plan, having knowledge cemented with love, death to the old nature having perfect place in us, so that the life-power can be manifested.

I once went for weekend meetings, and when I arrived on Saturday night, it was snowing hard, and the man meeting me stood at the door of the hall laden with packages. As we walked home, when we reached the first lamppost, I said, "Brother, are you baptized in the Holy Spirit?" Then I said, "Say you will be tonight." As we went along, at every lamppost (nearly a hundred), I repeated the question, "Say you will be baptized tonight." So he began wishing I was not staying at his house. At last we reached the gate to his house. I jumped over it and said, "Now, don't you come in here unless you say you will be baptized with the Holy Spirit tonight." "Oh," he said, "I feel so funny, but I will say it." We went in. I asked his wife, "Are you baptized in the Holy Spirit?" She said, "Oh, I want to be—but supper is ready, come in." I said, "No supper until you are both baptized in the Holy Spirit."

Did God answer? Oh yes, soon they were both speaking in tongues. Now, I believe that God will baptize you. Put up your hands and ask Him to. Also, those seeking healing and salvation, do the same, and God will meet you, every one.

CHAPTER FIFTEEN

AFTER YOU HAVE
RECEIVED POWER

I n Acts 1:8, we read, *"You shall receive power when the Holy Spirit has come upon you."* Oh, the power of the Holy Spirit— the power that quickens, reveals, and prevails! I love the thought that Jesus wanted all His people to have power, that He wanted all men to be overcomers. Nothing but this power of the Holy Spirit will do it—power over sin, power over sickness, power over the Devil, power over all the powers of the Devil (Luke 10:19)!

In order to understand what it means to have power, two things are necessary: one is to have *"ears to hear"* (Matt. 11:15), and the other is to have hearts to receive. Every born-again saint of God who is filled with the Spirit has a real revelation of this truth: *"He who is in you is greater than he who is in the world"* (1 John 4:4). I say this with as much audacity as I please: I know evil spirits are in abundance and in multitudes; Jesus cast them out as legion. (See Mark 5:2–15; Luke 8:26–35.) The believer, because of the Spirit who is in him, has the power to cast out the evil spirit. It *must* be so; God wants us to have this power in us; we must be able to destroy Satan's power wherever we go.

ALWAYS READY

After the Holy Spirit comes upon you, you have power. I believe a great mistake is made in these days by people waiting and waiting after they have received. After you have received, it is, *"Go"* (Mark 16:15). It is not, "Sit still," but *"Go into all the world and preach the gospel"* (v. 15). We will make serious havoc of the whole thing if we turn back again and crawl into a corner seeking something we already have. I want you to see that God depends on

357

us in these last days. There is no room for anyone to boast, and the person who goes around saying, "Look at me, for I am somebody," is of no value whatever. God will not often work through such a person. He will have a people who glorify Him. He is doing what He can with what He has, but we are so unwilling to move in the plan of God that He has to grind us many times to get us where He can use us.

Jesus was so filled with the Holy Spirit that He stood in the place where He was always ready. He was always in the attitude where He brought victory out of every opportunity. The power of the Holy Spirit is within us, but it can be manifested only as we go in obedience to the opportunity before us. I believe if you wait until you think you have power after you have received the Holy Spirit, you will never know you have it. Don't you know that the child of God who has the baptism is inhabited by the Spirit? Remember the incident in the Bible where the Jews were going to stone Jesus? He slipped away from them, and shortly afterward, He healed the man with the blind eyes. (See John 8:48–9:7.) Slipping away from the crowd that was trying to kill Him, He showed forth His power. Some people might think that Jesus should have run away altogether, but He stopped to heal. This thought has comforted me over and over again.

One day, as I was waiting for a streetcar, I stepped into a shoemaker's shop. I had not been there long when I saw a man with a green shade over his eyes. He was crying pitifully and was in great agony; it was heartbreaking. The shoemaker told me that the inflammation was intensely burning and injuring his eyes. I jumped up and went to the man and said, "You devil, come out of this man in the name of Jesus." Instantly, the man said, "It is all gone; I can see now." That is the only scriptural way: to begin to work at once, and to preach afterward. *"Jesus began both to do and teach"* (Acts 1:1).

GRACE ABOUNDING

You will find, as the days go by, that the miracles and healings will be manifested. Because the Master was *"touched with the feeling of* [the] *infirmities"* (Heb. 4:15 KJV) of the multitudes, they instantly gathered around Him to hear what He had to say concerning the Word of God. However, I would rather see one man saved than ten thousand people healed. If you should ask me why, I would call your attention to the Word, which says, *"There was a certain rich man who...fared sumptuously every day"* (Luke 16:19). Now, we don't hear of this man having any diseases, but the Word says that, after he died, *"being in torments in Hades ["hell,"* KJV], *he lifted up his eyes"* (v. 23). We also read that there was a poor man who was full of sores, and that, after he died, he *"was carried by the angels to Abraham's bosom* [in heaven]" (v. 22). So we see that a man can die practically in good health, but be lost, and a man can die with disease and be saved; so it is more important to be saved than anything else.

But Jesus was sent to bear the infirmities and the afflictions of the people, and to *"destroy the works of the devil"* (1 John 3:8). He said, *"The thief* [the Devil] *does not come except to steal, and to kill, and to destroy. I have come that they may have life, and that they may have it more abundantly"* (John 10:10). I maintain that God wishes all His people to have the more abundant life. We have the remedy for all sickness in the Word of God! Jesus paid the full price and the full redemption for every need, and where sin abounds, grace can come in and much more abound (Rom. 5:20), and dispel all the sickness.

When I was traveling by ship from England to Australia, I witnessed for Jesus, and it was not long before I had plenty of room to myself. If you want a whole seat to yourself, just begin to preach Jesus. However, some people listened and began to be much affected. One of the young men said to me, "I have never heard these truths before. You have so moved me that I must have a good conversation with you." The young man told me that his wife was a great believer in Christian Science, but that she was very sick now. Although she had tried everything, she had been unable to get relief, and so she was consulting a doctor. But the doctor gave her no hope whatsoever, and in her dilemma, and facing the reality of death, she asked that she might have an appointment with me.

When I went to see her in her cabin, I felt it would be unwise to say anything about Christian Science, so I said, "You are in bad shape." She said, "Yes, they give me no hope." I said, "I will not speak to you about anything, but will just lay my hands upon you in the name of Jesus, and when I do, you will be healed." That woke her up, and she began to think seriously. For three days, she was lamenting over the things she might have to give up. "Will I have to give up cigarettes?" "No," I said. "Will I have to give up dancing?" she asked. And again I replied, "No." "Well, we do a little drinking sometimes and then we play cards also. Will I have to give—." "No," I said, "you will not have to give up anything. Only let us see Jesus." And right then she got such a vision of her cruci-fied Savior, and Jesus was made so real to her, that she at once told her friends that she could not play cards anymore, could not drink or dance anymore, and that she would have to go back to England to preach against this awful thing, Christian Science. Oh, what a revelation Jesus gave her! Now, if I had refused to go when called for, saying that I first had to go to my cabin and pray about it, the Lord might have let that opportunity slip by. After you have re-ceived the Holy Spirit, you have power; you don't have to wait.

The other day, we were going through a very thickly populated part of San Francisco when we noticed that a large crowd had gathered. I saw it from the window of the streetcar I was riding in, and I said that I had to get out, which I did. There in the midst of the crowd was a boy in the agonies of death. As I threw my arms around the boy, I asked what the trouble was, and he answered that he had cramps. In the name of Jesus, I commanded the devils to come out of him, and at once he jumped up and, not even taking time to thank me, ran off perfectly healed. We are God's own chil-dren, quickened by His Spirit, and He has given us power over all the powers of darkness (Luke 10:19). Christ in us is the open evi-dence of eternal glory. Christ in us is the Life, the Truth, and the Way (John 14:6).

THE GREATNESS OF THE POWER

We have a wonderful salvation that fits everybody. I believe that a person who is baptized in the Holy Spirit has no conception of the power God has given him until he uses what he has. I main-tain that Peter and John had no idea of the greatness of the power they had, but they began to speculate. They said to the lame man who asked them for alms, "Well, as far as money goes, we have none of that, but we do have something; we don't exactly know what it is, but we will try it on you: *In the name of Jesus Christ of Nazareth, rise up and walk*" (Acts 3:6). And it worked. (See verses 1–10.)

In order to make yourself realize what you have in your pos-session, you will have to try it; and I can assure you, it will work all right. One time I said to a man that the Acts of the Apostles would never have been written if the apostles had not acted; and the Holy Spirit is still continuing His acts through us. May God help us to have some acts.

There is nothing like Pentecost, and if you have never been baptized in the Holy Spirit, you are making a big mistake by waiting. Don't you know that one of the main purposes for which God saved you was that you might bring salvation to others through Christ? For you to think that you have to remain stationary and just get to heaven is a great mistake. The baptism is to make you a witness for Jesus. The hardest way is the best way; you never hear anything about the person who is always having an easy time. The preachers always tell of how Moses crossed the Red Sea when he was at his wits' end. I cannot find a record of anyone in the Scriptures whom God used who was not first tried. So if you never have any trials, it is because you are not worth them.

God wants us to have power. When I was traveling on the train in Sweden early in the morning, a little lady and her daughter got onto the train at a certain station. I saw at once that the lady was in dreadful agony, and I asked my interpreter to inquire as to the trouble. With tears running down her face, she told how her daughter was taking her to the hospital to have her leg amputated. Everything possible had been done for her. I told her Jesus could heal. Just then the train stopped, and a crowd of people entered until there was hardly standing room; but friends, we never get into a place that is too awkward for God, though it seemed to me that the Devil had sent these people in at that time to hinder her healing. However, when the train began to move along, I got down, although it was terribly crowded, and, putting my hands upon the woman's leg, I prayed for her in the name of Jesus. At once, she said to her daughter, "I am healed. It is all different now; I felt the power go down my leg." And she began to walk around. Then the train stopped at the next station, and this woman got out and walked up and down the platform, saying, "I am healed. I am healed."

Jesus was the *"firstfruits"* (1 Cor. 15:20), and God has chosen us in Christ and has revealed His Son in us so that we might manifest Him in power. God gives us power over the Devil, and when I say the Devil, I mean everything that is not of God. Some people say we can afford to do without the baptism in the Spirit, but I say we cannot. I believe that any person who thinks there is a stop between Calvary and the glory has made a big mistake.

Chapter Sixteen

How to Be an Overcomer

I n the first chapter of Mark, we read of John the Baptist, who, as we learn in Luke, was filled with the Holy Spirit *"from his mother's womb"* (Luke 1:15). Because of this mighty infilling, there was mighty message on his lips. (See Mark 1:1–4.) It was foretold of John by the prophet Isaiah that he would be *"the voice of one crying in the wilderness"* (Isa. 40:3). He was to lift up his voice with strength, and cry to the cities of Judah, *"Behold your God!"* (v. 9). And so we find John, as he pointed to Jesus at the Jordan River, crying out, *"Behold! The Lamb of God who takes away the sin of the world!"* (John 1:29). In this way, he proclaimed Jesus to be the One of whom Abraham prophesied when he said to his son Isaac in Genesis 22:8, *"God will provide for Himself the lamb"*—the Lamb of God and God the Lamb.

John was so filled with the Spirit of God that the cry he raised moved all Israel (Mark 1:5). This shows that when God gets hold of a person and fills him with the Spirit, he can have a cry, a message, a proclamation of the Gospel that will move people. A person who does not have the Spirit of the Lord may cry out for many years and not have anybody take notice of him. The person who is filled with the Spirit of God needs to cry out only once and people will feel the effect of it.

Be Filled with the Spirit of God

This should teach us that there is a need for every one of us to be filled with the Spirit of God. It is not sufficient just to have a touch of God or to usually have a desire for God. There is only one thing that will meet the needs of the people today, and that is to be immersed in the life of God—God taking you and filling you with

His Spirit, until you live right in God, and God lives in you, so that *"whether you eat or drink, or whatever you do,"* it will all be for the *"glory of God"* (1 Cor. 10:31). In that place, you will find that all your strength and all your mind and all your soul are filled with zeal, not only for worship, but to proclaim the Gospel message—a proclamation that is accompanied by the power of God (Rom. 1:16), which defeats satanic power, convicts the world, and contributes to the glory of God.

The reason the world is not seeing Jesus today is that *too many Christian people are not filled with the Spirit of Christ.* They are satisfied with going to church, occasionally reading the Bible, and sometimes praying. Beloved, if God lays hold of you by the Spirit, you will find that there is an end to everything of the old life. All the old things will have passed away, and all things will have become new—all things will be of God (2 Cor. 5:17–18). You will find that, as you are wholly yielded to God, your whole being will be transformed by the divine indwelling. He will take you in hand so that you may become *"a vessel for honor"* (2 Tim. 2:21).

Our lives are not to be for ourselves, for if we live for self, we will die. If we seek to save our lives, we will lose them, but if we lose our lives, we will save them (Matt. 16:25). If we, through the Spirit, *"put to death the deeds of the body"* (Rom. 8:13), we will live—live a life of freedom and joy and blessing and service, a life that will bring blessing to others. God wants us to see that we must *"be filled with the Spirit"* (Eph. 5:18), that we must every day *"live in the Spirit,...walk in the Spirit"* (Gal. 5:25), and be continually renewed in the Spirit.

Study the life of Jesus. It was quite a natural thing for Him, after He had served a whole day among the multitude, to want to go to His Father to pray all night. Why? He wanted a renewing of divine strength and power. He wanted fellowship with His Father. His Father would speak to Him the word that He was to bring to others, and would empower Him afresh for new ministry. He would come from those hours of sweet communion and fellowship with His Father clothed with His holy presence and Spirit, and, anointed with the Holy Spirit and power, He would go about doing good and healing all who were oppressed by the Enemy (Acts 10:38).

When He met sickness, it had to leave. He came from that holy time of communion with power to meet the needs of the people, whatever they were. It is an awful thing for me to see people who profess to be Christians but who are lifeless and powerless. The place of holy communion is open to us all. There is a place where we can be daily refreshed, renewed, and re-empowered.

In the fourth chapter of Hebrews, we are told, *"There remains therefore a rest for the people of God. For he who has entered His rest has himself also ceased from his works"* (vv. 9–10). Oh, what a blessed rest that is, to cease from your own works, to come to the place where God is now enthroned in your life, working in you day by day *"to will and to do for His good pleasure"* (Phil. 2:13), working in you an entirely new order of things.

God wants to bring you forth as a *"flame of fire"* (Heb. 1:7), with a message from God, with the truth that will defeat the powers of Satan, with an unlimited supply for every needy soul. So, just as John the Baptist moved all of Israel with a mighty cry, you too, by the power of the Holy Spirit, will move the people so that they repent and cry, *"What shall we do?"* (Luke 3:10, 12, 14).

BORN OF GOD

This is what Jesus meant when He said to Nicodemus,

Unless one is born again, he cannot see the kingdom of God....That which is born of the flesh is flesh, and that which is born of the Spirit is spirit. Do not marvel that I said to you, "You must be born again." (John 3:3, 6–7)

If we only knew what these words mean to us, to be born of God! They mean an infilling of the life of God, a new life from God, a new creation, living in the world but not of the world (John 17:11, 14), knowing the blessedness of this truth: *"Sin shall not have dominion over you"* (Rom. 6:14). How will we reach this place in the Spirit? By the provision that the Holy Spirit makes. If we live in the Spirit, we will find that all that is carnal in us is swallowed up in life. There is an infilling of the Spirit that gives life to our mortal bodies (Rom. 8:11).

Give God your life, and you will see that sickness has to go when God comes in fully. Then you are to walk before God, and you will find that He will perfect what concerns you. That is the place where He wants believers to live, the place where the Spirit of the Lord comes into your whole being. That is the place of victory.

Look at the disciples. Before they received the Holy Spirit, they were in bondage. When Christ said, *"One of you will betray Me"* (Matt. 26:21), they were all doubtful of themselves and asked, *"Lord, is it I?"* (v. 22). They were conscious of their human depravity and helplessness. Later, Peter said, *"Even if I have to die with You, I will not deny You!"* (v. 35). The others declared the same, yet they all forsook Him and fled when He was arrested. But after the power of God fell upon them in the Upper Room, they met difficulty like lions. They were bold. What made them so? The purity and power that is by the Spirit.

You Can Be an Overcomer

God can make you an overcomer. When the Spirit of God comes into your surrendered being, He transforms you. There is a life in the Spirit that makes you free, and there is an audacity about it, and there is a personality in it—it is God in you.

God is able to so transform you and change you that all the old order has to go before God's new order. Do you think that God will make you to be a failure? God never made man to be a failure. He made man to be a son, to walk the earth in the power of the Spirit, to be master over the flesh and the Devil, until nothing arises within him except what will magnify and glorify the Lord.

Jesus came to set us free from sin, and to free us from sickness, so that we will go forth in the power of the Spirit and minister to the needy, sick, and afflicted. Through the revelation of the Word of God, we find that divine healing is solely for the glory of God, and that salvation is walking in newness of life so that we are inhabited by Another, even God.

CHAPTER SEVENTEEN

FILLED WITH GOD

For a short time, I want especially to speak to those of you who are saved. God wants us to be holy. He wants us to be filled with a power that keeps us holy. He wants us to have a revelation of what sin and death are, and what the Spirit and the life of the Spirit are.

Look at the first two verses of Romans 8. They are full of meaning, sufficient to occupy us for two hours, but we must move on in order to help everybody. But look at these verses for a moment:

> *There is therefore now no condemnation to those who are in Christ Jesus, who do not walk according to the flesh, but according to the Spirit. For the law of the Spirit of life in Christ Jesus has made me free from the law of sin and death.* (Rom. 8:1–2)

"No condemnation." This is the primary phrase for me tonight because it means so much—it has everything within it. If you are without condemnation, you are in a place where you can pray through, where you have a revelation of Christ. For Him to be in you brings you to a place where you cannot but follow the divine leadings of the Spirit of Christ, and where you have no fellowship with the world.

I want you to see that the Spirit of the Lord desires to reveal to us this fact: if you love the world (worldliness), you cannot love God, and the love of God cannot be in you (1 John 2:15). God wants a straight cut—a complete severing from worldliness. Why does God want a straight cut? Because if you are *"in Christ,"* you are a *"new creation"* (2 Cor. 5:17). You are in Him; you belong to a new creation in the Spirit, and therefore you *"walk in the Spirit"* (Gal. 5:16) and are free from condemnation.

THE LAW OF THE SPIRIT

So the Spirit of the Lord wants you without condemnation, and desires to bring you into revelation. Now, what will this mean? Much in every way, because God wants all His people to be targets, to be lights, to be like cities set on a hill that cannot be hidden (Matt. 5:14), to be so "in God" for the world's redemption that the world may know that they belong to God.

That is the law of the Spirit. What will it do? *"The law of the Spirit of life in Christ Jesus* [will make you] *free from the law of sin and death"* (Rom. 8:2). Sin will have no dominion over you (Rom. 6:14). You will have no desire to sin, and it will be as true in your case as it was in Jesus' when He said, "Satan comes, but finds nothing in Me." (See John 14:30.) Satan cannot condemn; he has no power. His power is destroyed. This fact is expressed in Romans 8:10. What does it say? *"The body is dead because of sin, but the Spirit is life because of righteousness."* To be filled with God means that you are free—full of joy, peace, blessing, power, and strength of character; molded afresh in God and transformed by His mighty power, until you *live.* Yet it is not you who live, but Another lives in you (Gal. 2:20), manifesting His power through you as sons of God.

Notice these two laws: ***"The law of the Spirit of life in Christ Jesus*** [makes you] *free from **the law of sin and death"*** (Rom. 8:2, emphasis added). The same *"law of sin and death"* is in you as was in you before, but it is dead. You are just the same person, only you have been made alive; it is the same flesh, but it is dead. You are a new creation, a new creature. You are created in God afresh according to the image of Christ.

Now, beloved, some people come into line with this, but they do not understand their inheritance in Christ, and therefore they are defeated. However, instead of being weak and being defeated, you have to rise triumphantly over *"the law of sin and death."* You say, "Show us '*the law of the Spirit of life in Christ Jesus.*'" I will, God helping me. It is found in Romans 7, the last verse: *"I thank God; through Jesus Christ our Lord! So then, with the mind I myself serve the law of God, but with the flesh the law of sin"* (v. 25).

Is it a sin to work? No, it is not a sin to work. Work is ordained by God. It is an honor to work. I find that there are two ways to work. One way is working in the flesh, but the child of God should never allow himself to come into the flesh when God has taken him in the Spirit. God wants to show you that there is a place where you can live in the Spirit and not be subject to the flesh. Live in the Spirit until sin has no dominion. *"Sin reigned in death"* (Rom. 5:21), but Christ reigns, and so we reign in Christ, over sin and death. (See verses 17–21.) Reigning in life.

THE GREATNESS OF REDEMPTION

There is not a person here who, if he is sick, is truly reigning in life. There is satanic power reigning there, but God wants you to know that you have to reign. God made you like Himself, and Jesus bought back for us in the Garden of Gethsemane everything that was lost in the Garden of Eden, and restored it to us through His agony. He bought that blessed redemption. When I think of redemption, I wonder if there is anything greater than the Garden of Eden, when Adam and Eve had fellowship with God, and He came down and walked with them in the cool of the evening (Gen. 3:8). Is there anything greater?

Yes, redemption is greater. How? Anything that is local is never as great. When God was in the Garden, Adam was local—within the boundaries of the Garden; but the moment a person is born again, he is free and lives in *"heavenly places"* (Eph. 1:3). He has no destination except the glory. Redemption is greater than the Garden, and God wants you to know that He wants you to come into this glorious redemption, not only for the salvation of your soul, but also for your body—to know that it is redeemed from *"the curse of the law"* (Gal. 3:13), to know that you have been set free, to know that God's Son has set you free. Hallelujah! *"Free from the law of sin and death"* (Rom. 8:2)! How is this accomplished? Romans 8:3–4 tell us. They are master verses:

> *For what the law could not do in that it was weak through the flesh, God did by sending His own Son in the likeness of sinful flesh, on account of sin: He condemned sin in the flesh, that the righteous requirement of the law might be fulfilled in us who do not walk according to the flesh but according to the Spirit.*

Righteousness fulfilled in us! Brother! Sister! I tell you, there is a redemption, there is an atonement, in Christ—a personality of Christ to dwell in you. There is a Godlikeness for you to attain to—a blessed resemblance of Christ in you—if you will believe the Word of God. The Word is sufficient for you. Eat it; devour it. It is the living Word of God.

Jesus was manifested to *"destroy the works of the devil"* (1 John 3:8). God so manifested His fullness in Jesus that He walked this earth glorified and filled with God. In the first place, Jesus was with God from the beginning, and is called *"the Word"* (John 1:1). In the second place, He and God are united in their working, and the Bible says, *"The Word was God"* (v. 1).

The cooperation of oneness was so manifest that nothing was done without the Other. They cooperated in the working of power. You must understand that *"before the foundation of the world,"* this plan of redemption was completed (Eph. 1:4; 1 Pet. 1:20–21); it was set in order before the Fall. Notice that this redemption had to be so mighty, and to redeem us all so perfectly, that there would be no lack in the whole redemption. Let us see how it came about.

First, *"the Word became flesh"* (John 1:14); next He was filled with the Holy Spirit (Matt. 3:16); and then He became the voice and the operation of the Word by the power of God through the Holy Spirit. He became the Authority.

Let me go further. You are born of an incorruptible power—the power of God's Word—by His personality and His nature. (See 1 Peter 1:23.) You are *"born of God"* (1 John 5:18), and *"you are not your own"* (1 Cor. 6:19). Christ now lives in you, and you can believe that you have *"passed from death into life"* (John 5:24) and become an heir of God, a joint heir with Christ (Rom. 8:17), in the measure that you believe His Word. The natural flesh has been changed for a new order. The first order was the natural Adamic order; the last order is Christ—the heavenly order. (See 1 Corinthians 15:45–49.) And now you become changed by a heavenly power existing in your earthly body, a power that can never die; it can never *"see corruption"* (Acts 2:27), and it cannot be lost. If you are born of God, you are born of the power of the Word, and not of man. I want you to see that you are born of a power that exists within you, the power by which God made the world that you are in. It is *"the law of the Spirit of life in Christ Jesus [that makes us] free from the law of sin and death"* (Rom. 8:2). Did you accept it?

I want you all to see that what I have been preaching for two weeks in this place—divine life, divine healing, authority over satanic powers—is all biblical. If you will only believe it, you will be secure, for there is a power in you that is greater than in all the world (1 John 4:4). It is power over sin, power over death.

THE LAW OF SIN AND DEATH

Let us consider the contrast between two laws. First, let us look at the law without the Spirit—*"the law of sin and death"* (Rom. 8:2). Suppose there is a man here who has never known regeneration; he is led captive by the Devil at his will. There is no power that can convert men except the power of the blood of Jesus. Men try without it; science tries without it; all have tried without it; but all are left shaking on the brink of hell—without it. Nothing can deliver you but the blood of the Lamb. You can be free from the law of sin and death by the law of the Spirit of life in Christ Jesus. Then you will have clean hearts and pure lives.

Beloved, the carnal life is not subject to the will of God, nor indeed can it be (Rom. 8:7). Carnality is selfishness, uncleanness. It cannot be subject to God; it will not believe; it interferes with you; it binds you and keeps you in bondage. But, beloved, God destroys carnality. He destroys *"the works of the flesh"* (Gal. 5:19). How? By a new life that is so much better, by a *"peace...which surpasses all understanding"* (Phil. 4:7), by a *"joy* [that is] *inexpressible and full of glory"* (1 Pet. 1:8).

OUR NEW LIFE IN GOD

This new life in God cannot be described. Everything that God does is too big to tell. His grace is too big. His love is too big. Why, it takes all heaven. His salvation is too big to be told; one cannot understand it. It is so vast, mighty, and wonderful—so "in God." But God gives us the power to understand it. Yes, of course, He does. Do you not know that ours is an abundant God? His love is far exceeding and abundant, above all that we can ask or think (Eph. 3:20).

Listen to this carefully! After you were illuminated, glory to God, you were quickened by the Spirit, and you are looking forward to a day of rapture, when you will be *"caught up"* and lifted into the presence of God (1 Thess. 4:17). You cannot think of God on any small line. God's lines have magnitude; they are wonderful, glorious. God can manifest them in our hearts with a greater fullness than we are able to express.

Let me address an important point. Christ Jesus has borne the cross for us—there is no need for us to bear it. He has borne the curse, for *"cursed is everyone who hangs on a tree"* (Gal. 3:13). The curse covered everything. The Word says that when Christ was in the grave, He was raised from the dead by the operation of God through the Spirit (Rom. 8:11). He was made alive in the grave by the Spirit, and the same Spirit that dwells in you will *"give life to your mortal bodies"* (v. 11). Jesus rose by the quickening power of the Holy Spirit, and

> *if the Spirit of Him who raised Jesus from the dead dwells in you, He who raised Christ from the dead will also give life to your mortal bodies through His Spirit who dwells in you.* (Rom. 8:11)

What does this mean? Right now, you do not have an immortal body. Immortality can only be obtained in the future resurrection. He will give life to your mortal bodies.

If you will allow Jesus to have control of your bodies, you will find that His Spirit will give you life, will loose you. He will show you that it is the mortal body that has to be given life. Talk about divine healing! You can't take it out of the Scriptures, for they are full of it. I see this. Everyone who is healed by the power of God—especially believers—will find their healing an incentive to make them purer and holier. If divine healing was only to make you well, it would be worth nothing. Divine healing is a divine act of the providence of God coming into your mortal bodies and touching them with almightiness. Could you remain the same after being touched in this way? No. Like me, you would go out to worship and serve God. That is why I am here in Australia—because of the healing of God in my mortal body. I am not here to build new orders of things. I understand the fact that God wants me to preach so that everyone who hears me will go back to his own home with the energy and power of God and the revelation of Christ.

It is a fact that the more you are held in bondage and the more you shut your eyes to the truth, the more the Bible becomes a blank instead of life and joy. The moment you yield yourself to God, the Bible becomes a new Book; it becomes revelation, so that we have the fullness of redemption going right through our bodies in every way. Then we are filled with God, as Christ was filled with *"all the fullness of the Godhead bodily"* (Col. 2:9).

Filled with God! Yes, filled with God,
Pardoned and cleansed, and filled with God.
Filled with God! Yes, filled with God,
Emptied of self, and filled with God!

CHAPTER EIGHTEEN

THE POWER OF CHRIST'S RESURRECTION

That I may know Him and the power of His resurrection, and the fellowship of His sufferings, being conformed to His death, if, by any means, I may attain to the resurrection from the dead. Not that I have already attained, or am already perfected; but I press on, that I may lay hold of that for which Christ Jesus has also laid hold of me. Brethren, I do not count myself to have apprehended; but one thing I do, forgetting those things which are behind and reaching forward to those things which are ahead, I press toward the goal for the prize of the upward call of God in Christ Jesus.
—Philippians 3:10–14

What a wonderful Scripture passage! This surely means to press on to be filled with all the fullness of God. If we are not filled in this way, we will surely miss God, and we will fail in fulfilling the ministry He wants to give us.

The Lord wants us to preach by our lives and by our deeds, always abounding in service; to be living epistles, bringing forth to men the knowledge of God. If we went all the way with God, what would happen? What would we see if we would only seek to bring honor to the name of our God? In this passage from Philippians, we see Paul pressing in for this purpose. There is no standing still. We must move on to a fuller power of the Spirit, never satisfied that we have attained all, but filled with the assurance that God will take us on to the goal we desire to reach, as we press on for the prize ahead.

Abraham came out from Ur of the Chaldeans (Gen. 11:31). We never get into a new place until we come out from the old one.

There is a place where we leave the old life behind, and where the life in Christ fills us and we are filled with His glorious personality.

On the road to Damascus, Saul of Tarsus was apprehended by Christ. (See Acts 9:1–6.) From the first, he sent up the cry, *"Lord, what do You want me to do?"* (v. 6). He always desired to do the will of God, but we see in this passage, which he wrote to the Philippian believers, that he longed for a place of closer intimacy, a place of fuller power, of deeper crucifixion. He saw a prize ahead, and every fiber of his being was intent on securing that prize.

Jesus Christ came to be the *"firstfruits"* (1 Cor. 15:20)—the firstfruits of a great harvest of fruit like Himself. How zealous the farmer is as he watches his crops and sees the first shoots and blades. They are the pledge of the great harvest that is coming. In the passage from Philippians, Paul longed that the Father's heart would be satisfied, for in that first resurrection (Rev. 20:6), the Heavenly Husbandman will see a firstfruit harvest—a harvest of firstfruits that are like Christ, sons of God made conformable to the only begotten Son of God.

GOD DELIGHTS TO WORK IN DIFFICULT SITUATIONS

You say, "I am in a needy place." It is in the needy places that God delights to work. One time, when a great multitude of people came to Jesus for healing, it grew late in the day, and Christ asked Philip, *"Where shall we buy bread, that these may eat?"* (John 6:5). That was a hard place for Philip, but not for Jesus, for He knew exactly what He would do. The hard place is where He delights to show forth His miraculous power. And how fully was the need provided for! There was food enough for five thousand, and more to spare! (See John 6:7–13.)

Two troubled, baffled travelers were on the road to Emmaus after the crucifixion of Jesus. As they communed together and reasoned, Jesus Himself drew near, and He opened up the Word to them in such a way that they saw light in His light. Their eyes were prevented from recognizing the One who was talking with them. But oh, how their hearts burned within as He opened up the Scriptures to them. And at the breaking of bread, He was made known to them. (See Luke 24:13–35.) Always seek to be found in the place where He manifests His presence and power.

The resurrected Christ appeared to Peter and several of the other disciples early one morning on the shore of the Sea of Galilee.

He prepared a meal for the tired, tried disciples. (See John 21:1–13.) That is just like Him. Count on His presence. Count on His power. Count on His provision. He is always there just where you need Him.

Have you received Him? Are you to be *"found in Him"* (Phil. 3:9)? Have you received His righteousness, which is by faith? Abraham got to this place, for God gave His righteousness to him because he believed (Rom. 4:3); and as you believe God, He credits His righteousness to your account. He will put His righteousness within you. He will keep you in perfect peace as you fix your mind upon Him and trust in Him (Isa. 26:3). He will bring you to a rest of faith, to a place of blessed assurance that all that happens is working for your eternal good (Rom. 8:28).

COMPASSION IS GREATER THAN SUFFERING

The Bible tells us about a widow from the town of Nain whose son had died; she was taking him to be buried. (See Luke 7:11–17.) Jesus met that sad funeral procession. He had compassion on that poor woman who was taking her only son to the cemetery. His great heart had such compassion that death had no power—it could no longer hold its prey. Compassion is greater than suffering. Compassion is greater than death. Oh God, give us compassion! In His infinite compassion, Jesus stopped that funeral procession and cried to the widow's son, *"Young man, I say to you, arise"* (v. 14). And he who was dead sat up, and Jesus presented him to his mother.

Paul had a vision and revelation of the resurrection power of Christ, and so, in the passage from Philippians, he was saying, "I will not stop until I have laid hold of what God has laid hold of me for." (See Philippians 3:12.) For what purpose has God laid hold of us? To be channels for His power. He wants to manifest the power of the Son of God through you and me. May God help us to manifest the faith of Christ, the compassion of Christ, the resurrection power of Christ.

One morning, about eleven o'clock, I visited a woman who was suffering from a tumor. She could not live through the day. A little blind girl led me to her bedside. Compassion broke me up, and I wanted that woman to live for the child's sake. I said to the woman, "Do you want to live?" She could not speak. She just moved her finger. I anointed her with oil and said, "In the name of

Jesus." There was a stillness of death that followed; and the pastor, looking at the woman, said to me, "She is gone."

When God pours in His compassion, it has resurrection power in it. I carried that woman across the room, put her against a wardrobe, and held her there. I said, "In the name of Jesus, Death, come out." And soon her body began to tremble like a leaf. "In Jesus' name, walk," I said. She did, and then she went back to bed.

I told this story in the assembly. There was a doctor there, and he said, "I'll prove that." He went to the woman, and she told him it was perfectly true. She said, "I was in heaven, and I saw countless numbers, all like Jesus. Then I heard a voice saying, 'Walk, in the name of Jesus.'"

There is power in the name of Jesus. Let us take hold of the power of His resurrection, the power of His compassion, the power of His love. Love will break the hardest thing—there is nothing it will not break.

CHAPTER NINETEEN

MEN OF FAITH:
THE LIFE THAT VENTURES ON THE WORD
OF GOD

God has drawn us together, and He has something to give us. He is not ordinary, but extraordinary; not measured, but immeasurable, abounding in everything. There is nothing small about our God, and when we understand God, we will find out that there should not be anything small about us. We must have an enlargement of our conception of God. Then we will know that we have come to a place where all things are possible, for our God is an omnipotent God for impossible situations.

We are born into a family that never dies, and it is the plan of God to subdue all things that are natural to a supernatural order. Nothing about us has to be dwarfed. God comes in with His mighty power and so works in us that sin has no dominion (Rom. 6:14); evil is subdued, and God's Son begins to reign on the throne of your heart, transforming what was weak and helpless.

But there must be a revolution if we want the almighty God living in and controlling our mortal flesh. We must conclude that there is no good thing in the flesh (Rom. 7:18), and then we must know that God can come into the flesh and subject it until every mighty thing can be manifested through the human order.

Now, beloved, have you come for a blessing? Turn to Hebrews, chapter eleven.

The Christian life continues nonstop until you reach heaven. We must keep going on. If you ever stop between Calvary and the glory, it is you who blocked the way. There is no stop between Calvary and the glory except by human failure; but if we allow God to have His way, He will surely transform us, for His plan is to change us from what we are to what He intends us to be, and never to lose the ideal of His great plan for us. God wants to shake us loose and take the cobwebs away, and to remove all the husks from the wheat, so that we may be pure grain for God to work upon. In order for Him to do that, we must be willing to let go; as long as you hold onto the natural, you cannot take hold of divine life.

VENTURE THE IMPOSSIBLE

The child of God never has to speculate; he only has to have faith, with audacity to prove that God is what He has promised to be. You will not become strong in faith until you venture the impossible.

If you ask for anything six times, five of the times are unbelief. You are not heard for your *"many words"* (Matt. 6:7), but because you believe. If you pray around the world, you will get into a whirlwind, and spoil every meeting you get into.

Now God does not want anybody in the world, under any circumstances, to be in a place where he lives on eyesight and on feelings. Faith never looks and faith never feels. Faith is an act, and faith without an act is not faith, but doubt and disgrace. Every one of you has more faith than you are using.

Now this *"substance"* (Heb. 11:1) that I am speaking about cannot be looked at or handled. God wants us to have something greater than what we can see and handle. It is declared in the Scriptures that the earth is going to be melted with fervent heat and the heavens will depart (2 Pet. 3:10, 12), but this Word will remain (Matt. 24:35), and this is substance. So we must know whether we are living in substance that cannot be handled or living in the temporal, for everything you can see is going to be removed, and what you cannot see is going to remain forever.

God gives us this remarkable substance that is called faith. It consists of the Word of God, the personality of God, the nature of God, and the acts of God, and these four things are all in faith. Faith is a deep reality caused by God's personality waking up our humanity to leap into eternal things and be lost forever in something a million times greater than ourselves—to be possessed by and be the possessor of something a million times greater than ourselves!

GO ON WITH GOD

There is a growing in faith after we are saved. Backsliding is knowing the way of holiness but shutting the door. So if you know to do good and you do not do it, that is backsliding (James 4:17). What standard is holiness? There is none. A person who is new-born in Christ is as holy as the aged believer while he walks according to the light he has, and the oldest saint with more light is not more holy than the person who has just been saved and is walking in the light.

You cannot make anything without material, but I want to read to you of something being made without material: *"By faith we understand that the worlds were framed by the word of God, so that the things which are seen were not made of things which are visible"* (Heb. 11:3).

God took the Word and made this world out of things that were not there. He caused it all to come by the word of faith. You were born of, created by, made anew by the same Word that made the world. God, in His infinite mercy, brings His infinite light and power right into our finite beings so that we have revelations of the mighty God and of His wonderful power. That is the reason why I lay hands on the sick and know they will be healed.

God has included all ranks and conditions of people in the eleventh chapter of Hebrews. Samson made terrible mistakes, but he is included. Then there is Barak, who wouldn't go without Deborah. He couldn't have been a strong man if a woman had to go with him, but he is mentioned. Now why can you not believe that God will also include you?

The Acts of the Apostles finishes abruptly. It is not complete, and all who are in this place tonight must add to the Acts of the Apostles. It is an incomplete record, because when you get there, you will find that you are among the Acts of the Apostles.

LET NOBODY TAKE YOUR CROWN

You have to be zealous. You must not let anybody stand in your way. Salvation is the beginning; sanctification is a continuation; the baptism in the Holy Spirit is the enlargement of capacity for the risen Christ. God comes along and inspires your thoughts, and says, "Now, go forward, my child; it will be all right. Do not give in."

The Lord may permit your tire to be punctured many times, but you must not be discouraged that the air has gone out. You must pump it up again. The life that He began cannot be taken away from you. If you have an inspiration to "go forth," you cannot be stopped. You know you are called to an eternal purpose, and nothing will stand in your way. It is His purpose that we will be sanctified, purified, and renewed. We are a people who have been raised from the dead, and if Jesus comes, you will go to be with Him because you have resurrection in you.

When our forefathers had a good report, it was always because of faith, and if devastating winds blow, it does not matter.

RELYING ON THE THINGS THAT ARE NOT

Men of faith are not moved by anything they see or hear. The man of faith does not live in time. He has begun in eternity. He does not count on the things that are; he relies on the things that are not.

We must be in the place of buoyancy. The man of faith is subject to God, but never in subjection to the Devil. He is not puffed up. No, he lives in meekness and grows in grace. If you ask God to give you power, you have fallen from grace. You *have* power after the Holy Spirit has come upon you (Acts 1:8). Act in faith. Act in wisdom, *"for it is God who works in you both to will and to do for His good pleasure"* (Phil. 2:13).

CHAPTER TWENTY

THE POWER OF THE GOSPEL

I am convinced that there is nothing in the world that is going to persuade men and women of the power of the Gospel like the manifestation of the Spirit with the fruits. God has baptized us in the Holy Spirit for a purpose: that He may show His mighty power in human flesh, as He did in Jesus. He is bringing us to a place where He may manifest these gifts.

JESUS IS THE WORD

"No one speaking by the Spirit of God calls Jesus accursed, and no one can say that Jesus is Lord except by the Holy Spirit" (1 Cor. 12:3). Everyone who does not speak the truth concerning this Word, which is Jesus, makes Him the accursed; so all we have to do is to have the revelation of the Word in our hearts, and there will be no fear of our being led astray, because this Word is nothing else but Jesus.

In the gospel of John, we read that *"the Word was God"* (1:1), and that He *"became flesh and dwelt among us, and we beheld His glory, the glory as of the only begotten [Son] of the Father"* (v. 14). So it is revealed that He is the Son of God—the Word of God. The Bible is nothing else than the Word of God, and you can know right away—without getting mixed up at all—that everything that does not confess it is not of the Holy Spirit, and consequently you can wipe out all such things. There is no difficulty about saving yourselves, because the Word of God will always save.

WE RECEIVE THE ANOINTING OF THE HOLY ONE

There are diversities of gifts, but the same Spirit. There are differences of ministries, but the same Lord. And there are diversities of activities, but it is the same God who works all in all. But the manifestation of the Spirit is given to each one for the profit of all.   (1 Cor. 12:4–7)

My heart is in this business. I am brought face-to-face with the fact that now the Holy Spirit is dwelling within me, that He is dwelling in my body; as John said, the anointing of the Holy One is within (1 John 2:20). The anointing of the Holy One is the Holy Spirit manifested in us. So we see that right away, within us, there is the power to manifest and bring forth those gifts that He has promised; and these gifts will be manifested in the measure that we live in the anointing of the Spirit of God. Thus we will find out that those gifts must be manifested.

My brother here, Mr. Moser, was suffering from lack of sleep. He had not had a full night of sleep for a long time. Last night I said, "I command you, in the name of Jesus, to sleep." When he came this morning, he was well; he had had a good night's sleep.

THE GIFTS ARE FOR THE PROFIT OF ALL

Beloved, the power of the Holy Spirit is within us *"for the profit of all"* (1 Cor. 12:7). The Holy Spirit says in the Scriptures,

To one is given the word of wisdom through the Spirit, to another the word of knowledge through the same Spirit, to another faith by the same Spirit, to another gifts of healings by the same Spirit, to another the working of miracles, to another prophecy, to another discerning of spirits, to another different kinds of tongues, to another the interpretation of tongues. But one and the same Spirit works all these things, distributing to each one individually as He wills.   (1 Cor. 12:8–11)

Paul distinctly said that it is possible for a person not to *"come short"* (1 Cor. 1:7) in any gift, according to the measure of faith that he receives from the Lord Jesus. (See verses 4–9.) No doubt, some of you have sometimes thought what a blessed thing it would be if you had been the Virgin Mary. Listen, a certain woman said to Jesus, *"Blessed is the womb that bore You, and the breasts which nursed You!"* (Luke 11:27). But He answered, *"More than that, blessed are those who hear the word of God and keep it!"* (v. 28).

You see that a higher position than Mary's is attained through simple faith in what the Scriptures say. If we receive the Word of God as it is given to us, there will be power in our bodies to claim the gifts of God, and it will amaze the world when they see the power of God manifested through these gifts.

I believe that we are coming to a time when these gifts will be more distinctly manifested. What can be more convincing? Yes, He is a lovely Jesus. He went forth from place to place, rebuking demons, healing the sick, and doing other wonderful things. What was the reason? *"God was with Him"* (Acts 10:38).

Wherever there is a child of God who dares to receive the Word of God and cherish it, there God is made manifest in the flesh, for the Word of God is life and spirit (John 6:63), and brings us into a place where we know that we have power with God and with men, in proportion to our loyalty of faith in the Word of God.

Now, beloved, I feel somehow that we have missed the greatest principle that underlies the baptism in the Holy Spirit. The greatest principle is that God the Holy Spirit came into our bodies to manifest the mighty works of God, *"for the profit of all"* (1 Cor. 12:7). He does not manifest only one gift, but as God the Holy Spirit abides in my body, I find that He fills it, and then one can truly say that it is the anointing of the Holy One. It so fills us that we feel we can command demons to come out of those who are possessed; and when I lay hands on the sick in the name of the Lord Jesus, I realize that my body is merely the outer coil, and that within is the Son of God. For I receive the word of Christ, and Christ is in me, the power of God is in me. The Holy Spirit is making that word a living word, and the Holy Spirit makes me say, "Come out!" It is not Wigglesworth. It is the power of the Holy Spirit that manifests the glorious presence of Christ.

CHAPTER TWENTY-ONE

THE GIFT OF TONGUES

Pursue love, and desire spiritual gifts, but especially that you may prophesy. For he who speaks in a ["an unknown," KJV] tongue does not speak to men but to God, for no one understands him; however, in the spirit he speaks mysteries.
—1 Corinthians 14:1–2

I t is necessary that we have a great desire for spiritual gifts. We must thirst after them and covet them earnestly because the gifts are necessary and important, and so that we, having received the gifts by the grace of God, may be used for God's glory.

TONGUES ARE FOR INTERCESSION

God has ordained this speaking in an unknown tongue to Himself as a wonderful, supernatural means of communication in the Spirit. As we speak to Him in an unknown tongue, we speak wonderful mysteries in the Spirit. In Romans 8:27, we read, *"He who searches the hearts knows what the mind of the Spirit is, because He makes intercession for the saints according to the will of God."* Many times, as we speak to God in an unknown tongue, we are in intercession; and as we pray thus in the Spirit, we pray according to the will of God. And there is such a thing as the Spirit making intercession *"with groanings which cannot be uttered"* (v. 26).

Along these lines, I want to tell you about Willie Burton, who is laboring for God in the Belgium Congo (Zaire). Brother Burton is a mighty man of God and is giving his life for the heathen in Africa. At one point, he took fever and went down to death. Those who ministered with him said, "He has preached his last. What shall we do?" All their hopes seemed to be blighted, and there they stood, with broken hearts, wondering what was going to take place. They had left him for dead; however, in a moment, without any signal, he stood right in the midst of them, and they could not understand it. The explanation he gave was that when he came to himself, he felt a warmth going right through his body, and there wasn't one thing wrong with him.

How did this happen? It was a mystery until he went to London and was telling the people how he had been left for dead and then was raised up. A lady came up and asked for a private conversation with him, and they arranged a time to meet. When they met together, she asked, "Do you keep a diary?" He answered, "Yes." Then she told him, "It happened that, on a certain day, I went to pray; and as soon as I knelt, I had you on my mind. The Spirit of the Lord took hold of me and prayed through me in an unknown tongue. A vision came before me in which I saw you lying helpless; and I cried out in the unknown tongue until I saw you rise up and go out of that room." She had kept a note of the time, and when he looked in his diary, he found that it was exactly the time when he was raised up. There are great possibilities as we yield to the Spirit and speak to God in quiet hours in our bedrooms. God wants you to be filled with the Holy Spirit so that everything about you will be charged with the dynamite of heaven.

TONGUES ARE FOR PERSONAL EDIFICATION

"He who speaks in a tongue edifies himself, but he who prophesies edifies the church" (1 Cor. 14:4). I want you to see that he who speaks in an unknown tongue edifies himself, or builds himself up. We must be edified before we can edify the church. I cannot estimate what I, personally, owe to the Holy Spirit method of spiritual edification. I am here before you as one of the biggest conundrums in the world. There never was a weaker man on the platform. Did I have the capacity to speak? Not at all. I was full of inability. All natural things in my life point to exactly the opposite of my being able to stand on the platform and preach the Gospel. The secret is that the Holy Spirit came and brought this wonderful edification of the Spirit. I had been reading the Word continually as well as I could, but the Holy Spirit came and took hold of it, for the Holy Spirit is the breath of it, and He illuminated it to me. He gives me a spiritual language

that I cannot speak fast enough; it comes too fast; and it is there because God has given it. When the Comforter, or Helper, comes, *"He will teach you **all** things"* (John 14:26, emphasis added); and He has given me this supernatural means of speaking in an unknown tongue to edify myself, so that, after being edified, I can edify the church.

THE ANOINTING REMAINS IN YOU

In 1 John 2:20, we read, *"But you have an anointing from the Holy One, and you know all things."* Then, in verse 27, we read,

> *But the anointing which you have received from Him abides in you, and you do not need that anyone teach you; but as the same anointing teaches you concerning all things, and is true, and is not a lie, and just as it has taught you, you will abide in Him.*

Even when you are baptized in the Spirit, you may say, "I seem so dry; I don't know where I am." The Word says you have an anointing. Thank God you have received an anointing. In the above passage, the Holy Spirit says that He *"abides"* and that He *"teaches you concerning all things."* These are great and definite positions for you. The Holy Spirit wants you to stir up your faith to believe that this word is true—that you have the anointing and that the anointing abides. As you rise up in the morning, believe this wonderful truth; and as you yield to the Spirit's presence and power, you will find yourself speaking to God in the Spirit, and you will find that you are personally being edified by doing this. Let everything about you be a lie, but let this word of God be true. The Devil will say that you are the driest person and that you will never do anything; but believe God's word, that *"the anointing which you have received from Him abides in you."*

PROPHECY AND THE INTERPRETATION OF TONGUES

> *I wish you all spoke with tongues, but even more that you prophesied; for he who prophesies is greater than he who speaks with tongues, unless indeed he interprets, that the church may receive edification.* (1 Cor. 14:5)

386

God wants you to be continually in the place of prophecy, for everyone who has received the Holy Spirit has a right to prophesy. In 1 Corinthians 14:31, we read, *"You can all prophesy one by one."* Now prophecy is far in advance of speaking in tongues, except when you have the interpretation of the speaking in tongues, and then God gives an equivalent to prophecy. In verse 13, we read, *"Let him who speaks in a tongue pray that he may interpret."*

TWO TYPES OF TONGUES

After I received the baptism in the Holy Spirit and spoke in tongues as the Spirit gave utterance (Acts 2:4), I did not speak in tongues again for nine months. I was troubled because I laid hands on people so that they might receive the Holy Spirit, and they were speaking in tongues, but I did not have the joy of speaking in them myself. God wanted to show me that the speaking in tongues as the Spirit gave utterance, which I received when I received the baptism, was distinct from the gift of tongues that I subsequently received. When I laid hands on other people and they received the Holy Spirit, I used to think, "Oh, Lord Jesus, it would be nice if You would let me speak in tongues." He withheld the gift from me, for He knew that I would meet many who would say that the baptism of the Holy Spirit can be received without the speaking in tongues, and that people simply received the gift of tongues when they received the baptism.

I did not receive the gift of tongues when I received the baptism; however, nine months later, I was going out the door one morning, speaking to the Lord in my own heart, when a flood of tongues poured forth from me. When the tongues stopped, I said to the Lord, "Now, Lord, I did not do it, and I wasn't seeking it; therefore, You have done it, and I am not going to move from this place until you give me the interpretation." And then came an interpretation that has been fulfilled all over the world. Is it not the Holy Spirit who speaks? Then the Holy Spirit can interpret. Let him who speaks in a tongue ask for the interpretation, and God will give it. We must not rush through without getting a clear understanding of what God has to say to us.

PRAYING WITH THE SPIRIT AND WITH THE UNDERSTANDING

"What is the conclusion then? I will pray with the spirit, and I will also pray with the understanding. I will sing with the spirit, and

I will also sing with the understanding" (1 Cor. 14:15). If you pray in an unknown tongue in the Spirit, you do not know what you are praying; you have no understanding of it; it is unfruitful to those around you. But you have the same power to pray with the understanding under the anointing of the Spirit as you have to pray in an unknown tongue.

Some say, "Oh, I could do that, but it would be myself doing it." If *you* pray, it is yourself, and everything you do in the beginning is yourself. When I kneel down to pray, the first and second sentences may be in the natural; but as soon as *I* have finished, the Spirit begins to pray through me. Granted, the first may be yourself. The next will be the Holy Spirit, and the Holy Spirit will take you through, praise the Lord. Everything but faith will say, "That isn't right." Faith says, "It is right." The natural man says, "It isn't right." Faith says, "It is right." Paul said, *"I will pray with the spirit, and I will also pray with the understanding"* (1 Cor. 14:15), and he did it in faith.

The Devil is against it, and your own self-life is against it. May the Holy Spirit bring us into that blessed place where we may live, walk, pray, and sing in the Spirit, and pray and sing with the understanding, also. Faith will do it. Faith has a deaf ear to the Devil and to the working of the natural mind, and a big ear to God. Faith has a deaf ear to yourself and an open ear to God. Faith won't take any notice of feelings. Faith says, *"You are complete in Him"* (Col. 2:10).

It is a wonderful thing to pray in the Spirit and to sing in the Spirit—praying in tongues and singing in tongues as the Spirit of God gives you utterance. I never get out of bed in the morning without having communion with God in the Spirit. It is the most wonderful thing on earth. It is most lovely to be in the Spirit when you are getting dressed, and then when you come out into the world, to find that the world has no effect on you. If you begin the day like that, you will be conscious of the guidance of the Spirit all during the day.

TONGUES SHOULD BE SPOKEN IN AN ORDERLY WAY

I thank my God I speak with tongues more than you all; yet in the church I would rather speak five words with my understanding, that I may teach others also, than ten thousand words in a ["an unknown," KJV] *tongue.*

(1 Cor. 14:18–19)

Many people will come to you and declare that Paul said he would rather speak five words with the known tongue than ten thousand words without understanding. They will always leave out the part of the passage that reads, *"I thank my God I speak with tongues more than you all"* (1 Cor. 14:18). In this passage, Paul was correcting the practice of excessive speaking in tongues without interpretation, which would not edify the assembly. If there was no one with the gift of interpretation present, the people were simply to speak to themselves and to God.

Suppose someone was preaching and twenty or thirty people stood up in succession to speak in tongues. It would be a very serious problem. There would be confusion. The people attending the meeting would rather have five words of edification, consolation, and comfort (1 Cor. 14:3) than ten thousand words without understanding.

Just because you feel a touch of the Spirit, you are not obligated to speak in tongues. The Lord will give you a sound mind (2 Tim. 1:7), so that you will hold your body in perfect order for the edification of the church. But in 1 Corinthians 14:18, Paul said that he spoke in tongues more than all of the Corinthians; and, as it is evident that the Corinthian church was very considerably given to speaking in tongues, he certainly must have been speaking in tongues a great amount both day and night. He was so edified by this wonderful, supernatural means of being built up, that he could go to the church preaching in a manner in which they could all understand him, and could marvelously edify the believers.

Seek God's Best with All Your Heart

I will explain to you the most perfect way to receive the gift. Come with me to the second chapter of 2 Kings and I will show you a man receiving a gift. The prophet Elijah had been mightily used by God in calling down fire and in other miracles. Elisha, his chosen successor, was moved with a great spirit of covetousness to have this man's gifts. You can be very covetous for the gifts of the Spirit and God will allow it. When Elijah said to him, "I want you to stay at Gilgal," Elisha said, *"As the LORD lives, and as your soul lives, I will not leave you!"* (See 2 Kings 2:1–2.) There was no stopping him. Likewise, when Elijah wanted Elisha to stay at Jericho, he said, in essence, "I am not stopping." The man who stops gets nothing. Oh, don't stop at Jericho; don't stop at Jordan; don't stop anywhere when God wants you to move on into all of His fullness that He has for you.

Elijah and Elisha came to the Jordan River, and Elijah took his mantle and struck the waters. The waters divided, and Elijah and Elisha went across on dry ground. Elijah turned to Elisha and said, in essence, "Look here, what do you want?" Elisha wanted what he was going to have, and you may covet all that God says that you shall have. Elisha said, *"Please let a double portion of your spirit be upon me"* (2 Kings 2:9). This was the plowboy who had washed the hands of his master (1 Kings 19:19–20; 2 Kings 3:11); but his spirit got so big that he purposed in his heart that, when Elijah stepped off the scene, he would be put into his place.

Elijah said, *"You have asked a hard thing. Nevertheless, if you see me when I am taken from you, it shall be so for you"* (2 Kings 2:10). May God help you never to stop persevering until you get what you want. Let your aspiration be large and your faith rise until you are wholly on fire for God's best.

Onward they went, and as one stepped, the other stepped with him. Elisha purposed to keep his eyes on his master until the last. It took a chariot of fire and horses of fire to separate them, and Elijah went up by a whirlwind into heaven. I can imagine Elisha crying out, "Father Elijah, drop that mantle." And it came down. Oh, I can see it lowering and lowering and lowering. Elisha took all of his own clothes and tore them in two pieces, and then he took up the mantle of Elijah. (See vv. 11–13.) I do not believe that, when he put on that other mantle, he felt any different in himself; but when he came to the Jordan, he took the mantle of Elijah, struck the waters, and said, *"Where is the LORD God of Elijah?"* (v. 14). The waters parted, and he went over on dry ground. And the sons of the prophets said, *"The spirit of Elijah rests on Elisha"* (v. 15).

It is like receiving a gift; you don't know that you have it until you act in faith. Brothers and sisters, as you ask, *believe.*

Chapter Twenty-Two

The Gift of Prophecy

I n 1 Corinthians 12:10, speaking of the diversities of gifts given by the same Spirit (v. 4), Paul wrote, *"To another* [is given] *prophecy."* We see the importance of this gift from 1 Corinthians 14:1, where we are told to *"pursue love, and desire spiritual gifts, but especially that you may prophesy."* We also see that *"he who prophesies speaks edification and exhortation and comfort to men"* (v. 3). How important it is, then, that we should have this gift in manifestation in the church, so that believers might be built up and made strong and filled with the comfort of God. But with this, as with all other gifts, we should see that it is operated by the Spirit's power and brought forth in the anointing of the Spirit, so that everyone who hears prophecy—as it is brought forth by the Spirit of God—will know that it is truly God who is bringing forth what is for the edification of those who hear. It is the Spirit of God who takes of the *"deep things of God"* (1 Cor. 2:10) and reveals them, and anoints the prophet to give forth what is a revelation of the things of God.

Utterance in prophecy has a real lifting power and sheds real light on the truth to those who hear. Prophecy is never a reflection of our minds; it is something far deeper than this. By means of prophecy, we receive what is the mind of the Lord; and as we receive these blessed, fresh utterances through the Spirit of the Lord, the whole assembly is lifted into the realm of the spiritual. Our hearts and minds and whole bodies receive a quickening through the Spirit-given word. As the Spirit brings forth prophecy, we find there is healing, salvation, and power in every sentence. For this reason, it is one of the gifts that we ought to covet.

False versus True Prophecy

While we appreciate true prophecy, we must not forget that the Scriptures warn us in no uncertain terms concerning what is false. In 1 John 4:1, we are told, *"Beloved, do not believe every spirit, but test the spirits, whether they are of God; because many false prophets have gone out into the world."* John then went on to tell us how we can tell the difference between the true and the false:

> *By this you know the Spirit of God: Every spirit that confesses that Jesus Christ has come in the flesh is of God, and every spirit that does not confess that Jesus Christ has come in the flesh is not of God. And this is the spirit of the Antichrist, which you have heard was coming, and is now already in the world.* (1 John 4:2–3)

There are voices that seem like prophecy, and some believers have fallen into terrible darkness and bondage through listening to these counterfeits of the true gift of prophecy. True prophecy is always Christ-exalting, magnifying the Son of God, exalting the blood of Jesus Christ, encouraging believers to praise and worship the true God. False prophecy deals with things that do not edify and is designed to puff up its hearers and to lead them into error.

Many people picture Satan as a great, ugly monster with large ears, eyes, and a tail; but the Scriptures give us no such picture of him. He was a being of great beauty, but his heart became lifted up against God. He is manifesting himself everywhere today as an *"angel of light"* (2 Cor. 11:14). He is full of pride, and if you aren't careful, he will try to make you think you are somebody. This is the weakness of most preachers and most men—the idea of being somebody! None of us are anything, and the more we know we are nothing, the more God can make us a channel of His power. May the dear Lord save us from continually being sidetracked by pride—it is the Devil's trap. True prophecy will show you that Christ is *"all in all"* (Eph. 1:23), and that you are, in yourself, less than nothing and vanity. False prophecy will not magnify Christ, but will make you think that you are going to be someone great after all. You may be sure that such thoughts are inspired by "the chief of the sons of pride."

I want to warn you against the foolishness of continually seeking to hear "voices." The Bible tells us that the voice of God, *"who at various times and in various ways spoke in time past to the fathers by the prophets, [and] has in these last days spoken to us by His Son"* (Heb. 1:1–2). Do not run away with anything else. If you hear the voice of God, it will be according to the Scriptures of Truth given in the inspired Word. In Revelation 22:18–19, we see the danger of attempting to add to or take from the prophecy of this Book. True prophecy, as it comes forth in the power of the Spirit of God, will neither take from nor add to the Scriptures, but will intensify and quicken what already has been given to us by God. The Holy Spirit will bring to our remembrance all the things that Jesus said and did (John 14:26). True prophecy will bring forth *"things new and old"* (Matt. 13:52) out of the Scriptures of Truth and will make them *"living and powerful"* (Heb. 4:12) to us.

Some may ask, "If we have the Scriptures, why do we need prophecy?" The Scriptures themselves answer this question. God has said that in the last days He will pour out His Spirit upon all flesh, and that *"your sons and your daughters shall prophesy"* (Acts 2:17). The Lord knew that, in these last days, prophecy would be a real means of blessing to us, and that is why we can count on Him to give us, by means of the Spirit, through His menservants and His maidservants, true prophetic messages (v. 18).

THE DANGERS OF LISTENING TO FALSE VOICES

Again, I want to warn you concerning listening to voices. I was at a meeting in Paisley, Scotland, and I came in touch with two young women. They were in a great state of excitement. These two girls were telegraph operators and were precious young women, having received the baptism in the Spirit. They were both longing to be missionaries. But whatever our spiritual state is, we are subject to temptations. An evil power came to one of these young women and said, "If you will obey me, I will make you one of the most wonderful missionaries who ever went out to the mission field." This was just the Devil or one of his agents acting as an angel of light. The young women was captured immediately by this suggestion, and she became so excited that her sister saw there was something wrong and asked their work supervisor if they could be excused for a while.

As the sister took her into a room, the power of Satan, endeavoring to imitate the Spirit of God, manifested itself in a voice, and led this young woman to believe that the missionary enterprise would be unfolded that night, if she would obey. This evil spirit said, "Don't tell anybody but your sister." I think that everything of God can be told to everybody. If you cannot preach what you live, your life is wrong. If you are afraid of telling what you do in secret, someday it will be told from the housetops (Luke 12:3). Don't think you will get out of it. What is pure comes to the light. *"He who does the truth comes to the light, that his deeds may be clearly seen, that they have been done in God"* (John 3:21).

The evil power went on to say to this girl, "Go to the railroad station tonight, and there will be a train coming in at 7:32. After you buy a ticket for yourself and your sister, you will have sixpence left. You will find a woman in a railway carriage dressed as a nurse, and opposite her will be a gentleman who has all the money you need." The first thing came true. She bought the tickets and had just sixpence left. Next, the train came in at exactly 7:32. But the next thing did not come true. The two sisters ran from the front to the back of that railroad train before it moved out, and nothing turned out as they had been told. As soon as the train moved out, the same voice came and said, "Over on the other platform." All that night, until 9:30, these two young women were rushed from platform to platform. As soon as it was 9:30, this same evil power said, "Now that I know you will obey me, I will make you the greatest missionaries." It is always something big! They might have known it was all wrong. The evil power said, "This gentleman will take you to a certain bank at a certain corner in Glasgow, where he will deposit all that money for you." Banks are not open at that time of night in Glasgow. If she had gone to the street that this evil spirit mentioned, there probably would not have been a bank there. All they needed was a little common sense, and they would have seen that it was not the Lord. If you have your heart open for this kind of voice, you will soon get into a trap. We must always remember that there are many evil spirits in the world.

Were these sisters delivered? Yes, after terrible travail with God, they were perfectly delivered. Their eyes were opened to see that this thing was not of God but of the Devil. These two sisters are now laboring for the Lord in China and doing a blessed work for Him. If you do get into error along these lines, praise God, there is a way out. I praise God that He will break us down until all pride leaves us. The worst pride we can have is the pride of self-exaltation.

Paul wrote, at the commandment of the Lord,

Let two or three prophets speak, and let the others judge. But if anything is revealed to another who sits by, let the first keep silent. For you can all prophesy one by one, that all may learn and all may be encouraged. (1 Cor. 14:29–31)

If you are not humble enough to allow your prophecy to be judged, it is as surely wrong as you are wrong. Prophecy has to be judged. A meeting such as this one that Paul suggested would certainly be the greatest meeting you ever held. Praise God, the tide will rise to this. It will all come into perfect order when the church is bathed and lost in the great ideal of only glorifying Jesus. Then things will come to pass that will be worthwhile.

Coupled with prophecy, you should see manifested the fruit of the Spirit that is goodness (Gal. 5:22). It was *holy* men who spoke in prophecy in days of old as the Holy Spirit prompted them (2 Pet. 1:21); and so, today, the prophet who can be trusted is a man who is full of goodness, the goodness that is the fruit of the Spirit. But when he gets out of this position and rests on his own individuality, he is in danger of being puffed up and becoming an instrument for the Enemy.

I knew some people who had a wonderful farm; it was very productive and was in a very good neighborhood. They listened to voices telling them to sell everything and go to Africa. These voices had so unhinged them that they had scarcely had time to sell out. They sold their property at a ridiculous price. The same voice told them of a certain ship they were to sail on. When they got to the port, they found there wasn't a ship of that name.

The difficulty was to get them not to believe these false voices. They said perhaps it was the mind of the Lord to give them another ship, and the voice soon gave them the name of another ship. When they reached Africa, they didn't know any language that was spoken there. But the voice did not let them stop. They eventually had to come back brokenhearted, shaken through, and having lost all confidence in everything. If these people had had the sense to go to some men of God who were filled with the Spirit and seek their counsel, they would soon have been persuaded that these voices were not of God. But listening to these voices always brings about a spiritual pride that makes people think that they are superior to their fellow believers, and that they are above taking the counsel of men whom they think are not as filled with the Spirit as they are. If you hear any voices that make you think that you are superior to those whom God has put in the church to rule the church, watch out, for that is surely the Devil.

We read in Revelation 19:10 that *"the testimony of Jesus is the spirit of prophecy."* You will find that true prophetic utterance always exalts the Lamb of God.

Fire and Faith

No prophetic touch is of any use unless there is fire in it. I never expect to be used by God until the fire burns. I feel that if I ever speak, it must be by the Spirit. At the same time, remember that the prophet must prophecy according to the measure of his faith (Rom. 12:6). If you rise up in your weakness, but also in love because you want to honor God, and you just begin, you will find the presence of the Lord upon you. Act in faith, and the Lord will meet you.

May God take us on and on into this glorious fact of faith, so that we may be so in the Holy Spirit that God will work through us along the lines of the miraculous and along the lines of prophecy. When we are operating in the Spirit, we will always know that it is no longer we but He who is working through us, bringing forth what is in His own divine good pleasure (Phil. 2:13).

CHAPTER TWENTY-THREE

A TRUE PROPHET

The prophet's message is a word of the Lord that has become a burden upon the soul or a fire shut up in the bones—a burden, a pent-up fire, an anguish, and a travail. The word of the Lord is living flame. The symbol of Pentecost is a tongue of fire.

When the prophet Jeremiah had spoken his message, he felt as if God had let him down and exposed him to ridicule and mockery. He determined to speak no more, but in the silence, the fire burned in his bones. He was full of the fury of the Lord until he was prostrate with holding it in. The fire consumed him until he could no longer hold it in, until one day the fire suddenly leapt forth in forked lightning, or a flaming sword. (See Jeremiah 20:1–11.)

The moment comes when the prophet is full of power by the Spirit of the Lord. He may be called to *"declare to Jacob his transgression and to Israel his sin"* (Mic. 3:8). The fire constrains and consumes him, and his generation persecutes and despises his word.

The Lord Jesus came to bring fire (Luke 12:49). He was distressed in spirit, but the baptism that He had to endure was accomplished (v. 50). So it is with every servant of God who brings fire. There is a brooding—a questioning, reasoning, excusing, hoping, foreboding. The whole being is consumed. The very marrow of the bones burns. At first, speech may not, must not, or will not come. Then, in a moment, it suddenly flames out. The prophet becomes a voice through which Another speaks. Fire compels attention; it announces itself. You don't have to advertise a fire. When the fire comes, the multitudes come.

CHAPTER TWENTY-FOUR

YOU HAVE RECEIVED— NOW BELIEVE

G od wants to make us pillars: honorable, strong, and holy. God will take us further along in the faith. I am passionately inspired by the great fact of our possibilities in God. God wants you to know that you are saved, cleansed, delivered, and marching on to victory.

"Set your mind on things above" (Col. 3:2); get into the *"heavenly places"* with Christ (Eph. 2:6); *"be transformed by the renewing of your mind"* (Rom. 12:2). What a privilege to kneel and to get right into heaven the moment we pray—where the glory descends, the fire burns, faith is active, and the light dispels the darkness! Mortality hinders, but the life of Jesus eats up mortality. (See 2 Corinthians 5:4.)

MAKE CERTAIN YOU HAVE RECEIVED

The Acts of the Apostles deals with receiving the Holy Spirit, and the Epistles are written to believers baptized in the Holy Spirit. When I was in New Zealand, some brothers in Christ questioned me about this baptism. They quoted the Epistles, but before we are in the experience of the Epistles, we must go through the Acts. I asked them, "When did you speak in mysteries?" (See 1 Corinthians 14:2.) But they had not yet come into the baptism of the Holy Spirit.

JESUS IS GREATER THAN EVERYTHING

Jesus is the life and light of men (John 1:4). No one who has this light walks in darkness. (See 1 John 2:10–11.) *"When Christ who is our life appears, then* [we] *also will appear with Him in glory"* (Col. 3:4). Where His life is, disease cannot remain; where His life is full, deficiencies cannot remain. Is not He who indwells us greater than all? (See 1 John 4:4.) Yes, when He has full control. If we permit one thing into our lives that is outside the will of God, it hinders us in standing against the powers of Satan. We must allow the Word of God to judge us, lest we stand condemned with the world (1 Cor. 11:32). *"When Christ who is our life appears."* Have I any life apart from Him—any joy, any fellowship? Jesus said, *"The ruler of this world is coming, and he has* [finds] *nothing in Me"* (John 14:30). All that is contrary in us is withered by the indwelling life of the Son of God.

THE SPIRIT OF JESUS DWELLS IN US

"We who are in this tent groan, being burdened, not because we want to be unclothed, but further clothed, that mortality may be swallowed up by life" (2 Cor. 5:4). Are we ready; are we clothed? Has mortality been swallowed up by life? If He who is our life came, we should go with Him. We can live in a heaven on earth right now.

> Heaven has begun with me;
> I am happy, now, and free,
> Since the Comforter has come,
> Since the Comforter has come.

The Comforter is the great Revealer of the kingdom. He came to give us the more abundant life (John 10:10). God has designed the plan. Nothing really matters if the Lord loves us. God sets great store by us. The pure in heart see God (Matt. 5:8). There are no stiff knees, or coughs, or pain, in the Spirit; nothing ails us if we are filled with the Spirit.

> *If the Spirit of Him who raised Jesus from the dead dwells in you, He who raised Christ from the dead will also give life to your mortal bodies through His Spirit who dwells in you.* (Rom. 8:11)

THE OVERFLOWING LIFE OF THE SPIRIT

This is what it means to live in the Spirit:

399

> ➤ We are *"free from the law of sin and death"* (Rom. 8:2).
> ➤ The *"perfect law of liberty"* (James 1:25) destroys the natural [carnal, sinful] law in us.
> ➤ Spiritual activity takes in every passing ray of God's light.
> ➤ We live days of heaven on earth.
> ➤ We have no sickness, so that we are not aware that we have a body.
> ➤ The life of God changes us, bringing us into the heavenly realm, where we reign over principalities and all evil.
> ➤ We live a limitless, powerful, supernatural life through the Holy Spirit.

If the natural body decays, the Spirit renews. Spiritual power increases until, with one mind and one heart, the glory is brought down over all the earth, right on into divine life. The whole life is filled as we continue to live in faith.

This is Pentecost! Pentecost means to have the life of the Lord manifested through us wherever we are, whether we are on a bus or a train. We are filled with the life of Jesus unto perfection—rejoicing in *"hope of the glory of God"* (Rom. 5:2) and continually looking for our translation in Christ. The life of the Lord in us draws others as a magnet, and His life eats up everything in us that is not of Him. I must have the overflowing life of the Spirit; God is not pleased with less. It is a disgrace to live an ordinary existence after we are filled with the Holy Spirit. We are to be salt in the earth (Matt. 5:13); we are not to be lukewarm, but hot (Rev. 3:16), which means seeing God with abundance, liberty, movement, and power. Believe! Believe!

Smith Wigglesworth on

GOD'S
TRANSFORMING
POWER

CONTENTS

CHAPTER ONE

PREPARING FOR CHRIST'S RETURN

God has a plan for us that is greater than our thoughts, greater than words can say, and so I am not frightened of beginning with a sort of spiritual exaggeration. I dare to believe that God will help me to say things to you that will inspire you to dare to believe God.

Up to this present time, the Lord's word for us has been, *"Until now you have asked nothing"* (John 16:24). Surely you who have been asking great things from God for a long time would be amazed if you entered into it with clear knowledge that it is the Master, it is Jesus, who has such knowledge of the mightiness of the power of the Father and of the joint union with Him, that nothing is impossible for you to ask. Surely it is He alone who could say, *"Until now you have asked nothing."*

God wants me to press you another step further. Begin to believe on extravagant asking, believing that God is pleased when you ask large things.

If you will only dispose of yourself—for it is nothing but yourself that will hinder you—it may be today that God will so transform you that you will be an altogether different person, as you have never been before. Get rid of your human mind, get rid of your human measure, get rid of your strength, and get rid of all you have—this is a big thing for me to say—and let inspiration take charge of you entirely, and bring you out of yourself into the power of God.

INTERPRETATION OF A MESSAGE IN TONGUES:
Only the divine mind has divine thought to meet human order, for knowing us from the beginning and understanding us as a Father and pitying us as children, He begins with the blade and the head and the full grain in the head. He does

this so that we might know that He won't take us out of our death, but He will transform us moment by moment until we can come into full stature of the mind and thought and prayer and action. Hallelujah! God is on the throne.

Now, beloved in the Lord, I want to inspire you to believe that this day is for you as a beginning of days. You have never passed this way before. So I bring you to another day of passing over any heights, passing through mists or darkness. Dare to believe that the cloud is upon you, and it will break with an exceeding reward of blessing. Don't be afraid of clouds—they are all earthly. Never be afraid of an earthly thing. You belong to a higher order, a divine order, a spiritual order. Then believe that God wants you to soar high this day.

INTERPRETATION OF A MESSAGE IN TONGUES:
Fear not to enter in, for the Lord your God has you now in preparation. He is proving you, and He is chastising you, but His hand is not heavy upon you as you may think, for He is gentle and entreating to bring you into the desired place of your heart's affections. "Be still, and know that I am God." It is I and I alone who opens to you the good treasure. Oh, to be still, that my mind may be so free from the cares of this life that I might be able to enter into the joy and the bliss God has caused me to, for I have not passed this way until now!

God is going to speak to us about entering into something we have not entered into before.

LIVING IN PERFECT READINESS

The thoughts of this message are primary to the message of the coming of the Lord. There must be a place of preparation and a line of understanding, because of the purposes that God is arranging for us. I know He is at the door. Spiritual perception makes us know of His near return. But we must be so built on the line of truth that when He comes we are ready.

I am going to tell you about the revelation of Christ to me of the readiness, and what it is—the knowledge of it, the power of it, the purpose of it—until every vestige of our beings is so filled with it that it would be impossible for us to be out of it. We will be in the midst of it.

I have a message leading up to the knowledge of His coming. It is in Peter's second epistle, the third chapter:

Knowing this first: that scoffers will come in the last days, walking according to their own lusts, and saying, "Where is the promise of His coming? For since the fathers fell asleep, all things continue as they were from the beginning of creation." For this they willfully forget: that by the word of God the heavens were of old, and the earth standing out of water and in the water, by which the world that then existed perished, being flooded with water. But the heavens and the earth which are now preserved by the same word, are reserved for fire until the day of judgment and perdition of ungodly men. But, beloved, do not forget this one thing, that with the Lord one day is as a thousand years, and a thousand years as one day. The Lord is not slack concerning His promise, as some count slackness, but is longsuffering toward us, not willing that any should perish but that all should come to repentance. But the day of the Lord will come as a thief in the night, in which the heavens will pass away with a great noise, and the elements will melt with fervent heat; both the earth and the works that are in it will be burned up. Therefore, since all these things will be dissolved, what manner of persons ought you to be in holy conduct and godliness, looking for and hastening the coming of the day of God, because of which the heavens will be dissolved, being on fire, and the elements will melt with fervent heat? Nevertheless we, according to His promise, look for new heavens and a new earth in which righteousness dwells. Therefore, beloved, looking forward to these things, be diligent to be found by Him in peace, without spot and blameless; and consider that the longsuffering of our Lord is salvation. (2 Pet. 3:3–15)

I may deal with many things on the line of spiritual awakening, for this is what is needed this day. This day is a needy day of spiritual awakening, not so much as a knowledge of salvation but a knowledge of waking in salvation.

The seed of the Lord Jesus Christ is mightily in you. This seed is a seed of purifying, of truth and knowledge, a seed of life-giving, a seed of transforming, a seed of building another person in the body until the body that bears the seed only lives to contain the body that the seed has made. Then, that seed comes forth with glorious light and power until the whole body has yielded itself to another, to a fullness, to a manifestation of the perfect formation of the Christ in you. This is the great hope of the future day.

I want to speak to you very exactly. All the people who are pressing into and getting ready for this glorious, attained place where they will not be found naked, where they will be blameless, where they will be immovable, where they will be purified by the power of the Word of God, have within them a consciousness of the very presence of God. They know that God is working within them, changing their very nature and preparing them for a greater thing and causing them to be ready for translation.

THE WORLD IS RIPENING FOR JUDGMENT

You will find that this thing is not already in the world in perfection. There are millions and millions of real believers in Christ who are losing this great upward look, and in the measure they lose this upward look, they lose perfect purification. There is only perfect purification in looking upward to God.

When we see the Day dawning as *"the manifestation of the sons of God"* (Rom. 8:19 KJV) appears, just as these things come to us in light and revelation, we will find that it makes us know that everything is decaying. Millions of people who are Christians believe this world is being purified. All the saints of God who get the real vision of this wonderful transformation of the body are seeing every day that the world is getting worse and worse and worse and is ripening for Judgment. God is bringing us to a place where we who are spiritual are having a clear vision that we must, at any cost, put off the works of darkness; we must be getting ourselves ready for the glorious Day.

These are the last days. What will be the strongest confirmation of the last days?

There are two classes of believers in the world: believers who are disobedient—or I ought to say children who are saved by the power of God, but who are disobedient children—and children who are also saved by the power of God who are longing to be more obedient all the time.

406

In this factor, Satan has a great part to play. It is on this factor in these last years that some of us have been brought to great grief at the first opening of the door to carnal forces. We heard the word come rushing through all over—"new theology," that damnable, devilish, evil power that lived in some of these disobedient children who in these last days opened the door to the next new thing.

As soon as this new theology was noised abroad everywhere, everybody began to say, "What is new theology?" Why, new theology is exactly on the same level as the idea that men came from monkeys. What does it mean? I want to make a clean sweep of it. There is not a man who can think on those lines and not also think on the lines of atheism. Every person who touches a thing like that is an atheist behind all he has to say.

New theology was born in infidelity; it is atheism, and it opened the door for the early Jehovah's Witnesses, whose religion is full of false prophecy. Take a look at their beliefs, and go into the prophecy. What was the prophecy? In 1924 the prophecy was that the Lord would return. Jehovah's Witnesses hold false prophecy. Their belief system is exactly the perfect plan that will make the Man of Sin come forth. The Jehovah's Witnesses are preparing the door for the Man of Sin, and they are receiving openheartedly.

They had also declared that Jesus would come in 1914. I went to see a dear beloved brother of mine who was so deluded by this false prophecy that he was utterly deceived by it. I said, "You will be deceived as sure as you live."

He replied, "We are so sure it is true that if we are deceived we will give up all Jehovah's Witness beliefs and have nothing to do with them."

But what does false prophecy do? False prophecy always makes a way out. The moment it did not come to pass, they said they were mistaken in dates. That is the Devil. If it had been a true prophecy, Jesus would have come. And the Word of God says that if any prophecy does not come true, the prophet who spoke it has to prophesy no more.

But those people were deluded by the spirit of this world, the Devil, and instantly they allowed themselves to be gripped by it again. And the same prophet came forth saying that Christ was going to come in 1925.

In order to cover that, what did they do? They announced in almost every nation, in the big cities, the words, "Millions are alive who will never die," and they have been going at that now since 1925. They are dying all the time; their prophecy is still a cursed, evil prophecy, yet they go on.

The spirit of this age is to get you to believe a lie. If you believe a lie, you cannot believe the truth. When once you are seasoned with a lie against the Word of God, He sends you strong delusion so that you will believe a lie. Who sends it? God does. God is gracious over His Word. His Word is from everlasting; His Word is true.

When we see these things that are coming to pass, what do we know? We know the time is at hand. The fig tree is budding for these false prophecies and these positions.

Now, you see, they never stop at that. They go on to say Christ never has risen. Of course, if you ever believe a lie, if you ever turn from the Word of God to some other place, you cannot believe the truth after that.

WARDING OFF EVIL

Then the last days opened the door for that false demon power that is rampant everywhere in the world. This power is putting up the most marvelous buildings, including that of Christian Science, which is devilish, hellish, and deceiving. I am preaching to you this morning so that you will deliver yourself from this present-day evil. How will you do it? You can do it only on one line. Let the seed in. Let in the seed of truth, the seed of righteousness, this power of God, this inward incorruptible.

The seed of Christ is an inward incorruptible. The new birth, the new life, is a quickening power; it is incorruptible, dealing with corruptible, carnal, evil, sensuous, devilish things. And when it comes to the Word of God, the seed of the Word of God is the life of the Word, and you are living the life of the Word of God and are tremendously transformed all the time by the Word of the Lord.

These are the last days. You go out in the world, and there is no difficulty. What are you going to do now? Is this a fact? Is this true? Aren't people today almost afraid of sending their sons and daughters to the colleges and universities, because they come out more like devils than they were when they went in? Isn't atheism right in the seat of almost all these colleges? Then what should you do? How will you keep your soul in peace? How will you preserve your children? How will you help them? You say they have to go because you want them to come out with certain degrees to their names; you want them to progress in knowledge, but how will you save your children?

Nothing but the Word can save them.

I wish all the young people in this place would read these words in the second epistle of John: *"Young men...you are strong... and you have overcome the wicked one"* (1 John 2:14). By what have they overcome? By the Word.

These are mighty words we read in this Scripture. What does it say?

THE POWER OF REVELATION

The Word is holding these things, even the fires that are going to burn up all the world. The Word is holding them. What is the Word? The Word is the mighty power of the revelation to us of the Son of God. And the Son of God is holding all these powers today in the world, ready for the greatest conflagration that ever could be, when the heavens will be burned up, when the earth will melt with fervent heat (2 Pet. 3:10).

The Word of God is keeping these things reserved and all ready. What manner of men ought we to be? We ought to be purifying ourselves in all our actions. (See verse 11.)

Remember this about heaven: the glory, the revelation, the power, the presence, and all that makes heaven so full of beauty, is that time has no meaning there. It is so lovely; a thousand years are as a day, and a day as a thousand years (v. 8).

> **INTERPRETATION OF A MESSAGE IN TONGUES:**
> All the springs are in you, all the revelations are in your midst. It is He, the mighty God! It is He, the King of Kings! It is He, the Son of the living God, who is in the very innermost being of your human nature, making you to know that, before these things will come to pass, you will be preserved in the midst of the flame. Whatever happens, God will cover you with His mighty covering; and that which is in you is incorruptible and undefiled and does not fade away, which is reserved in the glory.

God says to us, *"By your patience possess your souls"* (Luke 21:19). How beautiful! How the enrichment of the presence of the power of the Most High is bursting forth upon our—what can I say?—our human frames. It is something greater than the human frame. Do you not know that what is born in you is greater than anything formed around you? Do you not know that He who has been begotten in you is the very God of power to preserve you and to bring forth light and truth and cause the vision to be made clearer?

THE ELECT OF GOD

Take note of this: there is an elect of God. I know that God has in this place people who are the elect of God, and if you would examine yourself, you would be amazed to find that you are one of them. People are tremendously afraid of this position because they have so often heard, "Oh, you know you are the elect of God! You are sure to be all right." There have been great churches in England that were founded upon these things. I thank God that they have all withered. If you go to England, you will find that those strong people who used to hold all these things are almost withered out. Why? Because they went on to say that, if you were elect, you were right in whatever you did. That is wrong.

The elect of God are those who are pressing forward. The elect of God cannot hold still: they are always on the wing. Every person who has a knowledge of the elect of God realizes it is important that he press forward. He cannot endure sin or darknesses or shady things. The elect are so in earnest to be elect for God that they burn every bridge behind them.

Know that first there will be a falling away (2 Thess. 2:3). God will bring into His treasury the realities of the truth and put them side by side: the false, the true; those that can be shaken, and those that cannot be shaken. God wants us to be so built upon the foundation of truth that we cannot be shaken in our minds, no matter what comes.

THE MAN OF SIN

When I was in Sydney, they said, "Whatever you do, you must see this place that they built for the man, the new man who is coming."

Theosophy, which is based on theories of reincarnation and other falsities, has a new man. Nothing but Theosophy could have a new man. The foundation of this Theosophy has always been corruptible. In the formation of Theosophy, it was connected to one of the greatest atheists of the day; so you can only expect Theosophy to be atheism. It sprang out of atheism.

The Man of Sin, as he comes forth, will do many things. There will be many false christs, and they will be manifestations of the forthcoming of the Man of Sin, but they will all come to an end. The Man of Sin will be made manifest.

These people are determined to have a man. They know some-one has to come. We Christians know who He is who is coming to us. But these people begin to make a man in this manner: they find a man in India, they polish him up as much as they can, and they make him as—well, in appearance they dress him up, but we are told by the Lord that soft clothing can go onto wolves' backs (Matt. 7:15).

We find that they are going to bring this man forth in great style. When I went around the amphitheater in Sydney that was made for this man to come, I saw as clearly as anything it was the preparation for the Man of Sin. But they do not believe that.

What will make you to know it is the Man of Sin? This: every religious sect and creed that are in the world all join to it. There is not a religion known that has not joined up to it.

Why, that is exactly what the Devil wants. He wants all the false religions joining right up, and the Man of Sin will be received with great applause when he comes.

Who will be saved? Who will know the day? Who now knows the Man of Sin? We feel him when we touch him, when he opens his mouth, when he writes through the paper, when we see his actions—we know who he is.

What has the Man of Sin always said? Why, exactly what Jehovah's Witnesses say. What? That there is no hell. The Devil has always said that. What does Christian Science say? No hell, no Devil. They are ready for him. The Devil has always said no hell, no evil. And these people are preparing, though they do not know it, for the Man of Sin.

We have to see that these days have to come before the Lord can come. There has to be a falling away. There has to be in this day a manifestation so clear, of such undeniable fact. I tell you, when they begin to build temples for the Man of Sin to come (though they don't know it), you know the Day is at hand.

A person said to me, "You see, the Christian Scientists must be right. Look at the beautiful buildings; look at all the people following them." Yes, everybody can belong to it. You can go to any brothel you like, you can go to any theater you like, you can go to any race course you like, you can be mixed up with the rest of the people in your life and still be a Christian Scientist. You can have the Devil right and left and anywhere and still belong to Christian Science.

When the Man of Sin comes, he will be hailed on all sides. When he is manifested, who will miss him? Why, the reverent, the holy, the separated will miss him. Why will they miss him? Because they will not be here to greet him!

READY FOR CHRIST'S RETURN

But there will be things that will happen prior to his coming that we will know. You can tell. I am like one this morning who is moving with a liquid, holy, indispensable, real fire in my bosom, and I know it is burning and the body is not consumed.

It is real fire from heaven that is making my utterances come to you to know that Christ is coming; He is on the way. God is going to help me tell you why you will know. You who have the breath of the Spirit, there is something moving now as I speak. As I speak, this breath of mighty, quickening, moving, changing, desirable power is making you to know, and it is this alone that is making you know that you will be ready.

No matter who else misses it, you will be ready. This is what I want to press upon you today, so that you will be ready. And you won't question your position. You will know. Ah, thank God, you are not of the night; you are of the day (1 Thess. 5:5). Christ's coming will not overtake you as a thief. You are the children of the day. You are not children of the night; you are not drunken. People are drunken in the night. You are not drunken. Oh, yes, you are. There is so much intoxication from this holy incarnation that makes you feel all the time you have to have Him hold you up. Praise the Lord! Holy intoxication, inspired revelation, invocation, incessantly inwardly moving your very nature, so that you know sure as anything that you do not belong to those who are putting off the day. You are hastening unto the Day; you are longing for day.

You say, "What a great Day!" Why do you say it? Because the creature inside the temple longs, travails, groans to be delivered, and will be delivered. Is this body the creature? No. This is the temple that holds the creature. It is the living creature. It is the new creature. It is the new creation. It is the new nature. It is the new life.

What manner of men ought we to be? *"The Lord is not slack concerning His promise, as some count slackness, but is longsuffering toward us, not willing that any should perish but that all should come to repentance"* (2 Pet. 3:9). I want you to notice this: this is not referring to the wicked who have repented. The epistles are always directed toward the saints of God. When I speak to you saints of God, you will find that my language will make you see that there is not within you one thing that has to be covered. I say it without fear of contradiction, because it is my whole life and is inspired by the Truth. You know that these things will purify you.

A Spiritual Teaching

It is on this line that you hear people speak. I do not mean it as a theory. This is not a theory. There is a great difference between a man standing before you on theory and one who stands on spiritual knowledge. The man of theory has chapter and verse, line upon line, precept upon precept (see Isaiah 28:13), and he works it out upon the scriptural basis. It is wonderful, it is good, it is inspiring; but I am not there. Mine is another approach. Mine is the spiritual nature showing you that the world is ripening for Judgment. Mine is a spiritual acquaintance bringing you to a place of separation and holiness unto God, so that you may purify yourself and be clean, ready for the great Day.

This is the day of purifying; this is the day of holiness; this is the day of separation; this is the day of waking. Oh, God, let us wake today! Let our inner spirits wake into consciousness that God is calling us. The Lord is upon us. We see that the Day is upon us. We look at the left side, we look at the right side, we see everywhere new theories. New things will not stand the light of the truth. When you see these things, you know there must be a great falling away before the Day. And it is coming; it is upon us.

Paul said he travailed in birth so that Christ might be formed in the saints (Gal. 4:19). Jesus did the same; John did the same. So, brothers and sisters, may God bless you and make you see that this is a day of travailing for the church of God, that she might be formed in readiness for putting on the glorious raiment of heaven forever and forever.

Therefore, since all these things will be dissolved, what manner of persons ought you to be in holy conduct and godliness, looking for and hastening the coming of the day of God, because of which the heavens will be dissolved, being on fire, and the elements will melt with fervent heat? Nevertheless we, according to His promise, look for new heavens and a new earth in which righteousness dwells. Therefore, beloved, looking forward to these things, be diligent to be found by Him in peace, without spot and blameless. (2 Pet. 3:11–14)

"Without spot and blameless." Do you believe it? What can do this for us? Only the blood of Jesus can do it. Oh, the blood of the Lamb! The blood of Jesus can do it. It can make us spotless, clean, and preserved for God.

Give the Devil the biggest chase of his life, and say these words: *"The blood of Jesus Christ* [God's] *Son cleanses us from all sin"* (1 John 1:7).

If you ever hear something about the blood of Jesus in any Christian Science meeting, go, and I will tell you they are being converted. If you ever hear talk of Jehovah's Witnesses getting excited over the blood of Jesus, I can tell you that God has dealt with them. If ever you hear about this new man in Theosophy getting excited about the blood of Jesus, you can tell them from Wigglesworth that there is a new order in the world. But they have no room for the blood of Christ. And yet we see the blood is preparing us for this great Day.

In that amphitheater in Sydney, when I spoke about the blood and when I spoke about this infernal thing, the whole place was upset. Be careful when anybody comes to you with a sugarcoated pill or with a slimy tongue. They are always of the Devil. The Spirit of the Lord will always deal with truth. These people never deal with truth. They always cover up the truth. They say, "Oh, you can be sure that we are all sons of God; we all belong to God." That is what people said when Jesus was here, and He said, "You are mistaken: you belong to the Devil" (John 8:44). And if Jesus dared to say things like that, I dare.

QUESTIONS ANSWERED

Q: Is it true if we believe a lie we cannot believe the truth?

A: That is not what I said. As soon as you believe the Word of God to be a lie, then you cannot believe the truth of the Word of God. The Word of God comes to you like life and revelation; but Satan in his spurious condition comes, as he has done with many, and moves you from believing in truth to believing in some theory of truth. Once Satan has this hold on people, they have a theory of something else that is not truth, and they have denied the truth to take hold of the theory. It is all theory when people have left the truth. The people who live in truth never have a theory; it is always fact.

Q: Because I have laid aside my Christian Science books, people are now using what they call "malicious magnetism" against me. I know Jesus is stronger than they.

A: This is a very important thing. There are many people so under delusion and so oppressed by the Devil on these lines that they join together to damage the character of others because they do not go their way. That is the Devil if nothing else is. The greatest fact about Christian Science's false position is that its followers are led captive by the Father of Lies. He has been a liar from the beginning. They have stepped out of truth and have been taken by this monster the Devil until they cannot believe the truth.

Jesus said, *"'I am the light of the world. He who follows Me shall not walk in darkness'* (John 8:12). I am the light *'which gives light to every man coming into the world'* (John 1:9)."

If you will go back to the time when you knew that the light of the truth was burning through you, you will find that there you turned from light to take something else that was not light. Remain in the light, and Satan can have no power over you, even if a hundred people were to come and stand around you and say to you, "We will join together to bind you, so that you will be crippled," or so that your mind will be affected, or anything. If you know you have the light, you can smile and say, "You can do nothing to me."

Never be afraid of anything. There are two things in the world: one is fear, the other faith. One belongs to the Devil; the other to God. If you believe in God, there is no fear. If you sway toward any delusion of Satan, you will be brought into fear. Fear always brings bondage. There is a place of perfect love for Christ in which you are always casting out all fear and you are living in the place of freedom. (See 1 John 4:18.) Be sure that you never allow anything to make you afraid. God is for you; who can be against you (Rom. 8:31)?

The reason why so many people have gone into Christian Science is that the church is barren; it does not have the Holy Spirit. Christian Science exists because the churches have a barren place where the Holy Spirit has not been allowed to rule. There would be no room for Christian Science if the churches were filled with the Holy Spirit. But because the churches had nothing, then the needy people went to the Devil to fill the void, and he persuaded them that they had something. Now the same people are coming out knowing they have got nothing—only a wilderness experience.

Let us save ourselves from all this trouble by letting the Holy Spirit fill our hearts.

> Will you be baptized in this faith,
> Baptized in the Holy Ghost?
> To be free indeed 'tis the power you need,
> Baptized in the Holy Ghost.

Don't depend on any past tense, any past momentum, but let the anointing be upon you, let the presence and the power be upon you. Are you thirsty, longing, desiring? Then God will pour out of His treasures all you need. God wants to satisfy us with His great, abounding, holy love, imparting love upon love and faith upon faith.

The cause of all deterioration is refusal of the Holy Spirit. If you have fallen short, it is because you refused the Holy Spirit. Let the Holy Spirit be light in you to lighten even the light that is in you, and no darkness will befall you; you will be kept in the middle of the road.

Look to the coming of the Lord. Set your house in order; be at peace; live at peace; forgive, and learn how to forgive. Never bear malice; don't hold any grudge against anybody. Forgive everybody. It does not matter whether they forgive you or not, you must forgive them. Live in forgiveness; live in repentance; live wholeheartedly. Set your house in order, for God's Son is coming to take what is in the house.

CHAPTER TWO

THE KING IS COMING

The life of the Lord Jesus should be so upon us that we are being prepared and made ready for the Rapture. The purpose of this meeting is that the very nature of the Son of God might be presented to us by the Word of Life, so that we may know what this life is. Do we have it? If we do not, can we have it? What will be the evidences of it?

I want you to be so acquainted with the Word of Life that you will have no doubt that you are coming to a similarly precious faith, or that you are coming to the divine life, or that you have a knowledge that One who is greater than you is working out this mighty power of redemption in your mortal bodies.

These are foundation lines. We need to have a foundation of faith before we can begin. God in His omnipotence can bring us into the faith even if we do not have a firm foundation, but I believe that people ought to have things already in line before they begin. The Spirit of the Lord is so mighty that, just as He brought Philip and dropped him down in the desert and brought him back out of the desert (Acts 8:26–40), the same Spirit can come upon the whole church.

There is a "knowledge of know," and those who know can speak with confidence about what they do know. I want you to know so that when you go away from here, you will be able to talk about what you know regarding what will happen when Jesus comes, and what will be the cause of the happening—for there has to be a cause of the happening.

INTERPRETATION OF A MESSAGE IN TONGUES:
Prepare your heart, for the Lord is at the door and waiting now to open your inner vision. For what is created in you is

what will come out of you, to be clothed upon with that which is from above. It is not that body, but it is the body that will be.

It is the spiritual body I am dealing with, not the natural body. Let us turn now to the Word of God, the first chapter of John.

HIS LIFE IN US

"In Him was life, and the life was the light of men" (John 1:4).

As we go into the Scripture, we will find that this same light, this same spiritual acquaintance or knowledge, this same divine power and authority, the life that is eternal, that is divine and eternal, that is incorruptible, that cannot see corruption—this life was in the Son of God, and He came to be the light and the life of men.

God wants us to comprehend this life that is in the Son, which is meant to be in us, which is to be resurrection, which is to overcome death, which is to have all power in the mortal body. This life is meant to transform the body in every way until it should be in you a manifestation of the invisible but spiritual, the unknown and well known, having nothing and possessing all things. It is to be in you, mightier than you, pulling down strongholds, triumphing graciously over everything.

Now look at the twelfth verse, which has another side to it: *"But as many as received Him..."* (John 1:12). Don't get the idea of receiving the Son of Man in His natural order. If you do, you will miss it. As many as received His life, also received the revelation that was made manifest by Him, the fact that He was in the midst of them with a new order, greater than His natural order, mighty in its production, with forceful language and acts divine, every move supernatural.

"To them He gave the right to become children of God, to those who believe in His name" (v. 12). As they received Him, they had power to become acquainted with this inward knowledge of what He was presenting to them. Not His hair, not His head, not His feet, not His hands, not His legs, but the very life that was in Him had to come with power into every living one who understood Him, who received Him.

Now let us look at what power it had to have: *"Who were born, not of blood, nor of the will of the flesh, nor of the will of man, but of*

God" (v. 13). Born of God. They know they are confronted with a life and a power that has to come to them, and they are to be absolutely created of it, born of it, made of it. Just as He was, we have to be inwardly, knowing that we are now born of another nature, quickened by another power living in us—a new revelation, having the same things that He had.

He came. Those who believed saw Him. In 1 John 1:1 we read,

That which was from the beginning, which we have heard, which we have seen with our eyes, which we have looked upon, and our hands have handled, concerning the Word of life.

This is not referring to His hands; this is not referring to His eyes. They were looking inward, and they were seeing a new creation; they were seeing a Word with power; they were seeing the nature of God; they were seeing the manifestation of God in human flesh. This is exactly what we are when we are born of this.

"The life was manifested, and we have seen, and bear witness, and declare to you that eternal life" (v. 2). Now here is another order, here is another stream. It is not a temporal thing. This is divine, with supernatural power. This is an eternal thing. This is something that cannot pass away. This is something that is to be given to us. This is something that is to be in us. This is the very nature of God. This is as eternal as God. This manifestation of the Son that the disciples were looking at is the Word, the eternal Power, the eternal Source.

INTERPRETATION OF A MESSAGE IN TONGUES:
It is the Lord. It is the Life from above. It is that which came by the Spirit. He left the throne, He came igniting humanity, until they became a living, quickened spirit of divine order. It is eternal life. "The life was manifested, and we have seen, and bear witness, and declare to you that eternal life which was with the Father and was manifested to us."

Now they had it, and they began manifesting it themselves; they began writing about it and knew that they were writing Life:

That which we have seen and heard we declare to you, that you also may have fellowship with us; and truly our fellowship is with the Father and with His Son Jesus Christ.

(v. 3)

First, eternal life comes into you, then your conduct turns heavenward. You begin to fellowship with the Father, and you become divinely acquainted with Him, until you know that what was in Him is in you. This is why they wrote; this is why they knew. And they expressed it by their mouths, and it became a quickened, powerful Spirit as they gave it, as it was when He gave it. I feel the same thing as I am breathing out this message. I know there is a supernatural, quickening power coming through me by the Holy Spirit.

INTERPRETATION OF A MESSAGE IN TONGUES:
Not that which was first; no. God moved away the first so that He might establish the second. The first was the natural man, but now the second is a spiritual man. In you, through you, by you, coming into manifestation. Awake! The vision, the life, the power is now revealed. Enter in, that you might not be naked when the King comes.

God wants to establish in our hearts the fact that we must be ready for the King. Now we are talking about the fact, which is greater than the possibility. Fact works possibilities. Possibilities are in the fact, but you must have the fact first before the possibilities.

JOY IN THIS LIFE

To continue with this Scripture in 1 John 1, brought in to show the life manifested, let us consider the fourth verse: *"And these things we write to you that your joy may be full."*

The Word of Life is to make your joy full. We must remember that what is absent in the world is joy. The world has never had joy; the world never will have joy. Joy is not in the five senses of the world. Feelings are there, happiness is there, but joy can only be produced where there is no alloy. Now, there is no alloy in heaven. Alloy means that there is a mixture. In the world there is happiness, but it is a mixture; very often it comes up very close to sorrow. Very often in the midst of festivities there is a place of happiness, and right underneath that there is a very heavy heart and a strange mixture. So, in those five senses that the world has, they have happiness.

But what we have is this: it is joy without alloy, without a mixture. It is inwardly expressive. It rises higher and higher until, if it had its perfect order, we would drown everything with a shout of praise coming from this holy presence.

We want all the people to receive the Holy Spirit because the Holy Spirit has a very blessed expression to the soul or the heart, and it is this: the Holy Spirit has an expression of the Lord in His glory, in His purity, in His power, and in all His blessed words. All these are coming forcefully through as the Holy Spirit is able to witness to you of Him. And every time the Son is manifested in your hearts by the Holy Spirit, you get a real stream of heavenly glory on earth: joy in the Holy Spirit—not in eating and drinking, but in something higher, something better. We all enjoy eating and drinking, but this is something higher, something better, something more substantial: joy in the Holy Spirit! And the Holy Spirit can bring this joy to us.

This is the first foundation of the truths of the coming of the Lord. The coming of the Lord is for the life of the Lord. The coming of the Lord is not for my body. Our bodies will never be in heaven; they will never reach there. They are terrestrial things, and everything terrestrial will finish upon a terrestrial line.

What is going to be there? The Life—the life of the Son of God, the nature of the Son of God, the holiness of the Son of God, the purity. The Life will be there, as well as the likeness and everything pertaining to it.

As we go on, we will see that He is in this life that is going to have a new body. This life will demand a new body; it is demanding it now. We cannot develop this theme in this moment, but I want to throw out some thought of it. This is a law of life. Now, you have a law of life in nature. But now you have to have a law of a spirit of life, which is free from everything of the natural order (Rom. 8:2). And this is the law of life, of the life of Christ that is in you, which I am taking you through or bringing you to, that you may be firmly fixed on the perfect knowledge that no matter what happens, you know you will go.

When I say "you," it is right to say you will go. You will go up, but you, as you now know yourself, won't go in. You will be dissolved as you go. But the nature of the Son, the new life, will go in with your new body.

We move on now to a further foundation. We turn again to the first chapter of John and read the fourteenth verse. They saw, they heard the Word. Now this is to be ours.

> *And the Word became flesh* [they saw it] *and dwelt among us* [it was right in the midst of them, and they couldn't help seeing the glory of it], *and we beheld His glory, the glory as of the only begotten of the Father, full of grace and truth.* (John 1:14)

Now you have to receive that—full of grace, full of truth, the glory of the Lord. You must remember that glory is not a halo around your head. In some paintings of the Lord Jesus or of saints, you will see a light patch painted just over their heads, the idea being to exhibit glory. Glory never is that way. Glory is expressive, and glory is impressive before it is expressive. Glory is not an outside halo; glory is and inward conception.

The more they were in the midst of glory, the more they were convinced of it and preserved it. It had two mighty powers with it: it not only had grace, which was the canopy of the mercy of the high order of God, all the time prevailing and covering and pressing Him, but it also had truth. Christ spoke so that every heart was filled with what He said.

And this is what we have to have. This is what will be caught up and expressed. Can expressiveness be taken up? Yes, because it is the nature of the new birth. Will truth be taken up? Yes, for truth is the very embodiment of the Son. Just as this life permeates through your body, it would be impossible for any saint ever to be free to give anything but absolute truth. The saint has to become an embodiment of truth, life, and Christ manifested. We have to be like Him, just as He was, filled with His glory, this divine order speaking out of fullness, greater than anything we have ever had. Our minds and souls must perceive the things of God so that we live, move, and act in this glory.

They saw it, and you have seen it this morning. The glory of the Lord, the presence of the Lord, the power of the Lord, the life of the Lord is being made manifest. I will tell you how you know it. As I speak, your hearts are burning, your very inward motions are crying out for more. Why? This is what will be taken. It is not you He is after: it is what has been created in you.

NEW LIFE THROUGH CHRIST

How did it come? It wasn't of flesh, it wasn't of blood, it wasn't through the mind of man, but it came by God (John 1:12–13). This new life came by God. You had the other three things before, but then the fourth came. What place did it take? The very thing that would bring you to death changes by beginning in life. The moment this change began in your life, it made you so different, so new, that you felt you had never called God "Father" before in your life; there was something new that said "Father" differently. You knew that you were now joined up to an eternal Fatherhood. You knew you were moved from earth and were joined up to heaven.

The greatest thing that I can talk about this morning is the Rapture, and I touch on it occasionally but cannot go into it yet. The greatest word there is in the world is *rapture*. The worst thing ever that man knows about in the world is death. Death makes you shudder. There is something about it that makes nobody want it. But this new life frees you from death. You know there is no death in it. It is life. This eternal life, this inward force, makes you know as you think about rapture that you are not here, you are far off. That is why I want to get you into thinking that you are far off, and I want you to live in a place of divine acquaintance with the Rapture. You have to get to know how to possess your souls in patience (Luke 21:19).

Now look at the third chapter of John:

Jesus answered, "Most assuredly, I say to you, unless one is born of water and the Spirit, he cannot enter the kingdom of God. That which is born of the flesh is flesh, and that which is born of the Spirit is spirit. Do not marvel that I said to you, 'You must be born again.' The wind blows where it wishes, and you hear the sound of it, but cannot tell where it comes from and where it goes. So is everyone who is born of the Spirit." Nicodemus answered and said to Him, "How can these things be?" (vv. 5–9)

So we see that no natural man who ever lived can understand these things. This is a supernatural teaching, and when we come to the line of this truth, we are able to put supernatural things into place to discern natural things. But we must be supernatural first, before we can deal with supernatural things. (See 1 Corinthians 2:14.)

Jesus was a supernatural evidence, and He was dealing with a supernatural process. Here, He was dealing with a man who was natural. This man who was natural could not comprehend how it could be possible for him, who had been born, say, forty-five or fifty years before, to be born again.

THE NEW BIRTH

Jesus spoke to Nicodemus as I am speaking to you this morning, and He told him that this birth, this new birth, is not flesh and blood; this new birth is the life of God. It is a spiritual life, as real as God, as true as God, and as forming as God. God is a formation, and we are formed after His formation, for He made us in His very image. But He is a spiritual God, and He has quickened us and made us to be like Him with an inward, spiritual life. Just as we have natural formation, so the new nature, the new power, is continually forming a new man in us after the order of Him. The first Adam was formed, and we are in the vision of him; the last Adam, the new creation, is going to have a vision and expression like Him. As we have borne the image of the earthly, we are going to bear the image of the heavenly (1 Cor. 15:49).

It is already in us, but the vessel is not broken. The container will be dissolved, and the heavenly nature, the heavenly body, will prove itself, and we will be like Him.

I want you to follow the word and rightly discern its meaning, asking yourself these questions: Am I in the faith? Do I have what Nicodemus was seeking?

I was once exactly where Nicodemus was, and said, *"How can these things be?"* (John 3:9). Then there came by faith a regenerating power that made me know I was born of God. It came like the wind. I could not see it, but I felt it. It had a tremendous effect upon my human nature, and I found that I myself was a new creation. I found I wanted to pray and to talk about the Lord. Oh, I will never forget saying "Father."

If you catch this truth, it does not matter where you are. If you are in exile somewhere—on a farm where no one is near you, exiled from everybody, and cannot get near anybody for comfort—if this life gets into you, you will know that when He comes again, you will go to meet Him.

This is the life that I want you to know, the life in the body. The new birth, the new creation, the quickening, the being made after Him, being begotten of God—these are very beautiful thoughts if you put them in this perfect order. When you are born of God, God's nature comes in. I won't call it the germ of eternal life, but the seed of God, because we are conceived by the Word, we are quickened by the power, we are made after His order. What is from above has entered into what is below, and you have now become a quickened spirit. You were dead, without aspiration, and without desire. As soon as this comes in, aspiration, desire, and prayer ascend, lifting higher and higher, and you have already moved toward heavenly things.

This is a new creation that cannot live on the earth. It always lives, soaring higher—higher and higher, loftier and loftier, holier and holier. This is the most divine order you could have. This is the spiritual order, God manifested in the flesh, quickening us by the Spirit, making us like Him. Hallelujah!

KNOW AND BELIEVE

Now turn to John 5:24:

Most assuredly, I say to you, he who hears My word and believes in Him who sent Me has everlasting life, and shall not come into judgment, but has passed from death into life.

"He who hears." Does this mean that the Word of Life can go into the ear? Yes, in through the ear, right into the heart—the word, the life, the nature of the Son of God.

What does it do? *"He who hears My word and believes in Him who sent Me has everlasting life."* Who can put limits on that?

There is a good deal of controversy about the length of time this life lasts. How long do you say it lasts? What does Jesus say it is? *"Everlasting life."* Some people say it might be for ten, fifteen, or twenty years. What do you say it is? *"Everlasting life."*

If you get there, there is no difficulty about being ready. But if you doubt the Word of God, how can you be ready? I am speaking to the wise, and a word to the wise is sufficient. It does not matter who brings a quarrelsome accusation against the Word. If he says anything about this everlasting life, ask him what he believes about it, for Jesus said this: *"He who hears My word and believes in Him who sent Me has everlasting life."*

Suppose you say, "Well, I doubt it." Then you will be done. Jesus said that if you doubt it, it is damnation; if you believe it, it is everlasting life. Do you believe it is everlasting life? Are you going to let your opinions rob you and bring you into condemnation? Or are you going to receive what the Word says?

What is the Word? The Word is truth. What is truth? Jesus is truth. Jesus said these words: *"He who hears My word and believes in Him who sent Me has everlasting life, and shall not come into judgment, but has passed from death into life."*

> Holy, holy, holy, Lord God of Hosts!
> Heaven and earth are praising Thee,
> O Lord, Most High!

These meetings will go higher and higher. I want you to get a foundation position, so that when you go out in the world of service, you will have laid down a fact in your heart as to what is the coming of the Lord. As I go on, I will be able to give you a clear distinction of its expression—a living expression of a living personality. Christ is now already manifested or being manifested in us. The sons of God are coming forth with power, and God will show us, as we go on with the Word of God, this living glorious fact, or hope, or crown of rejoicing.

May God the Holy Spirit sanctify us and purify us with a perfect purification, until we stand white in the presence of God. Let us do some repenting; let us tell God we want to be holy. If you are sure you have this eternal life in you, I want you to consider it worthy not to look back, keeping your eyes upon the plan, looking toward the Master. Believe that God is greater than your heart. Believe that God is greater than your thoughts. Believe that God is greater than the Devil. Believe that He will preserve you. Believe in His almightiness. And on the authority of God's faith in you, you will triumph until He comes.

> Bring me higher up the mountain,
> Into fellowship with Thee!
> In Thy light I see the Fountain,
> And the Blood that cleanseth me.

QUESTIONS ANSWERED

Q: You said there is no body in heaven. Is Jesus Christ sitting at the right hand of the Father in flesh or in spirit?

A: We will have bodies in heaven, but they will be spiritual, glorified bodies. I believe that Jesus is different from anyone else in the glory because of the marks of the Crucifixion. But I have Scripture to bear me out that there is no flesh and blood in heaven, but we will be different. We will have our hands, but they will be glorified hands, on glorified bodies. Your own character, your own crown, will be there.

How will the crown be made? The crown is this: the wood, the hay, the stubble will be burned, and the gold, the silver, and precious stones will be left. Everybody will know what kind of a crown or life they have had because the crown will be made up of their own gold and their own precious stones after they have gone through the fire.

Everybody will know. We will know as we are known; there will be no mistake about that. But it will be an expression of brightness, of glory. For instance, we will be really transparent in so many ways; the glory will be so wonderful.

Let us look at Jesus for a moment. When Jesus was with Peter and John on that holy mount, the very vesture, the very nature, everything that He had was turned to transparent glory until even His clothing was as white as snow and the whole of His body was transformed in that vision. (See Matthew 17:1–8.)

The very thing that was in each person on earth will be exactly expressed in heaven. Moses and Elijah were known in their glorified bodies. Jesus will be known to everybody as the Son of God and as the Lamb that was slain. The marks will be there, the glorified body with the marks of the cross. It will be very wonderful. We will be there. What will have passed away from us is this: the marks of sin, the marks of deformity, the marks of corruption, the marks of transgression. We will be there, whiter than snow, purified through and through.

The Lamb of God will be known; He will be different, He will have a glorified body, for flesh and blood do not enter into the kingdom of God. They could not stand the glory; they would be withered up in His presence; so the body has to be a changed body. God calls it in 1 Corinthians 15 the *"celestial"* body (v. 40).

Q: Didn't Christ after the Resurrection have a body of flesh and bones?

A: Yes, He did. When we get to heaven, what we will be most pleased about at first is that He will be the same Lord, just the same, only in a glorified body. He will be neither flesh nor bones.

Q: What did Job mean when he said, *"After my skin is destroyed, this I know, that in my flesh I shall see God"* (Job 19:26)?

A: That is a different thing altogether. I believe that everybody will see God perfectly and in a very wonderful way. The pure in heart will see God (Matt. 5:8). I believe we will see God and see Jesus in our flesh, but it will be the last time of the flesh; we will know Him no more after the flesh, but we will see Him in the spirit. You will never see Jesus anymore after that in the flesh.

Q: Will the celestial bodies and terrestrial bodies be gathered together?

A: Terrestrial bodies will never be in the presence of God. Terrestrial is always earthly. Celestial bodies in the glory will leave terrestrial bodies, and we will all be together—the angels, archangels, God—all will be there, perfect. The angels may never understand the fullness of our redemption, but they will all be there in perfect harmony. God will gather all into perfect harmony. Heaven will be a wonderful place. But in order to prepare us properly, He knows it will be necessary to have a new earth and a new heaven to fit the situation.

Q: Is there a Scripture that says that the Christians of today without the baptism of the Holy Spirit go up in the Rapture?

A: What is the Rapture but eternal life? Could you imagine that anything down here that has had eternal life within would not be in the Rapture? It is contrary to the mind of God, contrary to the teaching of God. It is impossible for anyone to have eternal life in them and not also have that life that will lead to heaven; for eternal life, the life within you, is the life and the nature of the Son, and when He comes it is impossible for you not to go with Him. *"When Christ who is our life appears, then you also will appear with Him in glory"* (Col. 3:4). What will make it? The life, the joint life.

Q: Will we see the Father as a personality, or will Jesus be the expression of the Father?

A: One thing will be certain: when we get to glory, we will be very much taken up with the Son, but we must not forget that the Son will not rob the Father of His glory. Rather, He will take us all, and He will take Himself in the great Day of all things, and He will present us all and Himself to the Father. So I know the Father will be in a glorious place in glory; and I know the Son will be in a wonderful place; and I know the Holy Spirit who has comforted us all—what a great joy it will be to see Him who has been the great Comforter and the great Leader and the great Speaker and the great Operator. We will surely give Him a great place in glory!

Q: Is it possible after a person has been truly born again to get away from the Lord and to be lost?

A: The Scripture says, *"He who believes in* [the Lord] *has everlasting life"* (John 6:47). The Word of God will not change for anyone. The Word of God is like a two-edged sword, dividing even the soul and the spirit (Heb. 4:12), and it is all the time putting away what man says and giving you what God says.

Q: You said if our eyes are open we could see the Lord right among us. We know that He ascended in one body. How could that be, provided there were half a dozen meetings going on at the same time—how could He be right in the midst?

A: The Holy Spirit is here and—I want to say it reverently—Jesus is not here. Don't misunderstand me. Has Jesus ever been here since He went to the glory? No. Is He coming to the earth the next time? No; He is coming in the heavens, and we will meet Him.

But what is here? The Holy Spirit, and He makes Jesus just as real to me as if He were here. That is the position of the Holy Spirit—to reveal the Father and the Son—and He makes them just as real to us as if they were here. The Holy Spirit fills the whole earth, and He could make a million assemblies see every spiritual thing possible. We do not want to see spirits; we want to see bodies filled with the Spirit of the living God.

429

For our comfort and consolation, He says, *"Lo, I am with you always"* (Matt. 28:20), and He is with us in power and in might. The Holy Spirit makes Him real to me. He is with me.

Q: *"Most assuredly, I say to you, he who believes in Me has everlasting life"* (John 6:47). Does not this verse hinge on the word *"believes"*? That is a present, continuous tense. He believes now, and he keeps right at it. Do gaining the glory and keeping the eternal life not depend on whether or not we keep believing? First John says, *"If our heart does not condemn us, we have confidence"* (1 John 3:21), and then we can believe. If I do something that makes my heart condemn me, how can I keep on believing?

A: If eternal life in you depends upon your always thinking about nothing else but eternal life, most of the people in this place would say, "Well, I am no good then." But we must remember that the blood of Jesus is not a past-tense cleansing power, but it is a present-tense cleansing power. When you are asleep at night, you know very well you neither try to believe nor think about believing anything. Even so, the blood of Jesus cleanses you in the night, and He cleanses you right now. Your salvation does not consist of your always shouting, "I believe!"

The new birth is a new life; it is regenerative, it is holy, it is divine, it is faith, it is Christ. He is with you always, moving you, changing you, thrilling you, causing you to live in the glory without pressure. It is a believing position. *"I delight to do Your will"* (Ps. 40:8). My condition of salvation is not something that pressures me continually to say I believe or else I will be lost. Faith is a life; life is a presence, a presence of changing from one state of glory to another.

My attitude of yieldedness to God continually keeps me in His favor. If I thought that my salvation depended upon that, I would know then that I had lost the knowledge that God was greater than my heart and greater than my life, for I am not kept by what I do, but I am kept by the power of God.

Q: Doesn't His keeping power depend on my doing the same things as I did when I gained His favor?

A: What you are doing is putting your weakness in the place of God's almighty power. If you believe, you are kept from falling. After God gives faith, He does not take it away.

Q: I know a number of people who have truly belonged to God, and the glory has been upon them, but today they are serving the Devil just as faithfully as they ever served the Lord. They have lost eternal life, have they not?

A: You are not responsible for them. They have had the light. Light has come to the world, and they refused light. They are in awful jeopardy and darkness and sorrow. If you do not allow God to be greater than your heart, you will be in trouble about them.

Q: I am not in trouble about them, but I cannot quite catch the thought that they are still saved.

A: I have not told you that they are still saved. I believe they have tasted, but they have never been converted. I tell you the reason why: Jesus said, *"My sheep...follow Me"* (John 10:27), and they are not of the fold if they do not follow. Jesus said it.

If I find people who want me to believe that they belong to God, and they are following the Devil, I will say, "Well, either you or the Word is a liar." I do not take it for granted that because a person says he has been saved that he is saved. He is only proving to me he is saved if he follows.

Don't you for a moment believe I am here standing for eternal security. I am trying to help you to see that God's eternal security can be so manifested in your mortal bodies that there could not be a doubt about rapture or life or anything. I want the Word of God to make you know that it is the eternal Word; it is the eternal life, and it is eternal power.

I have never known a moment in my life in which God has not made me long for more holiness. I have been saved for sixty years, and I have never lost the sense of that saving, peaceful place. *"He who believes in the Son of God has the witness"* (1 John 5:10). I cannot change the Word of God because a few people tasted and then went away. I believe that when you have really been born of God, you are either in deep conviction or you are on the top. It could not be otherwise.

Q: Will you please explain Ezekiel 18:24, which says, *"But when a righteous man turns away from his righteousness and commits iniquity, and does according to all the abominations that the wicked man does, shall he live?"*

A: We ought to see that our righteousness is greater than the righteousness of filthy rags. We ought to see that our holiness is so purified that we are not holy for the sake of being holy, but we are holy because of an incarnation of God in us making us holy.

It is necessary that we face the truth and get to know it. If we do not, what an awful awaiting will be ours! The books are not to be opened and the crown is not to be given until the end. But I know some crowns are being increased, and I know God is making a great preparation for the saints.

But I warn you today: see to it that your lives are holy; see to it that you do not give place to the Devil; see to it that you buy opportunities; see to it that your whole body is sanctified and made ready for God, as the Scripture says. See to it that no sin ever has anything to do with your life. Believe God that He can keep you from falling. Believe God that He can present you holy. Believe God that you can have a reward. I am going in for the reward. Because other people do not care for going in for the reward, it makes me all the more earnest for it.

CHAPTER THREE

LIFE EVERLASTING

You may be amazed, when you step into the heavenly glory, to find there the very Word, the very life, the very touch that has caused aspiration and inspiration. The Word is settled there. The Word creates right in our very nature this wonderful touch of divine inspiration, making us know that those who are in heaven and we who are on earth are of one spirit, blended in one harmonious knowledge, created in a new order. We are being made like Him by the power of the spirit of the Word of God, until we are full of hopefulness, filled with life, joyously expecting, gloriously waiting.

One word is continually sufficient for me:

> *Therefore, having been justified by faith, we have peace with God through our Lord Jesus Christ, through whom also we have access by faith into this grace in which we stand, and rejoice in hope of the glory of God.* (Rom. 5:1–2)

Salvation fills us with the *"hope of the glory of God,"* with a great access into the grace.

Let us turn to the sixth chapter of John. We are still on the foundation of the construction of the saint of God in the new order of the Spirit. We are still building upon the foundation principles of the living Word of God, not so that we may be like those who are drunk in the night, or those who are asleep, but so that we will be awakened. (See 1 Thessalonians 5:5–8.)

Being awakened does not mean particularly that you have been actually asleep; the word *sleeping* in this context doesn't mean a person is actually asleep. It means that he is dense to activity relating to the spiritual realm. Sleeping does not mean that you are fast asleep. Sleeping means that you have lost under-standing, you are dull of hearing, and your eyes are heavy because they are not full of the light that will light you. So God is causing us to understand that we have to be alive and awake.

Here is the word: *"Do not labor for the food which perishes"* (John 6:27). At the beginning of John 6, Jesus had been feeding the sheep, and because they were being fed by His gracious hands, the crowd came around Him again. He saw that they were of the natu-ral order, and He broke forth into this wonderful word, *"Do not labor for the food which perishes."*

INTERPRETATION OF A MESSAGE IN TONGUES:

The Lord Jesus, seeing the needy missing the great ideal of His mission, turned their attention by saying, "It is more needful that you get a drink of a spiritual awakening. It is more needful that you eat of the inner manna of Christ today, for God has sealed Him for that purpose and He has become the Bread for you."

The Master was in earnest when He said, *"Enter by the narrow gate; for wide is the gate and broad is the way that leads to destruc-tion"* (Matt. 7:13).

Strive to enter in at the narrow gate. Get a live, inward inheri-tance in you. The Master has food for us, bread enough and to spare.

INTERPRETATION OF A MESSAGE IN TONGUES:

It is the living Word. It is the touch of His own spiritual na-ture that He wants to breathe into our human nature today. It is the nature of the Son; it is the breath of His life; it is the quickening of His power; it is the savor of life unto life. It is that which quickens you from death into life; it is that which wakens you out of all human into the glorious liberty of the sons of God. It is the Spirit that quickens.

Let me read the Word:

Do not labor for the food which perishes, but for the food which endures to everlasting life, which the Son of Man will give you, because God the Father has set His seal on Him. (John 6:27)

Everlasting life is a gift. The Holy Spirit is a gift. But *"the gift of God is eternal life"* (Rom. 6:23), and we have this life in His Son (1

John 5:11). *"He who does not have the Son of God does not have life"* (v. 12), but he who has the Son *"has passed from death into life"* (John 5:24). This is the life that will be caught up; this is the life that will be changed in a moment; this is the life that will enter into the presence of God in a moment of time, because it is divine, because it has no bondage, because it is not hindered by the flesh.

THE BEGINNING OF LIFE

So God is pruning us, teaching us to observe that those who enter into this life have ceased from their own works (Heb. 4:10). Those who enter into this spiritual awakening have no more bondages. They have learned that *"no one engaged in warfare entangles himself with the affairs of this life"* (2 Tim. 2:4). They have a new inspiration of divine power. It is the nature of the Son of God.

But the verse says, *"Strive to enter through the narrow gate"* (Luke 13:24). Yes, beloved, this means you will have to work for it, because your own nature will interfere with you; your friends will often stand in the way. Your position will many times almost bring you to a place where you will be doomed if you take that stand.

I understand that Jesus could be interpreted in no other way but this: *"Whoever desires to save his life will lose it, but whoever loses his life for My sake will find it"* (Matt. 16:25). He will find the life that never ceases. Human life has an end; divine life has only a beginning. This is the life that the Son of Man was sealed to give. He was specially sealed; He was specially anointed; He was specially separated. He gave Himself over to God, so that He might become the firstfruit of the first-begotten of a new creation that was going to be in the presence of God forever. A new creation, a new sonship, a new adoption, a new place, a new power. Hallelujah! Are you in for it?

The apostle Peter had entered into this divine position just before Jesus made His statement, *"Whoever desires to save his life will lose it, but whoever loses his life for My sake will find it"* (Matt. 16:25). Peter had just gotten this new life; he had just entered into the place where he knew that Jesus was the Son of God, saying, *"You are the Christ, the Son of the living God"* (v. 16). Then Jesus began breaking the seal of His ministry. He said, *"The Son of Man must be delivered into the hands of sinful men, and be crucified, and the third day rise again"* (Luke 24:7).

Peter said, "This will not happen. I'll see to that! You leave that business with me. Let anybody touch you, and I will stand in your place; I will be with you." And Jesus said, *"Get behind Me, Satan! You are an offense to Me, for you are not mindful of the things of God, but the things of men"* (Matt. 16:23).

Anything that hinders me from falling into the ground, everything that interferes with my taking up my cross, dying to self, separating from the world, cleaning my life up, or entering through the narrow gate, anything that interferes with that is Satan's power. *"Unless a grain of wheat falls into the ground and dies, it remains alone"* (John 12:24).

Strive to enter in. Seek to be worthy to enter in. Let God be honored by your leaving behind the things that you know are taking your life, hindering your progress, blighting your prospects, and ruining your mind—for nothing will dull the mind's perceptions like touching earthly things that are not clean.

When God began dealing with me on holy lines, I was working for thirteen saloons, meaning that I was going to thirteen different bars. Of course, I was among hundreds of other customers. God dealt with me in this matter, and I cleared up the whole situation in the presence of God. That was only one thing; there were a thousand things.

God wants us to be holy, pure, and perfect the whole way through. The inheritance is an incorruptible inheritance; it is undefiled, and it does not fade away (1 Pet. 1:4). Those who are entering in are judging themselves so that they will not be condemned with the world (1 Cor. 11:32). Many people have fallen asleep. (See verses 27–30.) Why? Because they did not listen to the correction of the Word of the Lord. Some have been ill, and God dealt with them; they would not heed, and then God put them to sleep.

Oh, that God the Holy Spirit will have a choice with us today, that we will judge ourselves so that we are not condemned with the world! *"For if we would judge ourselves, we would not be judged"* (v. 31). What is it to judge yourself? If the Lord speaks, if He says, "Let it go," no matter if it is as dear as your right eye, you must let it go. If it is as costly as your right foot, you must let it go. It is far better to let it go. Strive to enter in.

INTERPRETATION OF A MESSAGE IN TONGUES:
God's Word never speaks in vain. It always opens to you the avenues where you can enter in. God opens the door for you.

He speaks to your heart; He is dealing with you. We are dealing with the coming of the Lord, but how will we be prepared unless all is burned? The wood, the hay, the stubble must be burned. The gold, the silver, and the precious stones will be preserved. Be willing, beloved, for the Lord Himself has to deal with you.

THE BREAD OF LIFE

Let us move on to another important lesson of Scripture:

Then Jesus said to them, "Most assuredly, I say to you, Moses did not give you the bread from heaven, but My Father gives you the true bread from heaven. For the bread of God is He who comes down from heaven and gives life to the world." (John 6:32–33)

Bread! Oh, beloved, I want God to give you a spiritual appetite so that you will have a great inward devouring place where you will eat the Word, where you will savor it with joy, where you will have it with grace, and also where it will be mingled with separation. As the Word comes to you—the Word of God, the Bread of Heaven, the very thing you need, the very nature of the life of the Son of God— and as you eat, you will be made in a new order after Him who has created you for His plan and purpose.

"Then they said to Him, 'Lord, give us this bread always'" (v. 34). I want that same expression to be made in our hearts because He is helping us into this.

"And Jesus said to them, 'I am the bread of life. He who comes to Me shall never hunger, and he who believes in Me shall never thirst'" (John 6:35).

The process of the Word of God must kindle in us a separation from the world. It must bring death to everything except the life of the Word of Christ in our hearts. I want to save you from judging, because to the degree that you have not come into the revelation of this eternal working in you, to that degree you will not come right through believing in the true principle of the Word of Life.

"He who comes to Me shall never hunger, and he who believes in Me shall never thirst."

The two things are necessary. I will never expect any person to go beyond his light. The Word of God is to give you light. The Spirit

437

of the Lord and the Word of the Lord—one is light, the other is life. We must see that God wants us to have these two divine properties, life and light, so that we are in a perfect place to judge ourselves by the Word of God. The Word of God will stand true, whatever our opinions may be. Scripture says very truly, *"For what if some did not believe? Will their unbelief make the faithfulness of God without effect?"* (Rom. 3:3). Will it change the Word? The Word of God will be the same whether people believe it or not.

In these meetings, God will sift the believer. This is a sifting meeting. I want you to get away from the chaff. Chaff is judgment; chaff is unbelief; chaff is fear; chaff is failing. It is the covering of the weak, and as long as it covers the weak, it hinders the weak from coming forth for bread. So God has to deal with the chaff; He has to get it away so that you might be the pure bread, the pure life, the pure word, and so that there will be no strange thing in you, no misunderstanding.

God has to deal with His people, and if God deals with the house of God, then the world will soon be dealt with. The dealing first is with the house of God, and then after that with the world (1 Pet. 4:17). When the house of God is right, all the people will get right very soon. The principle is this: all the world needs and longs to be right, and so we have to be salt and light to guide them, to lead them, to operate before them so that they see our good works and glorify our Lord.

I was preaching on these divine elements one day, and one person in the midst of the meeting said, "I won't believe! I won't believe! Nothing like that ever moves me. You cannot move me. Nothing can move me."

"I believe! I believe! I believe!" I responded.

I went on dealing with the things of God. This man was a well-known preacher. He had come to a place where the chaff had to be taken up, where God was dealing with him, where his life was opened out. He said again, "I won't believe!" It made no difference to me; I went on preaching. He was so aroused that he jumped up and went out, shouting as he closed the door, "I won't believe!"

The next morning, the pastor of the church at which the meeting was being held, got a note saying, "Please come immediately," and the pastor went. As soon as he got to the door, a woman met him, tears in her eyes, weeping bitterly.

"Oh," she said, "I am in great distress!"

She took him inside. When he got inside, the first thing that confronted him was the man who had shouted out, "I won't believe!" The man got a piece of paper and wrote, "Last night I had a chance to believe; I refused to believe, and now I cannot believe, and I cannot speak."

This man was made mute because he would not believe. Is he the only one? No. We read the story of Zacharias and Elizabeth. When Zacharias was in the Holy of Holies, God spoke to him, telling him that He was going to give him a son. But his heart was unmoved, and his language was contrary to faith; so Gabriel said to him, *"You will be mute and not able to speak...because you did not believe"* (Luke 1:20). And he came out of that place mute.

It seems to me that if we will not judge ourselves, we will be judged (1 Cor. 11:31). I am giving you the Word. The Word should so be in you that, as I speak, the fire should burn, the life should be kindled, the very nature of Christ should transform you. You should be so moved in this meeting that you are ready for rapture, and longing for it. You know that you have the life, and you know this life will be held until it gets loose.

You need the Bread to feed the life to you. The Word of God is the Bread. There is no famine going on now; God is giving us the Bread of Life.

"He who comes to Me shall never hunger, and he who believes in Me shall never thirst" (John 6:35). It is a constant satisfaction, an inward joyful expression, a place of peace.

> *All that the Father gives Me will come to Me, and the one who comes to Me I will by no means cast out. For I have come down from heaven, not to do My own will, but the will of Him who sent Me. This is the will of the Father who sent Me, that of all He has given Me I should lose nothing, but should raise it up at the last day.* (vv. 37–39)

Nothing—I will lose nothing! Do you believe that? Some people are still on the hedge, undecided. "After all, He may lose us." I would rather believe the Word of God!

ONLY BELIEVE

I find people continually deceived because they look around them, and many people have lost all because of their feelings.

439

There was one man in the Old Testament who was very terribly deceived because of his feelings—it was Jacob. He felt for Esau, but he was deceived. If you feel, you will be deceived.

God does not want us to feel. He wants us on one line only: believing. I would like you to understand that you did not come to Jesus. God gave you to Jesus. Where did He find you? He found you in the world, and He gave you to Jesus, and Jesus gave you eternal life. As He received everyone whom He had given His life for and given His life to, He said He would lose nothing; He would preserve them.

"Oh," you say, "that all depends."

Yes, it does, it depends upon whether you believe God or not. But I find people always getting outside of the plan of God because they use their own judgment.

I am not going to believe that all who say they are believers, believe. There was one group who came up to Jesus and said, "We are the seed of Abraham; we have Abraham for our father." (See John 8:39.) He said, "You are mistaken; you are the seed of the Devil." (See verses 39–44.)

"He who believes in the Son of God has the witness" (1 John 5:10), and we know that we are the sons of God because we do those things that please Him. We know we are the sons of God because we love to keep His commandments. *"His commandments are not grievous"* (1 John 5:3 KJV). And we know we are the sons of God because we overcome the world. (See verse 4.)

That is what every son of God has to do—overcome the world. And this life we receive from Him is eternal and everlasting and cannot see corruption. But God is feeding us this morning with that wonderful Word of promise, so that we might know that we have the inheritance in the Spirit, and so that we may know that we are going on to the place of "Ready, Lord, ready!"

Are you ready to go? I am here getting you ready to go, because you have to go. It is impossible for the life of God or the law of the life of the Spirit to be in you unless it is doing its work. The law of the life of the Spirit will be putting to death all the natural life and will quicken you continually with spiritual life until you will have to go.

When I see white hair and wrinkled faces, I say, "You have to go. It does not matter what you say, you cannot stop; you have to go. You will begin blossoming, and in a short time you will bloom and be off."

That is a natural plan, but I am talking about a supernatural plan. We know that as we have borne the image of the earthly, we are going to bear the image of the heavenly (1 Cor. 15:49). Mortality will be swallowed up in life. The very nature of the Son of God is in us, making life, immortality, and power. The power of the Word of the living Christ!

The Gospel of the grace of God has power to bring immortality and life. What is the Gospel? The Word, the Bread of the Son of God. Feed upon it. Feed upon it in your heart. It is immortality; it is life by the Word of quickening and by the Word of truth.

You look good, you are an inspiration, but you know there are many marks and blemishes. You know that as you pass through the weary days of toil, battling with sin on every line, there is a light in you, a life in you that is going to pass off, and you are going to be like Him. It will be the same face, but the marks, the scars, and the spots will have gone. What will do it? The Bread! Oh, Lord, ever more give us this Bread, the Bread of the Son of God!

"Most assuredly, I say to you, he who believes in Me has everlasting life. I am the bread of life" (John 6:47–48). Everlasting life means Bread. Men cannot live by bread alone, but by the Word of the living God (Matt. 4:4).

TRIED BY FIRE, ENRICHED BY GRACE

When I read this in the book of Revelation, my heart was moved: *"And His name is called The Word of God"* (Rev. 19:13). His name, the very name, is the Word of God, who gave His life for the world. And of His life, of His Spirit, of His grace, of His faith we have received. What does this mean? Oh, you tried ones, grace is being poured into you—grace from heaven, grace enriched, grace abundant. His grace is for your weakness, so that you might be sustained in the trial, in the fire, passing through it, coming out more like the Lord.

This inspires me. Why? Because time comes to an end. All the beautiful buildings in the world, the mountains, the heavens and all, will pass away. The heavens will be rolled up as a scroll (Isa. 34:4), and all things *"will melt with fervent heat"* (2 Pet. 3:10). But one thing cannot be burned; one thing cannot be changed; one thing can stand the fire, the water, persecution, and anything else. What is it? The same thing that went into the fire and remained untouched while the men on the outside were slain by the fire.

Shadrach, Meshach, and Abednego were in the fire, and it did not burn them. The king was amazed when he saw them walking. "Oh!" he said. *"Did we not cast three men bound into the midst of the fire?"* (Dan. 3:24).

"True, O king" (v. 24), his men replied.

"'Look!' he answered, 'I see four men loose, walking in the midst of the fire...and the form of the fourth is like the Son of God'" (v. 25).

There is no consuming. There is a life of the Son of God that cannot be burned, cannot see corruption, passes through fire, passes through clouds, passes through legions of demons and will clear them out of the way, passes through everything. Oh, that life! What is it? The life of the Son of God. He came to give life; He came to give life more abundantly. Oh, what a life, abounding life, resurrection life!

Do you have it? Is it yours? Are you afraid you will lose it? Do you believe He will lose you?

"What makes you say that?" you ask.

Because sometimes I hear doubters. So I am going to read a wonderful Scripture for the doubters.

> *My sheep hear My voice, and I know them, and they follow Me. And I give them eternal life, and they shall never perish; neither shall anyone snatch them out of My hand. My Father, who has given them to Me, is greater than all; and no one is able to snatch them out of My Father's hand.*
>
> (John 10:27–29)

Oh, that life—full of deity, full of assurance, full of victory, full of a shout. There is the shout of a King in the midst of you this morning. Will you be ready? How can you help it? Is it possible not to be ready? Why, it is not your life, it is His life. You did not seek Him; it was He who sought you. You cannot keep yourself; it is He who keeps you. You did not make the offering; it was God who made the offering. So it is all of grace. But what a wonderful grace!

INTERPRETATION OF A MESSAGE IN TONGUES:

The trumpet will blow and all will be brought forth, for God will bring them with Him, and those who are awake will not interfere with those who are asleep, but all with one breath will rise. What will rise? The life will rise to meet the Life that has preserved it, and we will be ever with the Lord.

What is going? The life. He gives everlasting life, and they will never perish.

Oh, where is your faith? Is your faith inspired? Are you quickened? Is there within you a truth that is saying, "I feel it, I know it. It moves me; I have it"? Yes, and you will be there in heaven—as surely as you are here, you will be there.

This thing that we are entering into is going to continue forever. Let us feed on this Bread; let us live in this holy atmosphere. This is divine nature that God is causing us to know, which will last forever.

Keep us, Lord, in a place of buying up opportunities, burning up bridges, paying the prices, denying ourselves so that we might be worthy of being Your own forever.

QUESTIONS ANSWERED

Q: Is there distinction in the Word between the life that brings forth the Rapture and eternal life where some first go down into the grave?

A: No. Those asleep in Jesus have the same life, but they are not asleep in the grave. They fall asleep to rest, but it is not a sleep or a rest of the spirit. The spirit never sleeps; the soul never sleeps. Solomon wrote, *"I sleep, but my heart is awake"* (Song 5:2). Remember that the moment the body is put to rest, the spirit requires no rest; it is always young, it will know nothing about time.

Whichever way the body goes, it will be the same. If it goes to the grave, what will happen? The body, all that is earthly, will pass away; it will come to dust. Suppose it goes up. The Word of God says it will be dissolved. The same thing, it will be dissolved either way it goes. Why? Because flesh and blood are not going there, but the life of the Son of God is. God will provide a new body, resembling the old in every way—likeness, character, everything. The human spirit will enter into a celestial body whether it goes up or down—only we want you all to go up.

Q: I have heard Revelation 3:5 brought up to prove that a name could be blotted out of the Book of Life. Will you please explain?

A: I am dealing with people who are receiving everlasting life, who are not going to be lost. I am persuaded of better things than that of you. I will never believe that any human being is greater than my God. I believe that God is greater than all and that God can preserve us all. But I do believe that there are any number of people who have tried to make people believe they are the seed of God when they have not really been born again.

The life of the new birth is always seeking after God; it has no time for falling away from God, no time for the world; it is always hungry for God. Unless you get this fundamental truth deep down in your heart, you will fail, because you have to go on to holiness, inseparableness. *"Holiness adorns Your house, O LORD"* (Ps. 93:5). How can you be anything but holy and long to be holy?

CHAPTER FOUR

THE ABIDING SPIRIT

G od seems to fascinate me with His Word. I read and read, and yet it is all something so new, remarkable, and blessed. I realize the truth of that saying, "The bride rejoices to hear the Bridegroom's voice" (John 3:29). The Word is His voice, and as we get nearer to Jesus, we understand that He came to take out for Himself a people that should be His bride. It is not only to be saved, my brother, but there is an eternal destiny awaiting us of all the wonderment that God has in the glory. I pray that we may see that God in His mercy has given us this blessed revelation of how He lived, loved, and had power to say to those disciples, "Some of you shall not see death until you see the kingdom of God coming in power." (See Mark 9:1.)

Oh, that blessed Christ, who could pray until His countenance was changed and became so glorious, until His raiment became white and glistening. He said, "I have power to lay down My life, and I have power to take it again." (See John 10:17.) It is true that by wicked hands He was taken and crucified, but He had to be willing, for He had all power and could have called on legions of angels to help Him and deliver Him from death. But oh, that blessed Christ had purposed to save us and bring us into fellowship and oneness with Himself. He went right through death so that He might impart unto us the blessed reconciliation between God and man.

So it is that the Man Jesus Christ, who is the Atonement for the whole world, who is the Son of God, is also the sinner's Friend. *"He was wounded for our transgressions"* (Isa. 53:5). This blessed Christ gave His disciples the glory that He had with the Father before the world was. (See John 17:5.) Oh, it is lovely, and I believe that God wants us to know that He will withhold *"no good thing...from those who walk uprightly"* (Ps. 84:11), including health, peace, joy in the Holy Spirit, and a life in Christ Jesus.

THE POWER OF THE BLOOD

Oh, brother or sister, God wants you to know that He has a redemption for you through the blood of Jesus, a new birth unto righteousness, a change from darkness into light, from the power of Satan unto God. This blessed salvation through the blood of Jesus will free you from all the power of Satan and make you a joint-heir with Christ. Oh, this is a glorious inheritance that we have in Jesus Christ. Glory to God! Jesus was manifested in the flesh, manifested to destroy the works of the Devil. Christ can make us overcomers, destroying the power and passion of sin and dwelling in us by His mighty power. He can so transform our lives that we will love righteousness and hate iniquity. And He can make us holy, because just as God dwelt in His Son by the power of the Holy Spirit, so God can dwell in us through Christ.

I want you to see that we receive sonship because of Christ's obedience. And do not forget what the Scripture says: *"Though He was a Son, yet He learned obedience by the things which He suffered"* (Heb. 5:8). If you turn to the Scriptures, you will see how the people reviled Him and how they tried to kill Him by throwing Him over the cliff. But He passed through the midst of the whole crowd, and as soon as He got out, He saw a blind man and healed him. He was in the world but not of it.

It is lovely—it is divinely glorious—this power of the new creation, this birth unto righteousness by faith in the Atonement. It can transform you so that you can be in Jesus Christ and know that it is another power dominating, controlling, and filling you, and making you understand that though you are still in the body you are governed by the Spirit. Oh, to live in all the beauty of the glory and grandeur of the Holy Spirit!

CHANGED BY HIS LOVE

There is a constraining power in this Christ that causes you to know that it is different from anything else in the world. In Scripture it is called an *"unfeigned love"* (1 Pet. 1:22 KJV), a real and sincere love. This has a tremendously deep meaning. What is it, exactly? Beloved, Jesus will tell you what it is. It is a denunciation of yourself as the power of Christ lays hold of you. He loved you when you were yet a sinner (Rom. 5:8), and He seeks your love in return. It is an unfeigned love, a love that can stand ridicule, persecution, and slander, because it is a love brought about in you by the power of the Holy Spirit changing you from one state of glory to another. Christ is King of Kings and Lord of Lords, and *"of His kingdom there will be no end"* (Luke 1:33). *"He shall see His seed, He shall prolong His days, and the pleasure of the LORD shall prosper in His hand"* (Isa. 53:10).

Oh, beloved, what a Christ we have at this very moment! I want you to see that there is nothing like Him. If you see Him today, you needy ones, and gaze at Him, you will be changed. As you look at Him, you will find that even your natural bodies will change. His strength will come into you, and you will be transformed. He is the God of the sinner; He is the God of the helpless; He is full of mercy. I like the thought of His calling Himself the God of Jacob. When He says He is the God of Jacob, there is room for everybody. I tell you, He is your God, and He is preparing to meet you exactly as He met Jacob.

Jacob had deceived someone in everything he had done. He had deceived Esau to get his birthright (Gen. 25:29–34) and Laban to get his cattle (Gen. 30:25–43). Truly, the Devil manipulated Jacob, but, praise God, there was one thing that Jacob knew: he knew that God had fulfilled His promise. In Bethel, God let Jacob see the ladder—a wonderful ladder, for it reached from earth to heaven—and Jacob saw the angels ascending and descending upon it. Bethel is the place of prayer, the place of changing conditions, of earth entering heaven. God brought Jacob right back to the same place, regardless of how he had wandered. Jacob had to let everything go, and he was left alone. The same old Jacob remained, and as long as God would let him wrestle with Him, he wrestled.

This is an example of holding on to this world—we never let go until we have to. God touched Jacob, and as soon as he was touched, he found out that he was no good. Then the Man said, *"Let Me go."* But Jacob answered, *"I will not let You go unless You bless me!"* (Gen. 32:26). Brother, God will bless you if you get to that point, but you are no good as long as you wrestle. When you come in helplessness and with a real cry of brokenness, then God will meet you. It is marvelous how God meets us in our distresses. When the cry comes from broken hearts, then God comes.

HIS MERCY ENDURES

It is so lovely to know that God's mercy never fails. When Jesus came down from the Mount of Transfiguration, He set His face to go to the cross for you and me. When He came down from the mountain, there was a man there who had a son whom the Devil had taken and thrown down and bruised. The man cried out, saying, "Lord, come and help me. Here is my son; the Devil takes him and tears at him until he foams at the mouth. I brought him to Your disciples, but they could not help him." (See Mark 9:17–18.)

Oh, brother, may God strengthen our hands and take away all our unbelief. Jesus said, *"O faithless generation, how long shall I be with you?...Bring him to Me"* (v. 19), and they brought him to Jesus, who cast out the evil spirit. But even in the presence of Jesus, those evil spirits tore the boy and left him as one dead until Christ lifted him up. (See verses 20–27.)

Just think of that satanic power. The Devil goes about to kill, *"seeking whom he may devour"* (1 Pet. 5:8), but Christ said, "I came to give life, and life more abundantly" (John 10:10). May God keep us in the place where the Devil will have no power and no victory. I pray God that the demon powers that come out of people in today's churches will never return again.

FILLED WITH THE SPIRIT

Oh, if I could only show you what it means to be delivered by the power of Jesus and what it means to lose your deliverance through your own foolishness! I know of a case like this. A man possessed by demonic power and sickness and weakness came to Jesus, and He cast the evil spirit out. The man was made whole. Then, instead of the man seeking the Holy Spirit and the light of God, he afterward went to the races. God save us! The healing power is for the glory of God, and it appears that this man was *"swept, and put in order"* (Matt. 12:44), but he did not receive Christ and the power of the Spirit. So the evil spirit went back and found he could gain an entrance again because the man had no other inhabitant in him. He took with him other evil spirits, and the man's case was worse than before. (See verses 43–45.)

If you want to be healed by the power of God, it means that your life has to be filled with God. We must make sure that the power of God comes to inhabit us. Are you willing to so surrender yourself to God today that Satan will have no dominion over you?

CHAPTER FIVE

LOOKING TOWARD OUR TRANSLATION

God has a plan for us in this life of the Spirit. We are to go and speak *"all the words of this life"* (Acts 5:20), this abundant life. Jesus came so that we might have life (John 10:10). Satan comes to steal and kill and destroy (v. 10), but God has for us abundance in full measure, pressed down, shaken together, and overflowing (Luke 6:38). God is filling us with His own personality and His presence, making us salt and light and glory, as a revelation of Himself. God is with us in all circumstances, afflictions, persecutions; in every one of our trials, He is girding us with truth. Christ the Initiative, the Triune God, is in control, and our every thought, word, and action must be in line with Him, with no weakness or failure. Our God is a God of might, light, and revelation, preparing us for heaven. *"Your life is hidden with Christ in God. When Christ who is our life appears, then you also will appear with Him in glory"* (Col. 3:3–4).

For we know that if our earthly house, this tent, is destroyed, we have a building from God, a house not made with hands, eternal in the heavens. For in this we groan, earnestly desiring to be clothed with our habitation which is from heaven, if indeed, having been clothed, we shall not be found naked. For we who are in this tent groan, being burdened, not because we want to be unclothed, but further clothed, that mortality may be swallowed up by life. Now He who has prepared us for this very thing is God, who also has given us the Spirit as a guarantee. (2 Cor. 5:1–5)

449

God's Word is a tremendous word, a productive word that produces things like itself. It is power, producing Godlikeness. We get to heaven through the Word of God, and we have peace through the blood of His cross. Redemption is ours through the knowledge of the Word. I am saved because God's Word says so. *"If you confess with your mouth the Lord Jesus and believe in your heart that God has raised Him from the dead, you will be saved"* (Rom. 10:9).

If I am baptized with the Holy Spirit, it is because Jesus said, *"You shall receive power when the Holy Spirit has come upon you"* (Acts 1:8). We must have one thing in mind, and that is to be filled with the Holy Spirit, to be filled with God.

INTERPRETATION OF A MESSAGE IN TONGUES:
God has sent His Word to free us from the law of sin and death. Unless we die, we cannot live, and unless we cease to be, God cannot be.

THE IMPORTANCE OF FAITH

The Holy Spirit has a royal plan, a heavenly plan. He came to unveil the King, to show the character of God, to unveil the precious blood. Since I have the Holy Spirit within me, I see Jesus clothed for humanity. He was moved by the Spirit and led by the Spirit. We read of some who heard the Word but did not benefit from it, because faith was lacking in them (Rom. 9:6–8). We must have a living faith in God's Word, a faith that is quickened by the Spirit.

A man may be saved and still have a human spirit. In many people who hear about the baptism of the Holy Spirit, the human spirit immediately arises against the Holy Spirit. The human spirit is not subject to the law of God, nor can it be. The disciples at one time wanted to call down fire from heaven, and Jesus said to them, *"You do not know what manner of spirit you are of"* (Luke 9:55). The human spirit is not subject to the law of God.

The Holy Spirit came forth for one purpose, and that was to reveal Jesus to us. Jesus *"made Himself of no reputation"* (Phil. 2:7), and He was obedient unto death (v. 8), that God should forever hold Him up as a token of submissive yieldedness. God highly exalted Him and gave Him a name above every name. *"Now He who has prepared us for this very thing is God, who also has given us the Spirit as a guarantee"* (2 Cor. 5:5). With the clothing upon of the Spirit, human depravity is covered, and everything that is contrary to the mind of God is destroyed. God must have bodies for Himself, perfectly prepared by the Holy Spirit, for the Day of the Lord. *"For in this we groan, earnestly desiring to be clothed with our habitation which is from heaven"* (v. 2).

Was Paul speaking here about the coming of the Lord? No! Yet this condition of preparedness is highly relevant. The Holy Spirit is coming to take back a church and a perfect bride. The Holy Spirit must find in us perfect yieldedness, with every human desire subjected to Him. *"No one can say that Jesus is Lord except by the Holy Spirit"* (1 Cor. 12:3). He has come to reveal Christ in us, so that the glorious flow of the life of God may bring rivers of living water to the thirsty land within.

"If Christ is in you, the body is dead because of sin, but the Spirit is life because of righteousness" (Rom. 8:10).

INTERPRETATION OF A MESSAGE IN TONGUES:
This is that which God has declared freedom from the law. If we love the world, the love of the Father is not in us.

"For all that is in the world; the lust of the flesh, the lust of the eyes, and the pride of life; is not of the Father but is of the world" (1 John 2:16).

The Spirit has to breathe into us a new occupancy, a new order. The Holy Spirit came to give the vision of a life in which Jesus is perfected. It is Christ

> *who has saved us and called us with a holy calling, not according to our works, but according to His own purpose and grace which was given to us in Christ Jesus before time began, but has now been revealed by the appearing of our Savior Jesus Christ, who has abolished death and brought life...through the gospel.* (2 Tim. 1:9–10)

We who are saved have been called with a holy calling, called to be saints—to be pure, holy, and Godlike; to be sons with power. It is a long time now since it was settled and death was abolished. Death has no more power. This was made known through the Gospel, which brought in immortality. Mortality is a hindrance. Sin has no more dominion over you. You reign in Christ, and you make rightful use of His finished work. Don't groan and travail for a

451

week. If you are in need, *"only believe"* (Mark 5:36). Don't fast to get some special thing, *"only believe."* It is according to your faith that God blesses you with more faith. *"Have faith in God"* (Mark 11:22). If you are free in God, believe! Believe, and it will be unto you even as you believe. (See Matthew 9:29.)

"Awake, you who sleep" (Eph. 5:14); put on light, and open your eyes. *"If then you were raised with Christ, seek those things which are above, where Christ is, sitting at the right hand of God"* (Col. 3:1). Stir yourselves up, beloved! Where are you? I am risen with Christ, planted in Him. It was a beautiful planting. I am seated with Him. God gives me the credit, and I believe Him. Why should I doubt?

INTERPRETATION OF A MESSAGE IN TONGUES:
Why do you doubt when faith reigns? God makes it possible. How many people have received the Holy Spirit, and Satan gets a doubt in? Don't doubt, believe! There is power and strength in God. Who dares to believe in God?

Leave Doubting Street; live on Faith-Victory Street. Jesus sent the seventy out, and they came back in victory (Luke 10:1–17). It takes God to make it real. Dare to believe until there is not a sick person, until there is no sickness, until everything is withered and the life of Jesus is implanted within your soul. *"The righteous will hold to his way"* (Job 17:9). God has reserved him who is godly for Himself (Ps. 4:3). Therefore, lift up your heads. The Devil makes you remember the day you failed, though you would give the world to forget about it. But God has forgotten when He forgives. He forgets.

FILLED WITH THE SPIRIT

God wants to make us pillars: honorable, strong, and holy. God will move us on. I am enamored with the possibility of this. God wants you to know that you are saved, cleansed, delivered, and marching to victory. He has given you the faith to believe. God has a plan for you! *"Set your mind on things above"* (Col. 3:2), and get into the heavenly places with Christ. *"Do not be conformed to this world, but be transformed by the renewing of your mind"* (Rom. 12:2).

You cannot repeat the name of Jesus too often. What a privilege it is to kneel and get right into heaven the moment we pray, where the glory descends, the fire burns, faith is active, and the light dispels the darkness. What is darkness? What is mortality? Mortality hinders, but the life of Jesus eats up mortality.

The book of Acts deals with receiving the Holy Spirit, and the epistles were written to believers who had been baptized in the Spirit. When I was in New Zealand, some believers came to me, questioning the baptism of the Holy Spirit. They quoted from the epistles, but before we may be in the experience of the epistles, we must go through the Acts of the Apostles. I asked them, according to 1 Corinthians 14:2, "When did you speak in mysteries?" But they had not yet come into the baptism of the Holy Spirit.

Jesus is the light and the life of men; no man can have this light and still walk in darkness. *"When Christ who is our life appears, then you also will appear with Him in glory"* (Col. 3:4). Where His life is, disease cannot remain. Is not He who dwells in us greater than all? Is He greater? Yes, when He has full control. If one thing is permitted outside the will of God, it hinders us in our standing against the powers of Satan. We must allow the Word of God to judge us, lest we stand condemned with the world.

"When Christ who is our life appears." Can I have any life apart from Him, any joy or any fellowship apart from Him? Jesus said, *"The ruler of this world is coming, and he has nothing in Me"* (John 14:30). All that is contrary in us is withered by the indwelling life of the Son of God.

> *For we who are in this tent groan, being burdened, not because we want to be unclothed, but further clothed, that mortality may be swallowed up by life.* (2 Cor. 5:4)

Are we ready? Have we been clothed with the Holy Spirit? Has mortality been swallowed up in life? If He who is our life came, we should go. I know the Lord. I know that the Lord laid His hand on me. He filled me with the Holy Spirit.

I know that the Lord laid His hand on me. It is heaven on earth. Heaven has begun with me. I am happy now, and free, since the Comforter has come. The Comforter is the great Revealer of the kingdom of God. He came to give us the more abundant life. God has designed the plan, and nothing else really matters if the Lord loves us. God sets great store in us. The pure in heart see God. There are no stiff knees, coughing, or pain in the Spirit. Nothing ails us if we are filled with the Spirit.

If the Spirit of Him who raised Jesus from the dead dwells in you, He who raised Christ from the dead will also give life to your mortal bodies through His Spirit who dwells in you. (Rom. 8:11)

The way into glory is through the flesh being torn away from the world and separated unto God. This freedom of spirit, freedom from the law of sin and death, is cause for rejoicing every day. The perfect law destroys the natural law. Spiritual activity takes in every passing ray, ushering in the days of heaven upon earth, when there is no sickness and when we do not even remember that we have bodies. The life of God changes us and brings us into the heavenly realm, where our reign over principalities and over all evil is limitless, powerful, and supernatural.

If the natural body decays, the Spirit renews. Spiritual power increases until, with one mind and one heart, the glory is brought down over all the earth, right on into divine life. When the whole life is filled, this is Pentecost come again. The life of the Lord will be manifested wherever we are, whether in a bus or on a train. We will be filled with the life of Jesus unto perfection, rejoicing in hope of the glory of God (Rom. 5:2), always looking for our translation into heaven. The life of the Lord in us draws us as a magnet, with His life eating up all else.

I must have the overflowing life in the Spirit. God is not pleased with anything less. It is a disgrace to be part of an ordinary plan after we are filled with the Holy Spirit. We are to be salt in the earth, not lukewarm (Rev. 3:16). We are to be hot, which means seeing God with eagerness, liberty, movement, and power. Believe! Believe!

CHAPTER SIX

THE APPOINTED HOUR:
LIFE OUT OF DEATH

The communion service is a very blessed time for us to gather together in remembrance of the Lord. I want to remind you of this fact, that this is the only service we render to the Lord. All other services we attend are for us to get a blessing from the Lord, but Jesus said, *"Do this in remembrance of Me"* (Luke 22:19). We have gathered together to commemorate that wonderful death, victory, triumph, and the looking forward to the glorious hope. And I want you, if it is possible at all, to get rid of your religion.

It has been so-called religion at all times that has slain and destroyed what was good. When Satan entered into Judas, the only people whom the Devil could speak to through Judas were the priests, sad as it is to say. They conspired to get him to betray Jesus, and the Devil took money from these priests to put Jesus to death. Now, it is a very serious thing, for we must clearly understand whether we are of the right spirit or not, for no man can be of the Spirit of Christ and persecute another; no man can have the true Spirit of Jesus and slay his brother, and no man can follow the Lord Jesus and have enmity in his heart. You cannot have Jesus and have bitterness and hatred, and persecute the believer.

It is possible for us, if we are not careful, to have within us an evil spirit of unbelief, and even in our best state it is possible for us to have enmity unless we are perfectly dead and we allow the life of the Lord to lead us. Remember how Jesus wanted to pass through a certain place as He was going to Jerusalem. Because He would not stop and preach to them concerning the kingdom, they refused to allow Him to go through their section of the country. And the disciples who were with Jesus said to Him, *"Lord, do You want us to command fire to come down from heaven and consume them, just as Elijah did?"* (Luke 9:54). But Jesus turned and said, *"You do not know what manner of spirit you are of"* (v. 55). There they were, following Jesus and with Him all the time, but Jesus rebuked that spirit in them.

I pray God that you will get this out of this service: that our knowledge of Jesus is pure love, and pure love for Jesus is death to self on all accounts—body, soul, and the human spirit. I believe that if we are in the will of God, we will be perfectly directed at all times, and if we desire to know anything about the mighty works of Christ, we will have to follow what Jesus said. Whatever He said came to pass.

KNOWING THE MIND OF GOD

Many things happened in the lives of the apostles to show His power over all flesh. In regard to paying taxes, Jesus said to Peter, "We are free, we can enter into the city without paying tribute; nevertheless, we will pay." (See Matthew 17:24–27.) I like that thought, that Jesus was so righteous on all lines. It helps me a great deal. Then Jesus told Peter to do a very hard thing. He said, "Take that hook and cast it into the sea. Draw out a fish, and take from its gills a piece of silver for you and Me" (v. 27).

This was one of the hardest things Peter had to do. He had been fishing all his life, but never had he taken a coin out of a fish's mouth. There were thousands and millions of fish in the sea, but one fish had to have money in it. He went down to the sea as any natural man would, speculating and thinking, "How can it be?" But how could it not be, if Jesus said it would be? Then the perplexity would arise, "But there are so many fish! Which fish has the money?" Believer, if God speaks, it will be as He says. What you need is to know the mind of God and the Word of God, and you will be so free that you will never find a frown on your face or a tear in your eye.

The more you know of the mightiness of revelation, the more every fear will pass away. To know God is to be in the place of triumph. To know God is to be in the place of rest. To know God is to be in the place of victory. Undoubtedly, many things were in Peter's mind that day, but thank God there was one fish that had the silver piece, and Peter obeyed. Sometimes, to obey in blindness brings the victory. Sometimes, when perplexities arise in your mind, obedience means God working out the problem. Peter cast the hook into the sea, and it would have been amazing if you could have seen the disturbance the other fish made to move out of the way, all except the right one. God wanted just one among the millions of fish. God may put His hand upon you in the midst of millions of people, but if He speaks to you, the thing that He says will be appointed.

On this same occasion, Jesus said to Peter and the others that when they went out into the city they would see a man bearing a pitcher of water, and they should follow him (Mark 14:13). In those days, it was not customary in the East for men to carry anything on their heads. The women always did the carrying, but this had to be a man, and he had to have a pitcher.

I know of one preacher who said that it was quite all right for Jesus to arrange for a colt to be tied before He ever instructed His disciples to go and find it. Another preacher said it was quite easy for Jesus to feed those thousands of people with the five loaves, because the loaves in those days were so tremendously big, but he didn't say that it was a little boy who had been carrying the five loaves. Unbelief can be very blind, but faith can see through a stone wall. Faith, when it is moved by the power of God, can laugh when trouble is near.

The disciples said to the man with the pitcher, *"Where is the guest room?"* (v. 14). "How strange it is that you should ask," the man must have replied. "I have been preparing that room, wondering who needed it." When God is leading, it is marvelous how perfectly everything works into the plan. He was arranging everything. You think He cannot do that today for you? For you who have been in perplexities for days and days, God knows how to deliver you out of trouble; He knows how to be with you in the dark hour. He can make all things work together for good to those who love Him (Rom. 8:28). He has a way of arranging His plan, and when God comes in, you always know it was a day in which you lived in Him.

Oh, to live in God! There is a vast difference between living in God and living in speculation and hope. There is something better than hope, something better than speculation. *"The people who know their God shall be strong, and carry out great exploits"* (Dan. 11:32), and God wants us to know Him.

THE APPOINTED HOUR

"When the hour had come, He sat down, and the twelve apostles with Him" (Luke 22:14). *"When the hour had come"*—that was the most wonderful hour. There never was an hour, never will be an hour like that hour. What hour was it? It was an hour when all of creation passed under the blood, when all that ever lived came under the glorious covering of the blood. It was an hour of destruction of demon power. It was an appointed hour of life coming out of death. It was an hour when all the world was coming into emancipation by the blood. It was an hour in the world's history when it emerged from dark chaos. It was a wonderful hour! Praise God for that hour! Was it a dark hour? It was a dark hour for Him, but a wonderful light dawned for us. It was tremendously dark for the Son of Man, but, praise God, He came through it.

There are some things in the Scriptures that move me greatly. I am glad that Paul was a human being. I am glad that Jesus became a man. I am glad that Daniel was human, and I am also glad that John was human. You ask, "Why?" Because I see that whatever God has done for other people, He can do for me. And I find that God has done such wonderful things for other people that I am always expecting that these things are possible for me. Think about this. It is a wonderful thought to me.

Jesus said in that trying hour—hear it for a moment—*"With fervent desire I have desired to eat this Passover with you before I suffer"* (Luke 22:15). Desire? What could be His desire? It was His desire because of the salvation of the world, His desire because of the dethronement of the powers of Satan, His desire because He knew He was going to conquer everything and make every man free who ever lived. It was a great desire, but what lay between Him and its fulfillment? Gethsemane lay between that and the cross!

Some people say that Jesus died on the cross. It is perfectly true, but is that the only place? Jesus also died in Gethsemane. That was the tragic moment! That was the place where He paid the debt. It was in Gethsemane, and Gethsemane was between Him and the cross. He had a desire to eat this Passover, and He knew that Gethsemane was between Him and the cross.

I want you to think about Gethsemane. There, alone and with the tremendous weight and the awful effect of all sin and disease upon that body, He cried out, *"If it is possible, let this cup pass from Me"* (Matt. 26:39). He could only save men when He was man, but here, like a giant who has been refreshed and is coming out of a great chaos of darkness, He comes forth: *"For this cause I was born"* (John 18:37). It was His purpose to die for the world.

Oh, believer, will it ever pass through your lips or your mind for a moment that you will not have a desire to serve Christ like that? Can you, under any circumstances, stoop to take up your cross fully, to be in the place of ridicule, to surrender anything for the Man who said He desired to eat the Passover with His disciples, knowing what it meant? It can only come out of the depths of love we have for Him that we can say right now, "Lord Jesus, I will follow You."

SPIRITUAL REVELATION

Oh, brother or sister, there is something very wonderful in the decision in your heart! God knows the heart. You do not always have to be on the housetop and shout to indicate the condition of your heart. He knows your inward heart. You say, "I would be ashamed not to be willing to suffer for a Man who desired to suffer to save me." *"With fervent desire"* (Luke 22:15), He said.

I know what it is to have the kingdom of heaven within me. Jesus said that even the least in the kingdom of heaven is greater than John the Baptist (Matt. 11:11), meaning those who are under the blood, those who have seen the Lord by faith, those who know that by redemption they are made sons of God. I say to you, Jesus will never taste again until we are there with Him. The kingdom will never be complete—it could not be—until we are all there at that great Supper of the Lamb where there will be millions and trillions of the redeemed, which no man can count. We will be there when that Supper is taking place. I like to think of that.

I hope you will take one step into definite lines with God and believe it. It is an act of faith that God wants to bring you into, a perfecting of that love that will always avail. It is a fact that He has opened the kingdom of heaven to all believers and that He gives eternal life to those who believe. The Lord, the omnipotent God, knows the end from the beginning and has arranged by the blood of the Lamb to cover the guilty and to make intercession for all believers. Oh, it is a wonderful inheritance of faith to find shelter under the blood of Jesus!

I want you to see that He says, *"Do this in remembrance of Me"* (Luke 22:19). He took the cup, He took the bread, and He gave thanks. The very attitude of giving thanks for His shed blood, giving thanks for His broken body, overwhelms the heart. To think that my Lord could give thanks for His own shed blood! To think that my Lord could give thanks for His own broken body! Only divinity can reveal this sublime act unto the heart!

The natural man cannot receive this revelation, but the spiritual man, the man who has been created anew by faith in Christ, is open to it. The man who believes that God comes in has the eternal seed of truth and righteousness and faith born into him. From the moment that he sees the truth on the lines of faith, he is made a new creation. The flesh ceases; the spiritual man begins. One is taken off, and the other is taken on, until a man is in the presence of God. I believe that the Lord brings a child of faith into a place of rest, causes him to sit with Him in heavenly places, gives him a language in the Spirit, and makes him know that he no longer belongs to the law of creation.

Do you see the bread that represents His broken body? The Lord knew He could not bring us any nearer to His broken body. The body of Jesus was made of that bread, and He knew He could bring us no nearer. He took the natural elements and said, "This bread represents my broken body." (See Luke 22:19.) Now, will it ever become that body of Christ? No, never. You cannot make it so. It is foolishness to believe it, but I receive it as an emblem. When I eat it, the natural leads me into the supernatural, and instantly I begin to feed on the supernatural by faith. One leads me into the other.

Jesus said, *"Take, eat; this is My body"* (Matt. 26:26). I have a real knowledge of Christ through this emblem. May we take from the table of the riches of His promises. The riches of heaven are before us. Fear not, only believe, for God has opened the treasures of His holy Word.

As the disciples were all gathered together with Jesus, He looked on them and said right into their ears, *"One of you will betray Me"* (v. 21). Jesus knew who would betray Him. He had known it for many, many months. They whispered to one another, "Who is it?" None of them had real confidence that it would not be he. That is the serious part about it; they had so little confidence in their ability to face the opposition that was before them, and they had no confidence that it would not be one of them.

Jesus knew. I can imagine that He had been talking to Judas many times, rebuking him and telling him that his course would surely bring him to a bad end. Jesus never had told any of His disciples, not even John who *"leaned on His breast"* (John 21:20). Now, if that same spirit of keeping things secret was in any church, it would purify the church. But I fear sometimes that Satan gets the advantage, and things are told before they are true. I believe God wants to so sanctify us, so separate us, that we will have that perfection of love that will not speak ill of a brother, that we will not slander a fellow believer whether it is true or not.

There was strife among them as to who should be the greatest, but He said, *"He who is greatest among you, let him be as the younger, and he who governs as he who serves"* (Luke 22:26). Then He, the Master, said, *"I am among you as the One who serves"* (v. 27). He, the noblest, the purest, was the servant of all! Exercising lordship over another is not of God. We must learn in our hearts that fellowship, true righteousness, loving one another, and preferring one another, must come into the church. Pentecost must outreach everything that ever has been, and we know it will if we are willing.

MOVING TOWARD PERFECTION

But it cannot be if we do not will it. We can never be filled with the Holy Spirit as long as there is any human craving for our own wills. Selfishness must be destroyed. Jesus was perfect, the end of everything, and God will bring us all there. It is giving that pays; it is helping that pays; it is loving that pays; it is putting yourself out for another person that pays.

> *I am among you as the One who serves. But you are those who have continued with Me in My trials. And I bestow upon you a kingdom, just as My Father bestowed one upon Me.* (Luke 22:27–29)

I believe there is a day coming that will be greater than anything any of us have any conception of. This is the testing road. This is the place where your whole body has to be covered with the wings of God so that your nakedness will not be seen. This is the thing that God is getting you ready for, the most wonderful thing your heart can imagine. How can you get into it? First of all, *"You...have continued with Me in My trials"* (v. 28). Jesus had been in trials; He had been in temptation. There is not one of us who is tempted beyond what He was (Heb. 4:15).

If a young man can be so pure that he cannot be tempted, he will never be fit to be made a judge, but God intends us to be so purified during these evil days that He can make us judges in the world to come. If you can be tried, if you can be tempted on any line, Jesus said, *"You are those who have continued with Me in My trials"* (Luke 22:28). Have faith, and God will keep you pure in the temptation.

How will we reach it? In Matthew 19:28, Jesus said,

In the regeneration, when the Son of Man sits on the throne of His glory, you who have followed Me will also sit on twelve thrones, judging the twelve tribes of Israel.

Follow Him in constant regeneration. Every day is a regeneration; every day is a day of advancement; every day is a place of choice. Every day you find yourself in need of fresh consecration. If you are in a place to yield, God moves you in the place of regeneration.

For years and years God has been making me appear to hundreds and thousands of people as a fool. I remember the day when He saved me and when He called me out. If there is a thing God wants to do today, He wants to be as real to you and me as He was to Abraham. After I was saved, I joined a church that consisted of a very lively group of people who were full of a revival spirit, and it was marvelous how God blessed us. And then there came a lukewarmness and indifference, and God said to me as clearly as anything, "Come out." I obeyed and came out. The people said, "We cannot understand you. We need you now, and you are leaving us."

The Plymouth Brethren at that time were in a conference. The Word of God was with them in power; the love of God was with them unveiled. Baptism by immersion was revealed to me, and when my friends saw me go into the water, they said I was altogether wrong. But God had called me, and I obeyed. The day came when I saw that the people of that church had dropped down to the letter of the law, only the letter, dry and barren.

At that time the Salvation Army was filled with love, filled with power, filled with zeal; every place was a revival, and I joined up with them. For about six years, the glory of God was there, and then the Lord said again, "Come out," and I was glad I came. It dropped right into a social movement, and God has no place for a social movement. We are saved by regeneration, and the man who is going on with God has no time for social reforms.

God moved on, and at that time there were many people who were receiving the baptism of the Holy Spirit without signs. Those days were days of heaven on earth. God unfolded the truth, showed the way of sanctification by the power of the blood of Christ, and in that I saw the great inflow of the life of God.

I thank God for that, but God came along again and said, "Come out." I obeyed God and went with what others called the "tongues folks"; they were regarded as having further light. I saw God orchestrating every movement I made, and even in this Pentecostal work, unless we see there is a real death, I can see that God will say to us, "Come out." Unless Pentecostalism wakes up to shake herself free from all worldly things and comes into a place of divine likeness with God, we will hear the voice of God saying, "Come out." He will have something far better than this.

I ask every one of you, Will you hear the voice of God and come out? You ask, "What do you mean?" Every one of you, without exception, knows that the only meaning of Pentecost is being on fire. If you are not on fire, you are not in the place of regeneration. It is only the fire of God that burns up the entanglements of the world.

When we came into this new work, God spoke to us by the Spirit, and we knew we had to reach the place of absolute yieldedness and cleansing, so that there would be nothing left. We were *"swept, and put in order"* (Matt. 12:44). Believer, that was only the beginning, and if you have not made tremendous progress in that holy zeal and power and compassion of God, we can truly say you have backslidden in heart. The backslider in heart is dead. He does not have the open vision. The backslider in heart does not see the Word of God in a fresher light every day. You can say that a man is a backslider in heart if he is not hated by the world. If you have the applause of the world, you do not have the approval of God.

A PLACE PREPARED FOR YOU

I do not know whether you will receive it or not, but my heart burns with the message of changing in the regeneration, for when you are changed, you will get a place in the kingdom to come where you will be in authority. This is the place that God has prepared for us, the place that is beyond all human conception. We can catch a glimpse of this glory when we see how John worshipped the angel, and the angel said to him, *"See that you do not do that! I am your fellow servant, and of your brethren who have the testimony of Jesus"* (Rev. 19:10). This angel was showing John the wonders of the glorious kingdom, and in the angel's glorified state, John thought the angel was the Lord. I wonder if we dare believe for it.

Let me close with these words: *"As we have borne the image of the man of dust, we shall also bear the image of the heavenly Man"* (1 Cor. 15:49). To us, this means that everything of an earthly type has to cease, for the heavenly type is so wonderful in all its purity. God is full of love, full of purity, full of power. But there is no power in purity itself! There is no open door into heaven only on the basis of the void of sin between man and God. The heavens open only where the Spirit of the Lord is so leading that flesh has no power. But we will live in the Spirit. God bless you and prepare you for greater days.

CHAPTER SEVEN

THE BREAD OF LIFE

The Lord has revealed to me a new order concerning the Word of God. It is called the Book of Life. It is called the Spirit of Life. It is called the Son of Life, the Word of Life, the testament of the new covenant, which has been shed in blood. Here it is, the Bible. I hold it before you, and it is no more than any other book without the Spirit of revelation. It is a dead letter; it is lifeless. It has no power to give regeneration; it has no power to cause new creation; it has no power to cause the new birth apart from the Spirit; it is only words printed on the page. But as the Spirit of the Lord is upon us and in us, we breathe the very nature of the life of the new creation, and it becomes a quickened book. It becomes a life-giving source; it becomes the breath of the Almighty; it becomes to us a new order in the Spirit.

INTERPRETATION OF A MESSAGE IN TONGUES:
We will not die, but we will live to declare the works of the Lord. We have passed from death unto life; we are a new creation in the Spirit. We are born of a new nature; we are quickened by a new power; we belong to a new association. Our citizenship is in heaven, from which we look for our nature, our Life, our All in All.

That is beautiful! The Spirit is moving, giving, speaking, and making life! Can't you hear the Master say, "My Word is spirit and life"? (See John 6:63.) Only by the Spirit can we understand what is spiritual. We cannot understand it on our own. We have to be spiritual to understand it. No man can understand the Word of God without his being quickened by the new nature. The Word of God is for the new nature. The Word of God is for the new life, to quicken mortal flesh.

Note these words from the gospel of John:

Most assuredly, I say to you, he who believes in Me has ev-erlasting life. I am the bread of life. Your fathers ate the manna in the wilderness, and are dead. This is the bread which comes down from heaven, that one may eat of it and not die. (John 6:47–50)

I hope you have this everlasting life, for I can tell you that it has changed me already. It is all new. The Word of God is never stale; it is all life. May we be so spiritually minded that it becomes life and truth to us.

Christ said, *"I am the living bread"* (v. 51). Living bread! Oh, can't you feel it? Couldn't you just eat it? Your gums will never be sore, and your teeth will never ache eating this bread. The more you eat, the more you will have life, and it won't wear your body out, either. Instead, it will quicken your mortal body (Rom. 8:11). This is the Living Bread. Feed on it, believe it, digest it. Let it have a real, new quickening in your body.

I could sit and listen to anybody read these verses all day, and I could eat it all day. Living bread! Eternal bread! Eternal life! Oh, the brightening of the countenance, the joy of the new nature, the hope that thrills us, and the bliss that awaits us when we eat of this Living Bread! The glory of it will never decay.

ON THE WAY TO HEAVEN

We long for that eternal day when all are holy, all are good, all are washed in Jesus' blood. But guilty, unrenewed sinners cannot come there. There is no sickness in heaven. There is no death in heaven. They have never had a funeral in that land. They have never known what it means to ring the death toll or to have the drum muffled. Never once has anyone died up there. There is no death there, no sickness, no sorrow.

Will you go there? Are you getting ready for it?

Remember this: you were created by the power of God for one purpose in particular. God had no thought in Creation but to bring forth through mortality a natural order so that you might be quickened in the Spirit, be received into glory, and worship God in a way that the angels never could. But in order for that to be, He has brought us through the flesh and quickened us by the Spirit, so that we may know the love, the grace, the power, and all the perfect will of God.

He is a wonderful God—His intelligence, His superabundance in all revelation, His power to keep everything in perfect order. The sun in all its glory, shining so majestically on the earth today, is the mighty power of our glorious God who can make a new heaven and a new earth, in which righteousness will dwell, where no sin will ever darken the place, where the glory of that celestial place will be wonderful.

"I, John, saw the holy city, New Jerusalem, coming down out of heaven from God, prepared as a bride adorned for her husband" (Rev. 21:2). This city—figurative, but not exactly figurative, for it is a luminous fact—will surely exist, and we cannot miss it. It will be a city greater than any city ever known, with millions, billions, trillions all ready for the marriage of the Lamb and His bride. It will make a great city—architecture, domes, pinnacles, cornices, foundations—and the whole city will be made up of saints coming to a marriage.

Oh, the glory of it! I'll be there. I will be one of its inhabitants. I do not know what part, but it will be glorious to be in it anyhow. All these billions of people will have come through tribulation, distress, brokenness of spirit, hard times, strange perplexities, weariness, and all kinds of conditions in the earth. They will be quickened and made like Him, to reign with Him forever and ever.

What a thought God had when He was forming creation and making it, so that we could bring forth sons and daughters in the natural, who are quickened by the Spirit in the supernatural and received up to glory, to be made ready for a marriage! May God reveal to us our position in this Holy Spirit order, so that we may see how wonderful it is that the Lord has His mind upon us. I want you to see security, absolute security, where there will be no shaking, no trembling, no fear, absolute soundness in every way, knowing that, as sure as the Celestial City is formed, you are going to that City.

Salvation takes us to glory. New life is resurrection; new life is ascension; and this new life in God has no place for its feet anywhere between here and glory.

The Spirit of the Lord is with us, revealing the Word. He does not bring eternal life to us, for we have that already, and we believe and are in this place because of that eternal life. But He brings to us a process of this eternal life, showing us that it puts everything else to death. Eternal life came to us when we believed, but the process of eternal life can begin today, making us know that now we are sons of God.

INTERPRETATION OF A MESSAGE IN TONGUES:

Let your whole heart be in a responsive place. Yield absolutely to the Spirit's cry within you. Do not be afraid of being so harmonized by the power of the Spirit that the Spirit in you becomes so one with you that you are altogether what He desires you to be. Do not let fear in any way come in. Let the harmonizing, spiritual life of God breathe through you that oneness, and when we get into oneness today, oh, the lift, oh, the difference will be great! When our hearts are all blended in one thought, how the Spirit lifts us, how revelation can come! God is ready to take us far beyond anything we have had before.

Notice some more verses in the sixth chapter of John:

The Jews therefore quarreled among themselves, saying, "How can this Man give us His flesh to eat?" Then Jesus said to them, "Most assuredly, I say to you, unless you eat the flesh of the Son of Man and drink His blood, you have no life in you. Whoever eats My flesh and drinks My blood has eternal life, and I will raise him up at the last day. For My flesh is food indeed, and My blood is drink indeed. He who eats My flesh and drinks My blood abides in Me, and I in him." (John 6:52–56)

There is another passage that is very lovely in the fourth chapter of the first epistle of John: *"He who abides in love abides in God, and God in him"* (v. 16). You cannot separate these divine personalities. If you begin to separate the life from the nature, you will not know where you are. You will have to see that the new nature is formed right in you.

RESURRECTION POWER

You get a glimpse of it in a very clear way in Hebrews 4:12. The Word of God—the Word, the Life, the Son, the Bread, the Spirit—is in you, separating you from soulishness. The same power, the same Spirit, separates soul and spirit, joint and marrow, right in you. The Life, the Word, is the same power that by the Spirit quickens the mortal body. It is resurrection force; it is divine order. The stiff knee, the inactive limb, the strained position of the back, the muscles, and everything in your nature takes on resurrection power by the Word, the living Word in the body, discerning, opening, and revealing the hidden thoughts of the heart until the heart cannot have one thing that is contrary to God. The heart is separated in thought and in life until the whole man is brought into divine life, living in this life, moving by this power, quickened by this principle.

Oh, this is resurrection! This is resurrection! Is it anything else? Yes, this is what will leave us.

I do not know how far this goes, but I am told that when the spiritual life of a man is very wonderfully active, his white blood cells are very mightily quickened as they are going through the body. However, after the spirit goes, these cells cannot be found in any way. I do not know how far that goes, but to me, it is a reality; the Spirit of the living God flows through every vein of my body, through every tissue of my blood, and I know that this life will have to go. It will have to go!

INTERPRETATION OF A MESSAGE IN TONGUES:

"It is not by might or power; it is by My Spirit," says the Lord. It is not the letter, but it is the Spirit that quickens. It is the resurrection that He brought into us. "I am the resurrection and the life. He who believes in Me has resurrection life in him, resurrection power through him, and he will decrease and the resurrection will increase."

May God manifest that through us and give us that. Oh, how I yearn for this spiritual, divine appointment for us today, to see this deep, holy, inward reviving in our hearts!

I must press on. I am pressing on. The only difficulty is, God is pressing in and keeping us in, holding on but laying hold. Not until these last days have I been able to understand Paul's words to Timothy when he told him he was to lay hold of eternal life. We cannot imagine any human being in the world laying hold of eternal life—it never could be—but a supernatural human being has the power to lay hold, to take hold. Thus, it is the supernatural and divine that lays hold, laying hold of eternal life.

Eternal life, which was with the Father, was brought to us by the Son and is of Him. *"As the living Father sent Me, and I live because of the Father, so he who feeds on Me will live because of Me"* (John 6:57).

Here is a divine principle. He had His life from the Father. "As I live by the Father and have life in Myself by the Father, so you will live by Me and have life from Me as I take it from the Father." Oh, that the Lord would inspire thought and revelation in our hearts to claim this today!

"This is the bread which came down from heaven; not as your fathers ate the manna, and are dead. He who eats of this bread will live forever" (v. 58). The manna was wonderful bread. It was a wonderful provision; but the people ate it, and they still died. But God's Son became the Bread of Life, and as we eat of this Bread, we live forever!

INTERPRETATION OF A MESSAGE IN TONGUES:

It is the Spirit who gives life, for He gives His life for us so that we, being dead, might have eternal life. For He came to give us His own life, that we henceforth should not die, but live forever.

LIVING IN THE SPIRIT

Breathe upon us, breathe upon us,
With Thy love our hearts inspire:
Breathe upon us, breathe upon us,
Lord, baptize us now with fire.

Thank God for the breath of the Spirit, the new creation dawning. Thank God for the spiritual revelation. Fire, holy fire, burning fire, purging fire, taking the dross, taking everything out, making us pure gold. Fire! *"He will baptize you with the Holy Spirit and fire"* (Matt. 3:11). It is a burning that is different from anything else, a burning without consuming. It is illumining, an illumination different from anything else. It illumines the very nature of the man in such a way that in the inner recesses of his human nature there is a burning, holy, divine purging that goes on until every part of the dross is consumed. Carnality in all its darknesses, and the human mind with all its blotches, are inadequate to reach out and are destroyed by the fire. We will be burned by fire until the very purity of Christ is through and through and through, until the body is, as it were, consumed.

It seems to me the whole of the flesh of Jesus was finished up, was consumed in the Garden, on the cross, in His tragic moments. He was consumed when He spoke about seed falling to the ground (see John 12:24), and when He said in great agony, with sweat upon His brow, *"If it is possible, let this cup pass from Me; nevertheless, not as I will, but as You will"* (Matt. 26:39).

There is a consuming of the flesh until the invisible becomes so mighty that what is visible will only hold its own for the invisible to come forth into the glorious, blessed position of God's sonship.

These things He said in the synagogue as He taught in Capernaum. Therefore many of His disciples, when they heard this, said, "This is a hard saying; who can understand it?" (John 6:59–60)

It may be difficult for some of you to clearly understand this ministry we are giving you. Now, I tell you what to do: if you are not sitting in judgment but are allowing the Spirit to come forth to you, you will find out that even mysteries will be unfolded to you, and difficulties will be cleared up. These people sat in judgment without being willing to enter into the spiritual revelation of it. As you read the following verse, I want you to see how it divided the situation: *"When Jesus knew in Himself that His disciples complained about this, He said to them, 'Does this offend you?'"* (v. 61).

Jesus was a perceptive person. We, too, may get to the place where we rightly understand these things and can perceive whether people are receptive or not. I am immediately sensitive to the fact when there is anybody in a meeting or church service who is sitting in judgment of the meeting. Jesus felt this and said unto them,

Does this offend you? What then if you should see the Son of Man ascend where He was before? It is the Spirit who gives life; the flesh profits nothing. The words that I speak to you are spirit, and they are life. (vv. 61–63)

We have been having the Word, which is *"life"* and *"spirit."* There is not a particle of your flesh that will ever be of any advantage to you as long as you live. It has pleased God to give you a body, but only so that it may be able to contain the fullness of the principles and life of the Godhead. (See Colossians 2:9.) Your body has only been given to you so that it might be so quickened with a new generation of the Spirit that you can pass through this world with salt in your life, with seasoning qualities, with light divine, with a perfect position. He wants you walking up and down the breadth of the land, overcoming the powers of Satan, living in this spiritual relationship with God until your body is only used to take the *"spirit"* and the *"life"* from one quarter of the globe to the other, quickened by the Spirit. The flesh never had anything for you; the Spirit is the only property that will help you any time. In my flesh there never has been, there never will be, any good thing; the body can only be the temple of the Holy One.

Oh, to live! "If I live, I live unto Christ; if I die, I die unto Christ. Living or dying, I am the Lord's." (See Romans 14:8.) This is a wonderful message given to us by Paul, a saintly, holy, divine person, full of holy richness. I want to say another thing about this holy man, Paul, who was so filled with the power of the Holy Spirit that the Spirit moved in his mortal life until his flesh was torn to pieces with the rocks. Though his fleshly body was all the time under great privation, the Spirit moved in his life. He often came close to death, but he was quickened again in the Spirit. He was laid out for dead but was again quickened and brought to life.

What a wonderful position! *"I am now ready to be offered"* (2 Tim. 4:6 KJV)—offered on the altar of sacrifice. By the mercy of God, Paul lived and moved by the Spirit, energized and filled with a power a million times larger than himself. He was imprisoned; he had infirmities and weaknesses and all kinds of trials, but the Spirit filled his human body; and in a climax, as it were, of soul and body mingled, he wrote the words, "'I am now ready to be offered.' There is the guillotine; 'I am now ready to be offered.'" Already he had been on the altar of living sacrifice, and he taught us how to do the same.

But here he came to another sacrifice: *"I am now ready to be offered."* I do not know how it was, but I thank God he was ready to be offered. What a life! What a consummation. Human life was consummated, eaten up by the life of Another; mortality itself was eaten up until it did not have a vestige of the human nature to say, "You will not do that, Paul." What a consummation! What a holy invocation! What an entire separation! What a prospect of glorification!

Can it be? Yes, as surely as you are in the flesh, the same power of the quickening of the Spirit can come to you until, whether in your body or out of your body, you can only say, "I am not particular, as long as I know that

> Christ liveth in me!
> Christ liveth in me!
> Oh! what a salvation this,
> That Christ liveth in me.

"But there are some of you who do not believe." For Jesus knew from the beginning who they were who did not believe, and who would betray Him. And He said, "Therefore I have said to you that no one can come to Me unless it has been granted to him by My Father." (John 6:64–65)

MAINTAINING THE DIVINE LIFE

It is so precisely divine in its origin that God will give this life only to those who attain unto eternal life. Do not get away from this. For every person who has eternal life, it is the purpose of the Father, it is the loyalty of God's Son, it is the assembly of the first-born (Heb. 12:23), it is the newly begotten of God, it is the new creation, it is a race designed for heaven that is going to equip you and get you through everything. As surely as you are seeking now, you are in the glory. There is a bridge of eternal security for you if you dare to believe in the Word of God. There is not a drop between you and the glory. It is divine, it is eternal, it is holy, it is the life of God; He gives it, and no man can take from you the life that God gives to you.

This is wonderful! It is almightiness. Its production is absolutely unique. It is so essential, in the first place; it is so to be productive, in the next place; it is so to be changed, in the third place; it is so to be seated, in the fourth place. It is the nature of God that cannot rest in the earth. It is His nature from heaven. It is a divine nature. It is an eternal power. It is an eternal life. It belongs to heaven; it must go back from where it came.

I hope no person will say, "Wigglesworth is preaching eternal security." I am not. I have a thousand times better things in my mind than that. My preaching is this: I know I have what will not be taken away from me. *"Mary has chosen that good part, which will not be taken away from her"* (Luke 10:42).

I am dwelling upon the sovereignty, the mercy, and the boundless love of God. I am dwelling upon the wonderful power of God's order. The heavens, the earth, and everything under the earth are submissive to the Most High God. Demon power has to give place to the royal kingship of God's eternal throne. *"Every knee shall bow"* (Isa. 45:23), every devil will be submitted, and God will bring us someday right into the fullness of the blaze of eternal bliss. And the brightness of His presence will cast every unclean spirit and every power of devils into the pit forever and ever and ever.

INTERPRETATION OF A MESSAGE IN TONGUES:

Why faint, then, at tribulation when these light afflictions, which are only for a moment, are working out for us an eternal, glorious weight of glory? For we see this: God, in His great plan of preparing, has delivered us from the corruption of the world and has transformed us and made us able to come into the image of the Most Holy One. We are made free from the law of sin and death because the life of Christ has been manifested in our mortal bodies. Therefore, we live— and yet we live by another Life, another Power, an eternal Force, a resurrection glory. Oh, Jesus! If our fellowship here is so sweet, if the touches of the eternal glory move our inspiration, it must be wonderful to be there!

From that time many of His disciples went back and walked with Him no more. Then Jesus said to the twelve, "Do you also want to go away?" But Simon Peter answered Him, "Lord, to whom shall we go? You have the words of eternal life." (John 6:66–68)

Where will you go? If you leave the Master, where will you go? Where can we go? If we need a touch in our bodies, where can we go? If we want life, where can we go? Is there anywhere? This world is a big world, but tell me if you can get it.

Could you get it if you soared the heights of the Alps of Switzerland and looked over those glassy mountains where the sun is shining? As I looked over one of those mountains one morning, I saw eleven glaciers and three lakes, like diamonds before me in the glittering sun. I wept and I wept, but I did not get consolation.

Then I dropped on my knees and looked to God—then I got consolation.

Where will we go? There are all the grandeurs and the glories of earth to be seen, but they do not satisfy me. They all belong to Time; they will all fold up like a garment that is laid aside; they will all melt with fervent heat (2 Pet. 3:10).

Where will we go? *"You have the words of eternal life"* (John 6:68). Jesus, You fed us with bread from heaven. Jesus, give us Your life. Oh, breathe it into us! Then we will eat and drink and breathe and think in God's Son until our own natures are eaten up with the divine life, until we are perpetually in the sweetness of His divine will and in the glory. In fact, we are already in it! Praise Him! You can always be holy; you can always be pure. It is the mind of the Spirit that is making you know holiness, righteousness, and rapture.

CHAPTER EIGHT

CHANGED FROM GLORY TO GLORY

Who also made us sufficient as ministers of the new covenant, not of the letter but of the Spirit; for the letter kills, but the Spirit gives life. But if the ministry of death, written and engraved on stones, was glorious, so that the children of Israel could not look steadily at the face of Moses because of the glory of his countenance, which glory was passing away.
—2 Corinthians 3:6–7

N otice especially the seventh verse, where we read that the glory that was on the face of Moses had to pass away. Why was it to be done away with? So that something else that had exceeding glory could take its place.

> *For if the ministry of condemnation had glory, the ministry of righteousness exceeds much more in glory. For even what was made glorious had no glory in this respect, because of the glory that excels.* (vv. 9–10)

I am positive that we have no conception of the depths and heights of the liberty and blessing of the *"ministry of the Spirit"* (v. 8). We must attain to this position of godliness, and we must be partakers of the divine nature (2 Pet. 1:4). The law was so glorious that Moses was filled with joy in the expectation of what it would mean. To us, there is the excellence of Christ's glory in the ministry of the Holy Spirit. *"In Him we live and move"* (Acts 17:28) and reign over all things. It is no longer, "Thou shalt not." Rather, it is God's will, revealed to us in Christ. *"I delight to do Your will, O my God"* (Ps. 40:8). And, beloved, in our hearts there is exceeding glory. Oh, the joy of this celestial touch!

When Peter was recalling that wonderful day on the Mount of Transfiguration, he said, *"Such a voice came to Him from the Excellent Glory"* (2 Pet. 1:17). If I were to come to you right now and say, "Whatever you do, you must try to be holy," I would miss it. I would be altogether outside of God's plan. But I take the words of the epistle, which says by the Holy Spirit, *"Be holy"* (1 Pet. 1:16). It is as easy as possible to be holy, but you can never be holy by your own efforts. When you lose your heart and Another takes your heart, and you lose your desires and He takes the desires, then you live in that sunshine of bliss that no mortal can ever touch. God wants us to be entirely eaten up by this holy zeal for Him, so that every day we will walk in the Spirit. It is lovely to walk in the Spirit, for He will cause you to dwell in safety, to rejoice inwardly, and to praise God reverently.

THE RIGHTEOUSNESS OF CHRIST

"The ministry of righteousness exceeds much more in glory" (2 Cor. 3:9). I want to speak about righteousness now. You cannot touch this blessedness without saying that the excellent glory exceeds in Christ. All excellent glory is in Him; all righteousness is in Him. Everything that pertains to holiness and godliness, everything that denounces and brings to death the natural, everything that makes you know that you have forever ceased to be, is always in an endless power in the risen Christ.

Whenever you look at Jesus, you can see so many different facts of His life. I see Him in those forty days before His ascension, with wonderful truth, infallible proofs of His ministry. What was the ministry of Christ? When you come to the very essence of His ministry, it was the righteousness of His purpose. The excellence of His ministry was the glory that covered Him. His Word was convincing, inflexible, and divine, with a personality of an eternal endurance. It never failed. He spoke, and it stood fast. It was an immovable condition with Him, and His righteousness abides. God must bring us there: we must be people of our word, so that people will be able to depend upon our word.

Jesus was true, inwardly and outwardly. He is *"the way, the truth, and the life"* (John 14:6), and on this foundation we can build. When we know that our own hearts do not condemn us (1 John 3:21), we can say to the mountain, *"Be removed"* (Matt. 21:21). But when our own hearts do condemn us, there is no power in prayer, no power in preaching. We are just *"sounding brass or a clanging cymbal"* (1 Cor. 13:1). May the Holy Spirit show us that there must be a ministry of righteousness.

Christ was righteousness through and through. He is lovely! Oh, truly, He is beautiful. God wants to fix it in our hearts that we are to be like Him—like Him in character. God wants righteousness in the inward parts, so that we may be pure through and through. The Bible is the plumb line of everything, and unless we are plumbed right up with the Word of God, we will fail in righteousness.

"For even what was made glorious had no glory in this respect, because of the glory that excels" (2 Cor. 3:10). You have to get right behind this blessed Word and say it is of God. Here, we come again to the law. I see that it was truly a schoolmaster that brought us to Christ (Gal. 3:24).

DIVINELY USED BY GOD

Law is beautiful when law is established in the earth. As far as possible in every country and town, you will find that the law has something to do with keeping things straight, and in a measure the city has some kind of sobriety because of the law. But, beloved, we belong to a higher, nobler citizenship, not an earthly citizenship, for *"our citizenship is in heaven"* (Phil. 3:20). If the natural law will keep an earthly city in somewhat moderate conditions, what will the excellent glory be in divine relationship to the citizenship to which we belong? What is meant by *excellent glory* is that it outshines. The earth is filled with broken hearts, but the excellent glory fills redeemed men and women so that they show forth the excellency of the grace of the glory of God.

> *Therefore, since we have such hope, we use great boldness of speech; unlike Moses, who put a veil over his face so that the children of Israel could not look steadily at the end of what was passing away.* (2 Cor. 3:12–13)

The man who is going on with God will have no mix-up in his oratory. He will be so plain and precise and divine in his speech, that everything will have a lift toward the glory. He must use great plainness of speech, but he must be a man who knows his message. He must know what God has in His mind in the Spirit, not in the

478

letter. He is there as a vessel for honor, God's mouthpiece; therefore, he stands in the presence of God, and God speaks through him and uses him.

I always say that you cannot sing a song of victory in a minor key. If your life is not in constant pitch, you will never ring the bells of heaven. You must always be in tune with God, and then the music will come out as sweet as possible. We must be the mouthpiece of God, not by letter, but by the Spirit, and we must be so in the will of God that He will rejoice over us with singing (Zeph. 3:17). If we are in the Spirit, the Lord of life is the same Spirit. *"Now the Lord is the Spirit; and where the Spirit of the Lord is, there is liberty"* (2 Cor. 3:17).

There is no liberty that is going to help the people so much as testimony. I find people who do not know how to testify in the right way. We must testify only as the Spirit gives utterance. You are not to use your liberty except for the glory of God. So many meetings are spoiled by long prayers and long testimonies. If the speaker remains in the Spirit, he will know when he should sit down. When you begin to repeat yourself, the people get wearied, and they wish you would sit down, for the anointing has then ceased.

It is lovely to pray, and it is a joy to hear you pray when you are in the Spirit; but if you keep going after the Spirit has finished, all the people get tired of it. So God wants us to know that we are not to use liberty simply because we have it to use, but we are to let the liberty of the Spirit use us. Then we will know when to end. The meetings ought to be so free in the Spirit that people can always go away with the feeling, "Oh, I wish the meeting had gone on for another hour," or, "Was not that testimony meeting a revelation!"

The last verse I want to discuss from 2 Corinthians is the most glorious of all for us:

> *But we all, with unveiled face, beholding as in a mirror the glory of the Lord, are being transformed into the same image from glory to glory, just as by the Spirit of the Lord.*
> (2 Cor. 3:18)

So there is glory upon glory, and joy upon joy, and a measureless measure of joy and glory. Beloved, we get God's Word so wonderfully in our hearts that it absolutely changes us in everything. And as we so feast on the Word of the Lord, so eat and digest the truth, and inwardly eat of Christ, we are changed every day from one state of glory to another. You will never find anything else but the Word that takes you there, so you cannot afford to put aside that Word.

I implore you, beloved, that you come short of none of these blessed teachings. These grand truths of the Word of God must be your testimony, must be your life, your pattern. *"You are an epistle of Christ"* (2 Cor. 3:3). God says this to you by the Spirit. When there is a standard that has not yet been reached in your life, God by His grace, by His mercy, and by your yieldedness can fit you for that place. You can never be prepared for it except by a broken heart and a contrite spirit, and by yielding to the will of God. But if you will come with a whole heart to the throne of grace, God will meet you and build you up on His spiritual plane.

CHAPTER NINE

HOW TO BE TRANSFORMED

Jacob was on his way to the land of his fathers, but he was very troubled at the thought of meeting his brother Esau. Years before, Jacob and his mother had formed a plan to secure the blessing that Isaac was going to give Esau. How inglorious was the fulfilling of this carnal plan! It resulted in Esau's hating Jacob and saying in his heart, "When my father is dead, then will I slay my brother Jacob." (See Genesis 27:41.) Our own plans frequently lead us into disaster.

Jacob had to flee from the land, but how good the Lord was to the fugitive. He gave him a vision of a ladder and angels ascending and descending it (Gen. 28:12). How gracious is our God! He refused to have His plans of grace frustrated by the carnal workings of Jacob's mind, and that night He revealed Himself to Jacob saying, *"I am with you and will keep you wherever you go, and will bring you back to this land; for I will not leave you until I have done what I have spoken to you"* (v. 15). It is the goodness of the Lord that leads to repentance. I believe that Jacob really did some repenting that night as he was made aware of his own meanness.

Many things may happen in our lives to show us how depraved we are by nature, but when the veil is lifted, we see how merciful and tender God is. His tender compassion is over us all the time.

From the time when Jacob had the revelation of the ladder and the angels, he had twenty-one years of testing and trial. But God had been faithful to His promise all through these years. Jacob could say to his wives, *"Your father has deceived me and changed my wages ten times, but God did not allow him to hurt me"* (Gen. 31:7). He said to his father-in-law,

Unless the God of my father, the God of Abraham and the Fear of Isaac, had been with me, surely now you would

481

have sent me away empty-handed. God has seen my afflic-
tion and the labor of my hands. (v. 42)

Now that Jacob was returning to the land of his birth, his heart was filled with fear. If he ever needed the Lord, it was just at this time. And he wanted to be alone with God. His wives, his children, his sheep, his cattle, his camels, and his donkeys had gone on, and *"Jacob was left alone; and a Man wrestled with him until the breaking of day"* (Gen. 32:24). The Lord saw Jacob's need and came down to meet him. It was He who wrestled with the supplanter, breaking him, changing him, transforming him.

Jacob knew that his brother Esau had power to take away all that he had, and to execute vengeance upon him. He knew that no one could deliver him but God. And there alone, lean in soul and impoverished in spirit, he met with God. Oh, how we need to get alone with God, to be broken, to be changed, to be transformed! And when we do meet with Him, He interposes, and all care and strife are brought to an end. Get alone with God, and receive the revelation of His infinite grace and of His wonderful purposes and plans for your life.

SECURING GOD'S BLESSING

This picture of Jacob left alone is so real to me, I can imagine his thoughts that night. He would think about the ladder and the angels. I somehow think that as he would begin to pray, his tongue would stick to the roof of his mouth. He knew he had to get rid of a lot of things. In days gone by, his focus had been upon himself. When we get alone with God, what a place of revelation it is! What a revelation of self we receive! And then what a revelation of the provision made for us at Calvary! It is here that we get a revelation of a life crucified with Christ, buried with Him, raised with Him, transformed by Him, and empowered by the Spirit.

Hour after hour passed. Oh, that we might spend all nights alone with God! We are occupied too much with the things of time and this world. We need to spend time alone in the presence of God. We need to give God much time in order to receive new revelations from Him. We need to get past all the thoughts of earthly matters that crowd in so rapidly. It takes God time to deal with us. If He would only deal with us as He dealt with Jacob, then we would have power with Him, and we would prevail.

Jacob was not dry-eyed that night. Hosea tells us, *"He [Jacob] wept, and sought favor from Him"* (Hos. 12:4). Jacob knew that he had been a disappointment to the Lord, that he had been a groveler, but in the revelation he received that night, he saw the possibility of being transformed from a supplanter to a prince with God. The testing hour came when, at the break of day, the angel, who was none other than the Lord and Master, said, *"Let Me go, for the day breaks"* (Gen. 32:26). This is where we so often fail. Jacob knew that if God went without blessing him, Esau could not be met. You cannot meet the terrible things that await you in the world unless you secure the blessing of God.

You must never let go. Whatever you are seeking—a fresh revelation, light on the path, some particular thing—never let go. Victory is yours if you are earnest enough. If you are in darkness, if you need a fresh revelation, if your mind needs relief, if there are problems you cannot solve, lay hold of God and declare, *"I will not let You go unless You bless me!"* (v. 26).

In wrestling, the strength is in the neck, the breast, and the thigh, but the greatest strength is in the thigh. The Lord touched Jacob's thigh. With his human strength gone, surely defeat was certain. What did Jacob do? He hung on. God intends to have people who are broken. The divine power can only come when there is an end of our own self-sufficiency. But when we are broken, we must hold fast. If we let go, then we will fall short.

Jacob cried, *"I will not let You go unless You bless me!"* And God blessed him, saying, *"Your name shall no longer be called Jacob, but Israel; for you have struggled with God and with men, and have prevailed"* (Gen. 32:28). Now a new order could begin. The old supplanter had passed away, and there was a new creation: Jacob the supplanter had been transformed into Israel the prince.

God Is All You Need

When God comes into your life, you will find Him to be enough. As Israel came forth, the sun rose upon him, and he had power over all the things of the world and over Esau. Esau met him, but there was no fight now; there was reconciliation. They kissed each other. How true it is that *"when a man's ways please the LORD, He makes even his enemies to be at peace with him"* (Prov. 16:7). Esau inquired, "Why have you brought all these cattle, Jacob?" "Oh, that's a present," replied Jacob. "Oh, I have plenty; I don't want your cattle. What a joy to see your face again!" (See Genesis 33.) What a wonderful change! The material things did not count for much after the night of revelation. Who brought about the change? God did.

Can you hold on to God as Jacob did? You certainly can if you are sincere, if you are dependent, if you are broken, if you are weak. It is when you are weak that you are strong (2 Cor. 12:10). But if you are self-righteous, if you are proud, if you are high-minded, if you are puffed up in your own mind, you can receive nothing from Him. If you become lukewarm instead of being on fire for God, you can become a disappointment to Him. And He says, *"I will vomit you out of My mouth"* (Rev. 3:16).

But there is a place of holiness, a place of meekness, a place of faith, where you can call to God, *"I will not let You go unless You bless me!"* (Gen. 32:26). And in response, He will bless you exceedingly abundantly above all you ask or think (Eph. 3:20).

Sometimes we are tempted to think that He has left us. Oh, no. He has promised never to leave us or forsake us (Deut. 31:6). He had promised not to leave Jacob, and He did not break His promise. He has promised not to leave us, and He will not fail. Jacob held on until the blessing came. We can do the same.

If God does not help us, we are no good for this world's need; we are no longer salt, we lose our savor. But as we spend time alone with God, and cry to Him to bless us, He re-salts us. He re-empowers us, but He brings us to brokenness and moves us into the orbit of His own perfect will.

The next morning, as the sun rose, Jacob *"limped on his hip"* (Gen. 32:31). You may ask, "What is the use of a lame man?" It is those who have seen the face of God and have been broken by Him who can meet the forces of the Enemy and break down the bulwarks of Satan's kingdom. The Word declares, *"The lame take the prey"* (Isa. 33:23). On that day, Jacob was brought to a place of dependence upon God.

Oh, the blessedness of being brought into a life of dependence upon the power of the Holy Spirit. Henceforth, we know that we are nothing without Him; we are absolutely dependent upon Him. I am absolutely nothing without the power and anointing of the Holy Spirit. Oh, for a life of absolute dependence! It is through a life of dependence that there is a life of power. If you are not there, get alone with God. If you must, spend a whole night alone with God, and let Him change and transform you. Never let Him go until He blesses you, until He makes you an Israel, a prince with God.

CHAPTER TEN

HE IS RISEN

G od anointed Jesus, who went about doing good, for God was with Him. Today we know for a fact that He is the risen Christ. There is something about this risen, royal, glorified Christ that God means to confirm in our hearts today. The power of the risen Christ makes our hearts move and burn, and we know that there is within us that eternal working by the power of the Spirit.

Oh, beloved, it is eternal life to know Jesus! Surely the kingdom of darkness is shaken when we come into touch with that loftiness, that holiness, that divine integrity of our Master, who was so filled with power. Indeed, the grace of God was upon Him. This blessed, divine inheritance is for us. Surely God wants every one of us to catch fire. We must grasp new realities; we must cease from our murmurings; we must get into the place of triumph and exaltation.

Let's look at Acts 4:1–32. Part of this passage reads, *"And when they had prayed, the place where they were assembled together was shaken"* (v. 31). You talk about a church that cannot shout—it will never be shaken. You can write over it, "The glory has departed." It is only when men have learned the secret of the power of praying and of magnifying God that God comes forth. I have heard people say, "Oh, I praise the Lord inwardly," and nothing comes forth outwardly.

There was a man who had a large business in London. He was a great churchgoer. The church was wonderfully decorated and cushioned, and everything was comfortable enough to make him sleep. His business increased and he prospered, but he seemed to be always in a nightmare and could not tell what was bothering him.

One day he left his office to walk around the building. When he got to the door, he saw the boy who minded the door jumping and whistling. "I wish I felt like that," he said to himself. He returned to his business, but his head was in a whirl. "Oh," he said, "I will go and see the boy again." Again he went and saw the boy who was whistling and jumping. "I want to talk to you in the office," he said to the boy.

"How is it," he asked the boy, when he got into the office, "that you can always whistle and be happy?"

"I cannot help it, sir," replied the boy.

"Where did you get it?"

"I got it at the Pentecostal Mission."

"Where is that?"

And the boy told him about it. This man came to the Pentecostal church and heard about the power of God. He was broken up, and God did a wonderful thing for that man, changing him altogether. One day he was in his office, in the midst of his business, and he suddenly found himself whistling and jumping. He had changed his position.

THE POWER WITHIN

Beloved, it cannot come out of you unless it is within you. It is God who transforms the heart and life. There must be an inward working of the power of God, or it cannot come forth outwardly. We must understand that the power of Pentecost, as it came in the first order, was to loose men. People are tired of things being just smoke and deadness; they are tired of imitations. We want realities, men who have God within them, men who are always filled with God. This is a more needy day than any, and men should be filled with the Holy Spirit.

We must be like our Master. We must have definiteness about all we say. We must have all inward confidence and knowledge that we are God's property, bought and paid for by the precious blood of Jesus. Now the inheritance is in us. People may know that Jesus died and that He rose again, and yet they may not have salvation. Beloved, you must have the witness. You may know today that you are born again, for he who believes has the witness of the Spirit in him (Rom. 8:16).

It is true today that Jesus was raised up by the power of the Holy Spirit. It is true today that we in this place are risen by the power of the Spirit. It is true that we are preaching to you divine power that can raise you up, and God can set you free from all your weakness. God wants you to know how to take the victory and shout in the face of the Devil and say, "Lord, it is done." (See Revelation 21:6.)

> *So when they heard that, they raised their voice to God with one accord and said: "Lord, You are God"....And when they had prayed, the place where they were assembled together was shaken; and they were all filled with the Holy Spirit, and they spoke the word of God with boldness.*
> (Acts 4:24, 31)

That was a wonderful time. That was a real revival, a proper meeting. God means for us to have life. The people perceived something remarkable in the power of God changing these fishermen on the Day of Pentecost. Brothers and sisters, it is the Holy Spirit. We must not say this is merely an influence, for He is the personality and power and presence of the third person of the Trinity. Many of us have been longing for years for God to come forth, and now He is coming forth. The tide is rising everywhere. God is pouring out His Spirit in the hearts of all flesh, and they are crying before God. The day is at hand. God is fulfilling His promises.

Oh, it is lovely, the incarnation of a regeneration, a state of changing from nature to grace, from the power of Satan to God. You who are natural are made supernatural by the divine touch of Him who came to raise you from the dead. The Holy Spirit comes to abide. He comes to reveal the fullness of God. Truly, the Holy Spirit is shedding abroad in our hearts the love of God (Rom. 5:5), and He takes of the things of Jesus and shows them to us (John 16:14).

I know this great salvation that God has given us today is so large that one feels his whole body is enraptured. Do you dare leap into the power of faith right now? Do you dare take your inheritance in God? Do you dare believe God? Do you dare stand upon the record of His Word? If you will believe, you will see the glory of God (John 11:40). *"All things are possible to him who believes"* (Mark 9:23). Do you dare come near today and say that God will sanctify your body and make it holy? He wants you to have a pure body, a holy body, a separated body, a body presented on the altar of God, so that you may be no longer conformed to this world, but transformed and renewed after His image (Rom. 12:2).

SIFTED AS WHEAT, TRIED LIKE GOLD

I believe there are people here who will be put in the place where they will have to stand upon God's Word. You will be sifted as wheat (Luke 22:31). You will be tried as though some strange thing happened to you (1 Pet. 4:12). You will be put in the most difficult places, where all hell seems to surround you, but God will sustain and empower you and will bring you into an unlimited place of faith. God will not allow you to be *"tempted beyond what you are able, but with the temptation will also make the way of escape, that you may be able to bear it"* (1 Cor. 10:13).

God will surely tell you when you have been tried sufficiently in order to bring you out as pure gold. Every trial is to prepare you for a greater position for God. Your tried faith will make you know that you will have the faith of God to go through the next trial. Who is going to live a dormant, weak, trifling, slow, indolent, prayerless, Bible-less life when he knows he must go through these things? And if you are to be made perfect in weakness, you must be tried as by fire in order to know that no man is able to win a victory unless the power of God is in him. The Holy Spirit will lead us day by day. You will know that these light afflictions, which are only for a moment, are working out for us an eternal weight of glory (2 Cor. 4:17).

Oh, beloved, what are we going to do with this day? We must have a high tide this afternoon. We must have people receive the Holy Spirit; we must have people healed in their seats; we must see God come forth. Some of you have been longing for the Holy Spirit. God can baptize you just where you are. There may be some here who have not yet tasted of the grace of God. Close beside you is the water of life. Have a drink, brother, sister, for God says, *"And let him who thirsts come. Whoever desires, let him take the water of life freely"* (Rev. 22:17). *"If we love one another, God abides in us, and His love has been perfected in us"* (1 John 4:12).

Chapter Eleven

Rising into the Heavenlies

I want to read to you a few verses from 1 Peter 1. I believe that God wants to speak to us to strengthen our position in faith and grace. Beloved, I want you to understand that you will get more than you came for. There is not a person in this place who will get what he came for, because God always gives more. No man gets his answers to his prayers—he never does—for God answers his prayers abundantly above what he asks or thinks.

Don't say, "I got nothing." You got as much as you came for, and more. But if your minds are not willing to be yielded, and your hearts are not sufficiently consecrated, you will find that you are limited on that line, because the heart is the place of reception. God wants you to have receptive hearts that will take in the mind of God. These wonderful Scriptures are full of life-giving power. Let us read the first and second verses. There are some words that I ought to lay emphasis on.

> *Peter, an apostle of Jesus Christ, to the pilgrims of the Dispersion in Pontus, Galatia, Cappadocia, Asia, and Bithynia, elect according to the foreknowledge of God the Father, in sanctification of the Spirit, for obedience and sprinkling of the blood of Jesus Christ: Grace to you and peace be multiplied.* (1 Pet. 1:1–2)

I want you to notice that in all times, in all histories of the world, whenever there has been a divine rising or revelation, God coming forth with new dispensational orders of the Spirit, you will find there have been persecutions all over. Take the case of the three Hebrew children, Shadrach, Meshach, and Abednego, and also Daniel and Jeremiah. With any person in the old dispensation, as much as in the new, when the Spirit of the Lord has been moving mightily, there has arisen trouble and difficulty. Why? Because of things that are very much against revelations of God and the Spirit of God.

ELECTED BY GOD

Humanity, flesh, and natural things are all against divine things. Evil powers work upon this position of the human life, especially when the will is unyielded to God. Then, the powers of darkness rise up against the powers of divine order, but they never defeat them. Divine order is very often in the minority, but always in the majority. Did I say that right? Yes, and I meant it, too. Wickedness may increase and abound, but when the Lord raises His flag over the saint, it is victory. Though it is in the minority, it always triumphs.

I want you to notice the first verse because it says *"Dispersion."* This was meant to say that these people did not have much liberty to meet together, so they were driven from place to place. Even in the days of the Scottish religious reformer John Knox, the people who served God had to be in very close quarters, because the Roman church set out to destroy them, nailed them to judgment seats, and destroyed them in all sorts of ways. They were in the minority, but they swept through in victory, and the Roman power was crushed and defeated. Take care that such a thing does not rise again. May God bring us into such perfect order that we may understand these days, that we may be in the minority, but we will always obtain the victory through God.

The Holy Spirit wants us to understand our privileges: we are *"elect according to the foreknowledge of God...in sanctification of the Spirit"* (1 Pet. 1:2). Now this sanctification of the Spirit is not on the lines of being cleansed from sin. It is a higher order than the work of redemption. The blood of Jesus is rich unto all powerful cleansing, and it takes away other powers and transforms us by the mighty power of God. But when sin is gone, yes, when we are clean and when we know we have the Word of God right in us and the power of the Spirit is bringing everything to a place where we triumph, then comes revelation by the power of the Spirit, lifting us onto higher ground, into all the fullness of God, which unveils Christ in such a way.

This is what is called sanctification of the Spirit: sanctified by the Spirit, elect according to the foreknowledge of God. I don't want you to stumble at the word *elect*—it is a most blessed word. You might say you are all elect. God has designed that all men should be saved. This is the election, but whether you accept and come into your election, whether you prove yourself worthy of your election, whether you have so allowed the Spirit to fortify you, whether you have done this I don't know, but your election, your sanctification, is to be seated at the right hand of God.

This word *election* is a very precious word to me. Foreordained, predestined—these are words that God designed before the world was, to bring us into triumph and victory in Christ. Some people play around with it and make it a goal. They say, "Oh, well, you see, we are elected, we are all right." I know many of them who believe in that condition of election, and they say they are quite all right because they are elected to be saved. I believe these people are so diplomatic that they believe others can be elected to be damned. It is not true! Everybody is elected to be saved, but whether they come into it, that is another thing.

Many don't come into salvation because the god of this world has blinded their eyes *"lest the light of the gospel of the glory...should shine on them"* (2 Cor. 4:4). What does that mean? It means that Satan has mastery over their minds, and they have an ear to listen to corrupt things. Be careful of things that do not have Jesus in them. I sometimes shout for all I am worth about Jesus, because I know there is no Jesus inside some things.

Beloved, I want you to catch a glimpse of heaven, with your heart always on the wing, where you grasp everything spiritual, when everything divine makes you hungry for it.

If I returned to this place in a year's time, I would see this kind of election gone right forward, always full, never having a bad report, where you see Christ in some vision, in some way in your lives every day, growing in the knowledge of God every day. But I cannot dwell there, for we have much to get through. It is through the sanctification of the Spirit unto obedience and the sprinkling of the blood of Jesus Christ. There is no sanctification if it is not sanctification unto obedience.

OBEDIENT TO THE WORD

There would be no trouble with any of us if we would come definitely to a place where we understood these words of Jesus:

491

"And for their sakes I sanctify Myself, that they also may be sancti-fied by the truth" (John 17:19). *"Sanctify them by Your truth. Your word is truth"* (v. 17).

No child of God ever asks a question about the Word of God. What do I mean? The Word of God is clear on the breaking of bread, the Word of God is clear on water baptism, the Word of God is clear on all these things, and no person who was going on to the obedience and sanctification of the Spirit by election would pray questioningly over that Word. The Word of God is to be swallowed, not prayed over.

If ever you pray over the Word of God, there is some disobedi-ence; you are not willing to obey. If you come into obedience on the Word of God, and it says anything about water baptism, you will obey. If it says anything about speaking in tongues, you will obey. If it says anything about the breaking of bread and the assembling of ourselves together, you will obey. If you come into the election of the sanctification of the Spirit, you will be obedient in everything revealed in that Word. And to the degree that you are not obedient, you have not come into the sanctification of the Spirit.

A little thing spoils many good things. (See Ecclesiastes 10:1.) People say, "Mr. So-and-so is very good, but...." Or, "Mrs. So-and-so is excellent, but...." "Oh, you know that young man is pro-gressing tremendously, but...."

There are no *buts* in the sanctification of the Spirit. *But* and *if* are gone, and it is *shall* and *I will* all the way through.

Beloved, if there are any *buts* in your attitude toward the Word of truth, there is something unyielded to the Spirit. I pray to God the Holy Spirit that we may be willing to yield ourselves to the sanctification of the Spirit, that we may be in the mind of God in the election, that we may have the mind of God in the possession of it. Perhaps to encourage you, it would be helpful to show you what election is, because there is no difficulty in proving whether you are elected or not.

THE SPIRIT MOVES UPON YOU

Maybe if you, as a believer, had to search your own heart as to why you have been attending these meetings, you would not have to say, "Because it was Wigglesworth." This would be a mistake. But if there was in you that holy calling, that inward, longing de-sire for more of God, you could say it was the sanctification of the

Spirit that was drawing you. Who could do that except He who has elected you for that?

It does not matter what age you are. If I were to say to you, "Stand up, you who never remember the time when the Spirit did not strive with you," it would be a marvelous thing how many people would stand. What do you call it? God bringing you in, moving upon you. Strange? Very strange!

When I think of my own case, I recall that on my mother's side and on my father's side there was no desire for God, and yet in my very infancy I was strangely moved upon by the Spirit. At the age of eight years, I was definitely saved, and at nine years I felt the Spirit come upon me, just as when I spoke in tongues. I was *"elect according to the foreknowledge of God"* (1 Pet. 1:2), and there are people in this place who have had the same experience. You might say, "When I was in sin, I was troubled." And there is a direct line of election between God and the human man, moving it, being wholly prepared for God.

It is a most blessed thought that we have a God of love, compassion, and grace, who does not will the death of even one sinner. God has made it possible for all men to be saved by causing Jesus, His well-beloved Son, to die for the sins of all people. It is true that He took our sins; it is true that He paid the price for the whole world; it is true that He gave Himself as a ransom for many; it is true, beloved. And you say, "For whom?" *"Whoever desires, let him take the water of life freely"* (Rev. 22:17).

"What about the others?" you ask. It would be a direct refusal of the blood of Jesus; it would have to be a refusal to have Christ to reign over them, that's it. It is *"whoever desires"* on this side and whoever does not on the other side. There are people living in the world who do not desire this. What is up with them? *"The god of this age has blinded* [them], *who do not believe, lest the light of the gospel of the glory of Christ, who is the image of God, should shine on them"* (2 Cor. 4:4).

PEACE AND HOPE

Elect according to the foreknowledge of God the Father, in sanctification of the Spirit, for obedience and sprinkling of the blood of Jesus Christ: Grace to you and peace be multiplied. (1 Pet. 1:2)

Through sanctification of the Spirit, according to the election, you will get to a place where you are not disturbed. There is a peace in sanctification of the Spirit, because it is a place of revelation, taking you into heavenly places. It is a place where God comes and speaks and makes Himself known to you, and when you are face-to-face with God, you get a peace *"which surpasses all understanding"* (Phil. 4:7), lifting you from state to state of inexpressible wonderment. It is really wonderful.

> Oh, this is like heaven to me,
> This is like heaven to me,
> I've stepped over Jordan to Canaan's fair land;
> And this is like heaven to me.

Oh, it is wonderful.

> *Blessed be the God and Father of our Lord Jesus Christ, who according to His abundant mercy has begotten us again to a living hope through the resurrection of Jesus Christ from the dead.* (1 Pet. 1:3)

We cannot pass that up, because this sanctification of the Spirit brings us into definite alignment with this wonderful hope of the glory of God. I want to keep before us the glory, the joy of this lively hope. A lively hope is opposite of a dead hope, exactly opposite to normal.

Lively hope is movement. Lively hope is looking into. Lively hope is pressing into. Lively hope is leaving everything behind you. Lively hope is keeping the vision. Lively hope sees Him coming! And you live in it—the lively hope. You are not trying to make yourself feel that you are believing, but the lively hope is ready and waiting. Lively hope is filled with joy of expectation of the King. Praise the Lord!

I want you to know that God has this in His mind for you. Do you know what will move them? The real joy in expectation that will come forth with manifestation and then realization. Don't you know?

Well, I pray God the Holy Spirit that He will move you that way. Come now, beloved, I want to raise your hopes into such activity, into such a joyful experience, that when you go away from this meeting you will have such joy that you would walk if you could not run, that you would jump in a car if you could not run, and that you would go at full speed if you knew you could be there any faster.

Now, I trust that you will be so reconciled to God that there is not one thing that would interfere with your having this lively hope. If you had any love for the world, it could not be, for Jesus is not coming to the world. Jesus is coming to the heavenlies, and all the heavenlies are going to Him, so you cannot have anything but joy with it. You could not have the pride of life. All these things are contrary to the lively hope because of the greatness and the magnificent, multitudinous glories of the regions of eternity, which are placed before you in joyful expectation.

INTERPRETATION OF A MESSAGE IN TONGUES:
The joy of the Lord is everything. The soul lifts up like the golden grain ready to be gathered in for the great sheaf. All ready, waiting, rejoicing, longing for Him, until they say, "Lord Jesus, we cannot wait any longer."

What a wonderful expression of the Holy Spirit to the soul in interpretation. How He loves us, hovers over us, rejoices in us! How the Lord by the Holy Spirit takes a great drink with us, and our cup is full and running over (Ps. 23:5)!

"The joy of the LORD is your strength" (Neh. 8:10). You have to be right in these glorious places, for it is the purpose of God for your soul. I hope you won't forget the lively hope. Do not live for tomorrow because you did not catch it today. Oh, it is wonderful. Hallelujah!

OUR INHERITANCE AS HIS CHILDREN

"To an inheritance incorruptible and undefiled and that does not fade away, reserved in heaven for you" (1 Pet. 1:4).

First, incorruptible. Second, undefiled. Third, does not fade away. Fourth, reserved in heaven for you. Glory to God! I tell you, it is great, it is very great. May the Lord help you to thirst after this glorious life of Jesus. Oh, brother, it is more than new wine; the Holy Spirit is more than new wine; the Holy Spirit is the manifestation of the glories of the new creation.

This is an incorruptible inheritance. *Incorruptible* is one of those delightful words that God wants all believers to grasp. Everything corruptible fades away; everything seen cannot remain. Jesus said, *"Where neither moth nor rust destroys and where thieves do not break in and steal"* (Matt. 6:20). None of these things are joined up with incorruptible. Incorruptible is what is eternal, everlasting, divine. Therefore, everything spiritual and divine reaches a place where God truly is—what shall I say?—where God truly is in the midst of it. He is in existence from everlasting to everlasting: holy, pure, divine, incorruptible.

This is one part of our inheritance in the Spirit, only one part. Hallelujah! It is an inheritance incorruptible and undefiled. Oh, how beautiful it is, perfected forever, no spot, no wrinkle, holy, absolutely pure, all traces of sin withered. Everything that is mortal has been scattered and has come into a place so purified that God is in the midst of it. Hallelujah! It is so lovely to think of that great and wonderful city we read about in Revelation: *"Then I, John, saw the holy city, New Jerusalem, coming down out of heaven from God, prepared as a bride adorned for her husband"* (Rev. 21:2).

Think about it, the Marriage. Oh, it is glorious. "I saw the holy city *'as a bride adorned for her husband,'"* undefiled, glorious, all white, all pure. Who were the people who are now the bride of Christ? They were once in the world, once corruptible, once defiled, but now they have been made holy and spiritual by the blood. They are now lifted from corruptible to incorruptible and are now undefiled in the presence of God. Hallelujah!

Oh, beloved, God intends this for us today. Every soul in this place must reach out to this ideal perfection. God has ten thousand more thoughts for you than you have for yourself. The grace of God is going to move us on, and you will never sorrow anymore as long as you live. You will never weep anymore, but you will weep for joy.

This inheritance is undefiled; it does not fade away. It does not fade away! What a heaven of bliss, what a joy of delight, what a foretaste of heaven on earth. Everything earthly will fade away in the splendor of that glorious day; it all withers when you get in the Spirit. You would cheerfully do the work you have to do because of tomorrow in the presence of the King. Oh, brother, what a hope, what a joyous possibility, within a short time to be in that mighty multitude.

But you say, "My burden is more than I can bear." Cheerfully bear the burden, for tomorrow you will be there. No sin will entice you, no evil spirit will be able to trip you, no, because tomorrow you will be with the Lord. With the Lord forever, an inheritance that does not fade away.

Now let us go on a little further. *"Who are kept by the power of God through faith for salvation ready to be revealed in the last time"* (1 Pet. 1:5). I would like to say something along the lines of salvation, because salvation is very much misunderstood. Salvation that comes to you in a moment of time, believing unto salvation, is only the beginning. Salvation is so tremendous, mighty, and wonderful, as the early apostles said: "Being saved every day." You begin with God and go right on to being saved day by day (2 Cor. 4:16). *"Forgetting those things which are behind and reaching forward"* (Phil. 3:13), through the power of the blood you go on unto salvation.

Salvation is like sanctification of the Spirit; it is not a goal, no. It is only a goal when you limit yourself. There is no limitation as we see the great preservation of the Master. We should never stand still for a moment, but we should mightily move on in God.

REJOICE IN BEING PURIFIED

"In this you greatly rejoice, though now for a little while, if need be, you have been grieved by various trials" (1 Pet. 1:6). Ah, what a blessing, you have no idea what God will mean to you in trials and temptations—it is purification of the Spirit.

> *That the genuineness of your faith, being much more precious than gold that perishes, though it is tested by fire, may be found to praise, honor, and glory at the revelation of Jesus Christ.* (v. 7)

Gold perishes, but faith never perishes; it is more precious than gold, though it may be tried with fire. I went into a place one day, and a gentleman said to me, "Would you like to see purification of gold this morning?" I replied, "Yes." He got some gold and put it in a crucible and put a blast of heat on it. First, it became bloodred, and then it changed and changed. Then this man took an instrument and passed it over the gold, drawing something off that was foreign to the gold. He did this several times until every part was taken away, and then at last he put it over again and said, "Look," and there we both saw our faces in the gold. It was wonderful.

Dear believer, the trial of your faith is much more precious than gold that perishes. When God so purifies you through trials, misunderstandings, persecution, and suffering because you are wrongfully judged, because you have not believed what people say to you, Jesus has given you the keynote: rejoice in that day.

Beloved, as you are tested in the fire, the Master is cleaning away everything that cannot bring out the image of Him in you. He is cleaning away all the dross from your life, and every evil power, until He sees His face right in the life, until He sees His face right in your life.

"Always carrying about in the body the dying of the Lord Jesus, that the life of Jesus also may be manifested in our body" (2 Cor. 4:10). It may not seem to any of us to be very joyous, because it is not acceptable to the flesh, but I have told you already that your flesh is against the Spirit. Your flesh and all your human powers have to be perfectly submitted to the mighty power of God inwardly, to express and manifest His glory outwardly. But you must be willing for the process and say "Amen" to God. It may be very hard, but God will help you.

It is lovely to know that in the chastening times, in the times of misunderstanding and hard tests when you are in the right and are treated as though you were in the wrong, God is meeting you and blessing you. People say it is the Devil. Never mind, let the fire burn; it will do you good. Don't begin complaining, but endure it joyfully. It is so sweet to understand this: *"Love suffers long and is kind"* (1 Cor. 13:4). How lovely to get to a place where you think no evil, you are not easily provoked, and you can bear all things and endure all things! Praise the Lord. Oh, the glory of it, the joy of it!

I understand what it means to jump for joy. I could jump for joy this morning. Why? Because of the Lord.

I know the Lord, I know the Lord,
I know the Lord has laid His hand on me.

"Whom having not seen you love. Though now you do not see Him, yet believing, you rejoice with joy inexpressible and full of glory" (1 Pet. 1:8). We love our Lord Jesus Christ, whom we have not seen. Oh, how sweet, there is no voice so gentle, so soft, so full of tenderness to me. There is no voice like His, and there is no touch like His. Is it possible to love the One we have not seen? God will make it possible to all. *"Though now you do not see Him, yet believing, you rejoice with joy inexpressible and full of glory."*

SUBMITTED TO THE LORD

Rejoice? Oh, what a salvation God has procured for us, and yet we are nothing; we are worthless and helpless in ourselves. I entreat you from the Lord to be so reconciled to Him that there will be no division between you and Him. When He laughs you will laugh, and when He sees you in tears His compassion will be all you need forever. Will you give Him preference? Will you give Him preeminence in all things? Should He not have His right place and decide for you the way and plan of your life?

Believer, when you allow Him to decide for you, when you want nothing but His blessed will, when He is Lord and Governor over all, heaven will be there all the time. The Lord bless you with grace today to leave all and say, "I will follow You, Lord Jesus."

All of you who are longing to get nearer Jesus this morning, I ask you in the name of Jesus to surrender yourselves to Him. But you say, "Wigglesworth, I did it yesterday." I know, but this morning you need to do it more. I know I want to get nearer to my Lord. Let us rise and get near to Him for a few minutes.

CHAPTER TWELVE

PREPARATION FOR THE RAPTURE

Our hearts are moved. God is moving us to believe that He is on the throne waiting for us to make application. Stretch out your hands to God to believe that the almightiness of His grace is for us in a most marvelous way. Whatever yesterday was, today is to be greater.

Are you ready? What for? To come to a place where you will not give way, where you will dare believe that God is the same today and will surely make you satisfied because He longs to fill you. Those who believe will be satisfied.

Are you ready? What for? That you may so apply your heart to the will of God, so yield yourself to His purposes, that God will have a plan through your life that never before has been.

Are you ready? What for? That today you may so come into like-mindedness with Christ, that you may have no more human desire but will be cut short from all human bondages and set free. The shoreline must never know you more. Come to God in all His fullness, His revelation, His power, that you may be clothed upon with God today.

I believe you all believe in the coming of the Lord and the Rapture that is to take place. I am going to deal with what will take you right up to the Rapture. To this end, read the fifth chapter of 2 Corinthians.

This is one of those divine propositions. It is one of those openings to the heart of enlarged ideas. It is one of those moments when we enter in by faith to see that we can be so occupied, so changed, so in Christ, so ready, so clothed upon, and so filled with Him until the very breath of the life of what is causing it would cause us to leave this place.

Do not allow your natural inclinations to interfere with supernatural evidences. You never will be what God has ordered you to be until you are willing to denounce your own failings, your unbelief, and every human standard. You must be willing to denounce them so that you might stand in place, complete, believing that you are a new creation in the Spirit. In a mighty way, God can so fill you with life and can destroy all that is natural that would interfere with the process of change until you are made alive unto God by the Spirit, ready for the coming of the Lord.

A HIGHER PLANE

Here we have a definite position. Paul had a great deal of revelation. In fact, Peter said that Paul said many things that are hard to understand. "Nevertheless," he said, "we know they are of the Lord." (See 2 Peter 3:15–18.) Paul had many hard things to see. Unless we are spiritually enlightened, we will not be able to comprehend the attitude of the place of ascension he had reached.

All your spiritual acquaintances must come into ascension. Always keep in mind that to be conformed to this world is all loss, but to be transformed from this world is all gain. And the transforming is the working in of His mighty power in the mind.

The body and the soul can be so preserved in this wonderful life of God until there is not one thing that could hinder us. We are dead to sin, alive unto God. Sin is destroyed, disease is absolutely put outside, and death is abolished in the life of the resurrection of Christ in the body.

The Spirit of the Lord is giving us revelation that will teach us a plane that is so supernatural in the human realm that you will live absolutely in a new creation if you dare to believe. You will go by leaps and bounds into all the treasury of the Most High as you believe.

Nothing will interfere with you but yourself, and I believe God can change even your mind. He can give you much aspiration and inflate you with holiness, with life from Himself. He will fill you with great ambition for purity, holiness, and transformation, which means that you will be transported toward heaven.

God has to cause revolution many times in the body before He can get the throne. He causes you to come to death, and then to death, and then to death. He will cause you to see that sin violates, that it hinders progress, and He will show you that anything of the natural is not divine. He will teach you that you have to have the divine mind; you have to have a new mind, a new will. He will show you that everything about you must be in the line of consecration, separated entirely unto perfection.

Believe it. Perhaps, as you examine yourself, you will think that it never could be. Get your mind off yourself; that is destruction. Get your mind on the Lord.

No building could be built without a plumb line and a straight edge. The Word of God is a true plumb line. God has given us a plumb line and a straight edge, causing us to be built in supernatural lines so that we may be an edifice in the Spirit. He causes us to be strong against the Devil.

INTERPRETATION OF A MESSAGE IN TONGUES:
Weakness may be turned into power, feeblemindedness into the mind of Christ. The whole body fitly joined together in the Spirit can rise and rise, until it is an edifice in the Holy Spirit. It is not what it is; it is what it is going to be. God has made preparation for us to be freed from the law of sin and death. He has gained the victory. He has overcome and vanquished the Enemy, and the last enemy that will be destroyed is death. Yes, deeper, deeper, higher, higher, holier, purer, purer, until God sets His seal upon us; we are His forever, bought with a price, not with silver and gold, but with the precious blood. Let the Spirit move you, chasten you, bring you to nothing, because you must be so chastened by the Lord in order to have the fruits of His holiness. He compares you this morning to that position of fruitfulness. Unless you die, you cannot live. So, in the very attitude of death, He causes resurrection force to come into your life, until you come out of all things into the living Head; until Christ is over you, nourishing you in the mind, in the body, and causing your spirit to live until you feel the very breath of heaven breathing upon you and the wings of the Spirit moving within you.

GETTING READY FOR THE FUTURE EXIT

For we know that if our earthly house, this tent, is destroyed, we have a building from God, a house not made with hands, eternal in the heavens. For in this we groan, earnestly desiring to be clothed with our habitation which is from heaven. (2 Cor. 5:1–2)

This verse speaks about a present tense that has to make us ready for a future exit. Present-tense lessons are wonderful. You miss a great deal if you do not live in the present tense. You must never put anything off until tomorrow. "Remember today if you will believe."

The Word of God says, *"The same yesterday, today, and forever"* (Heb. 13:8). God wants us to have everything today. Don't say, "Tomorrow I will be healed." Don't say, "Tomorrow I will be baptized." Don't say, "Tomorrow I will have more light." Today, if you will hear His voice, do not harden your heart, for the hearing of faith is wonderful.

Two things are real that must take place, but it is our responsibility to be in readiness for these things to take place. We should all wish that no one would die from this day forward. Whenever the Scriptures speak of death, it is *"sown in dishonor"* (1 Cor. 15:43). We know God is going to raise in power.

But there is a state in which we may go on to see that sin, disease, and death are destroyed, that we have come into a plan of such an enforcement of resurrection power that we need not die if we dare believe the truth. But we are on the edge and frightened all the time that it won't come to pass.

SURPASSING JOY

I want to help you today. If you are not moved in some way, God is not with you. One of two things has to happen: either you have to be moved so that you cannot rest, or you have to be made so glad that you cannot remain in the same place. I could not believe that anybody filled with the Spirit could speak to an assembly of people, and they would still be the same after he had finished. So I take it for granted that God has me here to move you, to make you very thirsty, or to cause a gladness to come into your heart that will absolutely surpass everything else along the lines of joy.

THE BODY MUST BE CHANGED

No flesh can come into the presence of God. If no flesh can come into the presence of God, then what is going into the presence of God? If you do die, the process is to get rid of all that there is in the body. The very body that you are in must be disposed of. If it goes away, it must come to ashes. There is no such thing as your body being in the presence of God. So your body has to give place to a resurrection order, to a resurrection life. It has to.

The Scriptures speak about dissolving. If your body does not go through the process of death—if it does not experience just what earthly cabbages, potatoes, corn, and wheat experience—if it does not go that way and get rid of all its acquaintances, then God will cause the old body to be turned into gases when it goes up. There will not be a bit of it left. But the very nature of Christ, the life of God, the very essence of life, in that moment, will be clothed upon with a body that can stand all eternity.

So be ready for a change. You say, "How can we be ready?" I will explain. Follow me very closely.

"*In this we groan*" (2 Cor. 5:2). There should be a groaning attitude, a place where we see that there is some defect, that there is not perfect purification going on. When we come to that attitude, knowing we are bound in the way, then we will groan to be delivered.

What is the deliverance? Will it be in this present world? Certainly. I am not in heaven yet; I am on the earth. I am dealing with people who are in the earth, who can be in the earth and have this supernatural abounding within them. Now let us see how this can be.

"*Having been clothed, we shall not be found naked*" (v. 3). I am dealing with clothing now. The first time the body was clothed with flesh; this time it is being clothed with the Spirit.

The very nature that came into you when you were born again was a spiritual quality of knowledge. It understands supernatural things. It has power to compare spiritual things with spiritual things, and only those who are born of God can understand spiritual things. The world that has never been saved cannot understand them. But the moment we are quickened, born again, and made anew, this nature will take its supernatural powers and will go on travailing and groaning to be delivered from the body. And it will go on crying and crying until the saints are seen in large numbers saying, "*Come, Lord Jesus!*" (Rev. 22:20), and the consummation will be most remarkable.

But I believe God has a plan for us even before that may happen. Carefully, thoughtfully read the fourth verse of 2 Corinthians 5: "*For we who are in this tent groan, being burdened, not because we want to be unclothed, but further clothed, that mortality may be swallowed up by life.*"

504

"Further clothed." We do not desire to go, but to stop, because we realize we are not exactly ready to go. But we want to be so clothed with the Spirit while we are in the body, clothed with the life from heaven, that not one natural thing will be evident. We are then absolutely made alive in Christ, and we live only for the glory and the exhibition of the Lord of life.

Paul said that nothing good dwelled in his flesh (Rom. 7:18). You know exactly what nakedness is. They knew, when Jesus walked the earth, that their nakedness was made bare. You know that nakedness is a sense of consciousness that there is something that has not been dealt with, has not been judged, and the blood has not had its perfect application. Nakedness means that you are inwardly conscious that there is some hidden thing, something that has not been absolutely brought to the blood, something that could not stand God, something that is not ready for the absolute glory of God.

Then there is the principle of life. I want to speak about the life of the Word of Life itself. The Word of Life is preached to you through the Gospel, and it has a wonderful power in it. It deals with the natural realm and brings immortality into the natural, until the natural realizes the first spring of supernatural power in the heart. From that moment, a man knows he is in the earth but belongs to heaven, and this life that is in him is a life that has the power to eat up mortality. A couple of verses from Romans 8 will help us here:

> *There is therefore now no condemnation to those who are in Christ Jesus, who do not walk according to the flesh, but according to the Spirit. For the law of the Spirit of life in Christ Jesus has made me free from the law of sin and death.* (Rom. 8:1–2)

The law of life is the law that came into you that is incorruptible, that is divine, that is the nature of the Son of God.

Suppose I were dealing with the coming of the Lord. The revelation that I have about the Lord's return is that all those who are going to be caught up are going to be eaten up—their old natures, their old desires, their old lives are going to be eaten up with His life, so that when He comes His life will meet the life that is in them. But the process we are going through now is to build us on the lines of readiness.

THE LIFE THAT EATS MORTALITY

Now I want to speak of the life that has power to eat up mortality. What is mortality? When I speak about mortality, you no doubt think of your physical body and say, "That is mortality."

That is not mortality. That is not what will be swallowed up or eaten up. As long as you are in the world, you will want the casket that your body truly is. But it is what is in the body that is mortal that has to be eaten up with immortality.

If I were to go through Mark, Luke, Romans, Galatians, Timothy, and Peter, I would find sixty-six different descriptions of mortality. I would find sedition, heresy, envy, strife, malice, hatred, murder, emulation, witchcraft. I would find covetousness, adultery, fornication. I would discover that all these were mortality. But I would also find a life in the supernatural that can eat them up, devour them, and destroy them until there is no condemnation in this body.

The Scriptures are very clear that we must allow ourselves to come into touch with this great Life in us, this wonderful Life divine, this Christ form, this spiritual revelation.

Do not forget that the Holy Spirit did not come as a cleanser. The Holy Spirit is not a cleanser; the Holy Spirit is a revealer of imperfection that can only be cleansed by the blood of Jesus. After the blood has cleansed you, you need the Word of God, for the Word of God is the only power that creates anew. Life comes through the Word. The Word is the Son; the Word is the life of the Son. He who has received the Son has received life; he who has not received the Son has not received life (John 3:36).

There are millions of people living today who do not have life. There is only one life that is eternal, and that is the life of the Son of God. One is a life of death, eternal death; the other is a life of eternal life. One is destruction; the other is eternal deliverance. One is bondage; the other is freedom. One is sorrow; the other is joy.

I want you to see that you are to live so full of this divine life, until you are not moved by any *"wind of doctrine"* (Eph. 4:14), or anything else that comes along.

People make the biggest mistake in the world, and they miss the greatest things today, because they turn to the letter instead of the Spirit. How many people have been ruined because they have gone mad on water baptism? You cannot prove to me through any part of Scripture that baptism can save you. It is only a form. And yet, people are mad and are firm in their belief that if you are not baptized, you must be lost. These people understand only the letter, and the letter always kills. The Spirit always gives life.

The person, whoever he is, who would turn you from the baptism of Matthew 28 to any other baptism, is a thief and a robber and is trying to destroy you. Do not be carnally minded. Be spiritually minded; then you will know the truth, and the truth will make you free (John 8:32).

See to it that you live and affirm and know that it is Christ who gives life. Division brings sorrow, remorse, trials, and difficulties. Let Christ dwell in your hearts richly by faith.

Don't go mad on preaching only the baptism of the Holy Spirit; you will be lopsided. Don't go mad on preaching water baptism; you will be lopsided. Don't go mad on preaching healing; you will be lopsided. There is only one thing that you will never become lopsided over, and that is preaching salvation. The only power is the Gospel of the kingdom. Men are not saved by baptism, not even by the baptism of the Holy Spirit, or by the baptism in water. They are saved and preserved by the blood of Christ.

The Lord wants to bring us to the place of real foundation truth. Build upon the foundation truth. Don't be twisted aside by anything. Let this be your chief motive: that you are living to catch more of the Spirit, and only the Spirit.

I clearly know that the Holy Spirit is not the only means of making me eligible for the coming of the Lord. Lots of people have gone mad because they have gotten baptized with the Spirit and think no one is right but those who are baptized with the Spirit. It is the biggest foolishness in the world. Why is it foolishness? Because the truth bears it out all the time. The thief on the cross went right up to meet Jesus in paradise. But just because a thief missed these things, will we miss them, too? No. It was the great grace and mercy of the Lord to have mercy upon him. There is not a gift, not a grace, not a position except those that God uses to loosen you from your bondages, and He wants you to be free in the Spirit. He wants to fill you with the Holy Spirit, wants to fill you with the Word, until He brings you to the place of the sealing of the Spirit.

You say, "What is the sealing of the Spirit?" The sealing of the Spirit is that God has put His mark upon you and you are tagged. It is a wonderful thing to have the tag of the Almighty. It seals you.

The Devil cannot touch you. The Lord has preserved you. There is a covenant between you and God, and the sealing of the Spirit has got you to the place where evil powers have no more dominion.

Don't go away with the idea that I am preaching a perfection in which you cannot sin. There is a place of perfection, of purifying as He is pure, so that we cannot commit sins. There is no man who can commit sin if he is being purified. But it is when he ceases from seeking deeper experience, a holier vocation, a deeper separation, a perfect place where he and Christ are one, that sin comes in. Only in Christ is there security.

Let no man think that he cannot fall because he stands. No, but let us remember this: we need not fall. Grace abounds where sin abounds, and where weakness is, grace comes in. Your very inactivity becomes divine activity. Where absolute weakness is so strong that you feel you cannot stand the trial, He comes in and enables you to stand. Life is ministered, and Christ takes the place of weakness, for *"when I am weak, then am I strong"* (2 Cor. 12:10), for then God touches me with His strength.

This is ideal. This is divine appointment. This is holy installation. This is God's thought from the throne. The Lord is speaking to us, and I would say with a trumpet voice through to the whole world, "Be holy!" Don't fail to see that God wants you ready for translation. Holiness is the habitation of God.

SPIRITUAL DRUNKENNESS

There is a place to reach in the Holy Spirit that is mystifying to the world and to many people who are not going on with God. Here is a most remarkable lesson. We can be so filled with the Spirit, so clothed upon by Him, so purified within, so made ready for the Rapture, that all the time we are drunk. *"For if we are beside ourselves, it is for God; or if we are of sound mind, it is for you"* (2 Cor. 5:13).

You can be so filled with the Spirit of life that you are absolutely drunken and beside yourself. Now, when I come in contact with people who would criticize my drunkenness, I am sober. I can be sober one minute; I can be drunk the next. I tell you, to be drunk is wonderful! *"And do not be drunk with wine, in which is dissipation; but be filled with the Spirit"* (Eph. 5:18). In this there is a lively hope, filled with indiscreetness in regard to what anyone else thinks.

508

Think of a man who is drunk. He stops at a lamppost, and he has a lot to say to it. He says the most foolish things possible, and the people say, "He's gone."

Oh, Lord, that I may be so drunk with You that it makes no difference what people think! I am not concerned with what people think. I am speaking to the Lord in hymns and spiritual songs, making my boast in the Lord. The Lord of Hosts is around me, and I am so free in the Holy Spirit that I am ready to be taken to heaven. But He does not take me. Why doesn't He take me? I am ready, and it is better for me to go, but for the church's sake it is preferable that I stop. (See Philippians 1:23–25.)

It is best that I am clothed upon with the Spirit, living in the midst of the people, showing no nakedness. I need to be full of purity, full of power, full of revelation for the church's sake. It is far better to go, but for the church's sake I must stop, so that I may be helpful, telling the people how they can have their nakedness covered, how all their imperfections can be covered, how all the mind can be clothed, how all their inward impurities are made pure in the presence of God. It is better that I am living, walking, and acting in the Holy Spirit. This may seem impossible, yet this is the height that God wants us to reach.

Here is another verse to help you. It is a keynote verse to many positions I am teaching here. *"And if Christ is in you, the body is dead because of sin, but the Spirit is life because of righteousness"* (Rom. 8:10). There is no such thing as having liberty in your body if there is any sin there. When righteousness is there, righteousness abounds. When Christ is in your heart, enthroning your life, and sin is dethroned, then righteousness abounds and the Holy Spirit has great liberty. This is one of the highest positions of the Scripture character.

"And if children, then heirs; heirs of God and joint heirs with Christ" (v. 17). My, what triumphs of heights, of lengths, of depths, of breadths there are in this holy place! Where is it? Right inside.

INTERPRETATION OF A MESSAGE IN TONGUES:

He who is dead is free from sin but is alive unto God by the Spirit, and is made free from the law of sin and death. He has entered into a relationship in God, and now God is his reward. He is not only a son, but he is also joined in heirship, because of sonship. In purity, he is joined together with Him. He will withhold no good thing from him who walks uprightly.

Every good thing is for us on the holy line, walking uprightly, being set free, being made God's property.

RECONCILIATION IN CHRIST

"All things are of God, who has reconciled us to Himself through Jesus Christ, and has given us the ministry of reconciliation" (2 Cor. 5:18). What is reconciliation? It is being absolutely joined in one atonement into Christ and being blended with Him in the reconciliation. You are in a glorious place: *"That is, that God was in Christ reconciling the world to Himself, not imputing their trespasses to them, and has committed to us the word of reconciliation"* (v. 19).

Once we are reconciled to Him, we are forever reconciled, made one, brought into conformity. The law of the liberty of the Christ of God reigns supreme over us in all things; that ought to make us leap for joy.

Now then, we are ambassadors for Christ, as though God were pleading through us: we implore you on Christ's behalf, be reconciled to God. For He made Him who knew no sin to be sin for us, that we might become the righteousness of God in Him. (vv. 20–21)

The blessed Son of God has taken our place in reconciliation, becoming the absolute position of all uncleanness, of every sin. God laid upon Him the iniquity of all, so that every iniquity might go, every bondage might be made free. Sin, death, and disease are erased by our resurrection, by our re-creation. When He comes, we will be not naked, but clothed upon, separated, filled within, and made like Him in every way.

I come to you only in the living fact of this realized testimony. To me, it is reality. I am living in it; I am moving in it; I am acting in it; and I am coming to you with the joy of it.

I know this is for us, this divine life, free from bondage, free from the power of Satan, free from evil thoughts, free from thoughts of evil. God reconciles me to Himself in a way that He abounds to me.

It is joy unspeakable and full of glory,
And the half has never yet been told.

CHAPTER THIRTEEN

PRESENT-TIME BLESSINGS
FOR PRESENT-TIME SAINTS

Read with me the first twelve verses of Matthew 5, the verses that we generally call the Beatitudes. Some people tell us that Matthew 5 is a millennial chapter and that we cannot attain to these blessings at the present time. I believe that everyone who receives the baptism in the Spirit has a real foretaste and promise of millennial blessing, but also that here the Lord Jesus is setting forth present-day blessings that we can enjoy here and now.

It is a great joy for me to be speaking to baptized believers. We have not reached the height of God's mind, but my personal conviction is that we are nearer by far than we were fourteen years ago. If anyone had told me that I would be happier today than I was fourteen years ago when the Lord baptized me in the Spirit, I would not have believed him. But I see that God has more ahead for us, and that, so far, we have only touched the fringe of things. As we let the truth lay hold of us, we will press on for the goal ahead and enter more fully into our birthright—all that God says.

It seems to me that every time I open my Bible I get a new revelation of God's plan. God's Spirit takes man to a place of helplessness and then reveals God as his all in all.

FOR THE POOR IN SPIRIT

"Blessed are the poor in spirit, for theirs is the kingdom of heaven" (Matt. 5:3). This is one of the richest places into which Jesus brings us. The poor have a right to everything in heaven. *"Theirs is."* Do you dare believe it? Yes, I dare. I believe, I know,

that I was very poor. When God's Spirit comes in as the ruling, controlling power of our life, He gives us God's revelation of our inward poverty and shows us that God has come with one purpose: to bring heaven's best to earth. He also shows that with Jesus He will indeed *"freely give us all things"* (Rom. 8:32).

An old man and an old woman had lived together for seventy years. Someone said to them, "You must have seen many clouds during those days." They replied, "Where do the showers come from? You never get showers without clouds." It is only the Holy Spirit who can bring us to the place of realization of our poverty; but, every time He does it, He opens the windows of heaven, and the showers of blessing fall.

But I must recognize the difference between my own spirit and the Holy Spirit. My own spirit can do certain things on natural lines—it can even weep and pray and worship—but it is all on a human plane. We must not depend on our own human thoughts and activities or on our own personalities. If the baptism means anything to you, it should bring you to the death of the ordinary, where you are no longer putting faith in your own understanding but, conscious of your own poverty, you are ever yielded to the Spirit. Then it is that your body becomes filled with heaven on earth.

FOR THOSE WHO MOURN

"Blessed are those who mourn, for they shall be comforted" (Matt. 5:4). People get a wrong idea of mourning. In Switzerland, they have a day set apart to take wreaths to graves. I laughed at the people's ignorance and said, "Why are you spending time around the graves? The people you love are not there. All that taking of flowers to the graves is not faith at all. Those who died in Christ are gone to be with Him, 'which,' Paul said, 'is far better' (Phil. 1:23)."

My wife once said to me, "Watch me when I'm preaching. I get so near to heaven when I'm preaching that some day I'll be off." One night she was preaching, and when she had finished, off she went. I was going to Glasgow and had said goodbye to her before she went to the meeting. As I was leaving the house, the doctor and policeman met me at the door and told me that she had fallen dead at the church door. I knew she had gotten what she wanted. I could not weep, but I was in tongues, praising the Lord. On natural lines she was everything to me; but I could not mourn on natural lines, and I just laughed in the Spirit. The house was soon filled with people. The doctor said, "She is dead, and we can do no more for her." I went up to her lifeless corpse and commanded death to give her up, and she came back to me for a moment. Then God said to me, "She is Mine; her work is done." I knew what He meant.

They laid her in the coffin, and I brought my sons and my daughter into the room and said, "Is she there?" They said, "No, Father." I said, "We will cover her up." If you go mourning the loss of loved ones who have gone to be with Christ—I say this to you out of love—you have never had the revelation of what Paul spoke of when he showed us that it is better to go than to stay. We read this in Scripture, but the trouble is that people will not believe it. When you believe God, you will say, "Whatever it is, it is all right. If You want to take the one I love, it is all right, Lord." Faith removes all tears of self-pity.

But there is a mourning in the Spirit. God will bring you to a place where things must be changed, and there is a mourning, an unutterable groaning until God comes. And the end of all real faith always is rejoicing. Jesus mourned over Jerusalem. He saw the conditions; He saw the unbelief; He saw the end of those who closed their ears to the Gospel. But God gave a promise that He would see *"the labor of His soul, and be satisfied"* (Isa. 53:11) and that He would *"see His seed"* (v. 10).

What happened on the Day of Pentecost in Jerusalem was a promise of what would be the results of His travail, to be multiplied a billionfold all down the ages in all the world. And as we enter in the Spirit into travail over conditions that are wrong, such mourning will always bring results for God, and our joy will be complete in the satisfaction that is thereby brought to Christ.

FOR THE MEEK

"Blessed are the meek, for they shall inherit the earth" (Matt. 5:5). Moses was headstrong in his zeal for his own people, and it resulted in his killing a man. (See Exodus 2:11–12.) His heart was right in his desire to correct things, but he was working on natural lines, and when we work on natural lines we always fail. Moses had a mighty passion, and that is one of the best things in the world when God has control and it becomes a passion for souls to be born again. But apart from God it is one of the worst things.

Paul had it to a tremendous extent, and, breathing out threats, he was sending men and women to prison. (See Acts 8:3.) But God changed him, and later he said he could wish himself accursed from Christ for the sake of his fellowmen, his kinsmen according to the flesh (Rom. 9:3–4).

God took the headstrong Moses and molded him into the meekest of men. He took the fiery Saul of Tarsus and made him the foremost exponent of grace. Oh, brothers and sisters, God can transform you in the same manner, and plant in you a divine meekness and every other thing that you lack.

In our Sunday school, we had a boy with red hair. His head was as red as fire, and so was his temper. He was such a trial. He kicked his teachers and the superintendent. He was simply uncontrollable. The teachers had a meeting in which they discussed the matter of expelling him. But they thought that God might somehow work in that boy, and so they decided to give him another chance. One day he had to be kicked out, and he broke all the windows of the church. He was worse outside than in. Sometime later, we had a ten-day revival meeting. There was nothing much going on in that meeting, and people thought it was a waste of time, but there was one result—the redheaded lad got saved.

After he was saved, the difficulty was to get rid of him at our house. He would be there until midnight, crying to God to make him pliable and use him for His glory. God delivered the lad from his temper and made him one of the meekest, most beautiful boys you ever saw. For twenty years he has been a mighty missionary in China. God takes us just as we are and transforms us by His power.

I can remember the time when I used to go white with rage and shake all over with temper. I could hardly hold myself together. But one time I waited on God for ten days. In those ten days, I was being emptied out, and the life of the Lord Jesus was being worked into me. My wife testified of the transformation that took place in my life. She said, "I never saw such a change. I have never been able to cook anything since that time that has not pleased him. Nothing is too hot or too cold; everything is just right." God must come and reign supreme in your life. Will you let Him do it? He can do it, and He will if you will let Him.

It is no use trying to tame the *"old man"* (Eph. 4:22). But God can deal with him. The carnal mind will never be subjected to God, but God will bring it to the Cross where it belongs and will put in its place, the pure, the holy, the meek mind of the Master.

FOR THOSE WHO HUNGER AND THIRST

"Blessed are those who hunger and thirst for righteousness, for they shall be filled" (Matt. 5:6). Note that the verse says, *"Shall be filled."* If you ever see a *"shall"* in the Bible, make it yours. Meet the conditions, and God will fulfill His Word to you. The Spirit of God is crying,

> *Everyone who thirsts, come to the waters; and you who have no money, come, buy and eat. Yes, come, buy wine and milk without money and without price.* (Isa. 55:1)

The Spirit of God will take of the things of Christ and show them to you so that you may have a longing for Christ in His fullness, and when there is that longing, God will not fail to fill you.

See the crowd of worshippers who have come up to the feast. They are going away utterly unsatisfied, but

> *on the last day, that great day of the feast, Jesus* [will stand] *and* [cry] *out, saying, "If anyone thirsts, let him come to Me and drink. He who believes in Me, as the Scripture has said, out of his heart will flow rivers of living water."* (John 7:37–38)

Jesus knows that they are going away without the living water, and so He directs them to the true source of supply. Are you thirsty today? The living Christ still invites you to Himself, and I want to testify that He still satisfies the thirsty soul and still fills the hungry with good things.

In Switzerland, I learned of a man who met with the assembly of the Plymouth Brethren. He attended their various meetings, and one morning, at their Communion service, he arose and said, "Brothers, we have the Word, and I feel that we are living very much in the letter of it, but there is a hunger and thirst in my soul for something deeper, something more real than we have, and I cannot rest until I enter into it." The next Sunday this brother rose again and said, "We are all so poor here, there is no life in this assembly, and my heart is hungry for reality." He did this for several weeks until it got on the nerves of these people, and they protested, "Sands, you are making us all miserable; you are spoiling our meetings. There is only one thing for you to do, and that is to clear out."

That man went out of the meeting in a very sad condition. As he stood outside, one of his children asked him what was the matter, and he said, "To think that they should turn me out from their midst for being hungry and thirsty for more of God!" I did not know anything more of this situation until afterward.

Days later, someone rushed up to Sands and said, "There is a man over here from England, and he is speaking about tongues and healing." Sands said, "I'll fix him. I'll go to the meeting and sit right up in the front and challenge him with the Scriptures. I'll dare him to preach these things in Switzerland. I'll publicly denounce him." So he came to the meetings. There he sat. He was so hungry and thirsty that he drank in every word that was said. His opposition soon petered out. The first morning he said to a friend, "This is what I want." He drank and drank of the Spirit. After three weeks he said, "God will have to do something new or I'll burst." He breathed in God, and the Lord filled him to such an extent that he spoke in other tongues as the Spirit gave utterance. Sands is now preaching and is in charge of a new Pentecostal assembly.

God is making people hungry and thirsty after His best. And everywhere He is filling the hungry and giving them what the disciples received at the very beginning. Are you hungry? If you are, God promises that you will be filled.

CHAPTER FOURTEEN

THE RICHES OF HIS GLORY

M ay the Lord of Hosts so surround us with revelation and blessing that our bodies get to the place where they can scarcely contain the joys of the Lord. He will bring us to so rich a place of divine order that forever we will know we are only the Lord's. What a blessed state of grace to be brought into, where we know that the body, the soul, the spirit are preserved blameless until the coming of the Lord! Paul took us one step higher and said, *"May your whole spirit, soul, and body be preserved blameless at the coming of our Lord"* (1 Thess. 5:23). What a blessed state of grace!

When our hearts are moved to believe God, God is greatly desirous for us to have more of His presence. We have only one purpose in mind in these meetings, and that is to strengthen you, to build you up in the most holy faith, and to present you for every good work so that you should be faultless in Him, quickened by the might of the Spirit, so that you might be prepared for everything that God has for you in the future. Our human nature may be brought to a place where it is so superabundantly attended to by God that in the body we will know nothing but the Lord of Hosts.

To this end, I bring you to the banquet that cannot be exhausted, a supply beyond all human thought, an abundance beyond all human extravagances. No matter how you come into great faith and believing in God, God says, "Much more abundantly, much more." So, I trust you will be moved to believe for more.

Are you ready? What for? That you might by the power of God be brought into His coffers with a new plan of righteousness, that you might be able as never before to leave the things of the world behind you and press on toward the prize of the high calling (Phil. 3:13–14).

Are you ready? What for? That you might be so in God's plan that you will feel God's hand upon you. You will know that He has chosen you, so that you might be a firstfruit unto God.

Are you ready? What for? That the Lord will have His choice, that His will and purpose will be yours, that the "Amen" of His character may sweep through your very nature, and that you may know as you have never known before that this is the day of the visitation between you and Him.

FROM HUMAN TO DIVINE

The Lord has been speaking to me about this meeting, and I believe we are going to study a Scripture that will be pleasing to Him, the third chapter of Ephesians.

I do thank God for this stupendous, glorious exit of human into divine. I do praise God for these studies, which are showing us the fullness of the pleasure of God.

It is the God of all grace who is bending over us with the fullness of recognition. He sees us; He knows us; He is acquainted with us. He is bending over us so that His infinite pleasure, His glorious, exhaustless pleasure may move us today. What can please Him more than to see His sons and daughters clothed, in their right mind (see Luke 8:35), listening to His voice, their eyes and ears awake, coming into the treasury of the Most High?

For this reason I, Paul, the prisoner of Christ Jesus for you Gentiles; if indeed you have heard of the dispensation of the grace of God which was given to me for you, how that by revelation He made known to me the mystery...which in other ages was not made known to the sons of men, as it has now been revealed by the Spirit to His holy apostles and prophets: that the Gentiles should be fellow heirs, of the same body, and partakers of His promise in Christ through the gospel. (Eph. 3:1–3, 5–6)

Oh, that we might be so clothed upon by the ministry of His grace, that we might so understand the mystery of His wonderful initiative! If only we could comprehend today more than ever before why the Gentiles have been brought into the glories of His treasury, to feed on the finest of the wheat, to drink at the riches of His pleasure, to be filled with the God of love that has no measure.

Without doubt, the greatest mystery of all time from the commencement of creation to now is Christ made manifest in human flesh. What can be greater than eternal life working mightily through eternal death? What can there be greater than the nature and appearance of Adam being changed by a new nature that has to be the fullness of the expression of the Father in heaven? *"And as we have borne the image of the man of dust, we shall also bear the image of the heavenly"* (1 Cor. 15:49).

Everybody recognizes the Adamic race, but may God today let us understand fullness, the divine reflection. May He put us in the glorious position so that we may be changed—the living manifestation of the power of God changing our vestige. May He allow us to see the very expression of the Father, until the terrestrial will pass away, the celestial will come, and the rightness of His glory will press through all our humanity. Heaven will have an exhibition in us that it never before could have, and all the saints will be gathered. The very expression of the Master's face and the very glory of the Father will be in us.

INTERPRETATION OF A MESSAGE IN TONGUES:

It is the life from heaven that changes what could not be changed. Only the very expression of the nature of the God of all grace moving in our human faculties makes us know that we are begotten from above, changed by His power, transformed by His love, until we are not, for God has taken us. Be still, for the grace that has come upon you is to so transform your fashion and so beautify your comeliness until right within you there will be the expression of the glory of God in the old creation, making the new creation just longing to depart.

Oh, that the breath of heaven would move us today until we would feel, whatever happened, that we must move on to get ready for exit!

OUR JOINT INHERITANCE

The fullness of the expression of the Holy Spirit order today is giving us a glimpse into what has been provided by the Father. We know that in the old Israel, from Abraham right down, God had a very special position. Jesus said, "Is not this a daughter of Abraham?" (See Luke 13:16.) Paul spoke about it, knowing that he belonged to that royal aristocracy of Abraham's seed.

But the Gentiles had no right to it. The Master said to the Syro-Phoenician woman, "Shall I take the bread of the children and give it to dogs?" (See Mark 7:27.) Did Jesus mean that the Gentiles were dogs? No, He did not mean that, but He meant that the whole race of the Gentiles knew that they were far below the standard and the order of those people who belonged to the royal stock of Israel. The Samaritans all felt it.

"But isn't it possible for the dogs to have some crumbs?" was the woman's question. (See verse 28.)

God has something better than crumbs. God has turned to the Gentiles, and He has made us of the same body, the same heirs. He has put no difference between them and us, but He has joined us up in that blessed order of coming into the promise through the blood of Christ.

Thank God! He met the need of all nations, of all ranks, of all conditions, and God so manifests His power that He has brought us into oneness, and we know we are sharing in the glory. We are sharing in the inner expression; we are sharing that beautiful position in which we know that we belong to the aristocracy of the church of God.

I want to bring you into very blessed privileges along these lines, for I want especially to deal with the knowledge of the inner working of that joint fellowship in this holy order with Christ. *"As it has now been revealed by the Spirit to His holy apostles and prophets"* (Eph. 3:5).

I want you to see that this revelation was given by the power of the Spirit, and I want you to keep in mind that revelations are within the very body where Christ is manifested in the body. When Christ becomes the very personality of the fullness of the Father's will, then the Spirit, the effectual working of the power of God, has such glorious liberty in the body to unfold the mystery and the glories of the kingdom, for it is given to the Holy Spirit to reveal them as He reveals them all in Christ.

It is wonderful to know that I am in the body. It is wonderful to know that the apostles and prophets and all those who have passed down the years, holding aloft the torch, going on from victory to victory, all will be in the body. But how wonderful if we may be in the body so that we might be chosen out of the body to be the bride! It will be according as you are yielded to the *"effective working of His power"* (v. 7).

POWER THAT BRINGS LIGHT AND LIFE

"The effective working of His power" means to say that it is always Godward. The Holy Spirit has no alternative; He is here to fulfill the Great Commission of the Executive of heaven. Therefore, He is in the body for one express purpose: to make us understand the fullness of the glories that are contained in what is in us, which is Christ in us—not only the hope of glory (Col. 1:27), but also all the powers of the manifestation of the glory of Christ to be revealed in us.

It is for us to know the mysteries that have been laid up for us. It is for us to know the glories that will be revealed in Christ. It is for us to know all the fullness of the expression of His deity within us. It is for us to know that in this purposing of Christ's being in us, we have to be loosed from everything else, and He has to be manifesting and declaring to us. We have to be subservient, so that He may reign, rule, and have perfect authority, until in the body we are reigning over principalities and powers and every evil thing in the world.

The greatest mystery that has ever been known in the world, or ever will be known, is not only the spiritual body, but it is also the Gospel that has a creative power within it that brings light, liberty, immortality, and life. It is not only that, but it is also that after the seed, which is the life of the Son of God, has been put within you, Christ may be so formed in you that every revelation God has designed is for you because of His divine power in the body.

After the revelation came, after God began speaking to Paul, he felt so unworthy of this that he said, "[I] *am less than the least of all the saints"* (Eph. 3:8). There is nothing but revelation that will take you to humility. If ever it goes the other way, it is because you have never yet under any circumstances been brought to a death like that of Christ.

All lifts, all summits, all glories, all revelation is in the death, when we are so dead to selfishness and self-desire, when we absolutely have been brought to the place of worthlessness and helplessness. Then, in that place, the power of the Holy Spirit works mightily through us.

"Less than the least of all the saints." What a blessed state of grace! Paul did not assert himself in any way. It did not matter where he saw the saint, he said, "I am less worthy than that." Oh,

what a submission! How the principle of Christ was working through him!

Jesus knew that He was cooperating, perfectly united, that there was not a thing between Him and His Father, so He was in perfect order. Yet He *"made Himself of no reputation"* (Phil. 2:7). He submitted Himself to the Father, and just in the submission of going down, down, down, even to the death of the cross, God said to Him: "Oh, my Son! You are worthy of ten thousand thrones. You are worthy of all I have, and I will give you a name above every name."

There is not a name like the name of Jesus. All through eternity, that name will swing through the great anthems when they bring all the singers and all the angels, and there will be one song above all, *"To Him who loved us"* (Rev. 1:5).

May that make you the least of all saints, make you feel, "How can I submit myself to God so He can have royal preeminence, so that I will not refer to myself but He will be glorified?"

Isn't Jesus lovely? It pleased the Father to give Him the place. Nothing but humility will do it. Always be careful when you begin bouncing about, thinking you are somebody. More grace means more death to self; more life means more submission; more revelation means more baseness.

Why? That the excellency of the power, of the light, of the glory, may be exhibited. It is not I, but Another.

And thus it is proper for Christ to fulfill all righteousness in our human bodies, so that we may come to a place where we cease to be, for God's Son has to be royal; He has to be all and in all.

> All in all! All in all!
> Strength in time of weariness,
> A light where shadows fall;
> All in all! All in all!
> Jesus is my all in all.

Christ wants to be glorified right in your mortal bodies, so that there will be a manifestation of this very revelation of Christ in you, the hope, the evidence of eternal glory.

A VISION OF THE CHURCH

For what purpose is the church formed? That the Lord's people should be in the great mystery. Abraham, Isaac, Jacob, and the twelve patriarchs laid wonderful store upon the promise of God, and there was no hope for us Gentiles at all. But they missed the opportunity. They might have gone on to have been the greatest miracle workers, the most profound teachers of the truth. They might have been everywhere, all over the world, bringing such glorious revivals, because they were entrusted to it. But they failed God.

A very few of the apostles—when there was no open door for the Gospel, when their bodies were just filled with luminous light and the power of God pressing them right on—felt sure that that inward power was not meant to be exploded at nothing, so God moved upon them to turn to the Gentiles. Then a special revelation was given to Paul that God had joined up all the Gentiles.

My daughter often speaks of the ebony that will be around the throne because of the Africans who will be there. The Chinese will look very lovely around the throne, too, and the Japanese. All nations, peoples, kindred, and tongues are to be in the great body in heaven—all nationalities, all colors. What a blending of beauty in the glory, when all races will be filled with the glory, every one in its own nationality and yet in the express image of the Father! What a sight!

It is coming. It is already working in the body, and the body is feeling now that we are members in particular. In order that there will be no schism in the body, the Holy Spirit must have a royal place, effectively working through your mind, through your will, through every member of your body, until, as the Word of God says, every part of you is sanctified for the purpose that He may have preeminence. God will work in you, mightily through you, in all ways making manifestation in the human flesh—Christ in you!

YOUR PART IN THE BODY

You have the vision of the body; now I want you to get the vision of your personality in the body. There is no greater language than this about the Lord, that all fullness dwells in Him. (See Colossians 1:19.) Christ is to be a manifestation in humanity, with all fullness.

Do not be afraid of claiming your right. It is not a measure that you have come to. Remember, John saw Him, and he said that he had a measure that could not be measured. Christ is coming to us with this measure that cannot be measured. Human calculation will not do.

Paul went on to say this remarkable thing: that we may be able to have some revelation of the mightiness of God in its fullness.

To me, who am less than the least of all the saints, this grace was given, that I should preach among the Gentiles the unsearchable riches of Christ, and to make all see what is the fellowship of the mystery, which from the beginning of the ages has been hidden in God who created all things through Jesus Christ; to the intent.... (Eph. 3:8–10)

God would have us to understand that those mighty words are to a certain intent. What is the intent?

To the intent that now the manifold wisdom of God might be made known by the church to the principalities and powers in the heavenly places. (v. 10)

The church is rising in all her vision and destroying the powers of darkness, ruling among the powers of wickedness, and transforming darkness to light by the power of the new creation in us. The church is doing all this to the intent that we might know the power that is working in us by the resurrection of the life of Christ.

So we are enriched with all enrichment; we are endued with all beatitudes; we are covered with all the graces; and now we are coming into all the mysteries, that the gifts of the Spirit may be so manifested in us that we might be a constancy of firstfruit.

People are always asking me what I belong to. It makes a lot of difference—they either have plenty of room for your company or not, it all depends where you belong. So I always say, and they do not seem to understand it, "I will give you my credentials, they are right here. I wrote them down so that I would always have them ready. They are, 'T.S.E.W.S.A.'"

"Oh! We never knew there were a people that had such credentials. What are they?"

"The Sect Every Where Spoken Against."

Glory to God! To the intent that this sect everywhere spoken against might be envisioned by an incarnation of glorious authority, Christ is in us mightier than death, mightier than sin, triumphing over principalities and powers.

There can be within you a mighty moving of this intent, of this habitual, divine activity of Christ being manifested in you, which was the revelation of Paul.

The second revelation of Paul, which never from the foundation of the world had been revealed, is that the Son of God, the very embodiment of the nature of the Most High, the very incarnation of His presence and power, could fill a human vessel to its utmost capacity, until the very nature of Him will sweep through by the power of God in the body.

You cannot enter into this without being enlarged, abounding, and superabundant. Everything in God is enlargement. God never wants a child of His in the world to be measured. You cannot measure your place. You might measure your land, you might measure your harvest, but you cannot measure the purposes of the Spirit life: they are boundless and infinite. They are for the finite, but all the riches of God are infinite and boundless. There is no such thing as measuring them. If ever you measure God, you will be thin and little and dwarfed. You cannot measure. You have an exhaustless place.

God's Son is in you with all the power of development, until you are so enriched by this divine grace that you live in the world knowing that God is transforming you from grace to grace, from victory to victory.

The Spirit in you has no other foundation than from glory to glory. Paul was so enlarged in the Spirit in this third chapter of Ephesians that his language failed to go on. And then, when he failed to go on in his language, he bowed his knees unto the Father. Oh, this is supreme! When language failed, when prophecy had no more room, it seems that he came to a place where he got down on his knees. Then we hear by the power of the Spirit language beyond all Paul could ever say: *"For this reason I bow my knees to the Father of our Lord Jesus Christ, from whom the whole family in heaven and earth is named"* (Eph. 3:14–15).

Paul realized that he was joining earth and heaven together. They are one, thank God! There is nothing between us and heaven. Gravity may hold us, but all in heaven and in earth are joined under one blood, with no division or separation. *"To be absent from the body* [is] *to be present with the Lord"* (2 Cor. 5:8).

MORE THAN WHAT YOU EXPECT

God has something here for us in the language of the Holy Spirit. He wants it to enlarge our hearts and take a breath of heaven. Let your whole soul reach out unto God; dare to breathe in heaven; dare to be awakened to all God's mind; listen to the language of the Holy Spirit. Paul was praying in the Spirit:

> *That He would grant you, according to the riches of His glory, to be strengthened with might through His Spirit in the inner man, that Christ may dwell in your hearts through faith; that you, being rooted and grounded in love, may be able to comprehend with all the saints what is the width and length and depth and height; to know the love of Christ which passes knowledge; that you may be filled with all the fullness of God. Now to Him who is able to do exceedingly abundantly above all that we ask or think, according to the power that works in us, to Him be glory in the church by Christ Jesus to all generations, forever and ever. Amen.* (Eph. 3:16–21)

This is the Gentile's inhabitation; this is the Gentile's position; this is the body that is being joined up—this spiritual body that has to come into a fullness beyond all expectations.

You cannot expect the fullness that He has waiting for you. If you cannot think of it, then I am sure you cannot expect it. If you cannot ask, then I am sure it is larger than you can expect.

The Holy Spirit takes these things and brings them before us this morning, to the intent that this wonderful, divine appointment will be ours.

How may I get nearer to God? How may I be in the place of helplessness—in my own place and dependent on God? I see a tide rising. *"Blessed are the poor in spirit, for theirs is the kingdom of heaven"* (Matt. 5:3). God is making us very poor, but we are rich in it because our hands are stretched out toward Him in this holy day of His visitation to our hearts.

Believe that He is in you. Believe that He is almightiness. Believe that He is all fullness. Then let yourself go until He is on the throne of your heart. Let everything submit itself to God's throne and the King. Yield yourself unto Him in so sublime a position that He is in perfect order over everything. Let God have His perfect way through you. If you will let go, God will take hold and keep you up.

Oh, to seek only the will of God, to be only in the purpose of God, to seek only that God will be glorified, and not I! We need to repeat the words over and over in our hearts: "Not I, but Christ." (See Galatians 2:20.)

How did it come to Paul? It came when he was *less than the least of all the saints"* (Eph. 3:8). The effective working of the power when he was *"less than the least of all the saints"* buoyed him up until God was manifested in that mortal flesh, for surely Paul reached into all the fullness of that mighty God.

I believe God wants to send you away filled with the Spirit. Oh, beloved, are you ready? What must you do? You must say, "Father, have your way. Do not let my human will spoil your divine plan. Father, take charge of me today in such a way that I will be wholly, entirely on the altar for Your service." And I am sure He will meet you in this.

CHAPTER FIFTEEN

THE GLORY OF THE INCORRUPTIBLE

God has wonderful things for us in this present tense. I wish to enlarge your capacity of thought and also your inward desire toward God, so that you may richly claim all the things God has for you today.

God has, from before the foundation of the world, made a provision for us all, and many are coming into the knowledge that they have been pre-thought about, predestined, and wonderfully changed in the operation of the Spirit.

Are you ready? What for? To obtain the strength of God by a living faith.

Be ready for the enduement of power (Luke 24:49), the enrichment of His grace, the oil that causes you to rejoice and be glad. Be full of expectation; be earnest; make your supplications without fear; be bold in the presence of God; dare to believe that you enter in through the blood into a very large place today.

Are you ready? What for? That you may be lost in God, wholly swallowed up in His divine plan; that you might be enriched above all enrichment of earthly things with divine capacity, with the knowledge of His sovereign grace, so that you may be filled with all His fullness.

A SUPERNATURAL ORDER

Our subject this morning belongs to the deep things of God. In these days, we need to be grounded in an inward knowledge of greater things. We need to be supernaturally built, changed by a living authority, to come into a divine construction where the mind is operated by the spirit and where we live because Another mightier than us lives in us.

Oh, for a revelation that we may be taken on with God—not left behind, but taken on with God into all His divine arrangement for us! This meeting, however beautiful it may be, is all arranged, divinely arranged. There is nothing out of order with God. God is so large in all of His providences; He is providing, arranging, so that these meetings are not just happening. God has had these in His perfect order.

Occasionally I see one of my hairs fall out of my head, but God knows the number that are left. I am not troubled about my hair, whether it grows white or remains its natural color. Some people try to change the color of their hair. They have forgotten that God has said you cannot make one hair black or white (Matt. 5:36).

We ought to see that God wants us in a supernatural order, not conformed to the world, with all kinds of make-up or fancy garments. Don't you know that you have to be pretty in the sight of the Lord, that prettiness is a meek and quiet spirit? It is where the Lord has the right-of-way of your heart. It is where you are not troubled about the natural physique, knowing that the supernatural physique is being made like Him. We have borne the image of the earthly, but we are going to bear the image of the heavenly (1 Cor. 15:49).

Oh, that we could be lost to these things, set apart for the glory of God, brought into the resurrection order, filled with audacity! This is our divine appointment, where the Lord is taking us on. Heights, depths, lengths, breadths, yes, everything in the mind of God—we are being taken higher, higher, higher!

For our study this morning, I want to take the first chapter of the first epistle of Peter. This chapter has a foundation line of truth. We cannot cover it all, but I want to deal with the incorruptible Word, the incorruptible seed, and the incorruptible life in the body, which are all based on an incorruptible plan, so that you may be able to understand how the mind of the Lord has to be so extravagantly in you, even to deny your own personality before you deny the power of the Word of the living God.

The days will come when your ministry and your own life will be tested on all lines. If you can get beyond your nature, beyond your natural line of thought, and beyond yourself into a plane of almighty provision for you in the flesh, quickened by the Spirit, you will survive. It will be as the Word of God says, *"Having done all...stand"* (Eph. 6:13). When the trial is on, when everything comes to a point where it seems it is the last strand in the rope, then the Lord will very mightily bring you into a land of plenty. Lord, let it please You to keep us in that place.

In order to reach this climax in divine order, let us read the first verse of the first epistle of Peter: *"Peter, an apostle of Jesus Christ, to the pilgrims of the Dispersion in Pontus, Galatia, Cappadocia, Asia, and Bithynia."*

Peter, like James, was speaking to us on this line because of a trying time. James was edifying us in a trying corner. Here we have the same thing.

PERSECUTION COMES AFTER BAPTISM

The people were scattered, and persecution had come in. They had had a good time at Jerusalem, and God knew—I say it reverently—God knows that we never make progress in an easy time. You may settle down in your ease and miss the great plan of God. God allowed strange things to happen in Jerusalem after the Holy Spirit came.

A man may be saved for many years without knowing much of anything about persecution. A man may be sanctified for many years without knowing much of anything about persecution. But it is impossible to be baptized with the Holy Spirit without entering into persecution.

The disciples had a wonderful time when they were with Jesus. They had no persecution, but there was One in the midst of them whom the people of Nazareth tried to throw over the brow of the hill. The priests joined together to kill Him.

After the Devil entered into Judas, the only people he could have conversation with were the priests. The priests were willing to talk to the Devil after he got into Judas.

INTERPRETATION OF A MESSAGE IN TONGUES:

Guard the door of your lips; see to it that your heart is perfect, that you have no judgment, that you do not stand in the way and condemn everybody that is in the way, for there are many today who are like the priests in their day: they will neither go in themselves nor let anybody else go in. But don't let this spirit be in you, for God wants to guard you, purify you, and present you as a chaste virgin, made ready for every good work.

Let us see to it, whatever happens, that there is no harsh judgment in us, no bitterness. We must see that we have been quickened, brought into, changed by a new authority, incorruptible in the corruptible. We must see that we have the divine life where death was, love where hatred was, the power of God reigning in the human, the Lord lifting upon us the light of His countenance right in the midst of death, and life breaking forth like rivers in the desert.

May the Lord bring us to a place in which hard judgment is past. May He make us meek and lowly in heart. This is the principle of the Master.

SATAN CANNOT BE MADE HOLY

There is no such thing as purifying the impure. Evil things never get purer, but more vile. All impurity, all evil must be cast out. You can never make Satan holy. He will be hellish and fiendish forever, and when the brightness of God comes by the express image of the Father, the very brightness against uncleanness, he will be glad to get in the pit and be there forever and ever.

There are some fools in this day who foolishly say that the Devil will be saved, and that they will go arm in arm with him. It is because they do not rightly understand the Word of God. You will never purify sin. Sin cannot be purified. *"The carnal mind...is not subject to the law of God, nor indeed can be"* (Rom. 8:7). Carnality has to be destroyed. Evil propensities must be rooted out.

God's plan is, "I will give you a pure heart and a right spirit." And this is the order of the new creation in God.

As surely as the Holy Spirit fell, James was beheaded, Peter was put in prison, they had a tremendous trouble at Jerusalem, and the saints were scattered. The scattering of the saints meant the proclamation of the Gospel. So here Peter was writing to the people who had been scattered.

SANCTIFICATION OF THE HUMAN SPIRIT

Elect according to the foreknowledge of God the Father, in sanctification of the Spirit, for obedience and sprinkling of the blood of Jesus Christ: Grace to you and peace be multiplied. (1 Pet. 1:2)

Notice that there is a sanctifying of the human spirit. It does not matter what you say, if your human spirit does not get wholly sanctified, you will always be in danger. It is that position where the Devil has a chance to work upon you.

Therefore, we are taught to come into sanctification where uncleannesses and corruption pass away because of incorruption abiding, where all kinds of lusts have lost their power.

This is the plan. Only in the ideal of pursuit of this does God so bless us in our purifying state that we lose our position because of the ascended position with Him in the glory. The saints of God, as they go on into perfection and holiness and understand the mind of the Spirit and the law of the spirit of life, are brought into a very blessed place.

For instance, it is the place of holiness, the place of entire sanctification, the place where God has the throne of the heart. It is the place where the mind is so concentrated in the power of God that a person thinks about the things that are pure and lives in holy ascendancy, where every day is an exchange into the power of freedom with God. God highly honors him, but He never exalts him. The Devil comes to exalt him, but it cannot be under the lines of the sanctification of the spirit.

There is a sanctifying of the human spirit during which the human spirit comes into such perfect blending with the divine mind of Christ that the person cannot be exalted. You can live in the body with all the glorious anointing, revelation, and power. The Spirit can sanctify your spirit until you will never vaunt yourself and will never say "I, I, I," but it will be "Christ, Christ, Christ." Then Christ will be glorified.

INTERPRETATION OF A MESSAGE IN TONGUES:
Into this death within, this inward deepening of all human weaknesses and human powers that would assert themselves, deeper, deeper into and on with God, learning only the principles of Christ, as He is, to be like Him in holiness, in righteousness and in purity, until you reign with Him, gloriously reigning in Him, through Him, by Him, over the powers of the Devil.

Holiness is power; sin is defeat. Sin is weakness; holiness is strength.

"Renewed in the spirit of your mind" (Eph. 4:23) is a place where you are always being lifted into clearer light, always seeing

more the hideousness of sin, always having a consciousness of the powers of evil and a consciousness of the powers of God over evil. So may the Lord grant unto us by His mighty power this spiritual intuition of divine association with the Father.

INTERPRETATION OF A MESSAGE IN TONGUES:
He is exalted far above all, and we are united in Him, closer than all, until there is no division. Holy as He is, pure as He is, life, truth revealed in us. Because of truth in us, He becomes Alpha, Omega; He has the last thought: He is all in all. We love Him! We say, "He is altogether lovely."

THE INCORRUPTIBLE SEED

Now consider 1 Peter 1:13–16:

Therefore gird up the loins of your mind, be sober, and rest your hope fully upon the grace that is to be brought to you at the revelation of Jesus Christ; as obedient children, not conforming yourselves to the former lusts, as in your ignorance; but as He who called you is holy, you also be holy in all your conduct, because it is written, "Be holy, for I am holy."

It is settled in the canon of Scripture that what came into you at the new birth had no corruption in it, had no defilement in it, and could not desire evil. That incorruptible seed, that divine life of the Son, that quickening of the Spirit, that regenerative power, that holy creative force within you, that divine position—all of these caused your very nature to bring forth a likeness to the Son of God. Even your very organs yearned with desire after its purity; you loved to sing of His holiness.

I remember, when I was a little boy, I used to lie on my back singing until heaven seemed to be let down, until it seemed like glory. It was wonderful! What was it? It was the new creation, longing, waiting. Oh, hallelujah! That was sixty years ago, and I have still greater desire and more longing for what came then to be met with the very life that gave it. There is something so remarkable about it, and it was so concentrated in my human life, that from that day to this, I have never lost that holy knowledge that I am His, wholly His.

I want all of you to be created anew after this fashion until you will become saints: holy, purified, and perfect. Don't be afraid of being called saints; don't be afraid of the word *holiness*; don't be afraid of the word *purified*; don't be afraid of the word *perfect*. Believe that in you there is a power that has no corruption in it, that has no desire to sin, that hates uncleanness, that is born of an incorruptible power, that has no evil in it. It is Godlike, it is sonship order, and it has to grow up in you until He is perfectly manifested in you—perfect sight in God, perfect feeling after God, holy feelings, no carnal desires, yearning after purity, longing after cleanliness, desiring after God. This is the inheritance of the saints: in the world, not of it, but over it.

He who has this faith, he who has this life, overcomes the world. *"Who is he who overcomes the world, but he who believes that Jesus is the Son of God?"* (1 John 5:5).

What does it mean for Him to be the Son of God to you and me? God is holy; God is light; God is love. Jesus was the fullness of the expression of the purpose of all fullness. The same fullness, the same life, the same maturity after the perfect standard of life has to be in you until you are dead indeed to the world and alive to God in the Spirit (Rom. 6:11).

> Holy, Holy, Holy, merciful and mighty,
> God in Three Persons, blessed Trinity.

Trinity, boundless affinity; holy, transforming power—such is the very nature of the Son of God, the very power of the world to come, the very nature of the wonderful Son, formed in us.

There are five senses in the world. When He is come, there are five senses of spiritual acquaintance: the hearing of faith, the feelings after God, the seeing supernaturally, the speaking after the mind of the operation of the Spirit, and the tasting after God's plan.

Yet God wants us to be so triune, perfectly joined, until Christ is formed in us with His very life manifested in the human, until we know we have no questions, no matter what other people say. We know in whom we have believed (2 Tim. 1:12).

There are things that can be moved, and there are things that cannot be moved; there are things that can be changed, and there are things that cannot be changed. We have within us an incorruptible place that cannot be moved. It does not matter who is moved or what is moved; the things that God has given us remain.

Some things can be wrapped up and folded like a garment. The heavens may be rolled up like a scroll (Isa. 34:4) and melt with fervent heat (2 Pet. 3:10). The very earth we are standing on may be absolutely melted. But we are as endurable as He is, for we have the same life, the incorruptible life, the eternal power. The everlasting King is moving in the natural things to cause the natural to know that this is eternal, this is divine, this is God. Hallelujah!

AN INHERITANCE OF RIGHTEOUSNESS

Seeing that these things are so, we must build in this order, for it is in this order that nothing can contaminate us. You are perfect over sin, if you will believe it. You are perfect over disease, if you will believe it. You are perfect over death, if you will believe it. You are perfect in the order of Enoch's translation, if you dare believe it.

There are always three things that are working silently but powerfully: the blade, the head, and the full grain in the head (Mark 4:28). God is developing us in a righteous line to know that we are of a royal aristocracy (1 Pet. 2:9); we belong to a new company; we belong to the firstborn; we have the nature of the Son; we belong to eternal workings. God, who is greater than all, has come through all and is now working in all to His glory, to His power.

You may not be able to take these things in because you know so much about gravity, and I am speaking so much about gravity being removed. There is no gravity to the spirit. There is no gravity to thought. There is no gravity to inspiration. There is no gravity to divine union with Christ. It is above all; it rises higher; it sits on the throne; it claims its purposes.

God has brought us to a place where all manner of evil powers are subdued. Reigning over them, being enriched by the new creation of God in the Spirit, you are not timid and afraid; you meet these things with joy, and you triumph over them in the place of blessing.

Some of you may say, "If I could talk to you about this, I would have to say so many things that I know are in me that are not in that." You must allow the Lord to move you out and bring you into that. Unbelief is the great dethroning place; faith is the great rising place. Many people lose great confidence in the spirit and cease to go on to perfection because they allow their own minds and lives, their own knowledge, their own associations, to continually bring then into a deplorable, low estate.

God says you are not of this world (John 15:19); you have been delivered from the corruption of the world (2 Pet. 1:4); you are being *"transformed by the renewing of your mind"* (Rom. 12:2). God says that you are *"a royal priesthood,"* a holy people (1 Pet. 2:9), belonging to the building of which Christ is the great cornerstone (Eph. 2:20).

The Holy Spirit is coming forth to help you to claim your inheritance. Do not be afraid of getting rich this hour. Do not be afraid of coming in, but be very afraid if you do not come in. Have God's mind on this: God says you have to overcome the world, that you have to have this incorruptible, undefiled position now within the human body, transforming your mind, even your very nature, realizing the supernatural power working through you.

It is lovely for me to be here speaking about this knowledge of this glorious incarnation of the Spirit, and I want you to know I would be the last man to speak about these things unless I knew they could be attained. This is our inheritance; this is where God wants to make you His own in such a way that you will deny yourself, the flesh, and the world so that you may rule over principalities and powers and over spiritual wickedness in high places (Eph. 6:12), so that you may *"reign in life"* (Rom. 5:17) by this lovely place in Christ Jesus.

SUPERNATURAL FULLNESS

I want to stir you up today. If I cannot make a person who is suffering from disease righteously indignant against that condition, I cannot help him. If I can make every sufferer know that suffering, disease, and all these things are the workings of the Devil, I can help him.

Let me give you a Scripture for it: *"The thief does not come except to steal, and to kill, and to destroy"* (John 10:10). That is the Devil. And if you know that, believe the other side of the story, that Jesus has come to give you life, life eternal and life abounding (v. 10).

If you can see that the Devil is after you, to kill you for all he is worth, believe that Christ is enthroned in your heart to destroy the very principles of the Devil in every way. Have the reality of this; build upon it by perfect soundness until you are in the place of perfect bliss, for to know Him is perfect bliss. Be so built in Him that you are not afraid of what comes on the line of all evil. You must

536

have a fullness that presses out beyond; you must have a life that is full of divine power; you must have a mind that is perfectly Christ; you must cease to be natural and begin to be supernatural.

God is on His throne and can take you a thousand miles in a moment. Have faith to jump into His supernatural plan.

Are you ready? What for? To be so changed by the order of God that you will never have this human order of fear anymore. Remember that *"perfect love casts out fear"* (1 John 4:18).

Step into the full tide of the life of the manifestation of God. Your new nature has no corruption in it. Eternal life is not just during your lifetime; it is forever. You are regenerated by the power of the Word of God, and it is in you as an incorruptible force, taking you on from victory to victory until death itself can be overcome, until sin has no authority, until disease could not be in the body. This is a living fact by the Word of God.

You may say, "How can I come into it?" Read carefully the first two verses of Romans 8:

> *There is therefore now no condemnation to those who are in Christ Jesus, who do not walk according to the flesh, but according to the Spirit. For the law of the Spirit of life in Christ Jesus has made me free from the law of sin and death.*

Right in this present moment, there is *"no condemnation."* This law of the Spirit of life is a law in the body; it is a law of eternity; it is a law of God, a new law. It is not the law of the Ten Commandments, but a law of life in the body, changing you in the body until there is no sin power, no disease power, and no death power.

You who desire to go a thousand miles through faith, beyond what you have ever gone before, leap into it. Believe the blood of Christ makes you clean; believe you have come into resurrection order; believe you are young again. Believe you are young. God will renew your youth. Believe it!

You say, "I will try, anyhow." All right, but trying is an effort, whereas believing is a fact. Don't join the Endeavor Society, but come into the Faith Society, and you will leap into the promises of God, which are *"Yes"* and *"Amen"* (2 Cor. 1:20) to all who believe.

Don't look down your nose and murmur anymore. Have a rejoicing spirit; get the praise of God in your heart; go forth from victory to victory; rise in faith, and believe it. You must not live in yourself; you must live in Christ. *"Set your mind on things above"* (Col. 3:2), and keep your whole spirit alive in God. Let your inheritance be so full of divine life that you live above the world and all its thoughts and cares.

A Prayer

O Lord, move away disease, move away blind eyes, move away imperfect vision. Give the Word; let us understand the blood; let us understand the spirit of prophecy and of testimony. Let us understand, O God, that You are still building the foundation on the prophets and on the apostles and on all who work Your wonderful Word. Build us in this fashion until every soul is filled with divine grace.

Questions Answered

Q: Is the baptism of the Holy Spirit essential to the Rapture?

A: No. It is a good thing to be baptized with the Holy Spirit because—and it is a wonderful thing to me—when the church goes, the Holy Spirit is not here anymore. So it appears that the Holy Spirit goes with the church. The Word of God says that He will bring with Him all who are asleep in Jesus. And there are thousands asleep in Jesus who were never baptized in the Holy Spirit, but He is going to bring them. So it is evident they are there.

Verses sixteen and eighteen of Luke 22 will help you: *"For I say to you, I will no longer eat of it until it is fulfilled in the kingdom of God....For I say to you, I will not drink of the fruit of the vine until the kingdom of God comes."* Jesus said, *"The kingdom of God is within you"* (Luke 17:21). He meant the new creation; He meant the new deposit of life that He had given, for He was and is the life of the world. It would be impossible, He said, for Him to eat or drink again until the kingdom was come.

Every person who has the kingdom of God within him will be there at the Rapture. The Bible doesn't say anything about the baptism; it says the kingdom will be presented at the Supper.

The baptism of the Holy Spirit is for revelation. The baptism of the Holy Spirit is to take the things of Jesus and reveal them. The baptism of the Holy Spirit is to be a focus.

Suppose you put a great magnifying glass onto the smallest thing. What would happen? The Holy Spirit is the great Magnifier of the life, the gifts, and the ministry of the King. And the King, when the Holy Spirit comes, is coronated. Coronation implies that when the Holy Spirit comes into the body, Jesus becomes King, and the Holy Spirit becomes the revealer of kingship.

Q: Is the church going through tribulation?

A: We have a clear teaching in Thessalonians about the Rapture, and it clearly says, *"Only He who now restrains will do so until He is taken out of the way"* (2 Thess. 2:7).

As sure as anything, the Devil is having power given to him at this day and will have more power given to him until he is manifested, right up until he has full liberty and becomes the prince of the earth. At the same time, there is increasing velocity and divine power and quickening and revelation of the saints. Today we are in a day of revelation of the Holy Spirit that possibly has never been. This is the great open door of ministry, and as He is letting in that power, He is filling us with power. If you are ready for translation, you are ready for anything.

Q: Will the bride be taken out after we get to glory?

A: Yes, the bride is in the body of Christ. She will not be seen until just before her marriage to Christ; until then, she will be veiled. Even now, God is quickening many people in a remarkable way, and they are bringing themselves to the place where they will pay the price for holiness and separation. This is intensely the desire of the bridal position.

Now, don't take it that you are in the bride because of this, but prove yourself worthy to be in the body, so that you might be worthy to be taken out of the body as the bride. But don't get ideas about it, because many people are being tremendously fooled, believing that they had within them a manifestation of the bride. That is absolute foolishness. The bride will be taken out right in the kingdom.

Q: Will there be anyone saved on the earth after the church is taken away?

A: The 144,000 who are perfectly Jewish. They will go through great tribulation because of the Word, and the people, if they are saved at all, will be saved by the Word, not by the Spirit. The Holy Spirit will have gone with the church body. But the 144,000 will be Jewish. They know the Word, and they will go through by the Word. They will even die for the Word.

Greater Works:
Experiencing God's Power
Smith Wigglesworth

Smith Wigglesworth was extraordinarily used by God to see souls saved, bodies healed, and lives changed. Even in the face of death, Wigglesworth did not waver in his faith because he trusted the Great Physician. Your heart will be stirred as you read in Wigglesworth's own words the dramatic accounts of miraculous healings of people whom the doctors had given up as hopeless. Discover how God can enable you to reach out to a hurting world and touch all who come your way with His love.

ISBN: 0-88368-584-1 • Trade • 576 pages

WHITAKER
HOUSE

www.whitakerhouse.com

Smith Wigglesworth on Heaven
Smith Wigglesworth

Illustrating his insights with many dramatic, real-life examples, Smith Wigglesworth has a dynamic message in store for those who are looking toward the Second Coming. He explains how to prepare for your future in eternity with God while experiencing the power and joy of the Holy Spirit in the present. Discover God's plans for you in this life and what He has in store for you in heaven. You can know victorious living—now and for all eternity.

ISBN: 0-88368-954-5 • Trade • 224 pages

WHITAKER HOUSE

www.whitakerhouse.com

Smith Wigglesworth on Healing
Smith Wigglesworth

Meet a bride who is dying of appendicitis, a young man who has been lame for eighteen years, a betrayed husband who is on his way to kill his wife, and a woman who is completely deaf. Discover what happens in their lives and what can take place in your own life. Not only can you be healed of your sicknesses, but God can use you to bring healing to others.

ISBN: 0-88368-426-8 • Trade • 208 pages

www.whitakerhouse.com

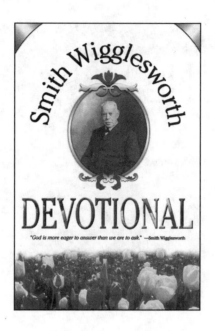

"God is more eager to answer than we are to ask." —Smith Wigglesworth

Smith Wigglesworth Devotional
Smith Wigglesworth

You are invited to journey with Smith Wigglesworth on a year-long trip that will quench your spiritual thirst while it radically transforms your faith. As you daily explore these challenging insights from the Apostle of Faith, you will connect with God's glorious power, cast out doubt, and see impossibilities turn into realities. Your prayer life will never be the same again when you personally experience the joy of seeing awesome, powerful results as you extend God's healing grace to others.

ISBN: 0-88368-574-4 • Trade • 560 pages

WHITAKER
HOUSE
www.whitakerhouse.com